Bruce
Byfield

Designing
with
LibreOffice

Editor & Publisher

Jean Hollis Weber, Friends of OpenDocument, Inc., 544 Carlyle Gardens, Beck Drive North, Condon, Queensland 4815, Australia. Please direct any comments or suggestions about this document to info@friendsofopendocument.com.

Reviewers

Jean Hollis Weber, Lee Schlesinger, Nicola Einarson, Terry Hancock, Charlie Kravetz, Michael Manning, Jean-Francois Nifenecker, Georges Rodier, Christina Teskey.

Special thanks also go to Marcel Gagné, Michael Meeks, and Carla Schroder for advanced reading.

Acknowledgments

Parts of this book's content were originally published, sometimes in different forms, by Linux Journal, Linux.com, Linux Pro Magazine, Open Content and Software, Wazi, and WorldLabel. My thanks for permission to re-use this material.

Publication date and software version

Published 15 March 2016. Based on LibreOffice Version 5.0.2.2 and later.

Photo credits

Cover photos and the photo on the interior title page are copyright by Bruce Byfield and released under the Creative Commons Attribution Sharealike License, version 3.0 or later.

They depict the Sun Yat Sen Classical Gardens in Vancouver, Canada. The gardens are based on the philosophy of feng shui, which, like typography, works deliberately to produce a natural, unnoticed effect.

Also included in the text are the following original works of art:: Nathan Wilson's "Tag'wa," Nigel Fox's "Butterflies #3," and Todd Stephen's "Jorja and I."

All three are in the collection of Bruce Byfield, and used by permission of the artists.

Table of Contents

Chapter 5

Chapter 8
193 Styling the page

Chapter 10

Chapter 11

Chapter 12

Chapter 13

Chapter 16

For Trish, Always

1

Introduction

Office suites are as old as the personal computer. Yet, after more than thirty years, few of us have learned how to use them.

Oh, we have learned how to get things done in them. Most of us can format a document and print it out, after a fashion. But what many of us haven't learned is to do these tasks efficiently, taking advantage of all the tools that are available.

It is as though we have learned enough about cars to go downhill in them and coast across level ground, but never learned about the ignition. We get things done, but with more effort and less efficiency that we should. Some tasks, like going uphill, we don't imagine are even possible because of our ignorance.

Using any office suite to its full potential means knowing how to design your documents – and nine-tenths of design is knowing how to use styles and templates. Knowing how to use styles and templates is the equivalent of being handed the key to that coasting car and shown the gas pedal – suddenly, you can take control of the vehicle, instead of getting by on clumsy makeshifts.

That is especially true of LibreOffice. Its Writer word processor in particular is structured around the concept of styles. Not only does Writer have more types of styles than other word processors, but many advanced features, such as tables of contents and master documents, take more effort to use without styles. And having spent the time to set up styles, you would prefer not to do the same work all over again for your next document, so templates also become an important part of your work flow.

Other parts of LibreOffice and OpenOffice are less dependent on styles than Writer, but are still more style-aware than their equivalents in Microsoft Office.

Much of this book is designed to explain not only what styles and templates are and how to use them, but also what you need to consider when selecting them. The rest is mostly about features that are not quite styles, or that are dependent on styles for full efficiency. Other sections are distinctly not about styles, but needed for a full discussion about design.

However, one thing that this book is not is a relentless death march in regimented order through every item in the menus. Instead, it looks at important features from the point of view of planning, as a variety of tactics that you can choose, and skips around as seems most useful for planning. It assumes that readers are either already familiar with LibreOffice and other office suites, or, at least, can tour the menus by themselves.

You might call this book an effort to make a single map out of two separate bodies of information: LibreOffice's features, and the standard practices of typography (designing with text).

By understanding both, you can take advantage of what publishers have been learning for over half a millennium about what works and what doesn't. The alternative is to spend more time on trial and error, and still end up (as likely as not) with something worse than if you had taken some advice.

What is typography?

People have strange ideas about typography. Many imagine that it is about design that screams for attention, like blinking text on a web page. Many, too, suppose that the main purpose is to show how clever the designer is.

The truth is, nothing could be more wrong. The real purpose of typography is to make the text more inviting and easy to read. Its focus is not abstract design, but practical concerns like providing margins wide enough so that readers can comfortably hold a book, or features that make a document easier to update.

Far from calling attention to itself, the best typography hides, noticed by casual readers only in a vague sense that a document is comfortable to read. The features that produce these characteristics should be noticeable only to eyes trained to be alert for them.

LibreOffice does not have all the tools needed for the highest levels of typography. However, it does have many of them, and far more than any other office suite. The more you know about typography, the more you can make it do what you want.

Still, in the end, *Designing with LibreOffice* is not about design in the abstract, but about getting everyday tasks done. Those who want to know more about typography and layout should look at Appendix C for more information.

What is LibreOffice? OpenOffice?

LibreOffice is an office suite that runs on 32 and 64 bit versions of Linux, OS X, and Windows. It is released under a free license that lets you use it legally on as many machines as you want, and share it with others. Since it is free software, you can even make your own changes in it if you have the skill.

LibreOffice is descended from OpenOffice.org, a free and open source software project run for years by Sun Microsystems. When Oracle bought Sun in 2010, LibreOffice started developing its own version of OpenOffice.org, as the code's license permits. Eventually, Oracle gave its rights in the code to The Apache Foundation.

Today, OpenOffice.org no longer exists, but Apache OpenOffice does. Despite having different version numbers, LibreOffice and Apache OpenOffice are extremely similar in most features. Unless I say otherwise, what I say about LibreOffice should also be true for OpenOffice.

Several other organizations repackage both LibreOffice and Apache OpenOffice, sometimes under different names. This practice is perfectly legal, but sometimes involves using different icons and making other minor changes.

Linux distributions are especially apt to make these cosmetic changes. You can tell if you are using an altered version because those installed from the repositories of distributions usually install to /usr/lib/libreoffice/. By contrast, installations directly from LibreOffice or OpenOffice downloads install to the /opt directory.

STOP Caution

> Some sources for LibreOffice and Apache OpenOffice charge a small fee. The license allows them to do so, but if you pay more than about ten dollars for shipping and handling, they are taking advantage of you.

Both LibreOffice and Apache OpenOffice are widely available at no cost to anyone with an Internet connection.

What is Open Document Format?

Both LibreOffice and Apache OpenOffice use Open Document Format (ODF), a file format consisting of zipped XML files.

You can use this format to exchange documents between the two, or with any other application that uses ODF, such as Calligra Suite or AbiWord. In both LibreOffice and OpenOffice, you can also save to most Microsoft Office formats, and open files from WordPerfect, Microsoft Works, and several other formats, although some formatting is sometimes lost in complex documents.

About this book

This book standardizes on LibreOffice on Linux, because that is what I use every day. However, most of the book applies to Apache OpenOffice as much as LibreOffice. Similarly, the content usually applies to OS X and Windows versions as much as the Linux versions.

Where important differences exist, I try to mention them, but they are surprisingly few. If you see a difference that I fail to mention, please let me know, so that I can make corrections.

About the writer

I have been writing about free and open source software for over a decade. I long ago lost count, but by now I've written over

1700 articles. A sizable minority have been about OpenOffice.org or LibreOffice.

My LibreOffice articles include:

- "11 Tips for Moving to OpenOffice.org," which was the cover article for the March 2004 *Linux Journal* (http://www.linuxjournal.com/article/7158).

- "Replacing FrameMaker with OpenOffice.org Writer"(http://archive09.linux.com/articles/39406).

- "How LibreOffice Writer Tops Microsoft Word" (http://www.datamation.com/applications/how-libreoffice-writer-tops-ms-word-12-features-1.html).

Before becoming a journalist, I was a technical writer and graphic designer. During that part of my working life, I had several chances to stress-test OpenOffice.org, including writing several manuals of over 700 pages. It met every challenge I threw at it, making me aware that the software had more to it than most people assumed.

LibreOffice is not perfect. Some parts of it are difficult to use, and others are undocumented in any meaningful way. A few seem to suffer from longstanding bugs. Some parts are frankly obsolete.

All the same, LibreOffice is not just a wannabe Microsoft Office. Rather, it is a powerful pieces of software in its own right, sometimes falling short of Microsoft Office, but just as often exceeding it. It remains by far the best office suite available today.

Some users complain about LibreOffice's reliance on styles and templates. Yet, without them, LibreOffice would not be nearly so powerful. They truly are the ignition key that most of us have been missing while coasting downhill.

Tip

Designing with LibreOffice is about layout, so it does not mention every available feature.

If you need information on features or selections that are not mentioned in this book, see the LibreOffice documentation page:

http://www.libreoffice.org/get-help/documentation/

Printed versions of the same manuals are available for sale at the Friends of Open Document store at:

http://www.lulu.com/spotlight/opendocument

2

Going in style

You have two ways to design a document in LibreOffice: by manual formatting and by applying styles. Or, as I like to joke: the wrong way and the right way.

Manual formatting (also called direct formatting) is how most people design a document. When you format manually, whenever you want to change the default formatting, you select part of the document – for example, a paragraph or a page – and then apply the formatting using the tool bars or one of the menus.

Then you do the same thing all over again in the next place that you want the same formatting. And the next, and the next.

If you decide to change the formatting, you have to go through the entire document, changing the design one place at a time.

Manual formatting is popular because it requires little knowledge of the software. In effect, you are using the office application as though it were a typewriter.

But although this approach gets the job done, it's slow. Not only that, but many features are awkward to use when you format manually – assuming you can use them at all.

By contrast, a style is a set of formats. For example, a character style might put characters into italics if they form the title of the book. A page style might list everything about how a page is designed, from the width of its margins to its orientation and the background color.

The advantage of styles is that you design everything once. Instead of adding all the characteristics every place where you format, you apply the style.

If you decide you want a different format, you edit the style once, and within seconds, every place where you applied the style has the new format as well.

You don't have to remember the details of the formatting, either – just the name of the style.

Example: Formatting with styles

To fully appreciate the difference between formatting manually and formatting with styles, imagine that you are preparing a twenty page essay for a university class. You have decided to use the DejaVu Serif typeface with a size of 10 points. Twenty minutes before you leave for class, you re-read the professor's instructions and realize that she only accepts essays in 12 point Times New Roman.

If you have manually formatted, you will be lucky to finish editing before you leave. But if you have used styles, you can change the font and its size in less than a minute, and print out a new copy of the essay with time to spare.

Then you can save the document as a template. The next essay you write for that professor, you can concentrate on content and not have to worry about formatting.

Other advantages of styles? You can mostly eliminate the need for tabs, especially at the start of a new paragraph, because you can create a style that automatically indents for you.

Similarly, instead of creating a separate frame for a section formatted differently from the rest of the document, you can include the different format in a set of styles and keep typing.

Another major advantage is that if you use heading styles, you can use them as bookmarks in Navigator to help you move around in a document. But unlike normal bookmarks, you don't have to define them in a separate task. Instead, headings are available for use the moment that you set the styles.

In the same way, headings let you generate a table of contents with a minimum of settings. Separate headers and footers for different pages are easier to maintain. You can give a uniform look to the frames around photos you add, set up a drop capital to mark the start of a new chapter, and automatically change page layouts, freeing yourself to focus on content.

However, the real saving comes when you save your design as a template. Once you have created your basic templates, the next time you start a document, you won't have to think about formatting at all – instead, you can open the template and start writing. Usually, the more you use styles, the more time you save.

Amazingly, some users view styles as an intrusion on their rights to work as they please. Of course they can do as they like, but not using styles means they work harder than necessary.

Debunking myths about styles

People who have never used styles often have bizarre ideas about them. Sometimes, these ideas may be excuses to rationalize not using styles, but often they are misunderstandings.

Here are some of the most common myths about styles that are repeated whenever the subject of manual formatting vs. styles is discussed:

Myth about styles	Reality
• Styles impose on users' right to work the way they choose.	• You can work without styles. But why demand the right to inconvenience yourself?
• Styles are hard to learn.	• Styles represent a different way of thinking than manual formatting. However, you can learn their basic concepts in ten minutes.
• Styles are for programmers, not ordinary users.	• Styles are for anybody who wants to work efficiently. Actually, just as many programmers format manually as anyone else.
• Styles require you to memorize their names.	• You don't need to memorize anything. You just need to read from the lists of styles in LibreOffice.
• What you set in styles applies to all the document, so styles more limited than manual formatting.	• A style affects only the parts of a document to which you apply it.
• Styles are too complicated.	• You don't need to understand every feature of every style. Often, you can just accept the defaults.

- Styles are limiting. You can't change what's built into them.

- Most aspects of styles can be fine-tuned, toggled on or off, or ignored until you need them. You can't do anything manually that you can't do with styles much more easily.

- Styles can conflict with each other.

- Only one style of a particular type can apply to a selection. You can have a character and a paragraph style applying to the same selection, but not two different character styles or two different paragraph styles.

- Manual formatting is preferable because you can make changes on the fly.

- You can change styles on the fly, too. In fact, changing styles is quicker; you only have to make a change once to apply it through the entire document.

Example: Styles save time

Just how much time do you save by using styles? Let's imagine that you have a heading paragraph that you want to format extensively.

Specifically, you want to set the font, font size, font weight, font color, and the space above the paragraph. In addition, you want to edit the heading so that it starts with a number.

The shortest way to make these changes manually is:

Steps	Action
1	Highlight the text of the header.
2–4	Open the font list in the tool bar, scroll, and select the font.
5–6	Open the font size in the tool bar, scroll, and select the font size.
7	Select font weight from the tool bar icon.
8–9	Open FONT COLOR in the tool bar and select the color.
10–14	Select from the menu FORMAT > PARAGRAPH > INDENTS & SPACING, edit the SPACE ABOVE field, and click OK.
15	Add a numbered list from the tool bar.

If you are lucky, you might save a few actions if you don't have to scroll for a setting, but this series of steps is a good average. You would have to repeat these steps, of course, for every header in the document.

By contrast, setting up a style would take 21 steps. Once the style is ready, here's how you would make the same changes using styles:

Steps	Action
1	Place the cursor anywhere in the header paragraph.
2	Press F11 to open the STYLES AND FORMATTING floating window.

3   Change the display in STYLES AND FORMATTING to ALL STYLES (or another view that shows the style you want).

4   Scroll to the paragraph style you want.

5   Select the paragraph style.

This example is extremely conservative. If you are using styles, then probably the STYLES AND FORMATTING window is already open. Often, too, you may not need to change the view.

However, even being conservative, applying the style requires one-third the number of actions than making the changes manually. When you change one paragraph's style, you also change every other use of the style in the same document. That means that if the document has more than two instances of the heading, using styles saves you effort.

When should you use styles?

The short answer is, "Whenever it saves time." Still, in practice, even experts sometimes use manual formatting in certain circumstances.

Format manually if:

- The document is short (1-2 pages), and you have no templates that you can use.

- The document will be used once and never reused.

Use styles if:

- The document is long (over 3 pages).

- The document is going to be used over and over.

- The document will only be edited by a single person.

- Any editing will only take place within a few days of finishing the document.

- Some people who will edit the document have no idea how to use styles, and refuse to learn.

- A consistent format doesn't matter for some other reason. For example, the document is informal, and won't affect your company's branding.

- You are experimenting with styles while building a template. Until you finalize the styles, you will make so many changes that creating styles is mostly wasted effort.

- The document's formatting is extremely simple and regular, like an essay.

- The document will be edited by more than one person.

- The document will be edited weeks, months, or even years after the first version.

- The document belongs to a standard class of documents, such as a letter, a fax, or memo.

- The document design must match that of other documents from you or your company or organization.

- You want to use the document in a number of different ways, each of which requires some minor changes: for example, printing it on both a white and a red background.

- The document is highly formatted, like a brochure.

The more circumstances that apply, the clearer your decision.

However, even if all indications are to use manual formatting, check the templates you have saved. You may find one close enough to your needs to re-use.

The types of styles

Most office suites confine themselves to paragraph and character styles in their word processors. However, LibreOffice adds three more styles in Writer (plus a pseudo-style for tables), and other styles for spreadsheets, presentations, and diagrams.

These additional styles greatly extend what LibreOffice can do. They make Writer less a word processor than an intermediate desktop publishing tool. Writer may not have all the precision of a tool like InDesign, but it compares favorably with a tool like FrameMaker for text-heavy documents. In fact, I know of several publishers who use Writer for designing their books.

Admittedly, styles are less useful in other applications. The layout in their files tends to be less uniform than in Writer. However, in other applications, styles do help to centralize frequently used settings, which is a benefit by itself.

The styles available are:

Style	Comment
Writer	
PARAGRAPH	PARAGRAPH styles are the most commonly used style. A paragraph begins and ends when you press the ENTER key. Common paragraph styles include those for body text

and headings. Equivalent to manual formatting with FORMAT > PARAGRAPH, plus some extras.

CHARACTER

CHARACTER styles modify selected letters in a paragraph style. Common character styles are bold lettering for emphasis, italics for a book title, and underlining and a different color for a web link. An exact equivalent to manual formatting with FORMAT > CHARACTER.

FRAME

All objects inserted to a Writer document are contained by a frame. By customizing FRAME styles, you can automatically adjust elements such as the border around objects and how text flows around them. Right-click on a selected frame for the manual equivalent.

PAGE

PAGE styles are the most reliable way to format pages differently, including headers and footers and footnotes. The main drawback is that you cannot easily set an object to reoccur on every page that uses the same page style. Exact equivalent to manual formatting with FORMAT > PAGE.

LIST

Styles for configuring bullet lists and numbered lists. LIST styles can be applied directly to a list, or, more elegantly,

	associated with one or more paragraph styles. Equivalent to manually formatting with FORMAT > BULLETS AND NUMBERING.
(TABLES)	Technically, Writer has no table styles. However, you can save and apply table designs in a style-like way by selecting TABLE > AUTOFORMAT > ADD.

Calc

CELL	CELL styles set both the appearance of cells and the types of content in them, such as percentages or currency. They also can automatically set the number of decimal places used by the cell, and automatically wrap and hyphenate the contents of a style.
PAGE	PAGE styles set how to arrange selected sheets or cells to print to paper.

Draw & Impress

GRAPHIC	Styles for drawing objects, including graphic text.
PRESENTATION	Styles for the contents of slides (Impress only).

Working with styles

To open the STYLES AND FORMATTING window, do one of the following:

• Select FORMAT > STYLES AND FORMATTING from the menu bar.

- Press the F11 key.

- Click the MORE... link at the bottom of the style list in the FORMATTING tool bar.

- Select the STYLES AND FORMATTING button on the sidebar.

Tip

You can also highlight an entry in the tool bar's style list and select EDIT to open the style's dialog window.

In LibreOffice releases before 4.4 and in Apache OpenOffice, you can click the first icon on the left on the FORMATTING tool bar (the bottom default tool bar).

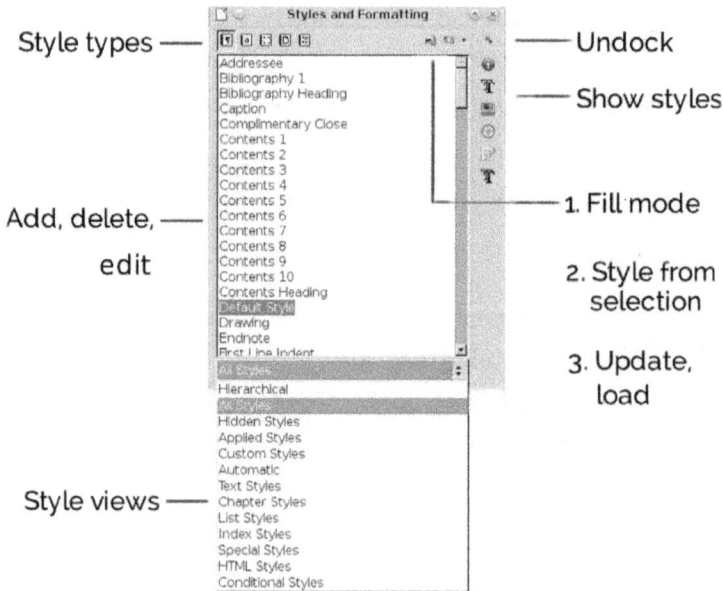

Writer's version of the STYLES AND FORMATTING window.

Undocking the Styles and Formatting window

Until LibreOffice version 4.4, the STYLES AND FORMATTING window opened as a floating window. The floating window could be placed anywhere on the screen, or dragged to be docked on either side of the editing window. However, starting in version 4.4, it opens in the sidebar.

To undock the window (or any other display in the sidebar), click the drop-down list of commands on the top right of the tool bar and select UNDOCK. When the window is undocked, select DOCK from the drop-down list to redock it. LibreOffice remembers whether the window is docked or undocked when you restart it.

Tip

The sidebar remains undocked, even after you exit and restart LibreOffice.

In OpenOffice and many earlier LibreOffice versions, drag the floating window by its title bar to the left or right edge of the editing window. When a frame appears, release the floating window, and it is docked. Dragging on the title bar of the docked window should undock it, although the reliability of the feature varies with the release.

Changing the style type

On the top left of the window are icons for each type of style. If you hover the mouse over them, you will see what type of style each icon represents. Click an icon to display the styles for its particular type.

Characters   Pages

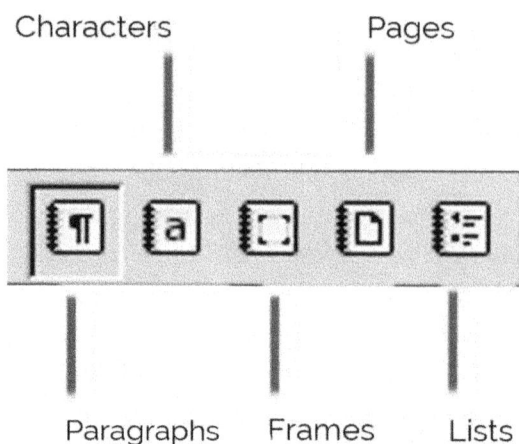

Paragraphs   Frames   Lists

The types of styles in Writer. Paragraph styles are currently selected.

Viewing styles

Because the list of styles is long, the drop-down list at the bottom of the window has filtered views that need less scrolling.

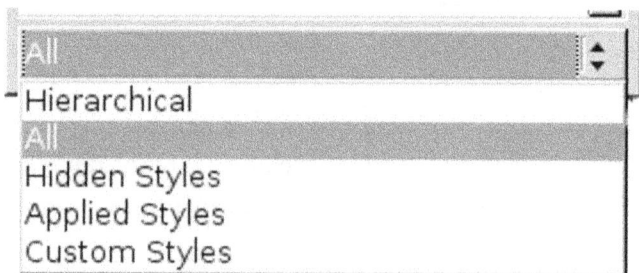

Style views filter the styles that display.

The best view depends on what you are doing. For example, when you are designing, the HIERARCHICAL view helps you work with related styles. By contrast, after you have written a few pages, the APPLIED STYLES view minimizes the styles displayed.

The basic views vary with the application. The most common ones are:

- HIERARCHICAL: Shows how styles are related to each other (See "The hierarchy of styles," page 25). Helps you decide where to make changes in multiple styles by editing just one of them.

- APPLIED STYLES: The styles used in the current document. This view is useless with a new document, but as you continue to work, it reduces the number of styles displayed.

- CUSTOM STYLES: The styles you have created, as opposed to the pre-defined ones.

- AUTOMATIC: A minimalist list of pre-defined styles. AUTOMATIC is the default view when you open a new document.

- ALL STYLES: Especially when you are viewing paragraph styles, the ALL STYLES view can give you so many names to scan that using it is counter-productive. Use ALL STYLES only when you are completely unable to find the style you want.

- HIDDEN STYLES: Styles you have removed from the other views to reduce the clutter.

Paragraph styles have a number of additional views. Most are self-explanatory divisions of the uses for styles, such as HTML STYLES and INDEX STYLES.

Styles that don't fit into any other category, such as CAPTION, FOOTER LEFT, or TABLE CONTENTS are listed as SPECIAL STYLES.

Tip

The HTML view shows the paragraph styles that LibreOffice has mapped directly to specific HTML tags.

Finding current styles

The STYLES AND FORMATTING window always opens with the style for the current cursor position highlighted. If you change the type of style displayed in the STYLES AND FORMATTING window, then the highlighted style also changes, if possible.

For example, if you are using the TEXT BODY paragraph style and switch the display to character styles, ordinarily the DEFAULT STYLE will be highlighted. However, if you switch to the list styles, nothing will be highlighted unless the cursor is at a position where a list style is being used.

In Writer, you can identify current styles in other places in the editing window. When closed, the list of paragraph styles on the FORMATTING tool bar always displays the current style.

Similarly, the current page style is shown, third from the left, in the indicators at the bottom of the editing window. As you scroll through a document, it is updated automatically.

In addition, you can select EDIT > FIND & REPLACE > OTHER OPTIONS > SEARCH FOR PARAGRAPH STYLES to locate where a style is used in a document. Finding character styles is not directly possibly, but FIND & REPLACE's OTHER OPTIONS do include search by settings of character styles using ATTRIBUTES and FORMAT.

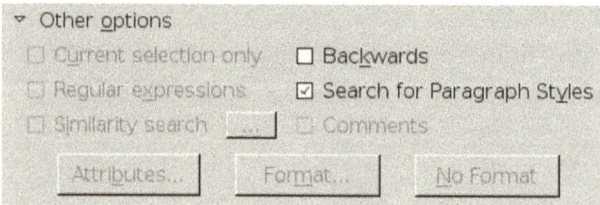

SEARCH FOR PARAGRAPH STYLES is an essential option for editing format and structure.

The nature of styles

LibreOffice has pre-defined styles that you can modify but not delete. In each style type, especially paragraph and character styles, the pre-defined styles are well thought out, and might be all that you need. In fact, one school of thought holds that you have less trouble if you use only pre-defined styles, even though that may limit your designs. Whether that is true is uncertain, but the pre-defined styles are useful references for what you can do with styles.

In addition, you can create custom styles that are based on pre-defined ones, or entirely new ones by clicking on any pre-defined style. Custom styles provide the specialized needs that the pre-defined styles do not.

Both custom and pre-defined styles behave similarly. Understanding their behaviors is essential for working with all styles.

The hierarchy of styles

Many styles in LibreOffice are hierarchical (although for some reason a few, such as LIST styles, are not). In other words, they are ordered in a tree, with each style taking its characteristics from the one at the top and modifying some of them.

A style that is one level above another is called the parent of the style directly below it. Similarly, styles that are one level below another one are called its children. Changing a parent style also changes its children.

This relationship can be confusing, especially the first time a style apparently changes its characteristics spontaneously. However, by making changes to the parent, you save the time you would spend changing its children one at a time.

```
▽Heading
    Bibliography Heading
    Contents Heading
    Heading 1
    Heading 2
    Heading 3
    Heading 4
    Heading 5
    Heading 6
    Heading 7
    Heading 8
    Heading 9
    Heading 10
```

A style hierarchy for paragraph styles in Writer. Changes to the HEADING style will change all the styles below it.

Changing the style hierarchy

You can manipulate the style hierarchy using the INHERIT FROM field on the ORGANIZER tab. The style inherited from is the current style's parent – the style from which the current style inherits characteristics.

Tip

In Apache OpenOffice and earlier LIbreOffice releases, the INHERIT FROM field is called LINKED WITH.

Sometimes, you may want to use the field to set an arbitrary parent. For example, if you created two paragraph styles for bullets, differing only in the list style each used, you could save time by setting one of the styles as the parent of another. Either one would do – the point is to make changes only once, not twice.

The Default styles

The only styles that do not have a hierarchical parent are those at the top of the entire tree. In paragraph and character styles, this style is called DEFAULT. All other styles of the same type are based upon the DEFAULT style.

You can choose to edit the DEFAULT style so that it includes the basic formatting you have chosen for the document. Alternatively, you can leave the DEFAULT style unchanged, so that you can exchange documents easily with people on other machines.

This second choice is not always possible because different versions of LibreOfice may set different DEFAULT styles, but is worth trying. In effect, this approach uses another style such as TEXT BODY as an unofficial default, leaving the DEFAULT style to function like FORMAT > CLEAR DIRECT FORMATTING.

Either way, the DEFAULT styles are useful when pasting formatted text from inside or outside the current document creates formatting problems.

The easiest way to solve these problems is to strip out most of the formatting by applying the DEFAULT character and/or paragraph style, then to apply the formatting you want.

Tip

Lists sometimes leave bullets or numbers behind after you apply the default paragraph style to them. When that happens, press the BACKSPACE key until the bullet or number disappears.

The Organizer tab

The window for each style throughout LibreOffice is divided into tabs. Many tabs, such as the BORDER and the AREA tabs, display identical features throughout LibreOffice; so, in later chapters, the book gives cross-references to prevent repetition.

Of all the tabs, the ORGANIZER tab is most important. It summarizes the style and its relation to other styles.

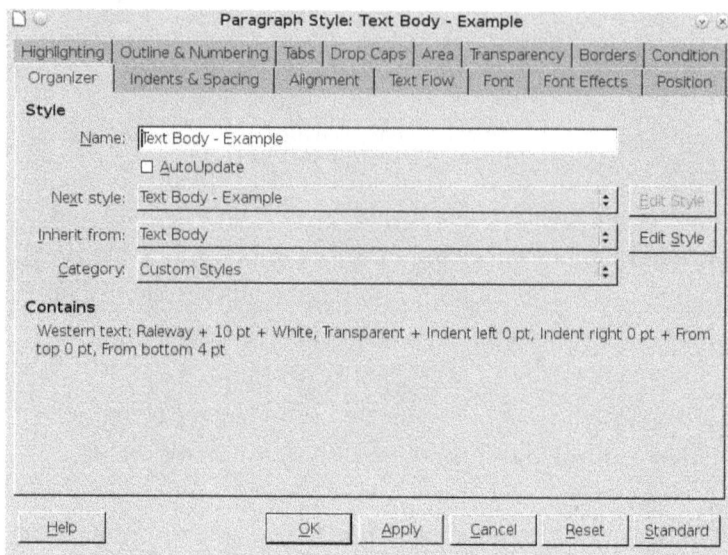

```
                   Paragraph Style: Text Body - Example                    ⌄ ✕

Highlighting | Outline & Numbering | Tabs | Drop Caps | Area | Transparency | Borders | Condition
  Organizer  |  Indents & Spacing  |  Alignment  |  Text Flow  |  Font  |  Font Effects  |  Position

  Style
       Name:  |Text Body - Example                                              |
              ☐ AutoUpdate
  Next style:  Text Body - Example                                      ⬍|  Edit Style
  Inherit from: Text Body                                               ⬍|  Edit Style
   Category:   Custom Styles                                            ⬍|

  Contains
     Western text: Raleway + 10 pt + White, Transparent + Indent left 0 pt, Indent right 0 pt + From
     top 0 pt, From bottom 4 pt




     Help                    OK    |   Apply   |  Cancel  |  Reset  |  Standard
```

To change a style's parent, change the INHERIT FROM field on the ORGANIZER tab (may be called LINKED WITH).

The ORGANIZER tab can include four fields:

- NAME: The entry that appears in the STYLE AND FORMATTING window. It should be descriptive or suggest the style's function.

- NEXT STYLE: The style that is automatically used next when you press the ENTER key. For instance, HEADING 1 is often followed by TEXT BODY. Since a heading is almost never followed immediately by another heading, this is a reasonable choice. By contrast, TEXT BODY's NEXT STYLE is usually TEXT BODY, because several paragraphs in a row are likely to be text.

- INHERIT FROM (LINKED WITH): The parent style in the hierarchy. Changes to the parent style will change the current style, so you don't have to make changes to every related style.
- CATEGORY: The view in which the style is listed. By default, styles you create are displayed in CUSTOM STYLES, but you can choose any other view instead.

> ## Tip
> You can sometimes make a view more effective by changing which category each of your custom styles displays in.

In addition, the ORGANIZER tab shows a summary of all the formatting options selected for the style, similar to the one that WordPerfect gives.

The fields in the ORGANIZER tab are grayed-out in types of styles where they would make no sense. For example, two frames seldom occur one after the other, so a FRAME style window omits the NEXT STYLE category. Similarly, the CATEGORY field is grayed out, because only one view is necessary for frames.

Applying styles

To apply a style, you must select part of the document. A paragraph or page is selected when the mouse cursor is anywhere in or on them, but frames or drawing objects must be selected by clicking in them so the frame and its eight handles displays. You can also drag the mouse to select multiple paragraphs or spreadsheet cells.

You have several options for applying a style: the STYLES AND FORMATTING window, the FORMATTING tool bar, FILL FORMAT mode, pasting from your system's clipboard, and applying keyboard shortcuts.

Using the Styles and Formatting window

With the STYLES AND FORMATTING window open, you can apply a style with a single mouse-click – or maybe two as you select another style category to list.

For many users, the STYLES AND FORMATTING window is the most efficient way to apply styles. Some users keep it docked in the sidebar, which can mean that a maximized window is necessary, depending on the size of your monitor.

If you prefer not to work in maximized windows, undock the window and place it where it is close enough to the editing window to minimize mouse motions, but far enough away that it doesn't block what you are doing.

Starting with version 5.0, the STYLES AND FORMATTING window shows a preview of the current font formatting. This preview is useful when dealing with character styles, but omits most of the information in a paragraph or a list style. With frame and page styles, it is mostly a distraction.

Using the Formatting tool bar

In Writer, you can apply paragraph styles to a selection by opening the drop-down list of styles that is on the left on the FORMATTING tool bar (the default bottom tool bar).

Tip

When applying a style, always click on the left of a list item. Otherwise, you risk being entangled in the menu.

```
Default Style          ▼
Clear formatting
Default Style
Text Body
Quotations
Title
Subtitle
Heading 1        ▼
Heading 2    Update to Match Selection
Heading 3    Edit Style...
More Styles...
```

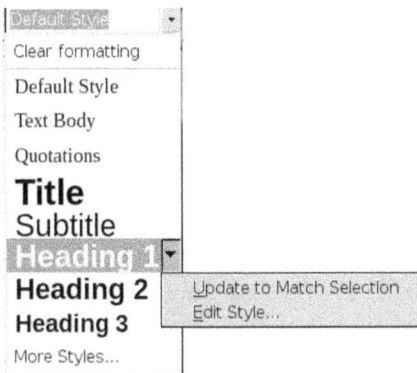

The styles list in the FORMATTING toolbar.

When you first open a document, the list includes only a half
dozen commonly used styles. Gradually, though, other paragraph
styles are listed as they are used in the document. Clicking the
MORE STYLES... link at the bottom of the list opens the STYLES AND
FORMATTING window, while selecting EDIT STYLE from a style's
drop-down menu opens the dialog window for the style.

Similarly, UPDATE TO MATCH SELECTION edits the style based on
the formatting of the text you select before opening the drop-
down list.

The list has the advantage of offering a preview of each
paragraph style. Unfortunately, that preview is only the name of
the style, which means that many formatting elements are not
shown in the preview.

Consequently, the list is a limited tool at best. At most it
serves as a reminder of what the style looks like.

Using Fill Format Mode

With the STYLES AND FORMATTING window, you also have the
option with some style categories of reversing the basic
application technique, choosing the style first, and where to apply

it second. When applying character styles, it is almost like painting with the cursor, as its icon in the STYLES AND FORMATTING window suggests.

To use FILL FORMAT:

1   Select a style.

2   Click the FILL FORMAT MODE button (the second from the right at the top of the STYLES AND FORMATTING window).

When FILL FORMAT is available, the cursor changes to a paint bucket.

If the button is grayed out, you cannot use FILL FORMAT with the style category selected.

3   Drag the cursor over the part of the document you wish to format. You need to drag the cursor for only a few characters to apply the style to a paragraph or a page. However, to apply a character style, you need to drag the cursor across all the characters you plan to format.

4   Click the FILL FORMAT MODE button a second time to turn the mode off.

STOP Caution

Right-clicking anywhere in a document when FILL FORMAT MODE is turned on stops it from being applied.

Pasting styles

The rules for copying and pasting styles are simple regardless of whether you use PASTE or PASTE SPECIAL, or are copying from one document to another:

- When source material formatted in a style with the same name as a style in the target is copied into a paragraph, then the target's style is used.

- When source material formatted in a style not in the target is copied into a new paragraph, then the formatting is kept and the style name is added to the target document.

- Any formatting done manually or with a character style in the source is copied wherever it is pasted.

These rules hold true for all types of styles.

They also hold true for any Open Document Format file, including those created in Apache OpenOffice or Calligra Suite, the free office program designed for the KDE desktop.

You can remove most of this formatting by selecting CLEAR FORMATTING from the top of the drop-down list of paragraph styles on the FORMATTING tool bar.

Unfortunately, some of the original formatting, including the text color and any underlining, sometimes remains when available system memory is low. When it does, applying the DEFAULT character style may remove it. If some formatting still persists, retype the material.

Tip

When you paste material, click the arrow beside the PASTE icon in the top toolbar and select UNFORMATTED TEXT. The extra step may prevent formatting difficulties.

Applying styles using keyboard shortcuts

Pressing CTRL+1 ... CTRL+10 applies the HEADING 1-10 styles. These shortcuts can be useful in documents such as an outline, in which you are using only Heading paragraph styles. You can set keyboard shortcuts for other styles from TOOLS > CUSTOMIZE > FUNCTIONS > STYLES.

Keyboard shortcuts can save stress on your wrists and hands when you are typing for long periods, so you may want to record additional macros and assign them to keyboard shortcuts. The DEFAULT STYLE and TEXT BODY paragraph styles are likely candidates for macros, and so are the EMPHASIS and STRONG EMPHASIS character styles.

STOP Caution

To record macros in LibreOffice, you first need to select TOOLS > OPTIONS > LIBREOFFICE > ADVANCED > ENABLE MACRO RECORDING (LIMITED). The menu item RECORD MACRO is then listed under TOOLS > MACROS without any need to re-start LibreOffice.

Creating and modifying styles

LibreOffice has styles for most ordinary purposes, so one way to save time is to use only pre-defined styles, changing no more attributes than necessary. On the whole, the styles have intelligent defaults, and you usually only have to make a few changes while designing.

However, if you decide to edit styles, you have several options in Writer:

- Right-click on a style in the STYLES AND FORMATTING window and select NEW to create a style that clones the selected style (in other words, one that is a child of the selected style in the hierarchy). Be sure to rename it immediately. If you forget to rename, you can find the new style at the bottom of the list of styles, named something like UNTITLED1.

- Right-click on a style in the STYLES AND FORMATTING window and select MODIFY to edit the selected style.

- Manually format and select part of the document. Open the drop-down list on the top right of the STYLES AND FORMATTING window and select NEW STYLE FROM SELECTION. This option is handy for creating styles on-the-fly or if you have a hard time visualizing settings while you are planning a design.

- Select a passage and drag it to the STYLES AND FORMATTING window when it displays paragraph or character styles. A dialog window opens so that you can give the new style a title.

- Select the AUTOUPDATE check box on the ORGANIZER tab of a style. When this box is selected, any manual formatting you do automatically updates the style.

- Edit styles from the tool bar. In LibreOffice 4.4 and later, you can update styles by highlighting part of the document, then selecting a style in the tool bar's drop-down list and clicking UPDATE TO MATCH SELECTION.

STOP

Caution

Only select AUTOUPDATE if everyone editing the document uses styles. Otherwise, the result could be stylistic chaos. In fact, when using styles, discourage any editors from doing any manual formatting.

You also have the option of copying styles from a template into the current document. See "Changing templates," page 61.

Hiding and deleting styles

Hiding styles reduces the clutter in the STYLES AND
FORMATTING window. To hide a style, select HIDE from the right-
click menu, one style at a time. If you need to use the style again,
you can restore it from the HIDDEN STYLES view.

A custom style that is no longer needed can be deleted using
the right-click menu. You cannot delete a pre-defined style. Styles
installed from an extension can only be deleted by removing the
extension in TOOLS > EXTENSION MANAGER.

Naming styles

Especially in Writer, styles are named for their functions,
followed by their position in the file hierarchy. For instance, USER

INDEX1 is the paragraph style for the first level of text in an index. Similarly, character styles include EMPHASIS and INTERNET LINK.

Other names for pre-defined styles are descriptive, such as OBJECT WITHOUT FILL in Draw.

Tip

Since you will probably be using at least some pre-defined styles, you may decide to use the same conventions for custom styles.

However, to save yourself scrolling endlessly through the STYLES AND FORMATTING window, consider prefacing any custom styles with "C-" or some other unique preface. That way, you can easily find and apply custom styles without having to change the view.

In Writer, you sometimes find that you use different categories of styles in the same design. For example, a list style can have a character style associated with it so that you can have colored bullets or numbers. In addition, the same list style can be assigned to a paragraph style so that it is used whenever you choose the paragraph style. To help you find each of these styles later, give them the same name. Since each is in a different category, neither you nor LibreOffice should confuse them.

Automating style application

In most documents, some styles follow one another in a set pattern. A TITLE paragraph style is usually followed by a SUBTITLE, and a TEXT BODY paragraph style by another TEXT BODY. A FIRST PAGE style is usually followed by a LEFT PAGE, which is followed by a RIGHT PAGE.

You can take advantage of such patterns by filling in the NEXT STYLE field on the Organizer tab. With some types of styles, such as lists, having a NEXT STYLE makes no sense, and the field is grayed out. But with the NEXT STYLE field filled in, just starting a new paragraph or page will automatically apply the next style without your hands leaving the keyboard.

Another way of writing

Don't be surprised if you need time to get used to the idea of styles. Using styles involves more planning beforehand than manual formatting. Yet the basic concepts are straightforward, and already you might be starting to see how styles can automate formatting.

In the next chapter, you'll see how templates can help you recycle document designs to save you even more time.

3

Recycling using templates

No one has time to design a document every time they sit down to write. It's inefficient. Nor do you want everyone working on a project to design their own documents. The solution to both these problems is templates – files to store formatting and structure to re-use or share.

Templates are handled differently from ordinary documents. Before you use them, they need to be registered, so that LibreOffice is aware of them. They also have their own menus and menu items that normal files do not use.

Mostly, templates store formatting. However, they can also store structure, either in the form of outlines, or of fields that automatically fill in standard information or indicate with placeholders what kind of information should be added.

This structural use of templates tends to be under-emphasized. However, you can find examples of it in some releases of LibreOffice or OpenOffice in the Impress templates entitled "Introducing a New Strategy" and "Recommendation of a Strategy."

Both these templates include not only formatting, but a standard set of slides for developing a presentation with certain goals in mind. You can develop equally detailed structural templates to automate your work.

An Impress slide with a formal placeholder for the title and informal ones for other information. Placeholders help you to rough out a design without requiring specific information.

Tip

If you are a long-time user of office suites, you may be wary of templates because of how easily they became corrupted in Microsoft Word when you made any changes or tried to mix templates.

If so, don't worry. LibreOffice templates are designed to eliminate the problems that caused the corruption in Word. Mostly, they succeed, although sometimes at the cost of restricting what you can do with templates.

When to use templates

As with styles, the short answer is, "Whenever possible." Not only are templates more efficient than designing from scratch, but using them consistently helps you get used to the concepts behind them.

Over the years, I have heard users claim that templates are impractical because every document they do is different.

However, when I probe such claims, I usually find that the problem wasn't that every document was different, but that the person making the claims didn't think in terms of structure. Nor did they realize that a consistent general format can be part of corporate or personal branding.

A more plausible reason for not using templates is that setting them up takes time. Yet even that excuse fails to survive scrutiny.

Example

The all-purpose template I first designed in 2002 took several hours to design, and maybe another two to fine-tune.

Since then, I have used that all-purpose template for hundreds of documents. Each time I used it, I could start to write immediately and without worrying about how it was formatted.

At a minimum of three hours per template design, I have easily saved over a month's time thanks to that one template alone.

Other templates I have made over the years have seen less use. But always, the initial hours lost to template design have still been regained countless times over the years.

Using templates does mean planning ahead. But this new work flow rapidly repays the effort to change your work habits.

How templates work

Unlike Microsoft Word, LibreOffice does not display a NORMAL template anywhere in its menus. This omission eliminates the possibility of a document being corrupted by too much editing of the DEFAULT template.

The only way that you can alter LibreOffice's default formats without using templates is to change the font settings in TOOLS > OPTIONS > LIBREOFFICE WRITER > BASIC FONTS (WESTERN). Default formatting such as page and list styles cannot be edited at all.

However, you can also design a template with far more formatting information as default. Its settings will be used for every document when you select FILE > NEW, unless you specifically select another template.

Linking templates with documents

Whichever template you use, it must be properly registered before you can use it.

Only one template can be applied at one time to a document. This policy avoids the tendency to corruption that used to plague MS Word (and may still do, for all that I know).

STOP
Caution

Two styles of the same name in separate documents can have different formats.

If the template changes, the next time you restart LibreOffice and open the document, you are prompted to update the document. Styles shared by the template and the document are updated, but styles that are only in the document are not.

If you choose UPDATE STYLES, then the document continues to be linked to the template. However, remember to save the document after updating.

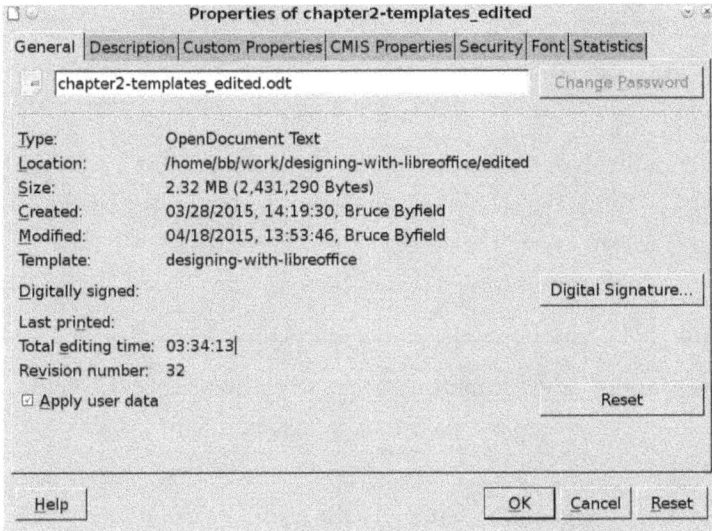

Properties of chapter2-templates_edited		
General Description Custom Properties CMIS Properties Security Font Statistics		

chapter2-templates_edited.odt   Change Password

Type: OpenDocument Text
Location: /home/bb/work/designing-with-libreoffice/edited
Size: 2.32 MB (2,431,290 Bytes)
Created: 03/28/2015, 14:19:30, Bruce Byfield
Modified: 04/18/2015, 13:53:46, Bruce Byfield
Template: designing-with-libreoffice

Digitally signed: Digital Signature...

Last printed:
Total editing time: 03:34:13|
Revision number: 32
☑ Apply user data   Reset

Help   OK   Cancel   Reset

FILES > PROPERTIES > GENERAL lists the template upon which the document was originally based. The layout of this tab is different in LibreOffice before release 4.3, with the template at the bottom of the window.

By contrast, if you choose KEEP OLD STYLES, it is unlinked from the template, and you are not prompted for further updates when the template changes again. However, the PROPERTIES window continues to list the template, even though it is irrelevant.

Tip

Documents whose templates have been edited are not always updated when closed and reopened. You may have to restart LibreOffice for the change to take effect.

When you open a document, you are warned that its template has been edited.

Generally, you want to avoid detaching documents from their templates. Since the whole point of using templates is to make uniform design easier, the best practices are usually:

- Change the formatting only on the template.

- Always keep documents connected to their templates.

- Never make any formatting changes in a document. Even deleting or adding a style can detach a document from its template.

- As soon as you make changes to the template, close and reopen the documents that use the template as soon as possible. This practice may disturb your work, but it means that you won't have to remember what changed, or wonder if you made an accidental change when you receive notice of the change the next time that you open the file.

Re-attaching styles

Macros and extensions are sometimes available for re-attaching styles to a document. Currently, Template Changer extension is available, but it has not had a release for some time. At any rate, any attempt to swap templates raises the possibility of corruption, so test the extension using duplicate files until you are confident that it works.

A more reliable solution is usually to copy and paste the file contents to a blank file created from the original template.

STOP

Caution

Any changes visible with EDIT > TRACK CHANGES > SHOW CHANGES are lost when you copy and paste.

By contrast, any comments or fields are copied.

Identifying a template

You can always identify a LibreOffice template file, because the second letter in its extension is always a "t." This pattern is used in both Open Document Format and the obsolete OpenOffice.org 1.0 format:

Application	ODF Format	OOo Format
Writer	.ott	.stw
Calc	.ots	.stc
Impress	.otp	.sti
Draw	.otg	.stf

Template extensions for Open Document Format and the older OpenOffice.org format.

Using the Template Manager

LibreOffice does not display template directories directly. Instead, it creates a virtual view of the contents of all the template directories listed in TOOLS > OPTIONS > PATHS > TEMPLATES in the TEMPLATE MANAGER window.

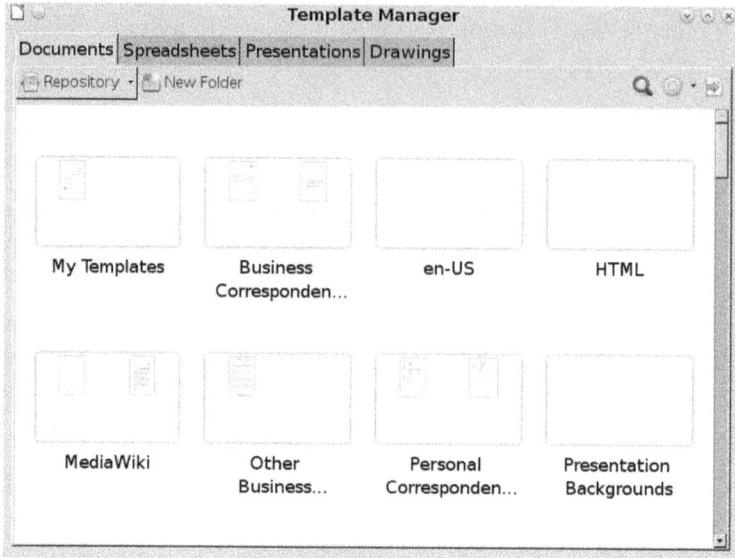

The Template Manager, showing sub-folders for different categories.

The Template Manager opens from several places in the menu. One is FILE > NEW > TEMPLATES. Depending on the version and operating system, it may also open from:

- FILE > SAVE AS TEMPLATE (not available in Apache OpenOffice or some operating systems).

- The TEMPLATES link on the introductory splash screen.

- FILE > TEMPLATES > MANAGE or FILE > TEMPLATEMENU, depending on the operating system and version.

STOP Caution

Each view of the Template Manager shows only the icons that apply to whatever is selected. For example, in Linux when you save from TEMPLATEMENU, you can only save, search, and view.

Designing with LibreOffice

The Template Manager is divided into tabs for different types of templates: DOCUMENTS, SPREADSHEETS, PRESENTATIONS, and DRAWINGS. Within each tab, sub-folders of the templates are shown as rectangles, and referred to as "categories."

As shown above, you might have sub-folders such as EN-US and EN-CA for templates that use American and Canadian English locales for dictionaries.

Other options might be sub-folders named for a client or project or specific themes, such as light or dark backgrounds – whatever works best for you. Click on these rectangles to zoom in on the available templates and select from them.

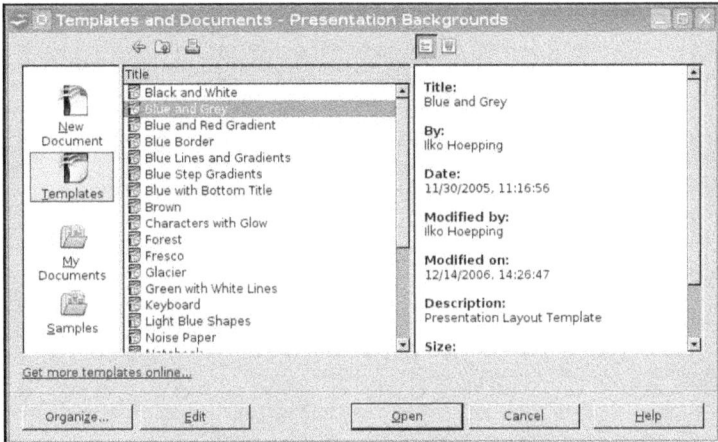

OpenOffice's Template Manager and versions of LibreOffice before 3.3 have an older design that is functionally equivalent.

Planning a template library

Whether you create or download your templates, start by assessing the types of documents you create regularly. Although you might be tempted to download or design every template available, installing or designing more templates than you generally need will only make finding the ones you actually use harder.

Begin your planning by considering what your general layout will be. If you work for a company, does it have corporate colors that you will constantly use? If so, begin by creating the colors in TOOLS > OPTIONS > COLORS so they are available for uses such as table borders and headings in color documents.

Are particular fonts part of your personal or corporate branding? Do you prefer a particular font size? All such items can go into an all-purpose template that can be the starting point for others. Call the result something like GENERAL or STANDARD.

Become more specific by recalling what documents you have written in the past. If you can't remember them:

- Open FILE > RECENT DOCUMENTS.

- Check the attachments in emails that you have sent.

- Keep a diary of the documents you produce over a week or a month and how often you write the same kind.

A carefully selected template can last you for years, so taking the time to classify your work is worth the effort.

Example: Assessing template requirements

Imagine that you are a financial account executive. You want your all-purpose template to use your company's branding.

After some consideration, you find that you are regularly writing one-page memos, short official letters, and longer monthly internal reports. You also write quarterly reports for the company newsletter, whose editor wants copy in HTML, and the occasional personal letter, whose design should make clear that you are not speaking officially for the company.

Basically, in planning your template library, you are answering the question: What documents do I regularly produce in LibreOffice?

If you are like most people, you will probably come up with at least three or four different templates that you will need regularly. If you don't download them, create them gradually as the need arises. Unless some of your templates are extremely similar, you probably won't want to design more than one at a time.

Naming templates

Like style names, template names should be as descriptive as possible. Descriptive titles are simply easier to find in a menu.

However, another practical reason for choosing template names carefully is that, if you copy a file to another computer, you might have a naming conflict. If that happens, your document will not be seen how you meant it to be seen. If you forgot to make a copy, you could have a lot of re-formatting to do.

To avoid such problems, make your template names as specific as possible. For instance, instead of LETTER.OTT, call your template PERSONAL-LETTER – or, better yet, something long and exact like PERSONAL-LETTER-FORMAL-STRUCTURE. The more specific the template's name, the easier it will be to find when you want it.

Readying templates for use

Once you have figured which templates you need, you can get the templates you need in several ways:

- Downloading and installing templates made by others, perhaps with minor modifications.

- Creating your own templates using LibreOffice's wizards as a guide.

- Designing your own templates from scratch.

Regardless of how you obtain templates, they must be registered before LibreOffice can take full advantage of them. See "Saving and registering templates," page 53.

Downloading templates

If you prefer not to design your templates from scratch, you can use pre-existing templates instead, modifying them as necessary. Appendix A lists some of the larger sites for templates.

Almost all the templates that you find online are released under free licenses, so you can generally modify them freely.

The disadvantage of using others' templates is that you have to sort through them to find what you want. At times, you may download two templates from different websites, only to discover that they are the same template with different names.

Often, too, you have to modify downloaded templates to get the exact design you want. In the end, you may not save time so much as exchange the time spent designing for searching and tweaking templates.

Another problem with these official sites is that each template must be downloaded and installed separately.

However, you can find extensions like the Professional Template Pack II that will install multiple templates together from TOOLS > EXTENSION MANAGER after you download them. Using such extensions can save several hours of effort.

You can also open Microsoft Office templates and convert them to Open Document Format. This is an ideal solution for presentation backgrounds, but less so for word processor documents, especially those with complex formatting, which may not import or export well.

STOP

Caution

Using Microsoft Office templates is illegal if you do not have a copy of Microsoft Office. To avoid any legal difficulties – however remote – avoid using templates designed for Microsoft Office except for personal, non-commercial use.

Creating templates with wizards

If designing your own templates is too large a step, start by using the wizards that LibreOffice installs.

These wizards illustrate the kinds of decisions that you make when designing, and can give you a sense of the sorts of decisions you need to make when designing your own templates.

In addition, they are good examples of how to add structure to templates. However, despite their best efforts to provide variety, the wizards do tend to create unimaginative, outdated results.

Wizards are available from the FILE > WIZARDS sub-menu. Some of the wizards give you the option of using a LibreOffice Base database or the address book of an email client for filling in fields, which is convenient for mass mail-outs.

When you are finished setting options for the template, the wizard defaults to saving the resulting template to a subdirectory of your personal template directory, registering them for immediate use.

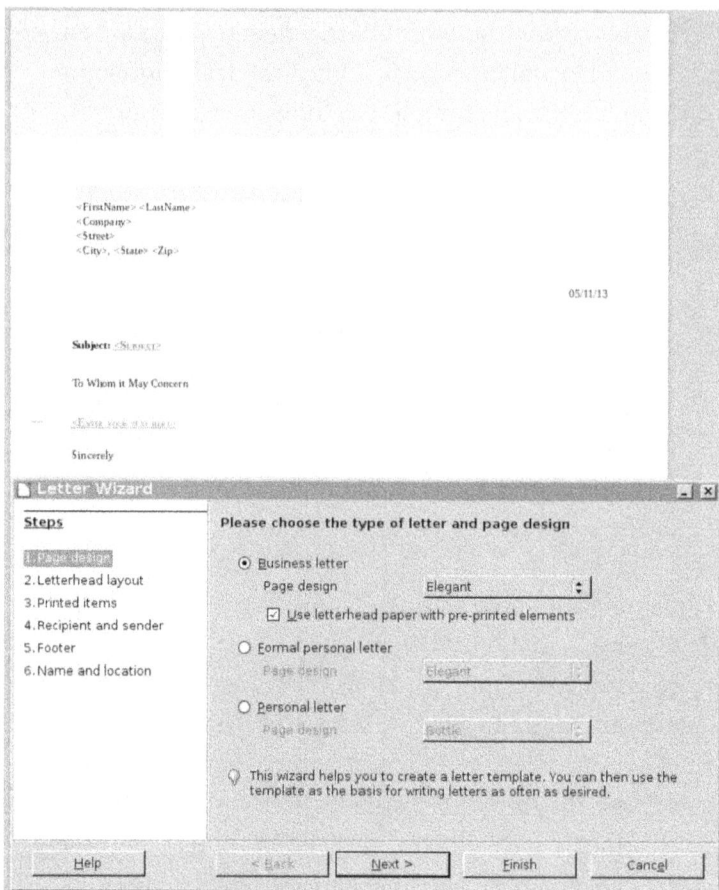

```
<FirstName> <LastName>
<Company>
<Street>
<City>, <State> <Zip>


                                                    05/11/13


Subject: <Subject>

To Whom it May Concern


<Enter your text here>

Sincerely
```

Letter Wizard

Steps	Please choose the type of letter and page design
1. Page design	⦿ Business letter
2. Letterhead layout	Page design Elegant
3. Printed items	☑ Use letterhead paper with pre-printed elements
4. Recipient and sender	○ Formal personal letter
5. Footer	Page design Elegant
6. Name and location	○ Personal letter
	Page design Bottle

This wizard helps you to create a letter template. You can then use the template as the basis for writing letters as often as desired.

[Help] [< Back] [Next >] [Finish] [Cancel]

LibreOffice's letter template wizard. Although often more elaborate than strictly necessary, these wizards can give you a starting point to studying templates.

The PRESENTATION template is particularly useful. It is designed as a wizard to guide you through the basic formatting and structural decisions for building a slide show.

Once, Impress opened in its template wizard. It remains a useful reminder of the structural decisions you need to make.

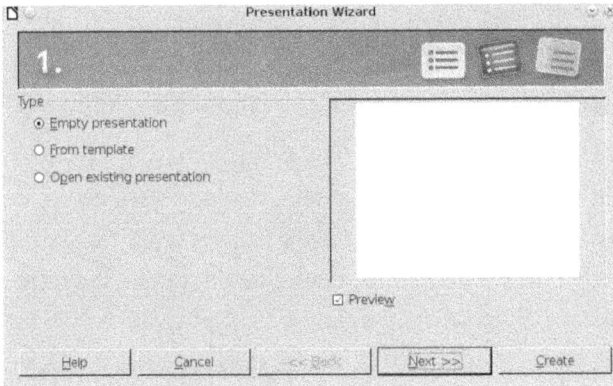

The Presentation Wizard in Impress.

Saving and registering templates

A regular file only needs to be saved in order to be ready for use. By contrast, each template must be registered with LibreOffice before you can use it, just as databases and address books must be.

What this means is that you cannot simply save a template.

True, if you save a file using FILE> SAVE or FILE > SAVE AS, you can select a LibreOffice template from the drop-down list of formats in the SAVE dialog window. This approach is useful for such purposes as saving a template so you can install it on another computer, or give a copy to a friend.

However, a conventional SAVE does not register and activate the new template for use on your system. To make a template available, follow these steps:

1 Save it with FILE > SAVE AS TEMPLATE, FILE > TEMPLATES > SAVE AS TEMPLATE, or FILE > TEMPLATEMENU > SAVE AS TEMPLATE (all these options may not be available in all versions of LibreOffice).

In each case, the TEMPLATE MANAGER opens, offering a virtual depiction of the templates saved for all users on the system and for your personal use only. The rectangles are sub-folders of the main directories listed in the paths.

You can either click down through the window or use the icons in the upper right to search and sort by name. If you have recently made several templates, you might need to click REFRESH to have all existing templates display.

2   Click a sub-folder in the display if you want to specify where the template displays in the Template Manager.

STOP Caution

If you do not select a sub-folder, the template is saved to the appropriate tab for its file format, rather than to a sub-folder.

3   Click the SAVE icon at the top left, and give the new template a name. If necessary, you can overwrite an existing template.

The newly saved template is now available for use.

Saving multiple templates

If you have downloaded a large number of templates, you can register a large number of them by moving them to one of the directories listed in the PATHS section of TOOLS > OPTIONS. Alternatively, select from the template manager tool bar REPOSITORY > LOCAL or REPOSITORY > NEW REPOSITORY.

Setting a new default

The default template for each module in LibreOffice is based on several assumptions. It assumes that most users want a generic font, like Times New Roman or Liberation Serif. It assumes that a connection exists between language locale and paper size, so that an installation that defaults to American English will use letter-sized paper, while one that defaults to United Kingdom English will use A4 paper.

These are reasonable assumptions. However, if they don't serve your needs, you can avoid making changes to every generic document that you start by changing the default template.

To change the default template:

1   Create and register the replacement template.

2   Open the Template Manager. Select the replacement default template.

3   Click the SET AS DEFAULT button.

Now, each new document will use the default template unless you specifically choose another template. LibreOffice reverts to its original DEFAULT template (the default DEFAULT) if you delete the replacement default.

Storing template structure

Discussions of templates usually emphasize storing formats in them. However, templates can store everything from return addresses to standard boilerplate such as corporate backgrounders – any information that you re-use but do not care to reinvent or type again. Instead, you can begin writing similar documents either immediately or with only minor modifications.

Such information is especially easy to store in Impress, in which each piece of information can be placed on one slide and easily deleted or rearranged.

Using placeholders

Placeholders are fields that mark the type of information needed at a certain spot, but leave you to fill in the details by clicking them.

Impress has built-in placeholders for slide titles, body text, and inserted objects.

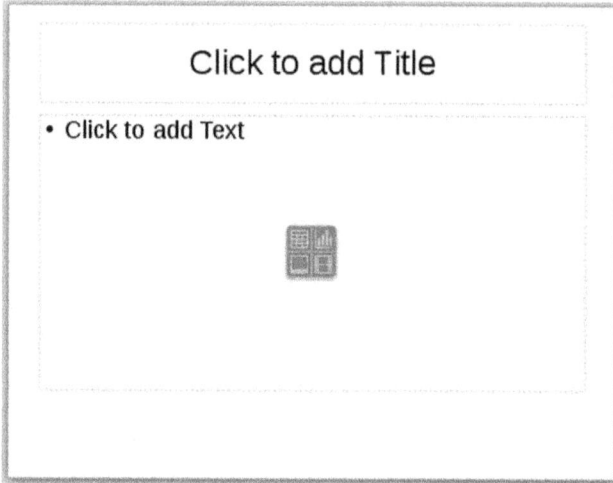

An Impress slide, with placeholders for the title and text, and a generic placeholder for tables, charts, images, and movies in the middle.

Placeholders are fields that mark the type of information needed at a certain spot, but leave you to fill in the details by clicking them.

Impress has built-in placeholders for slide titles, body text, and inserted objects.

However, you can also use placeholders for text and objects in Writer from INSERT > FIELDS > OTHER > FUNCTIONS. Select FORMAT, then give the placeholder a name in the PLACEHOLDER field. The REFERENCE field can be ignored.

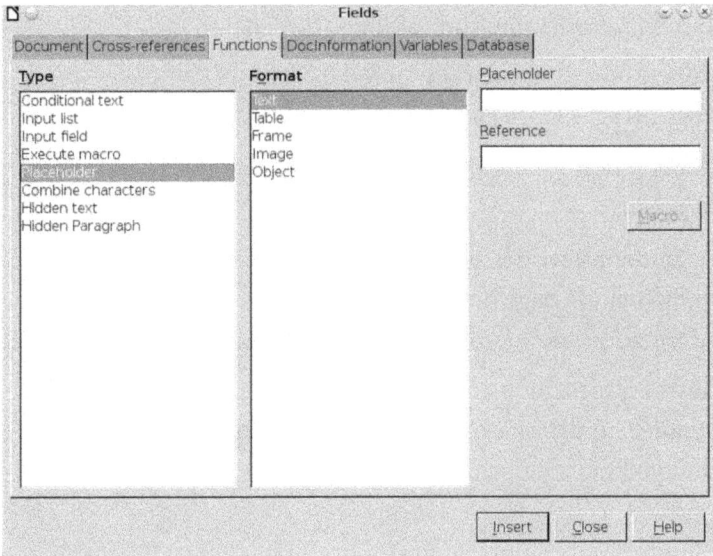

The FIELDS dialog window for adding placeholders in Writer.

The placeholders are added as fields in the document. When you are ready to insert the information, click the placeholder field to replace it.

<SALUTATION> <TITLE> <LAST NAME>

PLACEHOLDER fields in Writer for the opening of a letter.

> **Tip**
>
> Placeholders have their own character style, which makes them easy to find using EDIT > FIND & REPLACE.

Using fields in templates

Fields are another way to store information in templates. Four kinds of fields are likely to be useful:

- System information, such as date and time.

- General user information, stored in TOOLS > OPTIONS > LIBREOFFICE > USER DATA.

- Document information, stored or displayed in FILE > PROPERTIES.

- Document statistics, generated as you create the document. They include page numbers, page counts, and other information commonly placed in the header or footer.

As this information changes, the fields in the template will also change, updating each time that you open the document without you having to change it manually.

Tip

Date and time fields are of two kinds. Fixed fields add the current information and never change. By contrast, variable fields always update to the current date and time when anyone opens a document or update the fields.

Both have uses. For example, you could place a fixed date field beside a witness' signature, and a variable date field at the top of a letter template.

Date and time fields also support a number of formats, defaulting to the one listed for the current language. LibreOffice offers no way to change the default formats permanently.

Although a Month-Day-Year format is common in the United States, increasingly international use favors a consistent sequence – either Year-Month-Day or, less frequently, a Day-Month-Year format. All these formats can have two or four digits for the year.

Example: Using placeholders & fields

LibreOffice includes a tool for designing do-it-yourself business cards. The tool is designed so that you add information on one sample card, then add the information automatically to the rest.

To create the sample card:

1   Go to FILE > BUSINESS CARDS, and select the label sheet to use. Click the NEW DOCUMENT button to continue.

2   Adjust the zoom so you can work comfortably on the sample card.

3   Create two frames of equal width and height from INSERT > FRAME. One is for a graphic on the left, and the other for text on the right.

4   Place the cursor in the left hand frame and select INSERT > FIELDS > OTHER > FUNCTIONS > PLACEHOLDER.

5   Create an Image placeholder and call it GRAPHIC. Click the INSERT button to continue. You do not have to close the FIELDS dialog window to continue.

6   Place the cursor in the right hand frame and create one placeholder per line for AUTHOR, POSITION, COMPANY, EMAIL, and PHONE.

Tip

The AUTHOR field is filled automatically with the name entered in the User Data for LibreOffice's general use.

7   Give each line a right alignment. You can further adjust the look of the placeholders by editing the PLACEHOLDER character style.

8   Save the document. The BUSINESS CARD template is now ready for any user to complete by clicking on each placeholder and replacing it with actual information.

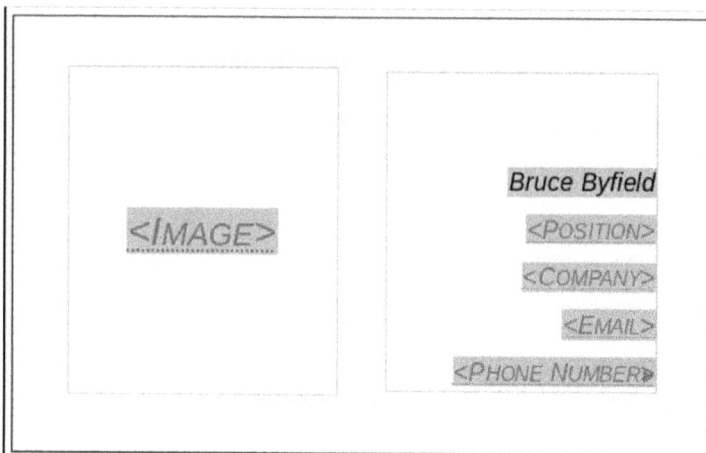

A basic business card template. Placeholders are used for information, and the name is filled in using the AUTHOR field, which borrows information from TOOLS > OPTIONS > LIBREOFFICE > USER DATA > FIRST / LAST NAME.

Editing templates

Unless you are extremely well-organized or lucky, you won't make a perfect template in one sitting. Instead, the first few times you use a template, you are likely to find countless ways to improve it so that it meets your needs without requiring endless manual adjustments.

To open a template for editing, select FILE > TEMPLATES > MANAGE to open the Template Manager, select a template, and click EDIT on the tool bar above the templates.

Once a template is open, you can edit it exactly the same as any other document. However, remember to register your changes by saving with FILE > TEMPLATES > SAVE AS TEMPLATE.

Deleting templates

You can delete custom or imported templates. You cannot delete templates installed with LibreOffice, through an extension, or for the entire system, although you can delete the extension from TOOLS > EXTENSION MANAGER.

From within the Template Manager, select the template to delete, then click the DELETE button.

STOP

Caution

The Template Manager does not include confirmation dialogs. A selected file is deleted as soon as you click the DELETE button. Nor can the deletion be undone.

Exporting templates

You can export a template from the Template Manager. Select the template to export, then click the EXPORT button. Exporting a template takes a copy of the template, de-registers the copy, and saves it to the directory of your choice.

Changing templates

Except with Template Changer or another extension, you cannot directly change which template is used by a document. Nor is there any means to apply multiple templates to the same document. However, you can use three workarounds.

The first is to open a document based on another template, then copy and paste into it. This method works best when all styles in both documents have the same names, because the styles in the original document will take on the formatting of the new document.

Tip

If you experience some problems with graphics, try copying and pasting a few pages at a time instead of all at once.

In addition, any custom-named styles in use in the original document are copied over to the new document. By contrast, custom-named styles that are defined but not in use, as well as tracked changes, will not appear in the new document.

A second method is to create a new master document with a different template. If you import the template-less document into the master document, it will be reformatted while being used from within the master document. When not opened from the master document, it will revert to its original formatting.

The third and most practical method is to transfer styles between documents.

Transferring styles is convenient when two people have been working on a document, but made their own changes to the template (something that happens, although you shouldn't encourage it).

You might also use the feature to transfer manual formatting of a document to its template, although making changes to the template is generally a more reliable practice.

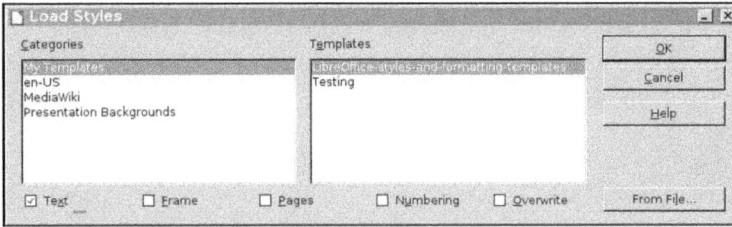

Transferring styles between documents. PARAGRAPH and CHARACTER styles are listed together under TEXT. Click OVERWRITE to replace existing styles of the same name.

To transfer styles between documents:

1 Press F11 to open the Styles and Formatting window.

2 From the pull-down menu at the far right of the icon bar, click LOAD STYLES.

The Load Styles window opens. The CATEGORIES pane shows the sub-folders in the Template Manager, while the template pane shows the templates of the current sub-folder.

3 Either select one of the templates in the Template pane or click the FROM FILE button and select a document template using the file manager.

4 Select the types of styles to import by selecting the boxes along the bottom of the LOAD STYLES window.

Tip

The LOAD STYLES window uses TEXT to refer to both PARAGRAPH and CHARACTER styles.

5 If you want to replace any styles in the current document that have the same name as the ones in the template or document

from which you are importing styles, click the OVERWRITE button.

STOP Caution

Carefully check styles that were supposed to be overwritten. They may not be consistently overwritten if you have large documents and a computer with limited memory.

If you do not want to replace styles, leave the OVERWRITE box unselected. You will import only styles that have names not found in the current document.

6   Click the OK button on the top right. You receive no confirmation, but the importing is complete in a matter of seconds.

Tip

Transferring styles does not change the template listed in FILE > PROPERTIES > GENERAL. If you are unsure whether a document is still associated with a template, make a minor change in the template and see if the document updates the next time that you open LibreOffice.

Working with templates in a file manager

LibreOffice includes all the features you need to interact with templates. Sometimes, however, you may want to deal with templates from outside LibreOffice, either because LibreOffice is not open or because you are dealing with more than one template at a time. Or perhaps you want to organize your installation by adding sub-folders to the main template directories.

In these cases, you can interact with templates through a file manager. The storage directory for templates varies with the operating system and software release, but you can find which directories your installation is using by going to TOOLS > OPTIONS > PATHS > TEMPLATES.

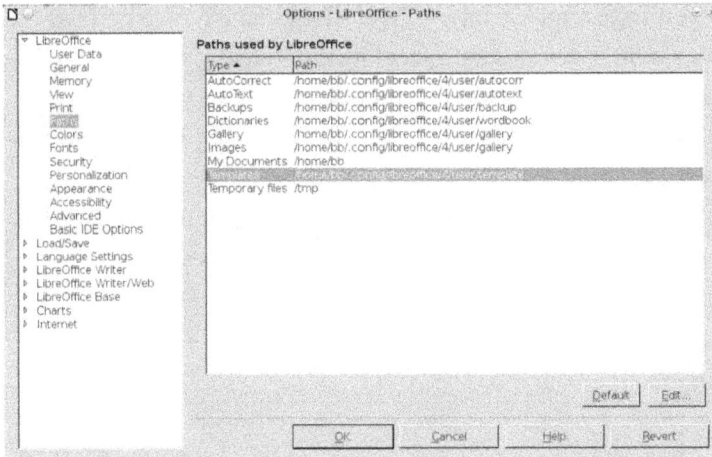

The directory (or directories) where templates are stored is listed in TOOLS > OPTIONS > LIBREOFFICE > PATHS. The exact path differs with operating systems and LibreOffice releases.

You can add directories to the template path, separating them from each other with a semi-colon. If you want to make directories accessible to all users on the system, log in as root or administrator and go to the directory in which LibreOffice was installed. For example, if you downloaded a Linux version directly from The Document Foundation, this directory will be in something like /opt/libreoffice4.4/share/template. In other cases, the top two directories may be different, but the bottom two should be the same.

If you are installing a large number of templates, placing them all in one directory, adding to the path, and re-starting LibreOffice is the quickest way of registering them.

The complete basics

If you have read Chapter 2, you should now have a general sense of how styles and templates work. Neither is difficult in theory, although some of the ways that templates work may seem needlessly complicated until you realize that they exist to prevent file corruption.

The next few chapters explain the points you need to consider to design useful and beautiful styles and templates.

4

Fonts, color, and the magic number

The first step in designing a document is to choose its fonts. Your choices will determine not only the look of your document, but, in a well-designed document, other details of your design as well.

As you select fonts, constantly ask yourself: How appropriate is a font to your subject matter and requirements?

Often, answering this question is a matter of imagination. Typography may have worked out a general set of principles, but it remains an art more than a science. For instance, a modern geometric font may seem futuristic, and therefore more appropriate for science fiction.

At other times, the answer will be exact. For example, some fonts have characters that are so thin that they are invisible online or with a low resolution printer. Others may be so gray they are hard to read, or so black that their effect is overwhelming on the page.

However, whatever the conditions, the fonts you choose should never be more noticeable than the content. The choice of fonts is meant to enhance your content, not to make the layout the center of attention.

Finding fonts to use

Many users never venture beyond the fonts installed on their computers when they design documents. Nothing is wrong with that choice, but nothing is particularly right with it, either.

By using fonts that everyone has seen many times, you greatly increase the chance of creating an impression of blandness. Familiar fonts like Times Roman or Helvetica can work against you, because they encourage readers to pay less attention or unconsciously question the originality of your ideas.

Traditionally, more computer fonts are designed for sale like any other software. Design houses like Adobe sell hundreds, including official versions of famous fonts like Gill Sans or Didot.

For years, the only alternative to paying for fonts was to use public domain fonts, which were often low quality.

However, hundreds of free-licensed fonts are now available. Sometimes designed by more than one person and often for love of typography rather than for money, the best free-licensed fonts like Gentium easily rival commercial fonts.

Many Linux distributions include a few free-licensed fonts in their package repositories. For other places where you can find free-licensed fonts, see Appendix C, "Where to get free-licensed fonts," page 487.

Installing fonts for LibreOffice

Both LibreOffice and Apache OpenOffice support PostScript (.pfb), TrueType (.ttf), and OpenType (.otf) font file formats.

Other font formats exist, and may be supported by your operating system, but these formats may be limited in selection and quality.

If you have administration privileges, you can install additional fonts through your operating system. Otherwise, you can install fonts only for LibreOffice by placing their files in the /share/fonts folder in the system path listed at TOOLS > OPTIONS > PATH and restarting LibreOffice.

Choosing fonts in LibreOffice

The first step in design is to choose the fonts. They are chosen on the FONT tab of a paragraph or character style.

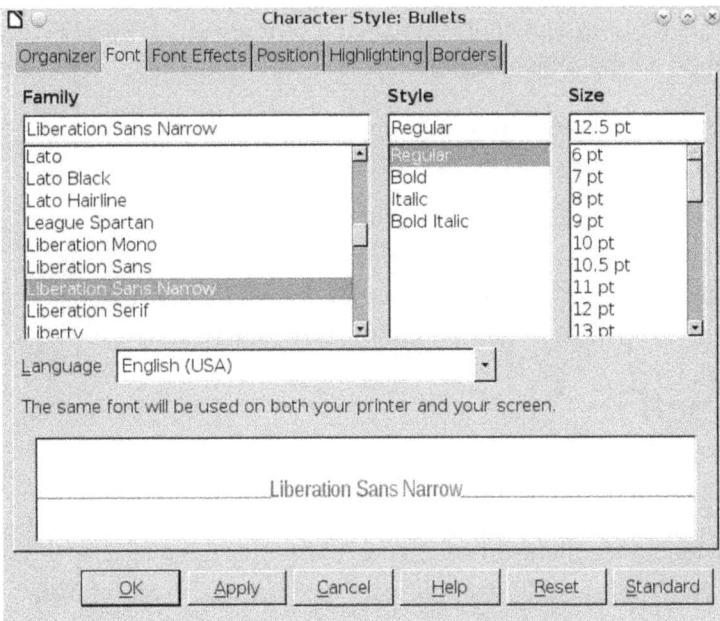

The FONT tab for character and paragraph styles.

On the FONT tab, each font has three basic characteristics: its family, its style or typeface (depending on the version and platform), and size. Fonts can be further modified by features on the FONT EFFECTS tab. See "Font effects," page 79.

Font families

In LibreOffice, related fonts are called a family. The six main font families are:

- Serif: Fonts whose lines end with a foot or a hook.

  A sub-category of serifs is called slab serifs, and uses very large serifs, making them suitable for posters and online.

Serif **Slab**

Left: Serif font (Goudy Bookletter 1911). Right: Slab serif font (Chunk). The serifs on the slab serif are much thicker than on the ordinary serif.

- Sans serif: Literally, fonts whose lines lack the foot that characterizes serifs. Sans serif fonts often read well online.

  When the New Typography of the early twentieth century favored them as part of the general simplification of design, sans serif fonts gained a reputation for modernity that they still keep today. They are informally called Sans.

Sans Serif

Font: Raleway. A recent design, Raleway hints at a serif for the lower case "a," but its general tendency is sans serif.

- Monospace: Fonts in which every letter occupies exactly the same amount of horizontal space. By contrast, in most fonts, letters take up different amounts of space, with "i" taking up the least and "m" the most.

  Monospace fonts can be either serif or sans serif, but the sans serif monospace fonts usually look more contemporary.

Because of their association with typewriters, monospace fonts are unpopular today, except for specific uses such as writing code or movie scripts.

Monospaced

Font: Deja Vu Sans Mono. This font is included in most Linux distributions.

- Display: Unusual fonts, usually used only in short lines in a heading or on a pamphlet or ad.

DISPLAY

Font: Cinzel, a font based on Roman inscriptions.

- Script: Fonts that imitate cursive handwriting.

Script

Font: Pinyon-Script.

- Dingbat: Fonts in which pictures replace letters. Hundreds of dingbat fonts are available, from practical ones useful in charts and diagrams to fun ones with dinosaurs and medieval figures. Their advantage over clip art is that they are scalable; their disadvantage is that they only display in one color.

Font: Entypo.

Font styles

Different members of a font family are often called weights. This term is a reference to the thickness of the lines that make up the individual letters. In character and paragraph styles, LibreOffice refers to a weight as a font style or typeface.

The most common styles are:

- Roman: This is the font style most often used for body text. It may also called Regular, Book, or Medium, although these are not always exact synonyms in individual font families.

  Sometimes a Narrow or Condensed version is available, in which the characters take up less width.

Roman
Font: ADF Romande.

- Italic: A cursive font, slanted to the right, used mainly for emphasis and book titles. In modern fonts, the Italic is sometimes replaced by an Oblique style, which is similar to the Roman, only inclined to the right.

Italic Oblique
Left Font: ADF Baskervald. Right Font: ADF Gillus.

- Bold: A version of the font with heavier lines on each character. Used for strong emphasis and headings, this weight sometimes replaces Italic online.

  Variants may have names like Black, Semi-bold, Demi-bold, Extra, or Heavy, sometimes each with a different thickness of line. The thicker variations are usually intended for use at large font sizes in media like posters.

Bold Heavy
Left: Lato Bold. Right: Lato Ultra Black.

- Old Style Figures: Numbers which have no common baseline, originally designed in the Renaissance. Those who have studied typography often prefer them, even though, to a modern eye, they can look stuffy and be difficult to read. Their opposite, which most fonts have, are called lining figures, and are the numerals generally in use today.

1234567890
1234567890

Above: Old style figures. Font: Goudy Bookletter 1911.
Below: Lining figures. Font: Liberation Sans.

STOP

Caution

Avoid using old style figures in spreadsheets or in diagrams in which you want to align numbers. Their lack of a common baseline is distracting in long columns or tables of numbers, and they are difficult to position manually.

- Small Capitals (Small Caps): Specially designed upper case letters intended to make more than two capitals in a row more readable.

Tip

If you use old style figures for numbers, use small caps beside them. Normal caps look outlandishly large beside old style figures.

SMALL CAPS

REGULAR CAPS

Top: True small caps, created using the font's metrics.
Bottom: Regular upper case letters. Small capitals are not
only smaller than regular capitals, but also proportioned
differently. Font: Fanwood.

Tip

In addition, some font families include styles such as
Bold Italic, Thin, and Outline. A few fonts take a different
approach, and divide fonts into Serif, Sans, and
Monospace.

Real fonts vs. manufactured ones

Some fonts store metrics for different weights within the same
file. Others have separate fonts for each weight, but if you change
the weight while using the regular weight, you get manufactured
versions of the different weights which have little resemblance to
the real ones.

This problem is common with TrueType fonts, and when you
change weights from the tool bar or a CHARACTER dialog window.

Italics

Italics

Top: Manufactured italics. Bottom: True italics. The angle on the
manufactured italics makes them awkward and harder to read,
and the letter shapes are frankly flights of fantasy. Font: Nobile.

bold

bold

Top: A manufactured bold style. Bottom: The bold style the designer intended. Notice the difference in spacing and letter shape. Font: Nobile.

SMALL CAPS

MANUFACTURED

REGULAR CAPS

Top: True small capitals. Middle: Manufactured small capitals for the same font. Bottom: Regular capitals. Font: Linux Libertine G.

Selecting fonts by font styles / typefaces

In theory, font styles should help you to choose fonts. However, in practice, font styles are inconsistent enough that the best they can give you is a rough indication of whether a font is suitable for your needs.

To start with, a font family traditionally contains four main styles: Regular, Italic, Bold, and Bold Italic. However, remember that just because two font styles have the same name does not mean you are under any obligation to use them together.

For instance, Nobile Italic is not actually an italic at all. Instead it is an oblique – the regular weight angled to the right. If you prefer an italic, you might go searching for something compatible with the regular weight.

Or perhaps an ampersand (&) figures in your design, but the font you want to use has a mundane design for ampersands. Just because the type designer thinks that font styles or individual characters fit together does not mean that you should accept their judgment.

& & & & &

Designers regularly borrow ampersands (and sometimes question marks) when they want an elegant touch. Fonts, from left to right: Cantarell, Quattrocento Roman, Goudy Bookletter 1911, Accanthis ADF Std., Lato.

Another point to consider is that you are rarely likely to need Bold Italic. Since the EMPHASIS character style uses Italic and STRONG EMPHASIS uses Bold, Bold Italic serves no regular purpose. It may be useful as a display or heading font, but often you can ignore a Bold Italic style if the other styles suit your needs.

Regular
Italics
Bold
Bold Italics

The four basic font styles in most font families. Up to a dozen other may also be included. Font: Nobile.

Another issue with font styles is that, through the years, various attempts have been made to standardize them. If you know CSS, you may recall how it categorizes font weights with three-digit numbers.

However, even in this summary, problems emerge. Italic and Oblique have no natural place, which is why you now see fonts designated as Italic or Oblique in their names. The same is true for Outline fonts, which show only the borders of characters but no fill.

Even more important, what looks like a well-regulated system at first glance is on closer look extremely arbitrary. The use of names is not standardized in 300-500, or 700-900, and, while in theory a font could have a weight of 350, what exactly would that mean, except in relation to other fonts in the same family?

100: Extra Light.	600: Semi-Bold/Demi-bold.
200: Light.	700: Bold.
300: Book.	800: Heavy, Extra, Black.
400: Regular, Roman.	900: Ultra, Extra.
500: Medium.	

Font styles in CSS. Many fonts use the same classifications.

These cautions do not mean that font styles are not useful in deciding what fonts to use. But you do need to remember that all systems are approximate and relative to the font family. Always experiment thoroughly before selecting a font.

Font sizes

Traditionally, fonts are measured in points. In the digital age, this measurement has been standardized as one-seventy-second of an inch or 2.5 centimeters. Previously, a point was actually slightly less, but points remain defiantly non-metric and a sign of typographic expertise.

Tip

When you are setting up paragraph and character styles, go to TOOLS > OPTIONS > LIBREOFFICE WRITER > GENERAL > SETTINGS and change the MEASUREMENT UNIT to points.

Using points will make designing much easier because you have a consistent measurement. You can always change the MEASUREMENT UNIT back to centimeters or inches when you start to add content to a template.

The font size refers to the amount of space given to each character and the empty space around it. However, how each font uses the empty space can vary tremendously. Each font uses a different amount of empty space, which explains why the actual height of fonts of the same size is inconsistent. In fact, the actual height can vary considerably.

A A A

The font size for each of these capitals is the same, but the height of the letters varies. Fonts, from left to right, are League Spartan, Oxygen Sans, and Liberation Sans.

The standard size for body text is usually 10–14 points. Text for captions and notes sometimes goes as low as 8 points, while headings and titles are rarely more than 28 points.

Tip

LibreOffice's pre-defined heading paragraph styles express size as percentages of the Headings styles.

Since the size of all headings are usually determined at the same time and in relation to each other, using percentages is logical.

However, as shown later in this chapter, many design elements are based on the size of the standard fonts, which are most conveniently measured in points. For this reason, setting headings in points as well only makes sense.

You can force LibreOffice to display the size in points by placing the cursor in the SIZE field of the FONT tab, and entering the size followed by "pt."

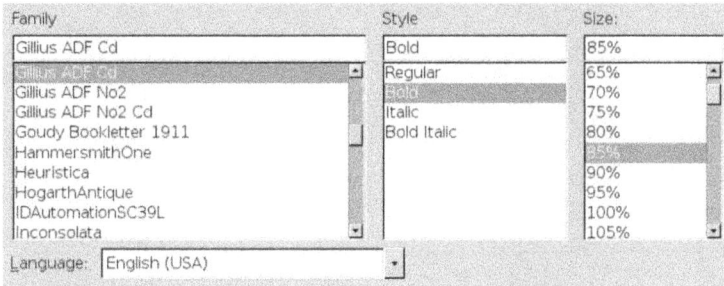

Family	Style	Size:
Gillius ADF Cd	Bold	85%
Gillius ADF Cd	Regular	65%
Gillius ADF No2	Bold	70%
Gillius ADF No2 Cd	Italic	75%
Goudy Bookletter 1911	Bold Italic	80%
HammersmithOne		85%
Heuristica		90%
HogarthAntique		95%
IDAutomationSC39L		100%
Inconsolata		105%

Language: English (USA)

Heading styles are measured by default in percentages because their size is often determined together.

Font effects

The FONT EFFECTS tab contains a variety of features, with widely differing degrees of usefulness.

In most circumstances, the FONT COLOR and EFFECTS fields are the most useful. In particular, the EFFECTS field includes the option for SMALL CAPITALS, which are used to make two or more upper case letters in a row more readable.

By contrast, OVERLINING, STRIKETHROUGH, and UNDERLINING have limited use in most circumstances. All three are largely for the automatic use of LibreOffice when displaying changes in a collaborative document.

In all other cases, use the FONT EFFECTS tab cautiously. Effects such as SHADOW, BLINKING, or RELIEF are leftovers from when word processors were new and users over-indulged in all the effects they suddenly had. All these effects break the basic purpose of typography by calling attention to themselves while doing nothing to enhance the main text.

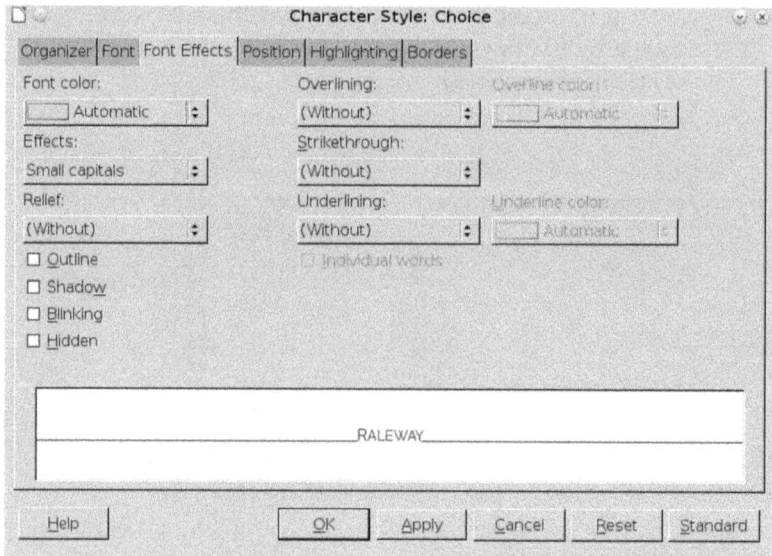

Character Style: Choice			

Organizer | Font | Font Effects | Position | Highlighting | Borders

Font color:
[Automatic]

Effects:
[Small capitals]

Relief:
[(Without)]

☐ Outline
☐ Shadow
☐ Blinking
☐ Hidden

Overlining:
[(Without)]

Strikethrough:
[(Without)]

Underlining:
[(Without)]

☐ Individual words

Overline color:
[Automatic]

Underline color:
[Automatic]

RALEWAY

Help   OK   Apply   Cancel   Reset   Standard

The FONT EFFECTS tab for character and paragraph styles. Many of the choices on this tab should be used sparingly, if at all.

Choosing basic fonts

The typographical convention is to limit each document to two font families: one for body text, and one for headings, headers, and footers. Any more tend to call attention to the design at the expense of the content.

However, this is not quite the limitation it sounds. The majority of fonts include a minimum of four font styles – Roman, Italic, Bold, and Bold Italic. Some have as many as nine, and a few have even more. Using so many font styles in the same document can look just as cluttered as too many different fonts, but nobody is likely to notice if you use several together.

A few fonts even come in pairs of a serif and a sans serif, and even a monospaced variation. These styles are more than enough for most needs. In fact, one font family is often all that is needed for effective design.

Judging fonts

To appreciate the differences between fonts, some typographical terms are useful:

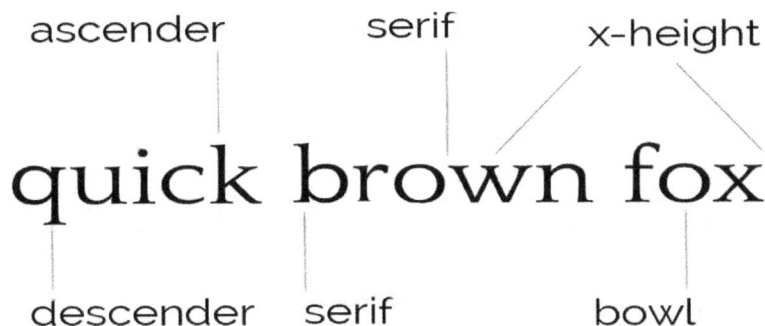

ascender   serif   x-height

quick brown fox

descender   serif   bowl

The basic terms to describe fonts physically.

- X-height: the height of a letter "x" and sixteen other letters.
- Ascenders and descenders: respectively, vertical strokes that rise above the baseline and descend below it.
- Bowls: The rounded parts of letters like "b," "d," and "o."
- Serifs: The small hooks at the bottom and top of ascenders and descenders found in some fonts.

If you study different font samples, you will see how these elements differ between fonts. This is the first step in learning how to appreciate fonts professionally. After all, if you have names for features, you can more easily observe them.

Choosing a body font

The first font you need is a body text. The main functional criterion for a body text font is that it must be easily readable by your audience in the conditions in which they are likely to see it.

For example, if you are designing a memo template for a low-resolution fax, you might prefer a larger, bold text style. Similarly, a brochure aimed at seniors might use a larger font size than usual out of respect for their failing eyesight. In other cases, you may be limited by a lower printer resolution or even a temporary shortage of toner to fonts with thick, consistent lines.

Tip

Often, a key feature for body text is the x-height. This is just what it sounds like: the height of the letter "x" and sixteen other lower case letters.

As a rule, the higher the x-height, the more readable a font is likely to be. However, if the ascenders and descenders are short, a high x-height might be less of an asset.

Choosing a heading font

The second font you probably need is for headings, headers, footers, and sub-headings – everything that guides readers through the document but is not actually content. It can belong to the same font family as the body text, but, if so, it should be a different font style, size, or color.

LibreOffice provides for up to ten heading levels, but this number is overkill. Any more than three or four levels of headings (including chapter titles) makes designing difficult and meaningless. Formatting ten heading levels so that each is distinct may just be possible, but neither the designer nor the reader is likely to be able to remember what all of them mean.

Other considerations for fonts

Choosing fonts begins with the impression you want to make. For instance, a commonly used font helps to put readers in an accepting mood, while a usual one might reinforce an impression of innovation.

At times, a font might need to fit the constraints of the page. A tall, narrow page, for example, might be matched with a similarly tall and narrow font. Or maybe a font has some association with the content – for instance, at least one edition of Arthur Conan Doyle's *The Hound of the Baskervilles* was printed in Baskerville font.

More general considerations can include:

* Where will the document be used? The North American convention is to use a serif font for body text, and a sans serif for headings. By contrast, in Europe typographers are much less likely to abide by this convention. You can use a sans serif for body text in North America, but it may be perceived as avant-garde.

* Is the document for paper or online use? Even today, text on a screen is lower resolution than professional printing, and may be processed differently by the brain than words on a page. For online use, you want fonts to have regular shapes, with a minimum of tapering. Often, that means designing mainly with sans serifs and the occasional slab serif.

* Will recipients have the fonts installed on their computers to display the document properly? If you only want recipients to view the document, you can send a PDF file. Otherwise, you

might be better off sticking to the standard Times New Roman, Arial or Helvetica, and Courier.

Tip

If you use Linux, and lack these fonts, look for the Liberation fonts, which are designed to take up the same space as the standard fonts.

- Is embedding fonts in the file a solution? LibreOffice has had font embedding since version 4.1.3.2. Embedding simplifies file-sharing, making it unnecessary for recipients to have the document's fonts.

  However, a file of 14 kilobytes balloons into one of 13.4 megabytes when only two fonts are embedded. Add more, and a file with embedded fonts may become too large to send as an attachment, especially to an account that can only receive attachments of a certain size.

Tip

Currently, Apache OpenOffice does not support embedding fonts.

- Do you prefer to use only free-licensed fonts? If so, you will be unable to use some of the best-known fonts, although you can sometimes find substitutes for them (see Appendix D, "Free-licensed equivalents for standard fonts," page 491).

  However, free-licensed fonts are often cost-free. They also mean that recipients only need an Internet connection to install the fonts they need.

Matching fonts

Modern typography usually uses separate fonts for body and heading text. Matching fonts is an art form rather than a science, but you can increase the odds of finding fonts that go together by selecting ones that:

- Share the same font family. Modern typographers sometimes design serif, sans serif, and monospaced fonts to be used together, which can be a great convenience.

STOP

Caution

An exception is the Liberation fonts, which are designed as replacements for Times Roman, Helvetica, and Courier, rather than for compatibility with each other.

- Are designed by the same typographer. A designer's preferences and habits may remain similar enough between fonts to give a common appearance.

- Have a large number of font styles, especially if you plan to use the same font for both body text and headings.

- Are inspired by the same historical era or are described in the same terms. Even if you are uncertain how a Humanist font (one based on Renaissance designs) differs from a Geometric font (one based on simple shapes), you can safely guess that the two are unlikely to go together. Of course, the more you know about the history of typography, the more you match fonts by their origins. See "Matching by historical categories," page 86.

- Occupy the same horizontal or vertical width. If nothing else, this criterion makes for a more symmetrical design.

However, no matter what criteria you use, the only way to be sure that fonts match is to experiment with them, both on-screen and by printing frequent hard copy samples.

Matching by historical categories

Fonts frequently defy easy categorizations. However, some general historical trends do exist, even though experts do not always agree on the features that identify trends, or where each font belongs.

Historical categories are not mentioned anywhere in LibreOffice, but you can sometimes match fonts by choosing ones from the same historical category.

Humanist serifs

Humanist serifs were originally fonts designed during the Renaissance, mostly by Italian designers – which is why a standard font is called Roman and a cursive font Italic. Humanist fonts are characterized by small x-heights, regular strokes, rounded bowls, small serifs, and a dark color. Some strokes may be angled, such as the crossbar on the lower case "e."

They are popular choices for body text today, although some designers think they look old fashioned.

The original Humanist fonts were also extremely dark, perhaps to make them more legible by candlelight. Modern imitations sometimes reduce the darkness to make them more acceptable to modern tastes.

Humanist serif

Font: Coelacanth, a free-licensed version of Bruce Roger's popular Centaur, which in turn was inspired by the work of Renaissance designer Nicholas Jenson.

Old Style

Sometimes an alternate name for Humanist serifs, "Old Style" is technically reserved for seventeenth-century designs or designs inspired by them.

Old Style fonts are characterized by wedge-shaped serifs, and their strokes show more variation in thickness than Humanist fonts. Like Humanist serifs, Old Style fonts are very popular for general purposes.

Old Style

Font: Linden Hill, a modern free-license rendering of Frederick Goudy's Deepdene.

Transitional

Also called Enlightenment, NeoClassical, and Modern, Transitional fonts first appeared during the Enlightenment. Their name refers to the fact that their serifs are small, anticipating the rise of sans serifs. Their strokes vary widely, their bowls are oval, and their serifs thin. Extreme versions, like the proprietary Didot, have strokes that are so thin that they almost disappear at small font sizes, or with a low-resolution printer.

Transitional

Font: Baskervald ADF, a free-licensed version of Hugo Baskerville's classic transitional font Baskerville.

Slab serifs

Slab serifs first appeared in the early 1800s. They are sometimes called Egyptian, because they were used in the publications of the research done in Egypt during Napoleon's invasion.

As their name implies, slab serifs have thick, broad serifs. Although often used for posters, some can be used for body text. Many are an exception to the conventional wisdom that serif fonts cannot be used online, and are often highly readable online or in slide shows.

Slab Serif

Font: Josefin Slab.

Sans serifs

Sans serif fonts are exactly what their French name implies: fonts without serifs. When they first appeared in the early nineteenth century, they were called "grotesque" and "gothic."

Modern sans serifs usually fall into one of two categories. Geometric fonts are marked by regular strokes and simple shapes, including circles for bowls. Geometric fonts were popular with Modernist schools for design.

Geometric

Font: Oxygen, the default for KDE's Plasma desktop in Linux.

By contrast, Humanist sans serif or Modern Humanist fonts are based on the clean lines of Roman inscriptions. Both the Arts and Crafts and Art Nouveau schools of design favored them, and they remain popular today.

Some Humanist sans serifs are versatile enough to be used for both headings and body text.

Humanist Sans

Font: Cantarell, the default font for the GNOME desktop in Linux.

Using dummy text to experiment

Dummy text is text unrelated to the document. It is used so you can focus on the result of formatting changes rather than the content.

The traditional dummy text in typography is the Lorem Ipsum, a passage so-called from its opening words. The Lorem Ipsum is fractured Latin, based on a passage from Cicero's essay, "The Extremes of Good and Evil," and can be downloaded from several sites.

Lorem ipsum dolor sit amet, consectetur adipisicing elit, sed do eiusmod tempor incididunt ut labore et dolore magna aliqua. Ut enim ad minim veniam, quis nostrud exercitation ullamco laboris nisi ut aliquip ex ea commodo consequat.

The start of the Lorem Ipsum, the popular dummy text passage.

The assumption behind the Lorem Ipsum is that, unless you can read Latin, you will not be distracted by the meaning of the words when you focused on formatting. For that matter, even if you read Latin, the passage is unlikely to distract you for very long, because you will see it so often that you will soon ignore the sense.

STOP Caution

Do not rely on the font preview in the FORMATTING tool bar or the sidebar. A single word is not enough to judge a font. At a minimum, you need several lines, while page design usually requires an entire page.

Study how the fonts you choose work together. They should not be jarringly different, but they should be sufficiently different for readers to tell them apart at a glance.

Look, too, for body text that fills a page or column without many hyphens. A sample riddled with hyphens is a sign that you will either have to change the font, or adjust its size or alignment.

As you work with a template, you will probably make changes the first few times you use it, including to the fonts.

However, you want a selection of fonts that will go together with a minimum of tweaking. If you need to fiddle too much with SCALE WIDTH or SPACING in a paragraph style, then finding another font is probably less effort for more aesthetic results.

Adjusting the page color

An important aspect of choosing fonts is the color of the body font. In this context, "color" does not refer to whether the text or the paper is black or green. Instead, color is the typographical term for how dark or light a passage or a page looks overall.

When you have found the line spacing that gives the color most pleasing to your eye, make a note of it. That line spacing is the magic number that can be the key to the rest of your design.

As you can see by opening professionally published books, you usually want the body text to be neither too black nor too washed out. Too black a color can be disturbing, while too washed out a color can be hard to read and looks like a publisher's error. Instead, you want a consistent dark gray.

The color of headings is usually darker than the body text, so it stands out when you are browsing. Otherwise, you can ignore the color of headings and concentrate on the body text.

Setting color through line spacing

The single most important influence on color is line-spacing.
In LibreOffice, line spacing is set in the LINE SPACING field on the
INDENTS & SPACING tab for paragraphs.

Line spacing is defined as the measurement from one baseline
(the imaginary line that the bottom of a letter like "n" or "m" sits
on) to the next one.

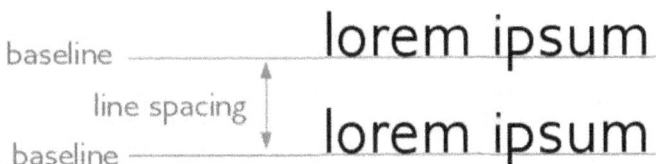

baseline ———————— **lorem ipsum**

line spacing

baseline ———————— **lorem ipsum**

Line spacing is the distance between two baselines.

In LibreOffice Writer, line spacing appears to be set by the
font size. The exact measurement is displayed when you set the
LINE SPACING field to FIXED.

For convenience, typographers notate line spacing after the
font size, so that a paragraph set in 12/14 has a 12 point font size
and 14 points of line spacing.

When a paragraph's font size and line space are identical – for
instance, 12/12 – then the paragraph is said to be "set solid."
However, you rarely see a paragraph set solid except for short
lines of text in brochures or ads, because the lines look crowded

except with a few fonts with small letter sizes with plenty of white space around them.

lorem ipsum dolor sit amet, consectetur adipiscing elit. Int dapibus diam. Sed nisi. Nulla quis sem at nibh elementum nec tellus sed augue semper porta. Mauris massa. Vestibu sociosqu ad litora torquent per conubia nostra, per incept dignissim lacinia nunc. Curabitur tortor. Pellentesque nibh. mattis. Sed convallis tristique sem. Proin ut ligula vel nunc suscipit quis, luctus non, massa. Fusce ac turpis quis ligula

A font set solid (in this case, 12/12). With so little line spacing, the text is cramped and hard to read. Font: Universalis ADF STD.

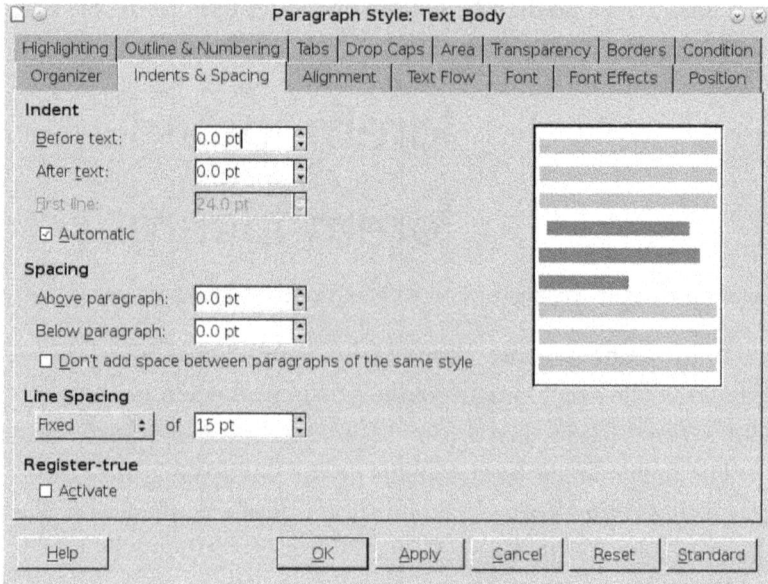

The INDENTS & SPACING tab. The color is adjusted mainly by setting the LINE SPACING field to a fixed distance.

LibreOffice sets a default line spacing based on the font size. For a 12 point font, that average is just over 14 points. However, because each font uses the space for characters differently, the default line spacing is not always ideal.

Tip

LibreOffice used to allow you to set line spacing to one-tenth of a point (1/720th of an inch). However, starting with the 4.2 release, you can only set line spacing to the nearest point. While you might not think such a small measurement would make a difference, it often can. By contrast, Apache OpenOffice still allows settings of 1/10 points.

When you have found the line spacing that gives the best color, make a note of it. That magic number can be the key to much of the rest of your design.

Caution

Typography calls line-spacing "leading," because of the pieces of metal that were once inserted between lines of text on a printing press.

However, LibreOffice uses "fixed" to refer to leading, and "leading" to refer to space in addition to the font size.

Contexts for changing color

Developing an eye for line spacing takes practice. Acceptable color may also depend to a degree on culture, era, and the principles of different design schools. However, certain contexts are more likely to need adjustments in line spacing than others. Experiment until you get acceptable results.

Increase spacing for:

- Fonts whose characters are narrow or have smaller spaces between them. (Adjusting SCALE WIDTH and SPACING on the POSITION tab may help as well.)

- A line of text greater than about 80 characters.

- Font sizes of less than 10 points, or more than 14.

- Roman fonts that are too black.

- Most sans-serif fonts.

- Any italic or oblique font.

Decrease spacing for:

- Fonts whose characters are broad and have relatively large spaces between them.

- A line of text less than 45 characters.

- Fonts of 10–14 points.

- Roman fonts that are light gray.

- Some serif fonts.

Deciding whether to increase or decrease font spacing.

Applying the magic number

Beginning typographers often wonder how to proportion documents. Over the years, countless theories have evolved, many of them uncomfortably elaborate. But the easiest is what I call – for want of a better name – the magic number.

The magic number is the line spacing that gives the preferred color with the chosen Body Text font. Its application is simple: whenever possible, any measurement in a document will be a multiple of the selected line spacing.

Not every design element can use the magic number, but most of the important ones can:

- Text indents.
- First line indent.
- Space above paragraph.
- Space below paragraph.
- Space between numbers/bullet and list items.
- The space above or below a graphic or any other inserted object.
- Tabs.
- Page margins.
- Header/footer height.
- Space between a header and footer and main text.
- The combination of heading font size, the space above/below.

Some design elements to be adjusted using multiples of the magic number.

At times, you might use half the line spacing instead of a whole multiple. In theory, you could use quarter-line spacing, or an even smaller fraction, but that is harder to track.

Just as importantly, half line-spacing quickly puts spacing back to the magic number itself. As you design, you may want to keep a calculator handy, or else jot down a palette – a list of the multiples or half-multiples that you will be using.

5	10	15	20	25	30	35	40	45	50	55	60	70
5.5	11	16.5	22	27.5	33	39.5	44	50.5	55	61.5	66	72.5
6	12	18	24	30	36	42	48	54	60	66	72	78
6.5	13	19.5	26	32.5	39	45.5	52	58.5	65	71.5	78	84.5
7	14	21	28	35	42	49	56	63	70	77	84	91
7.5	15	22.5	30	37.5	45	52.5	60	67.5	75	82.5	90	97.5

A line-spacing palette for typical body text. All measurements are in points and can be used for setting other sizes and spacing. Font: Cinzel.

Using the magic number is painstaking – but it is precise and unambiguous. You should have no trouble detecting a document designed with the magic number, because of its unified appearance.

Example: Solving the magic numbers

Page color can be affected by many variables, including the designer's eye, the paper, and the toner left in the printer. Sometimes, it can be subjective, particularly if your eyesight is imperfect. However, at the very least, you should be able to make the page color regular, even if the tone could be improved.

In fact, the variables are so numerous that, each time you use a font, you need to ask yourself if the circumstances are different enough that you need to re-test the color.

Do not assume that because a color worked once, it will work equally well under other circumstances. Choosing the page color is always highly contextual, and small changes in formatting can sometimes have large effects.

Always experiment systematically. Increase the font size and line-spacing a bit at a time, and work with different combinations systematically. Making large changes will only waste time by forcing you to backtrack.

If you are lucky, LibreOffice's default settings of 12/14 (font size = 12 points, line-spacing = 14 points) may require no tweaking. In my experience, 20–35% of fonts need no adjustments.

For example, here is Josefin Slab without modifications:

Lorem ipsum dolor sit amet, consectetur
diam. Sed nisi. Nulla quis sem at nibh el
sed augue semper porta. Mauris massa.
torquent per conubia nostra, per inceptos
Curabitur tortor. Pellentesque nibh. Aene
tristique

Font: Josefin Slab, 12/14.

The font size might be increased, but on the whole Josefin
Slab's default color is acceptable as is. That is just as well,
because a couple of extra points between each line can add
dozens of pages to a book and increase its production cost.

However, other fonts require testing, changing the font size and
line-spacing one at a time, and trying out different combinations.

For example, at the default 12/14, E. B. Garamond's color is
acceptable, but the height of the upper cases letters is
unusually high, and makes the lines a little pinched. Changing
the line spacing to 12/16 improves the layout:

Lorem ipsum dolor sit amet, consectetur ad
nisi. Nulla quis sem at nibh elementum imp
porta. Mauris massa. Vestibulum lacinia arc

Lorem ipsum dolor sit amet, consectetur adi
nisi. Nulla quis sem at nibh elementum imp
porta. Mauris massa. Vestibulum lacinia arc

Font: Above, E.B Garamond, 12/14. Below: E.B. Garamond, 12/16.

Humanist fonts designed in the Renaissance were often
designed to be very black by modern standards. Since that is

the way they are meant to be seen, trying to lighten them would fail to do them justice.

Not every modern Humanist Serif is as dark as its inspirations, but many are. An example is Colecanth:

Lorem ipsum dolor sit amet, conse cursus ante dapibus diam. Sed nisi. ipsum. Praesent mauris. Fusce nec arcu eget nulla. Class aptent taciti himenaeos. Curabitur sodales ligul Pellentesque nibh. Aenean quam. I tristique

Font: Humanist (Coelacanth), 12/14.

Should you encounter a modern font that remains very dark despite all adjustments, that is probably a sign that it Is designed for headings or as a display font, and should not be used for body text.

If you really want to use a font with a dark color, try changing the width of characters from POSITION > SCALING, or the spacing between fonts from POSITION > SPACING.

For example, after wrestling Heuristica to a setting of 12/16, I found it still too dark, so I set the Spacing to add .8 of a point more between characters.

Even then, the font was darker than ideal, but much more increased space between letters would have destroyed the look of the font completely.

Under the circumstances, this final modification was the best I could manage, and is still darker than ideal:

Lorem ipsum dolor sit amet, consectetur adipiscing elit. Integer nec odio. Praesent libero. Sed cursus ante dapibus diam. Sed nisi. Nulla quis sem at nibh elementum imperdiet. Duis sagittis ipsum. Praesent mauris. Fusce nec tellus sed augue semper

Lorem ipsum dolor sit amet, consectetur adipiscing elit. Integer nec odio. Praesent libero. Sed cursus ante dapibus diam. Sed nisi. Nulla quis sem at nibh elementum imperdiet. Duis sagittis ipsum. Praesent mauris. Fusce nec tellus sed augue semper

Font: Above, Heuristica 12/14. Below, Heuristica 12/16, with .8pts of extra spacing between characters.

At other times, if all else fails, try a different font style. Raleway Thin, to take one example, is too pale for body text. (Perhaps it is meant to add a shadow?) Changing the font size or the space between characters worked slightly, but not enough.

In the end, I concluded that I was using Raleway Thin for a purpose that it was simply not intended for, and switched to Raleway's Regular weight instead.

Lorem ipsum dolor sit amet, consec cursus ante dapibus diam. Sed nisi. ipsum. Praesent mauris. Fusce nec

Lorem ipsum dolor sit amet, conse cursus ante dapibus diam. Sed nisi ipsum. Praesent mauris. Fusce nec

Font: Above, Raleway Thin 12/14. Below: Raleway Regular, 12./14.

The lesson in these examples? LibreOffice's defaults may not be what you need, so experiment as widely as possible as you search for the best possible page color. Too much depends on it for you settle for anything less.

An unexpected journey

This chapter started with selecting fonts, but it ends well into character and paragraph styles. The next chapter continues where this one leaves off, going into more detail about character and paragraph styles.

5

Spacing on all sides

Paragraph styles are the most frequently used type of style in LibreOffice. However, they interact so closely with character styles that talking about one without the other is impossible – they even share several of the same tabs in their dialog windows.

Paragraph styles define the general formatting for any text-heavy document, while character styles provide brief variations. For short bursts of text – for example, a title, URL, or bullet point – character styles provide exceptions that give paragraph styles the flexibility they lack by themselves.

Chapter 3 ventured into some of the basics of paragraph and character settings while discussing fonts and how to find the ideal line spacing. This chapter completes the discussion of basic paragraph formatting, (including a more detailed discussion of line spacing), covering the options for vertical and horizontal spacing.

The next two chapters discuss special features and potential problems and advanced features.

Tip

Many of the tabs in character and paragraph style dialog windows reappear in the other LibreOffice applications. To minimize repetition, later chapters refer back to this chapter and the two following it.

Preparing to design

- Choose your fonts and ideal line spacing.

- Have a calculator and a list of multiples of the line spacing ready so you can check basic measurements.

- Set the default measure to points in TOOLS > OPTIONS > LIBREOFFICE WRITER > GENERAL > SETTINGS > MEASUREMENT UNIT. You can reset the default unit to centimeters or inches when you are done, but points are the most commonly used unit of measurement for general typography.

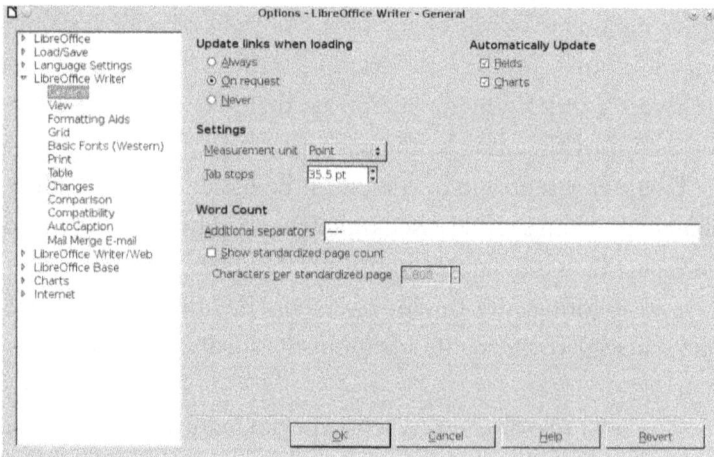

Before you design, set the MEASUREMENT UNIT to points.

- Set the zoom to 100% so you can judge the page color. Print or zoom in or out periodically so you can get a different perspective.

- In the status bar at the bottom of the editing window, set LibreOffice to display multiple pages, selecting the third button from the left. Unless you are struggling with a small monitor, a two-page spread helps you see the effect of your design choices.

Displaying multiple pages shows how the document will look when printed or else viewed on a wide screen monitor in a two-page spread.

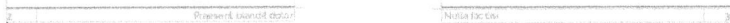

A multi-page display gives a design overview. Here, it confirms that footers are mirrored as intended.

- Open a second file where you can experiment and use dummy text to test formats.

- While you design, use manual formatting. Creating styles at this point is just an extra step until you have finished experimenting. When you have decided on the formatting choices, you can always drag a selected passage to the STYLES AND FORMATTING window to create a style from it.

- Use this chapter's headings as a checklist so you cover all the basic formatting.

STOP Caution

As you work, you may find that some of the settings you have already chosen require changing – even the magic number.

Rather than resisting the change, accept it as a natural part of the design process. The goal is to develop the best design you can, not to cling to a pointless consistency.

Planning text styles

You can save time while designing by working whenever possible with Writer's pre-defined styles. Later, as you write, you will find that some features, such as INSERT > FIELDS > OTHER DOCUMENT > CHAPTER > CHAPTER NAME field, depend on the pre-defined paragraph styles being in the document.

The pre-defined character and paragraph styles should cover most of your needs, but you can add other styles as needed..

Then go through the list of pre-defined styles and decide which ones you do not need. For example, paragraph styles

HEADING 5–10 are far more headings than anyone can manage. Perhaps, too, you have no use for paragraph styles like LIST 1 CONT., LIST 1 END, and LIST 1 START, and they will only clutter up the STYLES AND FORMATTING window. For each unnecessary style, select HIDE from the right-click menu. Should you decide that you need a hidden style after all, you can go to the HIDDEN STYLES view and select SHOW instead.

All these tasks are a lot of work. But you will also find that there are many styles in which you can keep the default settings.

For instance, line spacing may be unimportant in headings, since headings are often less than a single line in length.

Similarly, in a simple document, an automatic first line indent may completely remove the need to set tab stops. The fact that many defaults can be used unchanged or entirely ignored greatly reduces the amount of designing necessary to complete a template.

Setting vertical line spacing

Writer's LINE SPACING field is on the INDENTS AND SPACING tab of each paragraph style. It used to accept entries of $1/10$ of a point ($1/720$ of an inch), but, since LibreOffice 4.2, the field rounds entries to the nearest point ($1/72$) or an inch.

This rounding produces adequate results, but not always optimal ones. Believe it or not, $1/10$ of a point can make a large visual difference.

Tip

Apache OpenOffice still allows entries of 1/10 points.

If you used your choice of fonts to determine the magic number, then you have already adjusted this option using the FIXED setting in the LINE SPACING field. FIXED remains by far the best setting, because it is the only option that gives an exact measurement.

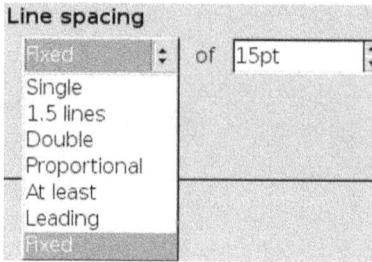

Line spacing

Fixed ‡	of	15pt ‡
Single		
1.5 lines		
Double		
Proportional		
At least		
Leading		
Fixed		

Line spacing options for paragraphs.

FIXED also has the advantage that documents will be register-true, regardless of whether the REGISTER-TRUE setting is turned on. In other words, lines will be in the same horizontal position on all pages, especially if the document uses only one font.

In addition, should you print on both sides of a page, the lines will overlap in most places, preventing the shadow of the other page showing through thin paper.

However, one problem with paragraph styles with larger font sizes, such as headings, is that they can have the tops or bottoms of letters cut off when FIXED is used. This problem can be solved by setting the LINE SPACING field using the AT LEAST option while keeping the line height unchanged.

Line-spacing problem with fixed setting

Cut-off characters are a sign that the FIXED line spacing needs to be either adjusted or replaced by AT LEAST.

The other options for line spacing are different ways of expressing line spacing. Except for quick, one-off documents, avoid the SINGLE, 1.5 LINES, and DOUBLE options. These options use Writer's standard defaults for line spacing, and are optimal for any given font only by luck.

The least useful option is PROPORTIONAL, in which line-spacing is expressed as a percentage of the automatically determined single space, and not an exact figure. In other words, this option places you two removes from the actual figure for line spacing.

Another vague option is LEADING. "Leading" is a term from the days of manual typesetting, when scraps of lead or anything else around the print shop were used to increase line spacing. "Leading" came to refer to the entire line spacing. However, LibreOffice uses the word to refer to only the extra space beyond the font size. For example, in LibreOffice, a paragraph set to 12/15 would be set with LEADING at 3 points.

Line spacing at small font sizes

You can sometimes find fonts specially designed to be readable at sizes below 10 points. More often, small font sizes need extra line spacing to make them readable.

Unfortunately, LibreOffice, like most word processors, treats line spacing for small font sizes the same as line spacing for any other size. As a rule, select FIXED to give small font sizes the extra line spacing they need.

Lorem ipsum dolor sit amet, consectetur adipiscing elit. Donec a diam lectus. Sed sit amet ipsum mauris. Maecenas congue ligula ac quam viverra nec consectetur ante hendrerit. Donec et mollis dolor. Praesent et diam eget libero egestas mattis sit amet vitae augue. Nam tincidunt congue enim, ut porta lorem lacinia consectetur. Donec ut libero sed arcu vehicula ultricies a non tortor. Lorem ipsum dolor sit amet, consectetur adipiscing elit. Aenean ut

Lorem ipsum dolor sit amet, consectetur adipiscing elit. Donec a diam lectus. Sed sit amet ipsum mauris. Maecenas congue ligula ac quam viverra nec consectetur ante hendrerit. Donec et mollis dolor. Praesent et diam eget libero egestas mattis sit amet vitae augue. Nam tincidunt congue enim, ut porta lorem lacinia consectetur. Donec ut libero sed arcu vehicula ultricies a non tortor. Lorem ipsum dolor sit amet, consectetur adipiscing elit. Aenean ut

Above: 8 point Liberation Serif with automatic single spacing. Below: 8/12 Liberation Serif. Font sizes of less than 10 points almost always require extra line-spacing for readability.

Spacing between paragraphs

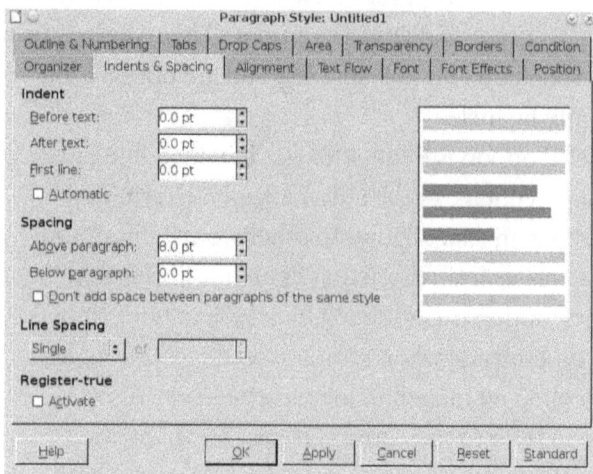

The INDENTS & SPACING tab, with the ABOVE PARAGRAPH and BELOW PARAGRAPH fields listed under SPACING.

Vertical spacing is set on the INDENTS AND SPACING tab in the SPACING > ABOVE PARAGRAPH and SPACING > BELOW PARAGRAPH.

Vertical spacing is also used to increase the effectiveness of headings. The rule is simple: Put a heading closer to the content it summarizes, and the relation between the heading and the content becomes clear at a glance.

vitae at nunc. Ut est nunc, malesuada nec ante sed, ullamcorper placerat orci. Duis volutpat dui at erat posuere fringilla. Duis interdum consectetur nisl porttitor pellentesque. Fusce tincidunt felis non nulla commodo varius. Nam dolor diam, laoreet blandit suscipit nec, lacinia eget nisi.

Vivamus sit amet convallis velit,

Nullam semper eu leo quis pulvinar. Morbi id consectetur nunc. Cras sollicitudin vehicula tellus quis feugiat. Cras vulputate arcu ac lorem placerat, sit amet dignissim erat ornare. Praesent eleifend pharetra sagittis. Ut turpis diam, sodales sit amet dolor lobortis, ultricies aliquet magna. Nulla libero dui,

Putting less space between headings and the passage they introduce helps the eye to associate them.

Extra spacing between paragraphs is one of the ways to indicate the start of a new paragraph (the other is an indentation of the first line). Usually, extra spacing is used in technical documents, but the only rule is not to use both at the same time.

Tip

The heading's font size, and the space above and below it, should total a multiple of the line spacing. In this way, heading paragraph styles matches the line spacing every few lines.

Use the same formula if spacing between body text paragraphs is used instead of a first line indentation.

nulla commodo varius. Nam dolor diam, laoreet blandit suscipit nec, lacinia eget nisi.

[15 pts]

[16 pts] Vivamus sit amet convallis velit
[6.5 pts]

Nullam semper eu leo quis pulvinar. Morbi id consectetur nunc. Cras sollicitudin vehicula

37.5 pts = 15 x 2.5

In this example, the line spacing is set to 15 points. Together, the spacing before the heading and after it plus the font size for the heading should equal a multiple of 15 or of 7.5 (half the line height).

Removing unexpected space.

The combined effect of BEFORE and AFTER settings for two subsequent paragraph styles can cause unexpectedly large spaces between paragraphs.

Minimize this problem by using only the BEFORE PARAGRAPH field and leaving the AFTER PARAGRAPH field set to zero for most paragraph styles.

In the case of pictures, you may want to vary the spacing to avoid extra large gaps.

Sometimes, the conflict may be between an image and a paragraph style. When that happens, modify the space below the image so that it matches the convention you have set and leave the paragraph style settings alone. After all, spacing around an image or any other object is manually set already.

Avoiding widows and orphans

Standard typography tries to avoid a single line at the bottom of a page – a widow – or a single line at the top of a page – an orphan.

Tip

You can distinguish widows from orphans by remembering that an orphan is left behind while a widow goes forward by herself.

Of course, avoiding widows and orphans is not always possible. Some paragraphs are a single line long. TOOLS > AUTOCORRECT does have an option to combine short paragraphs, but that is not always suitable to the sense of the passage.

Other paragraphs have a number of lines that do not fit Writer's settings. For example, if you have set last and first paragraphs on a page to each have two lines, something has to give when a three-line paragraph straddles two pages.

The TEXT FLOW tab, with ORPHAN CONTROL and WIDOW CONTROL under OPTIONS.

The TEXT FLOW tab of a paragraph style includes four options for avoiding both.

The main tools for avoiding widows and orphans are WIDOW CONTROL and ORPHAN CONTROL. For TEXT BODY and related styles, you should activate both, accepting the default of keeping two lines together, or three at the most. You do not need these settings for heading paragraphs, or in a case in which all paragraphs are short – in either case, the controls will have nothing to adjust.

As an alternative, keep WIDOW CONTROL and ORPHAN CONTROL unselected and select instead DO NOT SPLIT PARAGRAPH. This setting may keep important information together and therefore easier to read, but can result in page breaks well before the bottom of the page.

For headings, you may prefer KEEP WITH NEXT PARAGRAPH. When headings are meant to introduce the body text below them, having the heading and body text on separate pages makes no sense. However, this setting, too, may result in poorly positioned page breaks, so use it sparingly.

Spacing between paragraphs

Vertical spacing is set on the INDENTS AND SPACING tab in the SPACING > ABOVE PARAGRAPH and SPACING > BELOW PARAGRAPH fields.

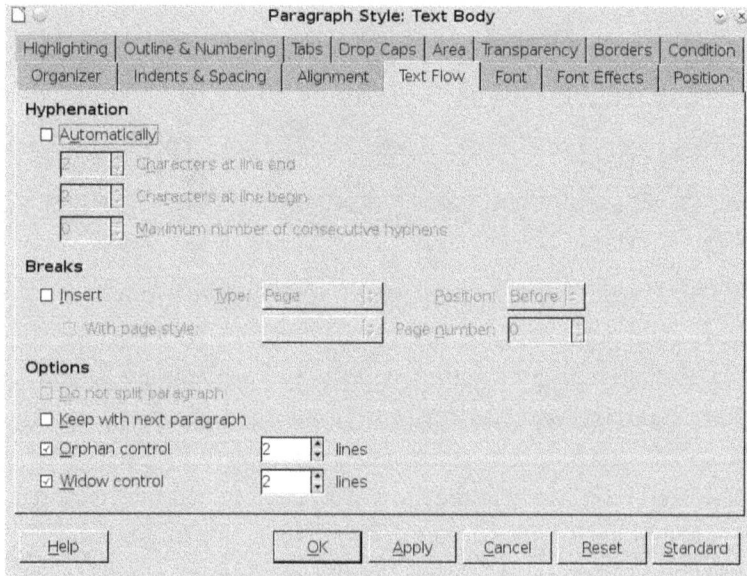

The INDENTS & SPACING tab, with the ABOVE PARAGRAPH and BELOW PARAGRAPH fields listed under SPACING.

Vertical spacing is also used to increase the effectiveness of headings. The rule is simple: Put a heading closer to the content it summarizes, and the relation between the heading and the content becomes clear at a glance.

Extra spacing between paragraphs is one of the ways to indicate the start of a new paragraph (the other is an indentation of the first line). Usually, extra spacing is used in technical documents instead of first-line indentation, but the only firm rule is not to use both at the same time.

vitae at nunc. Ut est nunc, malesuada nec ante sed, ullamcorper placerat orci. Duis volutpat dui at erat posuere fringilla. Duis interdum consectetur nisl porttitor pellentesque. Fusce tincidunt felis non nulla commodo varius. Nam dolor diam, laoreet blandit suscipit nec, lacinia eget nisi.

Vivamus sit amet convallis velit,

Nullam semper eu leo quis pulvinar. Morbi id consectetur nunc. Cras sollicitudin vehicula tellus quis feugiat. Cras vulputate arcu ac lorem placerat, sit amet dignissim erat ornare. Praesent eleifend pharetra sagittis. Ut turpis diam, sodales sit amet dolor lobortis, ultricies aliquet magna. Nulla libero dui,

Putting less space between headings and the passage they introduce helps the eye to associate them.

Tip

The heading's font size, and the space above and below it, should total a multiple of the line spacing.

Use the same formula if spacing between body text paragraphs is used instead of a first-line indentation.

Caution

The combined effect of BEFORE and AFTER settings for two subsequent paragraph styles can cause unexpectedly large spaces between paragraphs.

Minimize this problem by using only the BEFORE PARAGRAPH field and leaving the AFTER PARAGRAPH field set to zero for most paragraph styles.

Selecting an alignment

On the ALIGNMENT tab of a paragraph style, you have four choices for horizontal positioning: LEFT, RIGHT, CENTERED, and JUSTIFIED.

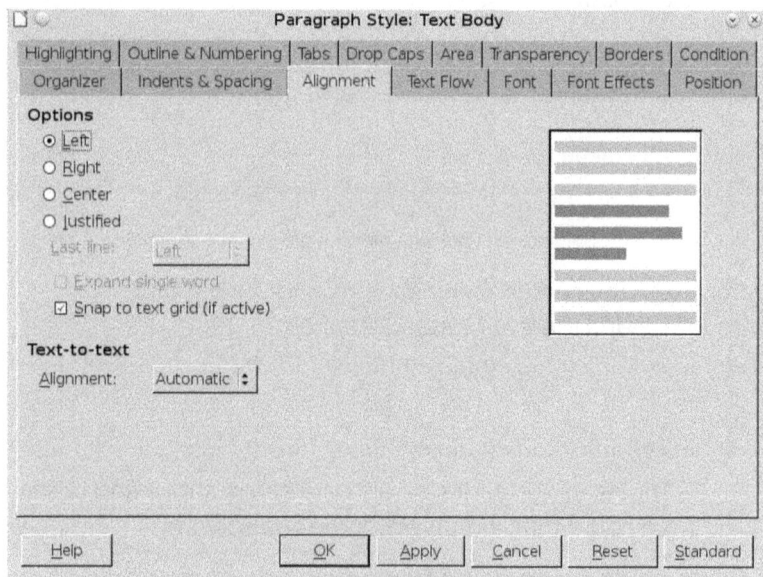

The ALIGNMENT tab, with the OPTIONS at the top of the window.

RIGHT is rarely used except in short, highly-formatted documents such as ads or diagrams, while CENTERED is generally reserved for titles and sub-titles. For most paragraph styles, your choice is likely to be LEFT or JUSTIFIED.

Whatever your choice of alignment, if you are using hyphenated styles, run TOOLS > LANGUAGE > HYPHENATION as a last step before publishing. This selection repairs any sub-optimal choices Writer might have made on the fly.

Using a Justified alignment

Many users prefer a Justified alignment, in which all lines start at the same position on the left and end at the same position on the right. Because commercial publications often use Justified, users often believe it looks more professional.

The preference may also be a reminder of the earliest days of word processing, the first time that a Justified alignment became practical. The vast majority of typewriters, of course, could only use a Left alignment.

The trouble is, a Justified alignment often requires more work. Too often, it results in irregular spacing between characters or words that looks far worse than Left alignment ever could. You almost always need to tinker to find the best distribution of characters and words on a line.

Generally, too, the shorter the line, the harder you have to work to make Justified work. As a rule, lines of less than 40 characters are too much effort to be worth justifying. A Left alignment can still cause problems, but they are often less severe, especially in columns or tables.

The easiest way to tell if a paragraph style can easily use Justified is to set it up with dummy text and count the number of lines that end in a hyphen and the blotches of irregular white space.

The more of these problems that appear, the more you need to change the hyphenation, the font, the font size, and/or the column width in the hope of a better fit. You can even go to the POSITION tab to expand or condense character spacing.

Lorem ip-	suere vitae,	tor elit id
sum dolor	molestie in	tempus dic-
sit amet,	mauris.	tum. Donec
consectetur	Nunc ac-	tempus
adipiscing	cumsan	eleifend
elit. Etiam	ante a	porta. Nam
mauris dui,	lorem port-	elementum
pellen-	titor pulv-	venenatis
tesque sit	inar. Ae-	nisi id ali-
amet po-	nean portti-	quet. Nunc

An example of the wrong alignment for the line length. The middle column has three hyphenated lines, while hyphenation causes awkward breaks throughout. Even worse, several lines are single words. Some lines even have more than one fault.

Setting the last line of justified text

The last line of justified text is only a complete line by luck. Almost always, it is an incomplete line.

LibreOffice offers several choices of how to handle this approach. Frankly, though, you have to wonder why. All but one leave large gaps between words or letters that anyone who cares about the design of their documents should find unacceptable.

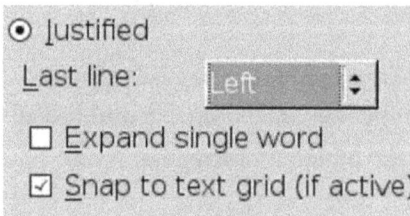

⊙ Justified

L̲ast line: [Left ▲▼]

☐ E̲xpand single word

☑ S̲nap to text grid (if active)

The LAST LINE options for justified text on the ALIGNMENT tab. The other options in the drop-down list are CENTERED and JUSTIFIED.

> **Tip**
>
> SNAP TO TEXT GRID (IF ACTIVE) uses the non-printing grid
> set in TOOLS > OPTIONS > LIBREOFFICE WRITER > GRID for
> positioning. Apache OpenOffice lacks this option.

The only consistently aesthetic choice is to set the LAST LINE field to LEFT. This selection is the only one that eliminates the impossible situation of trying to justify a line of text that is too short and has ugly gaps in it.

The other options – JUSTIFIED, CENTERED, EXPAND SINGLE WORD, and LEFT – all look awkward. The only reason to use any of them is to provide a sample of why they are unacceptable.

Lorem ipsum dolor sit amet, consectetur adipiscing elit. Integer nec odio. Praesent libero. Sed cursus ante dapibus diam. Sed nisi. Nulla quis sem at nibh elementum imperdiet. Duis sagittis ipsum. Praesent mauris. Fusce nec tellus sed augue semper porta. Mauris massa. Vestibulum lacinia arcu eget nulla. Class aptent

Lorem ipsum dolor sit amet, consectetur adipiscing elit. Integer nec odio. Praesent libero. Sed cursus ante dapibus diam. Sed nisi. Nulla quis sem at nibh elementum imperdiet. Duis sagittis ipsum. Praesent mauris. Fusce nec tellus sed augue semper porta. Mauris massa. Vestibulum lacinia arcu eget nulla. Class aptent

Lorem ipsum dolor sit amet, consectetur adipiscing elit. Integer nec odio. Praesent libero. Sed cursus ante dapibus diam. Sed nisi. Nulla quis sem at nibh elementum imperdiet. Duis sagittis ipsum. Praesent mauris. Fusce nec tellus sed augue semper porta
M   a   u   r   i   s

Lorem ipsum dolor sit amet, consectetur adipiscing elit. Integer nec odio. Praesent libero. Sed cursus ante dapibus diam. Sed nisi. Nulla quis sem at nibh elementum imperdiet. Duis sagittis ipsum. Praesent mauris. Fusce nec tellus sed augue semper porta. Mauris massa. Vestibulum lacinia arcu eget nulla. Class aptent

The justification of the last line. From top to bottom: JUSTIFIED, CENTERED, EXPAND SINGLE WORD, and LEFT.

You may be able to improve the look of JUSTIFIED by selecting SNAP TO TEXT GRID (IF ACTIVE) and adjusting the grid set in TOOLS > OPTIONS > LIBREOFFICE WRITER > GRID. However, getting an acceptable look is likely to take a lot of trial and error.

Using a Left alignment

When a paragraph has a Left alignment, all lines start at the same position on the left, but can end anywhere on the right. For this reason, a Left alignment is sometimes referred to as "ragged right." This is the default choice in Writer, probably because it is reasonably acceptable without tweaking, especially if lines are not hyphenated or are over about 40 characters long.

Generally, the shorter the line, the harder you have to work to make Justified look decent. That means that Left can be a better choice in columns or tables.

Setting hyphenation

Hyphenation options are set on the TEXT FLOW tab. Whether to hyphenate is one of the most important design decisions you will make when designing a document.

Hyphenation is a contentious issue in digital design. Most word processors hyphenate as you type, and while they make adjustments as the line lengths change, their on-the-fly solutions are not always optional. Short lines are especially hard to hyphenate well automatically.

These difficulties are one reason that many designers prefer a Left alignment or ragged right margin. A Left alignment does not always produce the best possible use of the line, but its shortcomings are rarely as severe as those with a Justified alignment.

Another choice is to turn off hyphenation completely, which is probably why the TEXT FLOW tab does not check the AUTOMATICALLY hyphenation box by default.

Other designers, more determined or more patient, try to improve hyphenation by adjusting the settings on the TEXT FLOW tab. The number of letters at the end and start of the line should be 1–4. The typographical convention is not to allow more than two lines in a row to end with a hyphen.

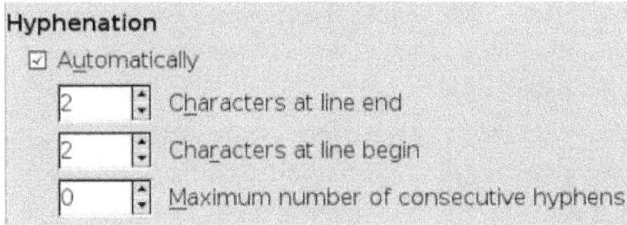

Hyphenation
☑ Automatically
> [2] [⇅] Characters at line end
> [2] [⇅] Characters at line begin
> [0] [⇅] Maximum number of consecutive hyphens

Detail of the TEXT FLOW tab, showing the hyphenation controls.

The CHARACTERS AT LINE END and CHARACTERS AT LINE BEGIN fields can sometimes be manipulated to improve hyphenation by playing one off against the other. Working by itself, the MAXIMUM NUMBER OF CONSECUTIVE HYPHENS field can also make a difference.

In many documents, only TEXT BODY and perhaps another handful of paragraph styles are used at such length that hyphenation can improve how they fall on the page. Headings, which are rarely more than a few words long and almost never more than two lines, generally do not need to be hyphenated at all. If anything, headings are easier to scan if not hyphenated.

You may want to change the hyphenation by adjusting:

* The HYPHENATION settings on the TEXT FLOW tab.

* The font weight or size.

* The choice of fonts.

* The settings for TOOLS > OPTIONS > LANGUAGE SETTINGS > WRITING AIDS > OPTIONS > MINIMAL NUMBER OF CHARACTERS FOR HYPHENATION. These settings are over-ridden by any formatting in the document itself.

- The SCALE WIDTH and SPACING fields on the POSITION tab to expand or condense character spacing. Frankly, these fields are a last desperate measure.

In addition, if you do hyphenate, the line divisions can be improved by running TOOLS > LANGUAGE > HYPHENATION as a final touch on the document.

This tool not only works interactively, giving you more control, but also generally does a better job than the on-the-fly hyphenation, if run when the document is complete.

Tip

For extra fine-tuning, go through a document when it is complete, and hand-hyphenate by positioning the cursor between syllables and pressing CTRL+ -. This key combination creates a conditional hyphen that only comes into play when it is in the hyphenation zone near the right margin.

Setting horizontal spacing

By default, paragraphs run from the left margin to the right margin – or, at least, to a region just before the right margin that LibreOffice must reach before starting a new line, with or without hyphenation.

However, on the INDENTS AND SPACING tab, you can indent a paragraph on the left by entering a value in the BEFORE TEXT field, or on the right by entering a value in the AFTER TEXT field.

Common uses for an indent include:

- The start of a new paragraph.

- A quotation of over three lines or 100 words. Typically, such long quotations are indented one line-space on the left and right. No quotation marks are used, since the indentation is enough to mark is a quotation.

- The space between a bullet or number and an item in a list. This space is set using the INDENT AT field on the POSITION tab for a list style.
- Notes, tips, or warning paragraph styles.
- Paragraph styles intended for single style outline numbering.
- Cases in which headers and footers are wider than body text.

Controlling the number of indents

Some paragraph styles that begin with an indentation are unavoidable in a text document. However, too many different indentations clutter the design, so indentations should be kept to a minimum. No need, for example, exists to have a bulleted or numbered list indented more than the TEXT BODY style. Instead, the indentation for a long quotation can be the same as the first line indentation, as well as the position where the text starts in a list item after a bullet or number.

Tip

Horizontal line spacing can also be a help in readability. Regardless of font or page size, typographic convention suggests that a line of body text should be 50–75 characters long for readability – or, to put things another way, two to three lower case alphabets long in a single-column layout.

In tables or multi-column layouts, the length should generally be 30–50 characters, regardless of alignment. Anything less risks cluttering the column with hyphens, single-word lines, and/or vast stretches of white space.

Lorem ipsum dolor sit amet, consectetur adipiscing elit. Donec a diam lectus. Sed sit amet ipsum mauris. Maecenas congue ligula ac quam viverra nec consectetur ante hendrerit. Donec et mollis dolor.
- Nam tincidunt congue enim, ut porta lorem lacinia consectetur.
- Donec ut libero sed arcu vehicula ultricies a non tortor.
- Lorem ipsum dolor sit amet, consectetur adipiscing elit.
  - Aenean ut gravida lorem.
  - Ut turpis felis, pulvinar a semper sed, adipiscing id dolor.
  - Pellentesque auctor nisi id magna consequat sagittis.

Lorem ipsum dolor sit amet, consectetur adipiscing elit. Donec a diam lectus. Sed sit amet ipsum mauris. Maecenas congue ligula ac quam viverra nec consectetur ante hendrerit. Donec et mollis dolor.
- Nam tincidunt congue enim, ut porta lorem lacinia consectetur.
- Donec ut libero sed arcu vehicula ultricies a non tortor.
- Lorem ipsum dolor sit amet, consectetur adipiscing elit.
  - Aenean ut gravida lorem.
  - Ut turpis felis, pulvinar a semper sed, adipiscing id dolor.
  - Pellentesque auctor nisi id magna consequat sagittis.

An example of why indents should be as few as possible. Starting at the left margin, the top passage has five indentations, and looks cluttered. The bottom passage looks less cluttered because it reduces the number of indentations to three.

Setting first line indentation

A first-line indent is one of the two ways to indicate a new paragraph. The other way is to add extra space between paragraphs.

Usually, a first line indent is used for more formal or literary works, while an extra space may be for technical manuals, but the rule is not absolute. The only firm convention is that you should use one or the other, but not both at the same time

Most people set an indent of 30–36 points – no doubt a legacy of typewriters, on which setting indentations precisely was difficult. However, that is excessive.

Unless a font is extremely small, the first line indent usually needs to be no more than the line spacing, and you might even manage with half a line-space, depending on the font size.

If you set the FIRST LINE field to AUTOMATIC, you can largely ignore tabs, except for features like tables of contents that rely upon them for some features.

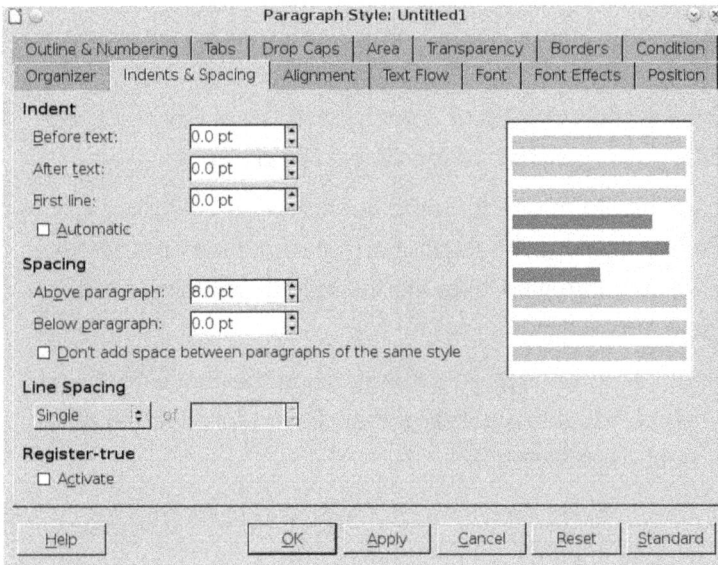

The first line indent is set in the FIRST LINE field of the INDENT section of the INDENTS & SPACING tab. You can use it either by pressing the TAB key or by selecting the AUTOMATIC box.

    Lorem ipsum dolor sit amet, consectetuer adipiscing elit, sed diam nonummy nibh

  Lorem ipsum dolor sit amet, consectetuer adipiscing elit, sed diam nonummy nibh

  Lorem ipsum dolor sit amet, consectetuer adipiscing elit, sed diam nonummy nibh

First line indentation. 36 points (top) can leave too much white space to the left, while half a line-space (bottom) can be hard to distinguish. Usually, a full line-space (middle) avoids both extremes.

Example: Designing a letter template

If you have been reading chapter by chapter, at this point you may want a sense of what goes into a template.

You can customize a letter template from FILE > WIZARDS > LETTER that uses frames to position different elements of the letter. As an alternative, here are the steps in building a letter template with styles.

The example ignores page settings, since they have not been covered yet. You can add margins and headers after you have read about page styles.

Choosing fonts

This template uses two fonts: One for the body of the letter, and one for information like addresses and the salutation – the equivalents of headers in other documents.

After some experimentation, I opted for two free-licensed fonts from the Arkandis Digital Foundry. Baskervald ADF Std. imitates the classic Eighteenth Century font Baskerville and is used for body text. Gillius ADF No.2, which imitates Gill Sans, is used for heading text (that is, anything not part of the body text).

If you download and install these two fonts on your system, you can build the template by following the description below.

Creating the basic font palette

To prepare Gillius ADF No.2, apply these settings to the HEADING paragraph style:

- Since this font is only for short lines, ignore elements such as first line indentation or widow and orphan control, which will not be used.

- Set the font size to 14 points for greater legibility on the FONT tab, and set the line space to 18 points. Experiments with page color show that anything less makes the color of the font too dark on the page.

To prepare Baskervald ADF Std, apply these settings to the TEXT BODY style:

- Select the AUTOMATICALLY box for hyphenation, ORPHAN CONTROL, and WIDOW CONTROL on the TEXT FLOW tab.

- Set the font size to 15 on the FONT tab. Baskervald's characters use more white space than most fonts, and therefore appear much smaller than the actual size.

- Set the LINE SPACING to FIXED > 18 POINTS on the INDENTS & SPACING tab. This setting gives Baskervald a color close to that of Gillius, which makes for a uniform look on the page.

Check these settings by printing samples of at least three lines for both fonts. All other styles will be based on the settings for these two, with variations for individual needs.

Setting up other styles

The best way to set up other styles is to start at the top of the document and note the styles that are needed:

- Use the pre-existing ADDRESSEE style for the return address. Change the INHERIT FROM field on the ORGANIZER tab from ADDRESSEE to HEADER, and change the alignment to RIGHT on the ALIGNMENT tab.

STOP

Caution

You may need to re-start LibreOffice for the changes to take effect. This problem may happen with any pre-existing style.

- Below the return address is the DATE style, which is followed by white space, then the ADDRESS. Create both as new styles linked to the HEADER style.

  Then make the following changes to the DATE style:

1 Set the NEXT STYLE field on the ORGANIZER tab to ADDRESS.

2 Change the alignment to RIGHT on the ALIGNMENT tab.

3 On the INDENTS AND SPACING tab, set SPACING > ABOVE PARAGRAPH to 54 points, and SPACING > BELOW to 126 points. Notice that these are multiples of the fixed line spacing of 18 points being used for Header and its subordinate style.

Tip

If you are using any page size other than Letter, increase SPACING > BELOW to a multiple of 18.

4 From the menu, select INSERT > FIELDS > OTHER > DOCUMENT > DATE. Select a format from the FORMAT pane, then click the INSERT button. Now, every time you select the DATE style, the current date will be automatically added.

5 The ADDRESS style is unmodified from the HEADER style. However, it is worth creating so you remember what style to use. Besides, you might eventually decide to modify it.

6   The next style is the SALUTATION. On the INDENTS & SPACING TAB, set SPACING > ABOVE PARAGRAPH to 36 points (2 lines), and SPACING > BELOW PARAGRAPH to 18 (1 line). Then, on the ORGANIZER tab, set the NEXT STYLE field to TEXT BODY.

7   The TEXT BODY style is already created. However, it needs a FIRST LINE INDENT setting on the INDENTS & SPACING tab. Set it to 18 points, the same as the line spacing.

8   Create a SIGNATURE style with the following settings:

•   On the ALIGNMENT tab, set the alignment to CENTER.

•   On the INDENTS AND SPACING tab, set SPACING > ABOVE PARAGRAPH to 18 points (1 line),

•   On the INDENTS AND SPACING tab, set SPACING > BELOW PARAGRAPH to 95 points (5 lines). Leave more space below if you have a large signature.

Creating character styles

The only character styles likely to be needed with this template are those for EMPHASIS (italics) and STRONG EMPHASIS (Bold). Base both on the Body Text (Baskervald ADF Std, 15 point).

Other points

Following these steps results in a useful, well-designed template. Formatting consists of six changes of paragraph styles, two of which are automatically changed when I press the ENTER key. Instead of worrying about formatting, I can concentrate on what I am saying.

However, you may prefer to organize the paragraph styles differently than I have done, and make other adjustments beyond the basics given here.

Building a template is a matter of trial and error, and you are unlikely to remember everything – or get all design elements perfect – after a single session.

For instance, after using the template for a few letters, I realized that the default margins created a somewhat narrow look. Changing the left and right margin to 72 points (a multiple of the line spacing for the TEXT BODY) improved the layout immensely.

Similarly, when I realized the template worked best for short letters, I added a page with a footer containing the page number for longer letters.

I could also have added a few touches, such as creating and attaching a list style to the SALUTATION paragraph style that automatically added "Dear" when I applied the paragraph style.

The text style basics

The settings discussed in this chapter are the ones you are likely to use in every document. The next two chapters explore special cases and advanced settings that you may want to use now and then.

6

Text tools and traps

Chapter 5 discusses settings that almost all documents use. This chapter is about less common character and paragraph settings. You might find several of these features in a single document, but rarely all.

Some of these features just have limited or specialized use. However, others you should consider carefully before using.

Some are design elements that seemed reasonable decades ago when Writer was first released, but have since become obsolete – and never were (to be polite) in the best typographical tradition.

Still others are obscure or difficult to use. In these cases, the same results can often be obtained with more options by choosing another method.

There is even a feature or two that LibreOffice technically supports but implements so poorly that you will get more satisfying results if you use another piece of software instead.

I was tempted to avoid talking about such features altogether, but the warnings are worth giving. Besides, possibly, they may have more practical uses than they appear to do. If anyone knows such a use, I would be glad to hear.

Of course, if you do find a use for some of the features I disparage, ignore my cautions and do as you think best. While typographic practice can advise, it should never be a set of conventions followed blindly. In the end, anything that makes the text more readable or easier to navigate or maintain is legitimate.

Setting borders

Borders are the lines surrounding an object on all four sides. All LibreOffice's applications include an identical BORDERS tab on at least one of their styles. In Draw and Impress, a similar feature is called LINE.

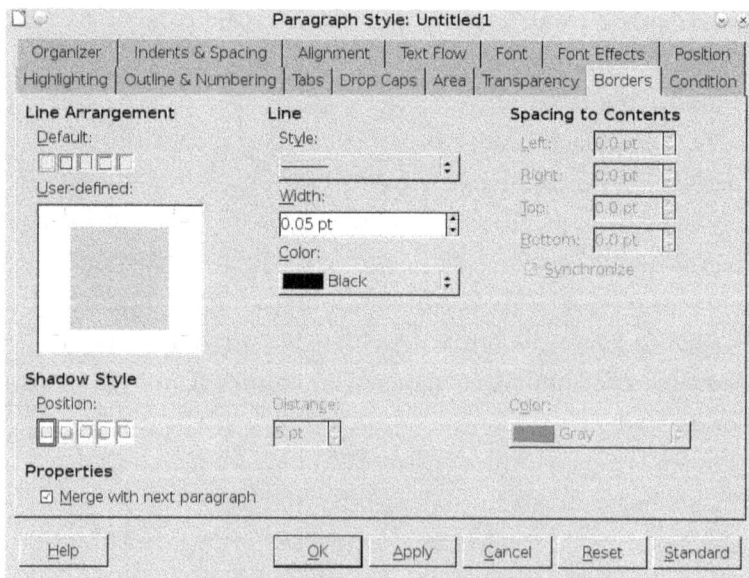

Similar BORDERS tabs are found throughout LibreOffice.

Adding borders

To set up borders:

1 Under LINE ARRANGEMENT, use either the DEFAULT or USER-DEFINED diagrams to choose on which sides you want a border.

   The DEFAULT diagram sets all sides together, offering pre-defined arrangements at a single click. With the USER-DEFINED diagram, you can set each side separately.

2 Set the line's STYLE, WIDTH, and COLOR. In most circumstances, choose the thinnest, plainest style possible. You may need to choose a thicker line so it is detectable on low-end printers.

3 Set the SPACING TO CONTENTS on each side. Generous spacing increases readability by avoiding a cramped look.

   When the SYNCHRONIZE check box is selected, you can fill in values for the LEFT and RIGHT sides or the TOP and BOTTOM sides at the same time.

> Lorem ipsum dolor sit amet, consectetur adipiscing elit. Integer nec odio. Praesent libero. Sed cursus ante dapibus diam. Sed nisi. Nulla quis sem at nibh elementum imperdiet. Duis sagittis ipsum. Praesent mauris. Fusce nec tellus sed augue semper porta. Mauris massa. Vestibulum lacinia arcu eget nulla. Class aptent taciti sociosqu ad litora torquent

> Lorem ipsum dolor sit amet, consectetur adipiscing elit. Integer nec odio. Praesent libero. Sed cursus ante dapibus diam. Sed nisi. Nulla quis sem at nibh elementum imperdiet. Duis sagittis ipsum. Praesent mauris. Fusce nec tellus sed augue semper porta. Mauris massa. Vestibulum lacinia arcu eget nulla. Class aptent taciti sociosqu

Above: BORDERS > SPACE TO CONTENTS set to 0 points. Below: Set to 5 points. The extra white space increases readability and prevents crowding against the borders.

Tip

Occasionally, borders may appear when you have set none. If that happens and you do not need borders, leave the LINE ARRANGEMENT blank, and select LINE > STYLE > NONE.

4   If you want a shadow as part of the border, select its POSITION, DISTANCE (from the border), and COLOR.

Caution

Shadows can help separate a picture from the background. However, if you cannot explain the reason for using a shadow, you should not use one. Shadows were so over-used in the mid-1990s that today they can look excessive and old-fashioned.

Lorem ipsum dolor sit amet, consectetur adipiscing elit. Proin bibendum maximus velit, blandit suscipit felis fermentum tristique. Aenean non neque magna. Praesent aliquam justo eros, ut aliquam arcu ullamcorper eu. In sit amet sapien non ligula pulvinar ultricies. Lorem ipsum dolor sit amet, consectetur adipiscing elit. Fusce et ullamcorper quam.

A paragraph with a border and shadow. Only use a shadow if you have a reason for doing so. The days are long past when people used shadows simply because they could.

Using borders in character and paragraph styles

Many beginning designers dislike empty space. To them, empty space is wasted space. As a result, they are tempted to corral it by putting borders around everything. This is a temptation that they should almost always avoid.

In text documents and presentation slides, the uses of borders are limited. The most obvious uses are to create a blank space to put an answer on a quiz, or to indicate a side bar in a newsletter.

Charles Darwin first explained evolution in his book .

Borders in character styles can be used for answer blanks.

Lorem ipsum dolor sit amet consectetur adipiscing elit. Integer nec odio. Praesent libero. Sed cursus ante dapibus diam. Sed nisi. Nulla quis sem at nibh elementum imperdiet. Duis sagittis ipsum. Praesent mauris. Fusce nec tellus sed augue semper porta. Mauris massa. Vestibulum lacinia arcu eget nulla. Class aptent taciti sociosqu ad litora torquent per conubia nostra, per inceptos himenaeos. Curabitur sodales ligula in libero. Sed dignissim lacinia nunc.

Curabitur tortor. Pellentesque nibh. Aenean quam. In scelerisque sem at dolor. Maecenas mattis. Sed convallis tristique sem. Proin ut ligula vel nunc egestas porttitor. Morbi lectus risus, iaculis vel, suscipit quis, luctus non, massa. Fusce ac turpis quis ligula lacinia aliquet. Mauris ipsum. Nulla metus metus, ullamcorper vel, tincidunt sed, euismod in, nibh. Quisque volutpat condimentum velit. Class aptent taciti sociosqu ad litora torquent per conubia nostra, per inceptos himenaeos. Nam nec ante.

Sed lacinia, urna non tincidunt mattis, tortor neque adipiscing diam, a cursus ipsum ante quis turpis. Nulla facilisi. Ut fringilla. Suspendisse potenti. Nunc feugiat mi a tellus consequat imperdiet. Vestibulum sapien. Proin quam. Etiam ultrices. Suspendisse in justo eu magna luctus suscipit.

Lorem ipsum dolor sit amet consectetur adipiscing elit. Integer nec odio. Praesent libero. Sed cursus ante dapibus diam. Sed nisi. Nulla quis sem at nibh elementum imperdiet. Duis sagittis ipsum.

Praesent mauris.
Fusce nec tellus sed augue semper porta. Mauris massa. Vestibulum lacinia arcu eget nulla. Class aptent taciti sociosqu ad litora torquent per conubia nostra, per inceptos himenaeos. Curabitur sodales ligula in libero. Sed dignissim lacinia nunc.

Curabitur tortor. Pellentesque nibh. Aenean quam. In scelerisque sem at dolor. Maecenas mattis. Sed convallis tristique sem. Proin ut ligula vel nunc egestas porttitor. Morbi lectus risus, iaculis vel, suscipit quis, luctus non, massa.

Fusce ac turpis quis
ligula lacinia aliquet. Mauris ipsum. Nulla metus metus, ullamcorper vel, tincidunt sed, euismod in, nibh. Quisque volutpat condimentum velit. Class aptent taciti sociosqu ad litora torquent per conubia nostra, per inceptos himenaeos. Nam nec ante.

Sed lacinia, urna non tincidunt mattis, tortor neque adipiscing diam, a cursus ipsum ante quis turpis. Nulla facilisi. Ut fringilla. Suspendisse potenti. Nunc feugiat mi a tellus consequat imperdiet.

Lorem ipsum dolor sit amet consectetur adipiscing elit. Integer nec odio. Praesent libero. Sed cursus ante dapibus diam. Sed nisi. Nulla quis sem at nibh elementum imperdiet. Duis sagittis ipsum. Praesent mauris. Fusce nec tellus sed augue semper porta. Mauris massa. Vestibulum lacinia arcu eget nulla. Class aptent taciti sociosqu ad litora torquent per conubia nostra, per inceptos himenaeos. Curabitur sodales ligula in libero. Sed dignissim lacinia nunc.

Curabitur tortor. Pellentesque nibh. Aenean quam. In scelerisque sem at dolor.

Borders in paragraph styles can be used to create side-bars. By placing a border around a small side discussion when the rest of the text has none, you emphasize that it is not part of the normal text flow. Font: Liberation Serif.

Often, however, borders are just another bit of unnecessary clutter. Enough empty space may achieve the same purpose as a border while looking less constricted. Sometimes a frame may be a better choice because it has more options.

No matter how you add borders, minimize their width and be generous with the SPACING TO CONTENTS settings. Borders that crowd the content only obscure.

Highlighting and setting backgrounds

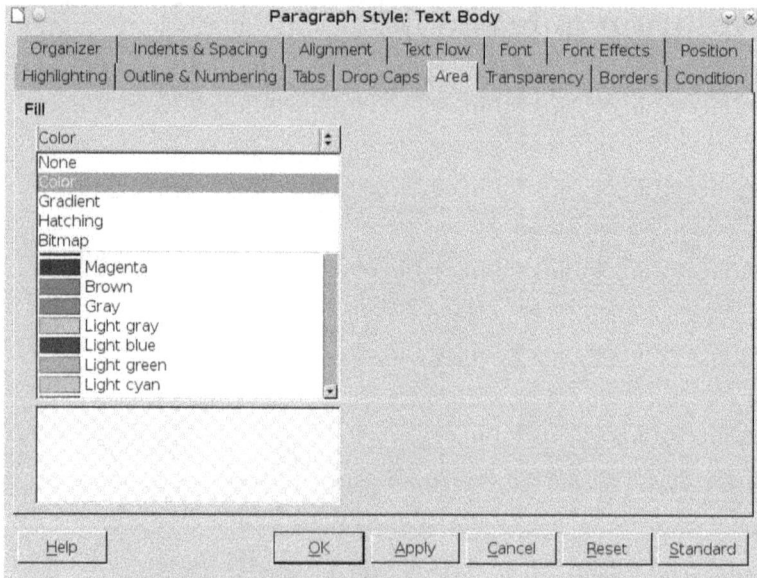

Like the BORDERS tab, the BACKGROUND/AREA tab is found throughout LibreOffice, sometimes allowing only color.

Highlighting is available in character styles, and most useful for emphasizing passages in informal documents. Backgrounds or areas are available in paragraph styles, and are basically the same feature as highlighting, except that highlighting is available only as a color, while a background or area can also be a gradient, hatching, or bitmap.

Tip

Using the AREA and TRANSPARENCY tabs, you can give a paragraph its own watermark. See "Creating watermarks," page 260.

If you are choosing a color background, make sure that the color you want is among LibreOffice's defined colors. If not, go to TOOLS > OPTIONS > LIBREOFFICE > COLORS to add it as a custom color, or make adjustments on the TRANSPARENCY tab (see "Setting transparency," page 136).

Similarly, before you add a graphic background, prepare its dimensions and transparency in a graphics editor such as GIMP.

Light Dark

The basic rule for backgrounds: text and background should contrast with each other.

For all backgrounds/areas, the basic rule is: combine light-colored text with a dark background, and dark-colored text with a light background. Without a strong contrast, your document loses readability. Dark text on a light background is easiest for many people to read, because that is the most commonly used.

Be careful, too, not to use backgrounds with too many different colors. Too often, the result will be illegibility.

Most foreground colors are lost on multi-colored backgrounds.

Tip

When adding backgrounds, consider whether you need to check the contrast for black and white as well as color printing. The two are not necessarily the same.

Using backgrounds in character and paragraph styles

Like borders, backgrounds have limited use in character and paragraph styles. Several character styles, each with a different color background, might be useful for highlighting when you are taking notes, or for a brochure, but the majority of text-heavy documents use a plain white background.

Most of the time, you have more options and more control if you use a frame instead, or perhaps apply the background to a page style.

Setting transparency

The TRANSPARENCY tab originated in graphic styles, and was added to paragraph styles in Writer in the 4.4 release.

The tab adds transparency when a selection is made on the BACKGROUND/AREA tab. 0% is no transparency, 100% complete transparency.

From the TRANSPARENCY tab, you can:

- Create a transparency to add quickly (if approximately) another color without formally defining a color in TOOLS > OPTIONS > LIBREOFFICE > COLORS.

- Edit the transparency of a background/area to improve the contrast between the foreground and background.

- Create a background gradient using degrees of transparency. A gradient makes a transition between two colors. (See "Designing area gradients," page 400.)

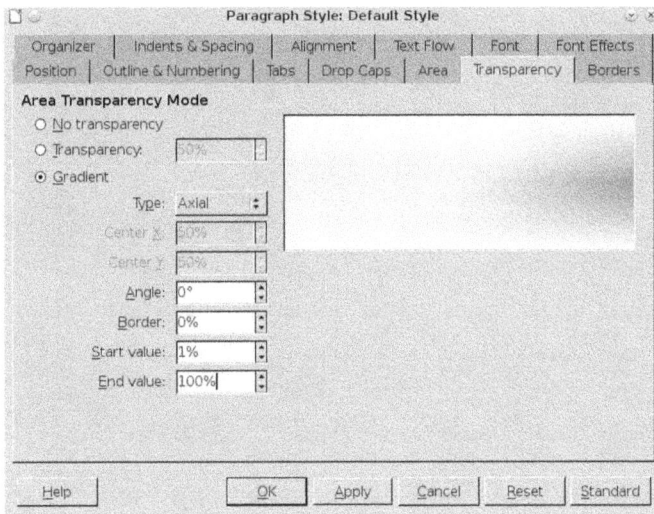

The TRANSPARENCY tab works with the AREA tab. Here, the controls to define a gradient are shown.

Setting tab stops

Tabs are set positions on a line. The place where a tab begins is called the tab position or tab stop.

Usually, tab stops should be multiples of the line-spacing, and kept to the minimum necessary. Much of the time, the standard typewriter tab stops of half or one inch will be far more than you need.

Tabs are sometimes used to create columns of text, but a table is usually a better option. If you use an automatic first line indent, in many cases the only reasons to use tab stops are from habit or because LibreOffice uses them in an advanced feature such as tables of contents.

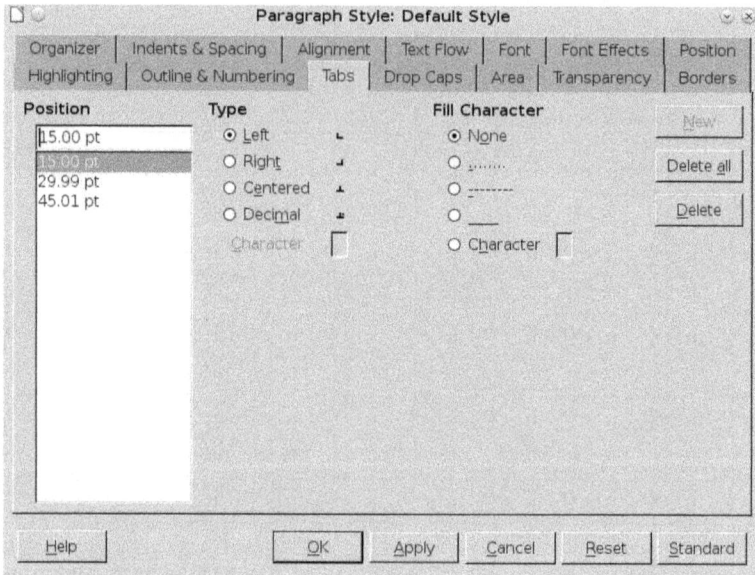

Organizer	Indents & Spacing	Alignment	Text Flow	Font	Font Effects		Position
Highlighting	Outline & Numbering	Tabs	Drop Caps	Area	Transparency		Borders

Paragraph Style: Default Style

Position	Type	Fill Character	
15.00 pt	⊙ Left	⊙ None	New
15.00 pt	○ Right	○	Delete all
29.99 pt	○ Centered	○ --------	
45.01 pt	○ Decimal	○ ____	Delete
	Character	○ Character	

Help	OK	Apply	Cancel	Reset	Standard

Use of tabs can be greatly minimized. When you do use tabs, make each a multiple of the line spacing.

The types of tabs are:
- LEFT: Places the left edge of the text column at the tab position, extending the text to the right. In most cases, this will be the most commonly used type, and often the only one.

- RIGHT: Places the right edge of the text at the tab, extending the text to the left. The most common use of this type is to position a column of text against the right margin.

- CENTERED: Places the center of the text at the tab position, extending it on both the left and the right. Often, this type can be replaced by setting the general alignment of the line to CENTERED.

- DECIMAL: Places the decimal at the tab position, and whole numbers and text to its left. You can set the decimal character according to the language locale. For instance, the decimal character is a period in most English locales.

Left   Center   4.35   Right

The four types of tab positions differ in where text appears in relation to the tab stop in the ruler.

The trouble with all the types of tabs is that they can be an unstable way of positioning characters. The smallest formatting change can sometimes throw them out of position.

Using tabs effectively

Even if you minimize the use of tabs yourself, you cannot avoid LibreOffice's built-in uses of them. For example, LibreOffice uses tabs to position text in relation to bullets and numbers in list styles, and as an option in customizing tables of contents or in the use of a conditional style.

Otherwise, consider whether you need tabs or can substitute another solution. Frames or tables with invisible borders are often a more stable choice.

When using tabs, do:	When using tabs, do not:
• Set them in the DEFAULT paragraph styles, or at the very least, as high up the hierarchical tree as possible. Otherwise, you will have to set tabs separately for each paragraph style.	• Use them to indicate the start of new paragraphs. Instead, create a FIRST LINE INDENT and check the AUTOMATIC box on the INDENTS AND SPACING tab.
• Make the tab positions multiples of the line spacing.	• Use them to position characters in a text frame, such as a header or footer. Instead, use a table with invisible borders and carefully adjusted column widths.
• Set the tab positions as late as possible in your designing. Otherwise, changes in features such as font or font size may force you to re-set them.	• Use fill characters in the blank spaces between tab positions. See "Avoiding the default TOC design," page 317.

The Dos and Don'ts of using tab stops.

Setting up drop capitals

Drop capitals are enlarged letters that mark the start of a new chapter or section. The DROP CAPS tab for a paragraph style automates the process of creating a text frame and setting the text flow around it.

Drop caps are more common in fiction than non-fiction, and in magazines than in an academic essay. They create an informality that is more at home in a novel than in most types of non-fiction. The exception are the highly decorated capitals found in illuminated manuscripts from the Middle Ages.

Before creating drop caps, consider what other indicators of a new chapter you have in your design. If your first page style starts lower down than the rest of your pages, or if the start is marked by a recurring design or by numbers, then drop caps may be more than you need.

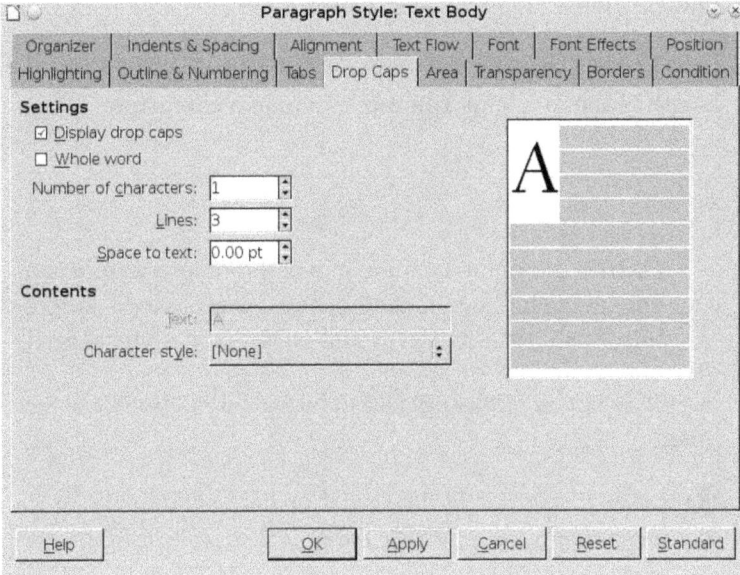

The DROP CAPS tab.

Creating drop caps:

To set up drop caps:

1 Choose the font for the drop caps. It can be the same font as for body text – perhaps in a different weight – a decorative font, or even a character from a dingbat set.

2 Use the DROP CAPS character style to define the font.

3   Create a DROP CAPS paragraph style. Most likely, it will be the child of TEXT BODY, differing only in having settings for DROP CAPS.

4   On the Drop Caps tab of the paragraph style, under Settings, select Display drop caps. This selection enables others on the tab, as well as the preview to the right.

5   Under CHARACTER STYLE, select DROP CAPS.

6   Select either NUMBER OF CHARACTERS or WHOLE WORD to set the length of the drop cap. You can use up to 9 characters.

Tip

Placing the entire first line in a different font weight is a very common layout choice. If you want to try it, ignore the DROP CAPS tab and create a FIRST LINE style instead.

7   Set the height of your drop cap in terms of the number of lines.

8   Set the SPACE TO TEXT. Unless the drop cap is extremely large, the magic number is probably too much, so try half of it first.

Caution

CONTENTS > TEXT is permanently grayed-out on the DROP CAPS tab. According to the online help, the field is supposed to give the text to use instead of a single letter.

However, the WHOLE WORD and NUMBER OF CHARACTER fields substitute adequately for it.

L orem ipsum dolor sit amet, consectetur adipiscing elit. In vitae sem non erat porta vestibulum. Pellentesque ut malesuada arcu. Praesent vel lectus blandit, molestie neque a, volutpat odio. Maecenas vitae lacus hendrerit, malesuada neque nec, molestie lorem. Phasellus elit quam, interdum vel massa nec, adipiscing gravida risus. Maecenas ornare tellus vitae

Lorem ipsum dolor sit amet, consectetur adipiscing elit. In vitae sem non erat porta vestibulum. Pellentesque ut malesuada arcu. Praesent vel lectus blandit, molestie neque a, volutpat odio. Maecenas vitae lacus hendrerit, malesuada neque nec, molestie lorem. Phasellus elit quam, interdum vel massa nec, adipiscing gravida risus. Maecenas ornare tellus vitae

L orem ipsum dolor sit amet, consectetur adipiscing elit. In vitae sem non erat porta vestibulum. Pellentesque ut malesuada arcu. Praesent vel lectus blandit, molestie neque a, volutpat odio. Maecenas vitae lacus hendrerit, malesuada neque nec, molestie lorem. Phasellus elit quam, interdum vel massa nec, adipiscing gravida risus. Maecenas ornare tellus vitae

L orem ipsum dolor sit amet, consectetur adipiscing elit. In vitae sem non erat porta vestibulum. Pellentesque ut malesuada arcu. Praesent vel lectus blandit, molestie neque a, volutpat odio. Maecenas vitae lacus hendrerit, malesuada neque nec, molestie lorem. Phasellus elit quam, interdum vel massa nec, adipiscing gravida risus. Maecenas ornare tellus vitae

L orem ipsum dolor sit amet, consectetur adipiscing elit. In vitae sem non erat porta vestibulum. Pellentesque ut malesuada arcu. Praesent vel lectus blandit, molestie neque a, volutpat odio. Maecenas vitae lacus hendrerit, malesuada neque nec, molestie lorem. Phasellus elit quam, interdum vel massa nec, adipiscing gravida risus. Maecenas ornare tellus vitae

Lorem ipsum dolor sit amet, consectetur adipiscing elit. In vitae sem non erat porta vestibulum. Pellentesque ut malesuada arcu. Praesent vel lectus blandit, molestie neque a, volutpat odio. Maecenas vitae lacus hendrerit, malesuada neque nec, molestie lorem. Phasellus elit quam, interdum vel massa nec, adipiscing gravida risus. Maecenas ornare tellus vitae

L *orem ipsum dolor sit amet, consectetur adipiscing elit. In vitae sem non erat porta* vestibulum. Pellentesque ut malesuada arcu. Praesent vel lectus blandit, molestie neque a, volutpat odio. Maecenas vitae lacus hendrerit, malesuada neque nec, molestie lorem. Phasellus elit quam, interdum vel massa nec, adipiscing gravida risus. Maecenas ornare tellus vitae

A selection of drop capitals. The last sample uses a character style to place the first line in italics.

Outlining and making lists

Lists have enough features that they are a separate type of style in Writer. However, as you might guess from the existence of the OUTLINE & NUMBERING tab, paragraph styles are essential to lists and outlining.

Specifically, on the OUTLINE & NUMBERING tab, you can:

- Associate list styles with paragraph styles so that they can be applied automatically. The same list style can be associated with multiple paragraph styles.

- Create an outline using a single paragraph style.

- Add a paragraph style to the default outline styles. Being included in the outline styles means that a paragraph using that style is listed in the Navigator, and used automatically in features like tables of contents.

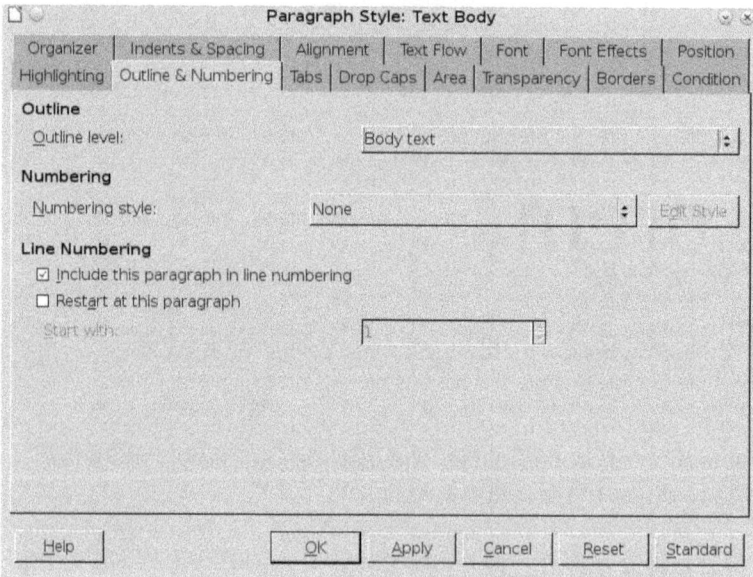

Associate a list style with a paragraph style in the NUMBERING section on a paragraph style's OUTLINE & NUMBERING tab.

Automating lists

An unordered list is another name for a bullet list, and an ordered list is another name for a numbered list.

Set up an ordered or unordered list in the dialog for list styles (see "Understanding the types of list," page 266). Then associate it with a paragraph style from the paragraph's OUTLINE & NUMBERING tab in the NUMBERING STYLE field.

Restarting paragraph numbering

You do not need to create a separate list style for each numbered list in a document.

To restart the numbering in any numbered list, select RESTART NUMBERING from a paragraph's right-click menu.

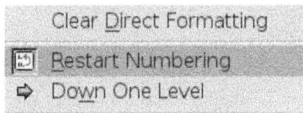

```
    Clear Direct Formatting
📑  Restart Numbering
⇨  Down One Level
```

Restart the numbering in a list from the right-click menu.

Caution

The RESTART AT THIS PARAGRAPH field on the OUTLINE & NUMBERING tab is for line numbering, not paragraph numbering.

Nesting lists

A nested list – a list within a list – is most common in an online text, where space is unimportant and structured text like lists and tables improve readability.

To nest a list, you have two choices. The first is to create a list style, and set up two or more list levels with different formatting choices on the POSITION and OPTIONS tabs. The advantage of list levels is that each level can be formatted separately, but all the levels remain connected. You can switch to the next level below by pressing the TAB key, or to the one above by pressing SHIFT+TAB.

The preview pane can help you set up each list level, and the customized list style is associated with a paragraph style for use.

To switch to a lower list level while using the associated paragraph style, press the TAB key before entering content; to switch to a higher list level, press SHIFT+TAB.

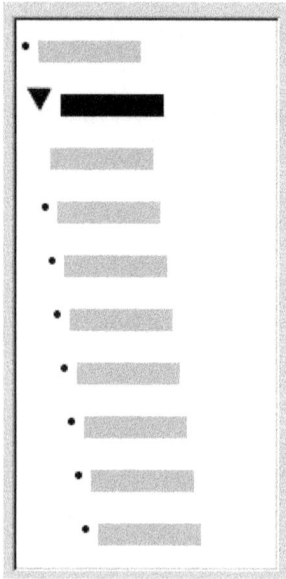

The PREVIEW pane for a bulleted list style with two list levels. The other list levels have not been customized, so they default to the same bullet as the top level.

The second choice is to create two separate list styles, then associate each list style with a separate paragraph style.

Neither choice has any advantage over the other, since you are still dealing with the same options. However, in both cases, each nested list is typically indented more than the list level above it. Typically, too, each list level will use a different bullet style or numbering system.

Style names like BULLETED and BULLETED 2 or NESTED will help to remind you of the relation between the two paragraph styles. For convenience, use the same names for both the PARAGRAPH and LIST styles, since they cannot be mixed up.

1ˢᵗ list style   1. Lorem ipsum dolor sit amet, consectetur adipiscing elit.

                   2. Sed et urna ac lorem malesuada venenatis ut et lorem.

2ⁿᵈ list style   • Phasellus imperdiet lorem turpis, at egestas neque egestas nec.

                   • Vestibulum a nibh ante.

                   • Sed accumsan orci at turpis tempor, sit amet pulvinar ipsum vehicula.

1ˢᵗ list style   3. Tincidunt ac magna.

Nested lists created using two separate list styles.

Outlining with paragraph styles

LibreOffice has several ways to outline using paragraph styles. With TOOLS > OUTLINE NUMBERING, you can choose a numbering style for each paragraph style, making it part of the Outline Levels (see "Outlining and making lists," page 143). Alternatively, you can ignore TOOLS > OUTLINE NUMBERING, and associate each Heading style with a separate list style using the STYLES AND FORMATTING window.

An even easier form of outlining is to create a single list style for outlining. If you want to, you can manually set up the different levels on the list style's OPTIONS tab. However, you can get much the same result by selecting a pre-defined pattern from the list style's OUTLINE tab instead.

To use the paragraph style, press ENTER + TAB to add a sub-level paragraph. The sub-level paragraph automatically uses the numbering pattern of the list style. To raise the level of a paragraph style, press ENTER + TAB + SHIFT.

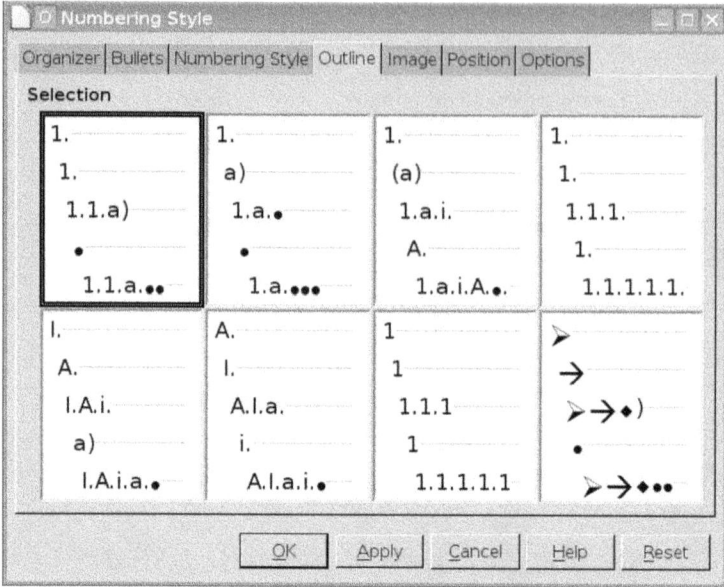

Numbering Style				_ □ ×

Organizer | Bullets | Numbering Style | **Outline** | Image | Position | Options

Selection

1.	1.	1.	1.
1.	a)	(a)	1.
1.1.a)	1.a.•	1.a.i.	1.1.1.
•	•	A.	1.
1.1.a.••	1.a.•••	1.a.i.A.•.	1.1.1.1.1.
I.	A.	1	➤
A.	I.	1	→
I.A.i.	A.I.a.	1.1.1	➤→•)
a)	i.	1	•
I.A.i.a.•	A.I.a.i.•	1.1.1.1.1	➤→•••

OK | Apply | Cancel | Help | Reset

The pre-defined formatting for outlines in the list styles window. An outline is typically a way of planning a document that readers never see, so often whether the pre-defined format is exactly what you prefer won't matter.

Creating outlines with a single paragraph style

To set up a single paragraph style for outlining:

1 Create a list style and associate it with one of the pre-defined formats on the OUTLINE tab.

2 Select or make a paragraph style for outlining. You cannot use the HEADING 1-10 styles. Presumably, this restriction prevents confusion between a single paragraph style outline and the registered outline levels.

3 On the ORGANIZER tab of the paragraph style, set the style to use itself as the NEXT STYLE.

4 Assign the list style to the paragraph style using the NUMBERING field on the paragraph style's OUTLINE & NUMBERING tab.

Adding paragraph styles to outline levels

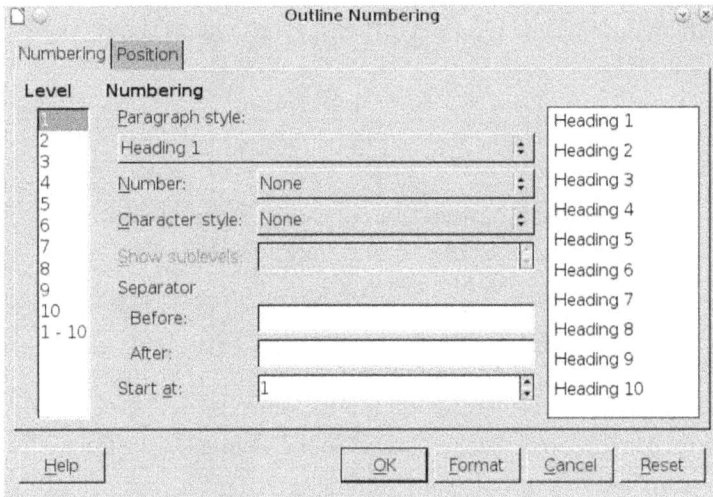

OUTLINE LEVELS default to Heading paragraph styles. You can add other paragraph styles using the OUTLINE LEVEL field on their OUTLINE & NUMBERING tabs.

Tip

In the drop-down list for the OUTLINE LEVEL field on the OUTLINE & NUMBERING tab, all paragraph styles not assigned to an outline level are identified as BODY TEXT. This designation has nothing to do with the TEXT BODY paragraph style.

Outline levels are a concept used throughout LibreOffice to automate advanced features. For example, outline levels determine which paragraph styles are displayed by default in the Navigator under HEADINGS, and in a table of contents .

By default, outline levels are mapped to the HEADING 1-10 paragraph styles. OUTLINE LEVEL 1 is mapped to HEADING 1, and so on.

You can change these mappings, or add another paragraph style to an outline level in the OUTLINE LEVEL field on the OUTLINE & NUMBERING tab.

Tip

You can assign more than one paragraph style to an outline level, but only one paragraph style displays in TOOLS > OUTLINE NUMBERING.

Skipping a paragraph in a list

In many lists, each paragraph is a list item and is therefore numbered. However, you sometimes need to break up a list with an unnumbered or unbulleted paragraph that gives more detail about a list item. Without such a paragraph, a list item may turn into a long paragraph, reducing the readability that is the whole point of using a list.

To create a style for such paragraphs, you can use the paragraph style with a list to create a linked paragraph that is mostly formatted identically. The exceptions are on the OUTLINE & NUMBERING tab, on which:

- OUTLINE LEVEL is set to BODY TEXT.

- NUMBERING STYLE is set to NONE.

- THIS PARAGRAPH IN LINE NUMBERING is unchecked.

If you have only a few horizontal indents, this style may be usable with multiple lists.

BODY TEXT INDENT is a pre-defined paragraph style that you can use for this purpose.

Tip

If you want to number paragraphs as lines in a poem, use TOOLS > LINE NUMBERING.

This tool is more comprehensive than the formatting available from within paragraph style formatting, with a selection of character styles and the exact positioning of numbers in relation to text.

Using multiple languages

LibreOffice supports over 110 languages, and many more locales. Locales are variants of a language that have unique vocabularies and spellings.

For example, in the United Kingdom English locale, the correct spelling is "neighbours," while in United States English, it is "neighbors." A complete locale consists of separate dictionaries for spell-checking, hyphenation, and thesauruses.

Many users use only the default language determined by the version of LibreOffice that they downloaded. However, you have two options for adding support for more languages and locales.

The most common way to add support for additional languages is to select them from the drop-down list at TOOLS > OPTIONS > LANGUAGE SETTINGS > WRITING AIDS > USER-DEFINED DICTIONARIES > NEW.

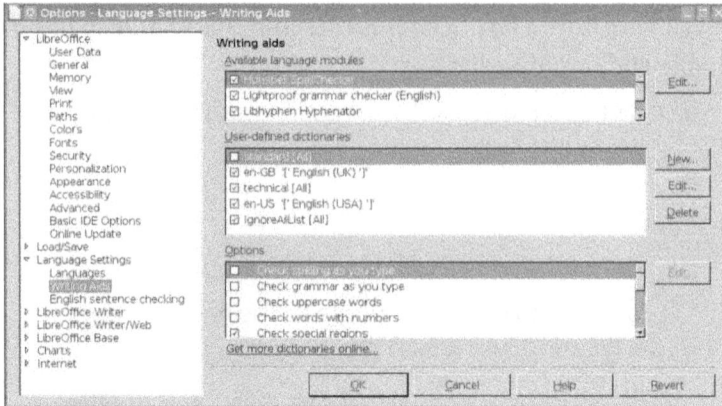

Use the general language settings to load as many languages and locales as you want.

In addition, the extension site also has packages for several languages, including Ancient Greek, Finnish, and Basque.

You can update extensions with TOOLS > EXTENSION MANAGER > NEW, which is an advantage when the dictionaries are still being developed and changing rapidly.

Setting up other language features

Adding dictionary locales may be only the first step in using another language. You may need to:

- Select a system keyboard layout for the language. An international English keyboard is adequate for most Western European languages. Without a suitable keyboard layout, you have to rely on INSERT > SPECIAL CHARACTER for accents and umlauts.

- Install a font for a language. A Greek style is of limited use if your installation of LibreOffice has no Greek font installed.

- Adjust the settings for East Asian or Bi-Directional Languages at TOOLS > OPTIONS > LANGUAGE SETTINGS > LANGUAGES > ENHANCED LANGUAGE SUPPORT.

- Create multiple styles with similar names in a multi-language document. For example, you might have paragraph styles called TEXT BODY – ENGLISH and TEXT BODY – FRENCH.

- Disable TOOLS > AUTOCORRECT OPTIONS in a multi-language document. If you don't use Autocorrect, uncheck the ENABLE WORD COMPLETION and COLLECT WORDS boxes at TOOLS > AUTOCORRECT OPTIONS > WORD COMPLETION.

- Set URLs or snippets of code to NONE In the LANGUAGE FIELD to spare yourself extra queries while spell checking.

Creating a block quote style

All forms of academic quotation have a special format for long quotations – that is, quotations that fill more than three lines or are longer than about 100 words.

Quotations that meet this criteria are presented in a block so that they are easier to read. The assumption is that a long quote would not be used unless it was important. Readers may wonder if the emphasis is misplaced if a block quotation is not especially relevant.

Typically, the paragraph style for a block quote is the child of the body text style. The standard format for a block quotation is:

- Do not use quotation marks, unless someone is quoted directly or speaking.

- Use the same font and font size as for the body text. Making the font size smaller only makes the block harder to read.

- Use an equal indentation on the left and right sides of the paragraph, based on the line spacing. Usually, 40–50 points on each side will be about right, the exact width depending on the font size.

> Lorem ipsum dolor sit amet, consectetur adipiscing elit. Praesent consequat tincidunt eros, nec dictum nulla ultrices in. Suspendisse id pharetra massa. Donec egestas massa nulla, eleifend hendrerit odio consectetur facilisis:
>
> > Fusce eget mattis augue. Sed sit amet semper lacus, eu malesuada lectus. Cras sodales faucibus ipsum, quis lobortis tellus.
> >
> > In ac commodo mi. Ut ac semper lectus. Vestibulum ante ipsum primis in faucibus orci luctus et ultrices posuere cubilia Curae; Vestibulum ante ipsum primis in faucibus orci luctus et ultrices posuere cubilia Curae.
>
> Sed nec neque vitae dolor auctor hendrerit. Aenean tempus in risus vitae gravida. Ut pretium porttitor nulla, auctor commodo quam ultrices eu.

The standard layout for a block quotation. The extra indentation is used instead of quotation marks.

- Indicate new paragraphs by either a first line indent or else an extra space between paragraphs. The indicator is not necessarily the same as the one used in the rest of the body text.

Writer includes a QUOTATIONS paragraph style by default, although you might prefer a custom style with a name like BLOCK QUOTATION for greater clarity.

Preparing styles for HTML

HTML has never been well integrated into LibreOffice Writer.

On the one hand, Writer includes VIEW > WEB LAYOUT so you can have an approximation of how an HTML page looks, but the view is not always reliable. It also includes VIEW > HTML SOURCE so you can see the code with which you are working.

On the other hand, you cannot save files as HTML in the template manager.

To add to the confusion, HTML is treated in a very individualist way. While LibreOffice uses FILE > DOCUMENT PROPERTIES to create a thorough collection of meta-tags, it also converts all graphics to .jpegs, with no provision for doing otherwise.

An even greater limitation is that only a limited number of character and paragraph styles are converted directly into HTML tags. Other styles, as well as fields, are converted to .css classes.

These peculiarities mean that HTML files exported from LibreOffice preserve as much of the formatting as possible.

Unfortunately, they also mean that LibreOffice does not produce clean HTML – that is, files with only HTML tags that are easy to use in other applications.

```
<!DOCTYPE HTML PUBLIC "-//W3C//DTD HTML 4.0 Transitional//EN">
<html>
<head>
  <meta http-equiv="content-type" content="text/html; charset=utf-8"/>
  <title>designing-with-..ibreoffice</title>
  <meta name="generator" content="LibreOffice 4.4.0.3 (Linux)"/>
  <meta name="author" content="Bruce Byfield"/>
  <meta name="created" content="2015-03-10T16:43:53.833362432"/>
  <meta name="changedby" content="Bruce Byfield"/>
  <meta name="changed" content="2015-03-12T14:27:31.680201186"/>
  <style type="text/css">
    @page:left { size: 432pt 648pt; margin-left: 88pt; margin-right: 64pt; margin-top:
72pt; margin-bottom: 88pt }
    @page:right { size: 432pt 648pt; margin-left: 88pt; margin-right: 64pt; margin-top:
72pt; margin-bottom: 88pt }
    @page:first { }
    p { text-indent: 24pt; margin-bottom: 0pt; line-height: 16pt; orphans: 2; widows: 2;
page-break-before: auto }
```

Looking at the source code for HTML generated by LibreOffice shows how cluttered it can be.

Unless you are prepared to write your own style sheet, or clean up HTML files exported from LibreOffice either manually or through a program like HTML Tidy, LibreOffice's exported HTML requires great effort while offering results that are usually mediocre at best.

You could, of course, create a series of macros for HTML tags, then save files as plain text, renaming them in a file manager. However, at that point, using a dedicated HTML editor is less trouble.

The only times that using LibreOffice's HTML output is advisable are when the output is only going to be used by itself and has a short life.

Problems with cluttered HTML are often compounded when the output files are used, or when someone uses a file without knowing its limitations.

Paragraph style	HTML tags	Comments
Heading 1-6	\<h1\> - \<h6\>	Notice that only 6 headings are available, while Writer has 10.
List Contents	\<p\>	Converts to the default paragraph tag. Use with list styles.
List Headings	\<dl\>, \<dd\>	Creates a definition list \<dl\> or adds the heading \<dd\>.
Preformatted text	\<pre\>	Appears in the web browser in a monospaced font (such as Courier).
Quotations	\<blockquote\>	Indents the text on both margins.
Sender	\<address\>	
Table Contents	\<p\>	Converts to the default paragraph tag.

Table Heading	<p>	Converts to the default paragraph tag.
Text body	<p>	The default HTML tag for contents.

How Paragraph styles are mapped to HTML tags.

Character style	HTML tags	Comments
Definition	<dfn>	Displays default font.
Emphasis	<em>	Displays as an italic font.
Endnote characters	References style sheet.	Defaults to default font.
Example	<samp>	Defaults to monospaced font.
Footnote characters	References style sheet.	Uses default font.

How Character styles are mapped to HTML tags.

Minimizing HTML problems

LibreOffice HTML code is generally best avoided. However, if you do decide to use it, follow these steps to minimize problems:

1 Select FILE > NEW > HTML DOCUMENT.

2 Press F11 to open the STYLES AND FORMATTING window. Notice that the ALL and HTML views are identical.

3 Select VIEW > WEB LAYOUT. This selection displays the file as a web page instead of a printed page.

4 Customize only by making changes to the pre-defined paragraph and character styles listed in the table above.

5 Save the document by selecting FILE > SAVE AS and selecting HTML DOCUMENT TEMPLATE (.OTT) as the format or file type. Notice that you cannot save an HTML document using TEMPLATES > SAVE AS TEMPLATE. If you try, you receive no error message, but nothing is saved. Instead, save the file as an HTML DOCUMENT TEMPLATE in a directory specifically set aside for that purpose.

6 If you want clean HTML output, do one (or both) of the following: Manually remove unnecessary tags or run the file through a tool such as HTML Tidy. In Linux, many major distributions have HTML Tidy in their repositories.

7 Open the file in at least one major browser such as Chrome, Firefox, or Internet Explorer to see whether any display problems exist.

To use the template, navigate to the directory in which the template was saved.

Moving beyond practical text

If you are reading this book from beginning to end, at this point all the features of character and paragraph styles that you might want to use regularly have been covered.

However, before the topic of text styles is wrapped up, Chapter 6 discusses some advanced features – ones that are not strictly necessary to your design, but ones that can automate your design and make template design more efficient.

7

Positioning and automating text

This chapter concludes the ongoing discussion about character and paragraph styles by talking about their advanced features. It explains the relationship between paragraph and list styles, how to position characters more precisely, and several specific ways to automate your work flows using text styles.

The automating features are easy to overlook, but they can be as important as features that affect the look of a document.

For example, a conditional style allows you to format the same style differently depending on its context, or set a paragraph style so that it always starts a new page. Although casual users may never be aware of such features, those who write as part of their work will soon become well aware of the time these feature save.

You will rarely use these features all the time, nor all of them at once. However, knowing what is available can help you to design your documents more intelligently and to work more efficiently when you write.

For example, the font effect HIDE sounds minor. Yet in one unimportant-looking toggle switch, HIDE provides an elegant solution for one of the most difficult tasks for professional documenters – maintaining multiple versions of the same document in a single file.

Fine-tuning characters

Like most word processors or layout software, LibreOffice does much of the housekeeping for design.

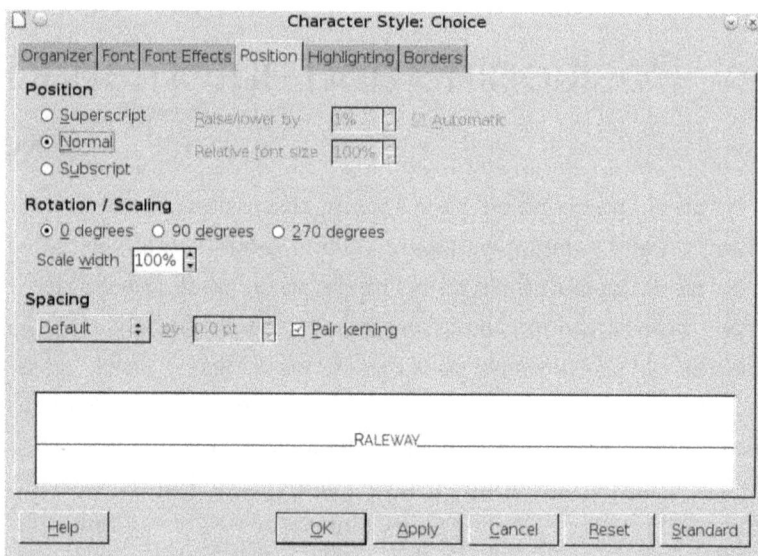

Unique to character styles, the POSITION tab is the main spot for adjusting individual characters.

For example, without consulting users, Writer examines font files to display characters properly. It also detects whether a font family includes italics or bold weights, and decides the size and placement of footnote numbers.

Most users are happy to let LibreOffice make these decisions. However, the software's decisions are not always ideal, so at times you might want to tweak the spacing between characters or reposition footnote numbers.

LibreOffice includes the tools you need for such tweaking. Many are on the POSITION tab for character styles, although others are scattered throughout the character and paragraph style dialogs.

Positioning superscript and subscript

The POSITION tab of a character style gives you several advanced options for adjusting superscript characters (above others on the same line) and subscript characters (below others on the same line). Another alternative for superscript characters is to adjust the vertical alignment of text on the same line (see "Aligning different-sized text on one line," page 165).

These adjustments are relatively common, because, depending on the font, LibreOffice's default superscript and subscript characters can sometimes be too too small for easy reading.

To understand superscript and subscript characters, you have to remember that all letters sit on an imaginary baseline. Many characters have what is called an x-height – the height of a letter x, but also of an m or r, as well as the bowl of a lower case b or p.

Still others like y have descenders, or lines that are lower than the baseline, while letters like k have ascenders, or lines that rise above the x-height. However, all characters are positioned relative to the baseline. The exact positions are part of the font's design and are stored in its files. There is no reason, though, why you should not modify the intended design if you care to make the effort.

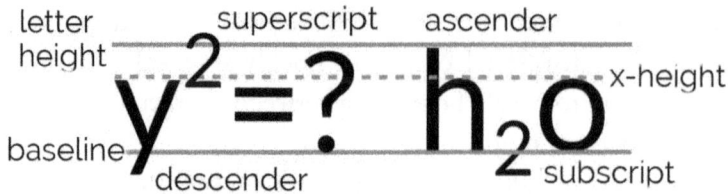

letter height — superscript — ascender — x-height

baseline — descender — subscript

$$y^2 = ?\ h_2o$$

Superscript and subscript characters. The superscript "2" on the left is higher than the ascenders or the question mark, and throws off the look of the line.

By contrast, the subscript "2" on the right is as low as the bottom of the descender on the "y," which gives a more consistent look to the line (Font: Lato).

Superscript characters, such as mathematical components or footnote numbers, are usually positioned somewhere between the x-height and the height of the ascenders.

Similarly, subscript characters, such as those in chemical equations, usually sit between the baseline and the low point of descenders.

The size of superscript and subscript characters is a trade off between being large and easily readable and being uncluttered but harder to read. To many users, LibreOffice's defaults are too small.

When adjusting both position and size, be prepared for several trials and errors before getting the best results, with the adjustments getting smaller as you move closer to the ideal.

To direct your experiments, consider these points:

* The exact size will vary with the font's white space, but 40–60% of the body text should be the usual range.

* If a font's characters use a lot of white space, so that they look small compared to fonts of the same size, increase its size.

- Unless the x-height is exceptionally large, using it for the bottom of superscript characters often makes for a consistent design. However, using this guide with a large x-height is likely to make the superscript characters too small.

- Avoid old style characters for superscript and subscript. Their lack of a common baseline means either an eye-disturbing clutter or a time-consuming positioning of each numeral separately.

- Aligning superscript characters with the top of ascenders and subscript characters with the bottom of descenders has the advantage of being symmetrical while giving you a visible target.

STOP

Caution

The fields for lowering or raising superscript or subscript characters read all input as percentages, rounded to the nearest number. You cannot use points in them.

STOP

Caution

The POSITION tab for characters and paragraph styles is specifically for blocks of text. To create formulas, open FILE > NEW > FORMULA or use the Math application.

Aligning different-sized text on one line

The TEXT-TO-TEXT option on the ALIGNMENT tab vertically aligns text of different sizes on the same line. It can be used with a brochure or poster than an essay, but its main use is probably to create superscript or subscript characters without the fuss of using the POSITION tab (see "Positioning superscript and subscript," page 163).

The setting can align font sizes by the TOP, MIDDLE, or BOTTOM of the letters, or the default BASE LINE. In each case, the largest characters remain on the baseline, while other characters are raised or lowered in relation to them. For example, if you select BOTTOM, then the smaller characters are positioned at the bottom of the largest characters' descenders (the lines below the base line). Similarly, with TOP selected, the smaller characters are positioned at the top of the largest characters' ascenders (the lines above the x-height).

However, mostly you can leave the setting on AUTOMATIC, which defaults so that all different font sizes are aligned by the base line. In other words, you can usually safely ignore the setting.

lorem ipsum **lorem ipsum** lorem ipsum

lorem ipsum **lorem ipsum** lorem ipsum

lorem ipsum **lorem ipsum** lorem ipsum

lorem ipsum **lorem ipsum** lorem ipsum

From top to bottom: The TEXT-TO-TEXT field on the ALIGNMENT tab set to AUTOMATIC (BASE LINE), BOTTOM, MIDDLE, AND TOP.

Rotating text

The POSITION tab for character style includes settings for rotating text 90 (right angle to the baseline and above) and 270 degrees (right angle to the baseline and below). These settings are mostly useful in a table heading, but both interfere with readability and should not be used if any alternative exists.

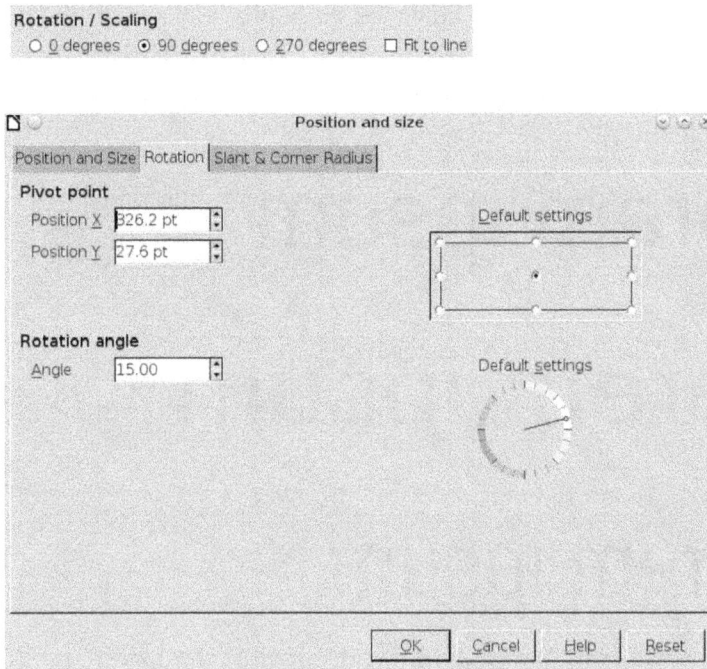

Above: Controls for rotating a character style on the POSITION tab. Below: Controls for rotating graphic text on a sample's right-click menu. Graphic text is text created with the DRAWING toolbar, and is treated as a drawing object rather than as text.

The rotation tools may be useful in brochure and ad designs, but they are very basic. You will have more precision than these settings offer if you use graphical text – text treated as a drawing object – and then right-click and select POSITION AND SIZE > ROTATION instead.

Adjusting font width

The width of characters is interpreted by LibreOffice's reading of each font's file. However, you can adjust it using the SCALE WIDTH field on the POSITION tab. This feature is especially useful when you have no condensed or expanded version in a font family.

lorem ipsum

lorem ipsum

lorem ipsum

From top to bottom: 100%, 115%, and 85% character width. Greater increases or decreases tend to look clumsy with most fonts, especially at smaller sizes. Font: Maven Pro.

In pre-digital typesetting, changing the width of a font would also include changing the design of many of the individual characters to keep the proportions in the shape of the letter. These adjustments do not happen with most digital fonts, and rarely to the same degree. Consequently, you can do little to change the width of some fonts without producing a disordered mess.

However, most fonts can stand 1–15% adjustments less or more than the default 100% without deteriorating too badly.

These adjustments can help improve the page color of the body text.

Adjusting character combinations (kerning)

Kerning is the spacing between characters. Professional printers sometimes adjust kerning to improve the appearance of awkward combinations of letters. Combinations such as "Va," "ll," and "ff" can be improved in most fonts, and individual fonts may benefit from the adjustment of other combinations as well.

VaVa ffff IIII

Changing the spacing between characters using the SPACING field on the POSITION tab.

Left: Reducing the space between characters improves the spacing.

Middle: Creating your own ligature by moving characters together.

Right: Sometimes, kerning means increasing the space between characters for easier reading. Font: Maven Pro.

Kerning has always been a concern in typography, but digital typography makes it more important than ever. Unlike in manual type, digital fonts usually do not have different spacing when the font size changes. Instead, the spacing is intended for a standard size.

Consequently, if you greatly decrease or increase font size, the kerning may be off. What is intended for 12 points may not work for 8 or 48 points.

Moreover, LibreOffice's general kerning tends to be very loose, and you can often improve on it if you are willing to make the effort and make small changes.

If you choose to handle your own kerning, create character styles with adjusted spacing. You may manage with only a single kerning character style for all your needs, but if you are really attentive to detail, you might decide on individual kerning character styles for different letter combinations – it all depends on your patience, the font you use, and your perfectionism.

However, you may want to change the spacing, either to improve legibility or for a short string of characters in a more graphical document, such as a brochure, by adjusting the SPACING field on the POSITION tab.

If you are manually adjusting justified lines, you might also want to make micro changes here and there.

No matter what your interest, you will want to select the PAIR kerning box beside the field.

Tip

Whether you worry about kerning depends on how much of a perfectionist not only you, but the font's designer, happens to be.

Often, you can reduce the amount of kerning by carefully choosing a font after looking at letter combinations that often need kerning. Gentium, for instance, is tightly kerned and even uses ligatures automatically.

By contrast, early versions of Cantarell had a reputation – since outgrown – for being poorly kerned, which made manual kerning much more difficult.

Manufacturing small capitals

Small capitals are designed to improve the look of two or more capital letters in a row. Although they have to be applied in individual cases, small caps are especially useful in improving the readability of text full of abbreviations.

SMALL CAPS

MANUFACTURED

REGULAR CAPS

From top to bottom: genuine small caps, manufactured small caps, and regular caps. If you compare the "A" in the genuine small caps with the other samples, you can see that small caps are not just a matter of size – the proportions of letters are also changed. Font: Linux Libertine G.

When a font does not include its own set of small caps, LibreOffice creates an imitation of them, usually making them smaller than ordinary capitals. However, these imitations are rarely more than adequate, because true small capitals are distinguished not just by size, but by an entire redesign of characters.

Still, not every font comes with small capitals, leaving you sometimes with no choice except to try making your own.

Making your own small caps

If a font lacks small capitals, LibreOffice manufactures some. However, you might want to see if you can improve on what

LibreOffice offers. If so, follow these steps to manufacture small caps for yourself:

1   Use the regular capitals for your experiments. Starting from manufactured capitals mean that you are inheriting all sorts of assumptions that are hard to pin down.

2   Start with a character style that is several points smaller than the paragraph font with which it will be used. Experiment until you find a suitable size.

3   Use the SCALE WIDTH field on the POSITION tab to make the characters slightly wider than those of the paragraph style it will accompany. Do not increase the width by more than a few percent, or it may look grotesque.

4   Increasing the width may have upset the spacing between characters, so experiment with the SPACING field on the POSITION tab. Because the small cap character style has a smaller font size, you probably will want to increase the spacing anyway to increase legibility.

When you have finished your tweaks, compare your effort to LibreOffice's manufactured small caps, and choose the best one to use.

Making line spacing consistent

Even advanced users puzzle over the REGISTER-TRUE setting on the INDENTS & SPACING tab. It's a large mystery for a simple setting. The REGISTER-TRUE feature makes lines consistent across the pages – or as near as possible if different-sized fonts are used.

When REGISTER-TRUE is selected, the lines of text in columns, mirrored pages, or on both sides of a page are spaced identically.

The setting improves the looks of both single and multi-column documents, and prevents shadows of the other side being from interfering with reading.

Usually, the spacing is that of the TEXT BODY font.

Tip

Setting REGISTER-TRUE for more than one paragraph style can negates the setting. Use the setting only for the paragraph style used most often – usually, TEXT BODY – and related styles – for example, TEXT BODY INDENT – that use the same line spacing.

Instead of using REGISTER-TRUE for Headings, make the font size, the space above, and the space below equal a multiple of the line spacing. That way, the Headings will rarely be out of sync for any length of time.

You can improve the effectiveness of the setting for pages printed on both sides by choosing a heavier weight of paper – which you probably want anyway if a document is important enough that you are concerned about line spacing.

There is no reason not to select this setting, but setting LINE SPACING to FIXED on the INDENTS & SPACING tab will produce much the same effect.

Tip

Page styles also have a REGISTER-TRUE setting, which allows you to set the line spacing by page, selecting the paragraph style to use. Choose the paragraph or the page REGISTER-TRUE setting, rather than using both.

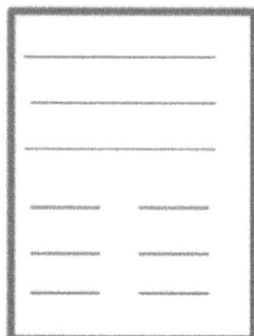

The REGISTER-TRUE feature on the INDENTS & SPACING tab makes lines consistent across the pages – or as near as possible if different-sized fonts are used.

Automating with styles

People think of typography mostly in terms of format – that is, the choices of fonts and spacing. However, digital typography is also about making a document easier to construct and maintain.

These concerns do not matter if you are writing a document that will be sent, read, and discarded in a matter of minutes. In fact, any attempt to implement them in a short-lived document is a waste of effort.

However, many other documents have longer life spans. For example, a technical manual may be revised a dozen times or more in its life cycle. In such circumstances, any formatting that gives you one less thing to think about is welcome.

This section introduces two features of paragraph styles that make documents easier to construct: using conditional styles, and setting page breaks by style.

In exchange for some extra setup, both features keep your hands on the keyboard as you work, allowing you to focus on content instead of distracting you with formatting issues.

Configuring conditional styles

A conditional style is an alternative way of using paragraph styles. Normally, you define a style, then set the NEXT STYLE field on the ORGANIZER tab.

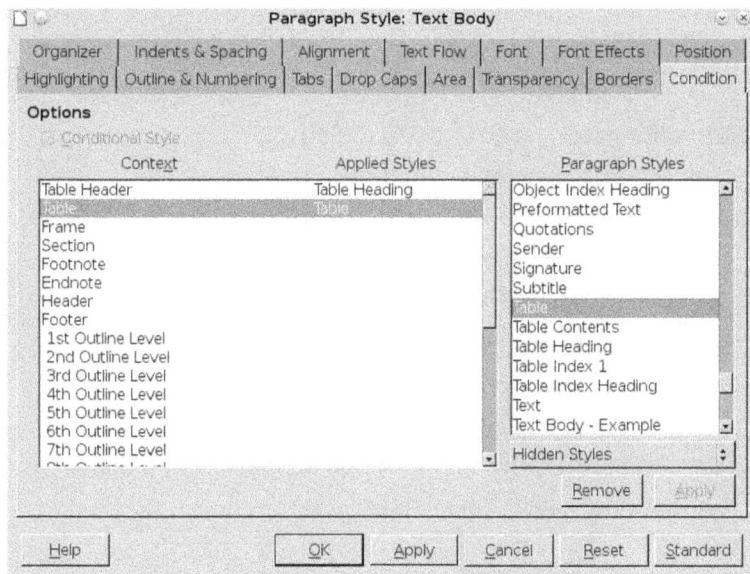

The CONDITION tab sets up one paragraph style to use the formatting of other styles in different contexts.

However, with a conditional style, you define the paragraph's format in each context, such as in a table or a footer. When the cursor moves to a new context, the style's format changes automatically.

STOP

Caution

Don't confuse a conditional paragraph style with a CONDITIONAL TEXT field available from INSERT > FIELDS. All that the two have in common is that each changes when their context changes.

Conditional styles are different enough from the normal use of styles that they puzzle many users, who scrupulously avoid them. However, they are easier to use than you might imagine. Each contextual format is defined by another paragraph style, then connected to the conditional style on the CONDITION tab.

Conditional styles do have limitations:

- You cannot make any pre-defined paragraph styles conditional except TEXT BODY. In fact, pre-defined paragraph styles display no CONDITION tab, although new (custom) paragraph styles created from them do.

- If you want a custom style to be conditional, you must set up at least one condition before you click the OK or ACCEPT button when you close the style dialog window for the first time. Otherwise, the next time you open the style's dialog window, the CONDITION tab is no longer available.

- A conditional style is limited to thirty pre-defined contexts. You might be able to think of at least two dozen more contexts that might be useful, but you cannot create custom contexts.

Still, even with these limitations, conditional styles can be useful, especially if the document structure is not too complex.

Defining conditional styles

Conditional styles are an answer to those who claim that styles are too difficult to remember. With conditional styles, you only need to remember the name of a single paragraph style per document or template, yet format quickly in different ways.

Admittedly, the available contexts are limited, but they may still be enough for many purposes. You might think of conditional styles as equivalent to single-style outlining – an advanced trick that can be useful and free you from thinking about formatting.

To create a conditional style:

1 Examine a CONDITION tab and make a note of the contexts you want to use. You cannot create new contexts.

2 Create or format a paragraph style for each context you plan to use. The only pre-defined style that you can use as a conditional style is TEXT BODY, but you can create a new style from any pre-defined one.

3 Create a new paragraph style and go to the CONDITION tab. Under OPTIONS, select the CONDITIONAL STYLE box.

Tip

To minimize confusion, name the style CONDITIONAL TEXT or something like SINGLE STYLE so you can identify it.

Otherwise, as you work, you might wonder why the formatting has changed but the style listed on the tool bar hasn't.

4 Highlight a context on the CONDITION tab.

5 In the PARAGRAPH STYLES pane on the CONDITION tab, select the paragraph style that you want to apply in the highlighted context. Click twice, and the selected style is listed under APPLIED STYLES on the right side of the CONTEXT pane.

6 Repeat Step 4–5 as often as needed.

STOP Caution

If you want to use conditions with a custom style, you must set at least one before you close the dialog window. If you do not set at least one condition, the tab will be unavailable the next time you open the style's dialog window.

So long as you have set at least one condition, you can add and delete conditions later.

7   Click the OK or APPLY button when all the contexts you plan to use are associated with a paragraph style.

Setting page breaks by style

The application of a particular paragraph style often coincides with the start of a new page.

For example, new chapters may always start with a paragraph style called CHAPTER NUMBER or TITLE, while a style called DIAGRAM TITLE might begin a new page to ensure plenty of space for a diagram.

This feature is set up in the BREAK section of the TEXT FLOW tab for a paragraph style.

Automating page breaks

To set up automatic page breaks:

1   Open the dialog window for the paragraph style that will coincide with the start of a new page.

2   Select TEXT FLOW tab > BREAKS > INSERT.

3   Set the TYPE to PAGE.

4   If the POSITION is BEFORE, you can select the WITH PAGE STYLE
    box, and choose the new page's style from the drop-down list.

5   When you select a page style to follow the break, you can also
    re-set the PAGE NUMBER. For example, you might have a page
    style for an introduction numbered in lower case Roman
    numerals, and ordinary pages that use Arabic numerals.

6   If you want the page number to continue sequentially from
    the previous page, leave the PAGE NUMBER field set to o.

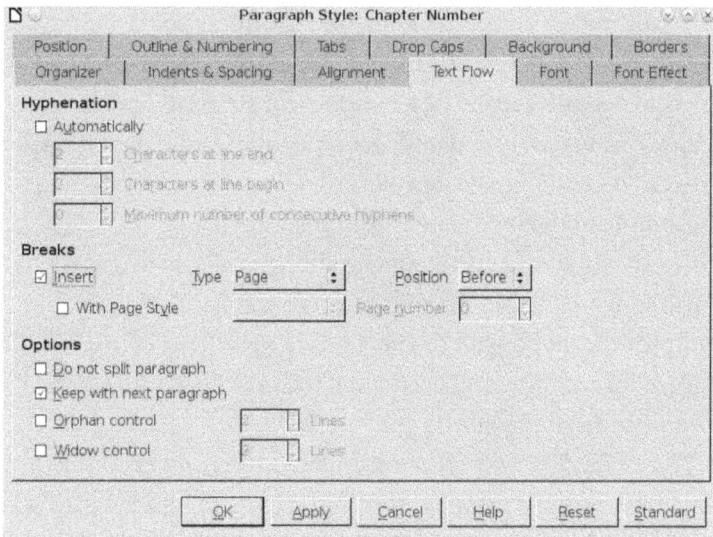

Automate page breaks in the BREAKS section of the TEXT
FLOW tab by associating them with a paragraph style. This
setting is used mostly to start new chapters in a long
document or a master document.

Other common uses include starting a page reserved for an
image that occupies an entire page, or inserting a landscape
page in an otherwise portrait-oriented document.

STOP Caution

The TYPE of break also includes the option of COLUMN. This selection may be useful in a multi-column section or a newsletter. However, it can be awkward and confusing. In many cases, you are likely to have less trouble with items shifting if you create a table instead.

Single-sourcing by hiding text

Multiple versions of documents that differ only in some details are common in business or academia. For instance, you might want one version of a handout for students, and another version for teachers that adds teaching goals and suggestions for use. Or, you might have one version of a software manual for users and another for system administrators.

The only trouble is that maintaining multiple versions of a document is difficult. Placing each version in its own file complicates keeping all the versions in sync. Forget just once to update all versions, and correcting the mistake can cost you several painstaking hours.

Yet in most word processors, maintaining all versions in a single file complicates printing, forcing you to create a duplicate copy first, and then to delete all the parts not needed for the version you are printing and hope that you don't make a mistake.

LibreOffice's solution to this dilemma is to create a single file in which selected words, paragraphs, or sections are hidden or revealed as needed. The tools include styles and fields. All the tools for hidden elements work with two versions of the text, but sections and some fields do not work with three or more versions.

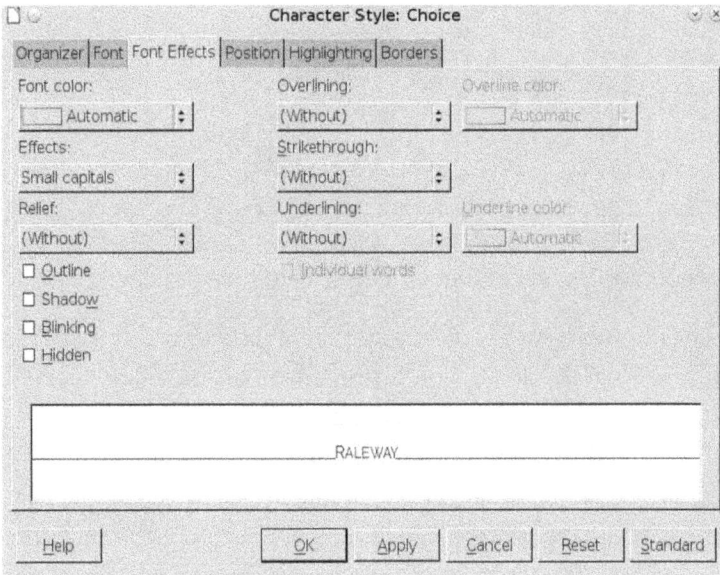

Character Style: Choice

Organizer | Font | Font Effects | Position | Highlighting | Borders

Font color:	Overlining:	Overline color:
Automatic	(Without)	Automatic
Effects:	Strikethrough:	
Small capitals	(Without)	
Relief:	Underlining:	Underline color:
(Without)	(Without)	Automatic
☐ Outline	☐ Individual words	
☐ Shadow		
☐ Blinking		
☐ Hidden		

RALEWAY

| Help | OK | Apply | Cancel | Reset | Standard |

Maintaining two copies of the same document in a single file is as easy as toggling on or off the HIDDEN box at the bottom left of the FONT EFFECTS tab.

Using hidden text is faster than manual formatting and reduces the chances of making mistakes. It also eliminates the need to print from copies, which with careless hands or tired brains can lead to the accidental over-writing of the original file.

Choosing a tactic for hiding/showing text

Features for hiding and showing text can be used in two ways.

If two versions of the document share common text, enter one using ordinary paragraph styles and create unique paragraph styles for the other that can be hidden and shown as needed. This method works with both styles and with sections and fields, but can be hard to organize.

User Always On	Admin On/Off	Coders On/Off

One way to structure single-sourcing is to have one set of styles, sections, or fields that are always visible and another set for each additional version that can be turned on and off.

The alternative is to create a special set of paragraph styles for each version of the document, turning them on and off as needed.

In this structure, each version could be distinct, and single-sourcing mainly a method of keeping related material together. Alternatively, each version could be mixed and matched. For example, if you were preparing user, developer, and admin guides for a piece of software, the published guide for administrators might require showing both the user and admin material, while the guide for developers might include both the admin and developer material. You might also create multiple bodies of content found in more than one version, although that might become too complex to work with. All these possibilities can be used by setting up multiple variables for fields (see "Hiding text using fields," page 184), one for each version, but are least confusing when working with styles only.

User On/Off	Admin On/Off	Coders On/Off

Another way to single source is to have separate sets of styles, fields, and sections for each version of the document, turning each on and off as needed

No matter how you work, single-sourcing can be confusing, so choose the name of styles and fields to help keep everything straight. You can even give each paragraph style a different font color to make it quickly recognizable. Each style's font color can be replaced quickly by using EDIT > FIND & REPLACE. If you are printing in black and white and use dark enough colors, you may not even need to change the colors when you print.

Hiding text using styles

To hide or reveal text, you can toggle the HIDDEN box on a style's FONT EFFECT tab. You can either choose part of the document to hide to produce one alternative version, or else create a different set of paragraph styles for each version.

Whatever method you choose:

1   Create one set of character and paragraph styles for text that appears in all versions of the document.

2   Create the common styles needed for each version of the text. For example, in a student quiz with an answer key, you might have one set of styles with names like USER – TEXT BODY and TEACHER – TEXT BODY. These styles are formatted exactly the same as the common styles, and hidden as needed.

Tip
You may not need to copy all the common styles for each version of the file. For example, in a quiz, the teacher's version might only need a single paragraph style called ANSWER KEY.

3   On the FONT EFFECT tab, toggle HIDDEN as needed before printing. Notice that spacing above or below a paragraph is

hidden along with the text. By contrast, you need to select the space after a string of hidden characters.

4   After you print a version from a single-source file, de-select HIDDEN so the complete file is visible the next time you open it.

Hiding text using fields

An alternate but more time-consuming way of single-sourcing is to place each passage in its own field. You can either toggle one version of the document, or else create a separate variable with a unique value for each version of the document. Usually, this second method is practical only for relatively short documents.

When you single-source, the FUNCTIONS tab of the FIELDS dialog contains several useful tools: HIDDEN TEXT, HIDDEN PARAGRAPH, and CONDITIONAL TEXT. Other types of fields exist, but, except for SET VARIABLE, are not relevant to single-sourcing.

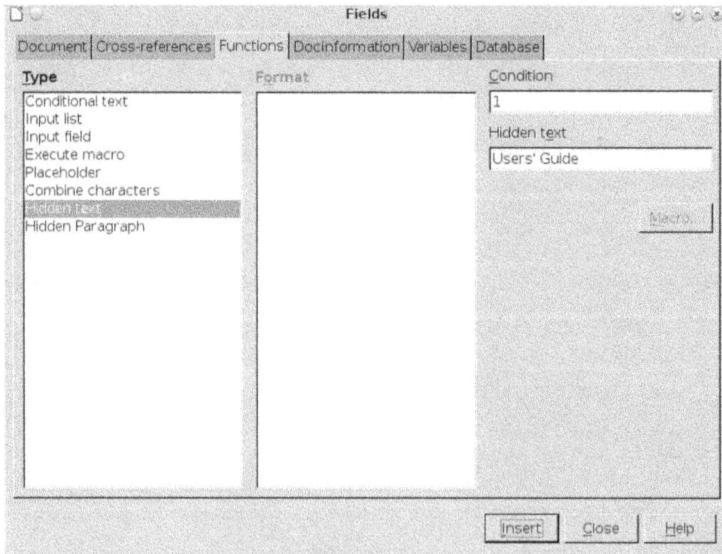

The HIDDEN TEXT field window.

For very limited uses, such as changing the title or the contents of a header or footer, you can use INPUT LISTS, which contains interchangeable items. However, input lists are impractical in a longer document, because each has to be changed separately.

The HIDDEN option in a character or paragraph style is the stylistic equivalent of some of the fields in INSERT > FIELDS > OTHER > FUNCTION > TYPE, such as HIDDEN TEXT and HIDDEN PARAGRAPH.

STOP

Caution

Make sure that VIEW > FIELD SHADINGS and VIEW > HIDDEN PARAGRAPHS are turned on when you use these fields. Otherwise, you will be lucky to find the hidden text or paragraphs.

The fields used for single-sourcing use an off or on condition for hiding and unhiding. A condition is merely a state of a document – or, if you prefer, a version with different content.

For instance, when a condition is set to o, then the content in the fields is hidden, creating one version of the file. When a condition is set to 1, then the content is shown, creating a second version. Alternatively, the condition that turns one version of a document on could be the name of the version, such as USER GUIDE. This arrangement is no different than checking or unchecking the HIDDEN box in a style.

Tip

A HIDDEN TEXT field can be awkward, because the field for entering it makes only a limited amount of text visible at one time. Hiding a section may be a simpler tactic to use.

Alternatively, in a CONDITIONAL TEXT field, a simple expression is set up using the CONDITION, THEN, and ELSE fields on the right side of the window. For instance, if the condition is 1, then the text that appears in the document is whatever is entered in the THEN field, such as USER'S GUIDE. However, change the condition to anything else, and the text in the document becomes whatever is entered in the ELSE field, such as SYSTEM ADMINISTRATOR'S GUIDE.

This arrangement is almost as handy as the HIDDEN box in a style. In effect, the CONDITION field becomes a password to limit who can change the condition.

The main disadvantage of this method is that each condition needs to be changed separately, while using the HIDDEN FONT effect means toggling a single box.

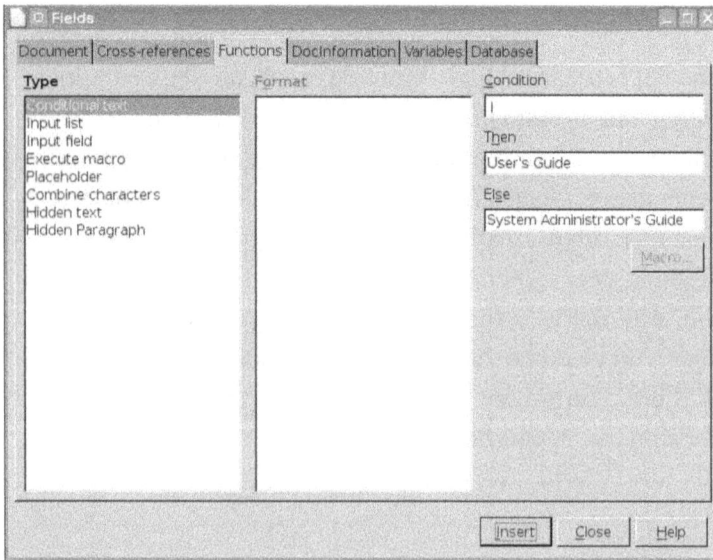

Do not confuse a CONDITIONAL TEXT field with a CONDITIONAL paragraph style. A CONDITIONAL TEXT field is similar to the HIDDEN check box on a paragraph style's FONT EFFECTS tab.

Hiding with sections

When documents have large areas to hide or show, you may prefer using sections.

Sections are areas that have properties that are different from the main body of text. These properties may be formatting, or content that is password-protected from editing.

You can also add a link to insert a separate file in the current document. Such links can be another sort of single-sourcing, allowing content used in several documents to be maintained in one place.

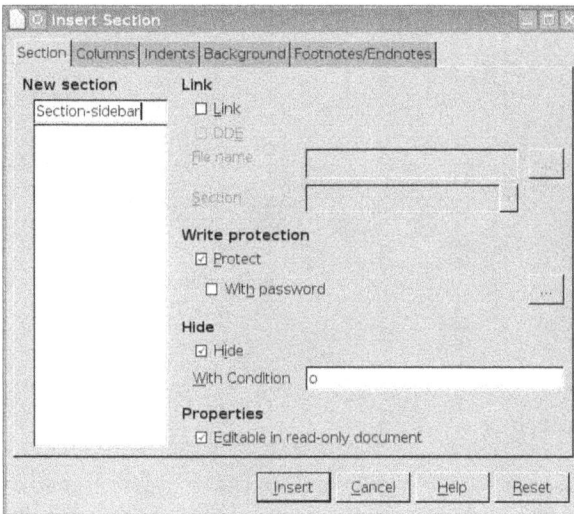

INSERT > SECTION can hide or reveal large sections of text.

Automating the use of fields and sections

Field windows stay open after you insert a field, allowing you to move to the next position for a field in the document. Section windows do not, although you can use the Navigator to jump from one section to the next as you edit.

However, changing the conditions for each field or section individually eats up time. If the same field appears more than once, you can copy and paste or use EDIT > AUTOTEXT so that you can add information with a couple of keystrokes, instead of making changes manually.

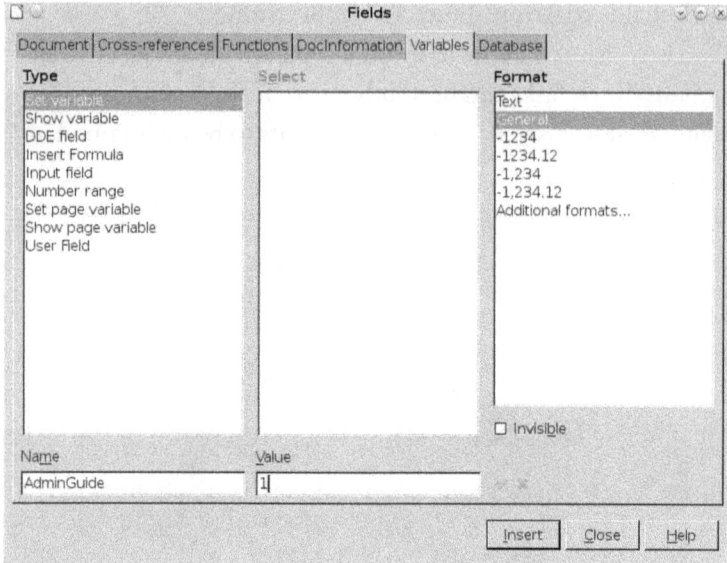

A variable can be a master control for turning all fields with the same condition on or off.

Better yet, you can set a general variable that toggles all fields at the same time:

1 Place the cursor at the start or end of the document, or anywhere else that is easy to locate.

2 Click INSERT > FIELDS > MORE FIELDS > VARIABLES > SET VARIABLE.

3 Set the FORMAT. You can leave it as GENERAL, or specifically as TEXT or a number format.

4   At the bottom of the window, give the variable a name. The name can indicate one of the document versions, or be something like MASTERSWITCH.

5   Enter a value. It can be text, or simply 0 or 1, but make sure that it uses the FORMAT entered.

6   Click the INVISIBLE box so that the variable cannot be seen in the document. Then click the INSERT button.

STOP

Caution

Locating the variable can be difficult, so you should place it in some easy to find place. You might choose to leave it visible while you work.

7   In all the CONDITIONAL TEXT, HIDDEN TEXT, and HIDDEN PARAGRAPH fields, as well as SECTIONS, set the condition to the variable name, followed by the value in quotation marks. For example: MASTERSWITCH "0" or ADMINGUIDE"1".

Condition
MasterSwitch "1"

Hidden text
Programmer's Guide

A HIDDEN TEXT field set up to work with a variable called MASTERSWITCH. The value of the variable follows its name.

Now you can show or hide all the fields in the document by changing only the variable, much as you would with a style.

If you have more than two versions of the document, you can create other variables to toggle each one off and on.

However, make sure that the values are different for each, and that each is placed where you can easily find them. The easiest way to find the values is to use EDIT > TRACK CHANGES > MANAGE CHANGES, especially when the document is complete and the only changes you are marking are hiding or showing different versions.

Using sections

Sections are yet another way to hide or unhide text. They can be used more easily than fields for long passages, but are less versatile than a paragraph style.

Sections work in much the same way as fields:

1   Place the cursor where you want an empty section, or else highlight existing text. Then select INSERT > SECTION. The INSERT SECTION dialog window opens.

2   Give the section a unique name that reflects its contents, and if desired protect it with a password.

3   Click the HIDE box, and/or set the WITH CONDITION field to 1. Either is necessary, but not both. When you close the dialog window, the section and the space above and below it are no longer visible in the document.

Tip

A section set to hide is visible until you remove the mouse cursor from it.

4   When you want to edit the section, click FORMAT > SECTIONS. The dialog window lists the document's sections, with an open or closed lock beside each name to indicate whether it is hidden. Sections can be formatted without unlocking them, but must be unlocked to edit the text.

Designing with LibreOffice

The limits to LibreOffice text design

If you read the last few chapters in sequence, you should start to understand why Writer can best be described as an intermediate desktop publisher. Using Writer, you can follow basic typographic principles and easily design complicated documents.

However, a few advanced features can be added only by tweaking a few settings in character and paragraph styles. Others cannot be set up in styles at all.

Probably the greatest lack is the easy insertion of non-standard characters, such as diagonal fractions or, in English locales, accented characters. The only way to mitigate this limitation is by choosing an international keyboard locale that includes accented characters and international currencies.

Even then, resources like small caps, old style figures, and ligatures – redrawings of groups of characters to make them easier to read – cannot be used automatically. Sometimes, these features are available in separate font families, but, in other cases, you might want to use features like macros, AutoText, and AutoCorrect to create libraries in your default template. The difficulty, of course, is remembering how to access such libraries.

Using the Typographic toolbar

SIL International, a maker of free fonts, also offers support for Graphite, a system which automatically uses small caps, old style figures, and ligatures where they are appropriate. However, a font has to be Graphite-aware before you can take advantage of the support – and, so far, only a handful of fonts are, such as Linux Libertine G and Linux Biolinum G.

If your fonts are Graphite-aware, consider installing the Typographic tool bar extension. This extension adds a tool bar to the LibreOffice window from which you can quickly add advanced typographical features manually. The help will also give you formulas that you can add to the end of the FAMILY field on the FONT tabs of character and paragraph styles that will automatically enable advanced features.

However, if these choices seem too fussy, stay with what you can do with standard character and paragraph styles. Modern typography tends to ignore these advanced features, so you might not even miss them.

Besides, while the arrangement of individual characters and paragraphs is a major part of typography, it is not the only part, as the next chapters will show.

8

Styling the page

Page styles are one of Writer's distinguishing features. Most word processors have character and paragraph styles, but having page styles elevates Writer to an intermediate desktop publisher, giving it immense flexibility.

Page styles matter because the design of pages is central to typography. Entire books have been written on the topic, many of them full of abstruse theories reinforced by complicated diagrams that often seem abstract from the practical issue of composition. In fact, until the rise of digital typography, the page was generally the main unit of composition.

Fortunately, however, you do not need to believe in obscure theories, much less follow them, in order to design a page.

The only drawback to page styles is that most users are unaccustomed to thinking in terms of pages. Why, many ask, should page numbers or footers and headers be associated with pages? Other word processors certainly do not make the same association. In fact, they frequently offer no sense at all of what the page looks like.

However, when you think, the page is really the most logical place for such features. It is other word processors that treat these features illogically.

Over the years, LibreOffice has added tools to make manual formatting of pages easier. For instance, while you still have to add new page styles to create new headers or footers, you can now apply them from the INSERT menu.

Yet despite these efforts, the basic logic of associating such features with pages remains strong despite its unfamiliarity. Learn to accept it, and possibilities open up that are not available in manual formatting – not the least of which are increased ease of use.

Understanding layout conventions

Page design is based on the two-page spread of left and right pages, because that is what you see when reading a book unless you are on the first or, sometimes, the final page.

While your document may be intended to be read online, a two-page spread is still a reasonable view to refer to regularly, because it means that you are less likely to miss any design problems.

Even more importantly, with wide screen monitors having become universal, a two-page spread is the most economical display of a document.

You can get a spread view by selecting BOOK VIEW from the zoom controls at the bottom right of the editing window.

Traditionally, a document's first page is a right page, modified to make clear that it is the start. Open any book and you immediately see why: On the left is the cover or binding, which leaves the first page to fall on the right.

A two-page spread in the zoom shows a document as readers will experience it in hard copy.

This tradition also means that right pages are usually odd numbered, and left pages even numbered. Master documents automatically add blank pages so that chapters will start with a right page.

Applying page styles

In theory, you can change the style of the page at any time by placing the cursor on a page and making a selection from the STYLES AND FORMATTING window. However, this practice can cause other pages in the document to change their style – not all the time, but often enough that the method is unreliable.

Lorem ipsum dolor sit amet, consectetur adipiscing elit. Integer nec odio. Praesent libero. Sed cursus ante dapibus diam. Sed nisi. Nulla quis sem at nibh elementum imperdiet. Duis sagittis ipsum. Praesent

35.

mauris. Fusce nec tellus sed augue semper porta. Mauris massa. Vestibulum lacinia arcu eget nulla. Class aptent taciti sociosqu ad litora torquent per conubia nostra, per inceptos himenaeos. Curabitur

A page break is marked in the editing window by a purple dotted line.

The only times this approach works reliably is when manual or automatic pages clearly mark the start and the end of a page.

Automating the next style

You do not want to be continually inserting a page break and selecting a page style as you work. As a result, the NEXT STYLE field on the ORGANIZER tab is even more important for page styles than for paragraph styles.

The most basic pattern is defined for you: a left page is followed by a right page, and a right page by a left page. If you use a FIRST PAGE style, its NEXT STYLE field defaults to LEFT PAGE.

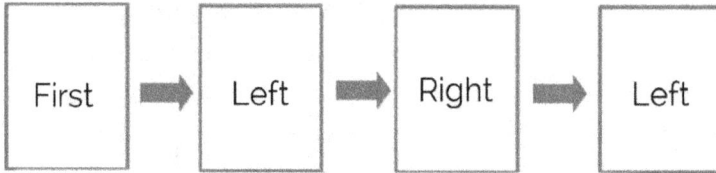

First ➡ Left ➡ Right ➡ Left

The default page succession. Usually, you can leave the default.

Tip

The NEXT STYLE field over-rides the PAGE LAYOUT field on the PAGE tab. For example, if a page is set to LEFT ONLY, the NEXT STYLE field allows you to use it as right page.

In some LibreOffice versions, a conflicting next style and page layout may cause layout problems, so make the two fields consistent.

Keep this default arrangement, and you should only have to think about setting page styles when you do something unusual, such as adding a landscape page to an otherwise portrait-oriented document. In these unusual circumstances, select INSERT >

MANUAL BREAK > PAGE BREAK and select the appropriate page style.

In other non-standard cases, you might create a paragraph style that is set on the TEXT FLOW tab to start a new page with a particular style. See "Setting page breaks by style," page 178.

Planning page styles

The default page designs are either for a specific dimension, such as ENVELOPE and LANDSCAPE, or for a specific purpose, such as ENDNOTE or INDEX.

You might also considering adding page styles for:

- Tables of contents.

- Front matter such as copyright notices and acknowledgments.

- Alphabetic index. If the entries are short, it can save space by being multi-columned.

- End notes in a scholarly work.

- A title page with the title and author's name. A title page is often centered, and in a larger font size than the body text.

- An epigraph, or short quote at the start of the document. Usually, an epigraph is indented vertically and horizontally. It may use an italic or script font.

- Poems, especially in a mixture of verse and prose.

- Dramatic scripts. Scripts have a very definite format, which you can find online.

- Legal documents that require a strict format.

- A page for a single page, chart, or diagram that may or may not be landscape-oriented.

For some documents, especially short ones, the DEFAULT STYLE is all you need.

However, the most basic page styles for any purpose are the LEFT PAGE, RIGHT PAGE, and FIRST PAGE. They are the ones that will be models for most of the other page styles.

Designing left and right pages

Unless you are using only the DEFAULT STYLE, page design almost always begins with the LEFT PAGE and RIGHT PAGE. They are most often mirror images of each other, part of a two-page spread.

You might choose to design only one of these styles for an online document, although many readers on tablets or wide screen monitors prefer a two-page spread online these days. You should also consider a spread if the online document is ever likely to be printed out. Unbalanced headers or footers may distract readers from the text with a clumsy design.

Designing the first page

The first page refers not to a title page, but the page on which a document or its first chapter begins. A first page is customarily a modified right page. It should be different enough that it is immediately obvious as the start of a new part of the document.

Tip

Designers sometimes pride themselves on a minimum of indicators, but better to use more indicators than are strictly necessary than have readers miss that you are starting a new chapter.

Sometimes, the main indicator of a first page may be a different header or footer from the rest of the pages – or perhaps the only ones. Usually, however, the indicators are more obvious:

A top margin that is 76–230 points taller than the top margin on a normal right page.

A chapter title and/or number. The titles may be in one or two styles.

An image or a dingbat, either above the text or in a text frame at the start of the first paragraph.

A drop capital of a single letter or a string of characters. This indicator is common in fiction. See "Setting up drop capitals," page 140.

Common tactics for indicating a first page. If headers are a different color from body text, you can also use the header color for the background color.

Setting the paper format

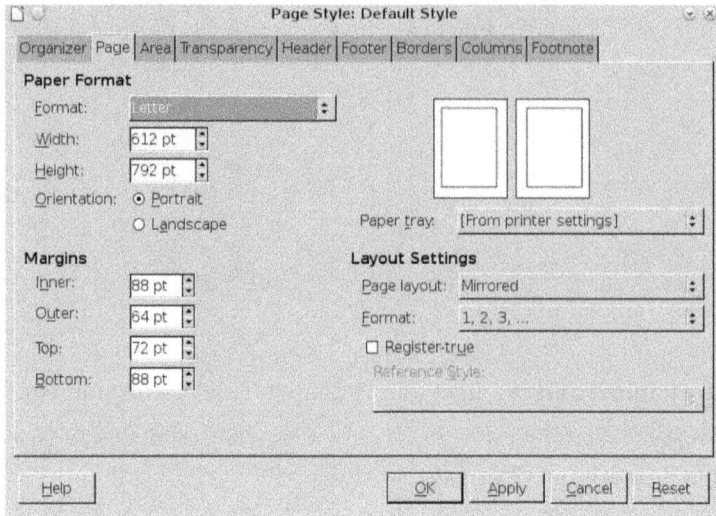

The PAGE tab for page styles.

Paper formats are set on the PAGE tab for a style.

The default page size is usually determined by your locale, and should be changed as necessary for your needs or printer. Throughout much of the world, the standard size is A4, but in North America, the standard size is LETTER.

Regardless of the page size, the standard orientation is portrait (taller than wide). The alternative is landscape (wider than tall).

Tip

To define your own page dimensions, start with any page size, and manually change the width and height. The FORMAT field changes automatically to USER.

Most printers will print non-standard page dimensions on whatever size they support. Some printers may not

Designing with LibreOffice

print non-standard dimensions at all from LibreOffice, but will support printing if you first export the document to PDF, especially if they support PostScript format.

All page formats assume a single sheet of paper. However, printing multiple pages to a sheet is more economical if you are using a large commercial printer. You can set up multiple page sheet printing through FILE > PRINT, or else by using text frames instead of pages.

All multiple sheets will of course need to be cut or folded later. LibreOffice does not support crop marks, but you can still cut pages down to size by making careful measurements.

For instance, single sheet brochures are often printed duplex (double-sided) with connected frames on one side for pages two and three, and frames on the other side for pages one and four.

If you are publishing online, neither paper size nor orientation matters unless the document might be printed to PDF or converted to an ebook format.

Example: A4/Letter combined template

A4 is a standard page size in most of the world, and Letter in the United States and Canada. They are also close in size: A4 has a width of 595 points and a height of 842 points, while Letter has a width of 612 points, and a height of 792 points.

If you have an international audience, a template that you can print on both sizes becomes a form of single-sourcing.

To create a combined A4/Letter template:

1   Create a user-defined page format with a width of 595 points, and a height 792 points. These are the smallest

measurements of the two formats. To display, all contents must fall within this area.

2   Decide on the left and right (or inner and outer) margins as though designing for the A4 format, the narrower of the two formats.

3   Decide on the top and bottom margins as though designing for Letter format, the smaller in height of the two formats.

The result is not completely satisfactory for either size. However, with this template, you can print from the same file to both sizes, rather than maintaining two files with the same content.

Setting layout settings

LAYOUT SETTINGS on the PAGE tab set the basic formats for a page. The PAGE LAYOUT setting offers four choices:

* MIRRORED: The page style is used for both left and right pages.

Tip

When you choose MIRRORED, the margin fields on the PAGE tab also change from LEFT and RIGHT to INNER and OUTER, with the INNER margin the one closest to the center of a two-page spread.

In a traditional hard copy book, the inner margin may have extra space so that the book can be bound. Be careful that enough space is allotted so that the binding does not become so tight that it obscures characters on the inner side of the page or requires readers to bend the binding to view the complete text.

In a mirrored layout, the INNER margin will be on the right side of left pages, but the left side of right pages.

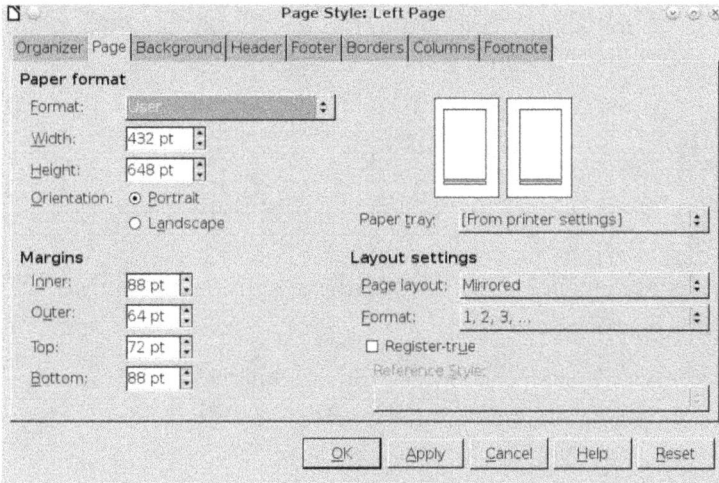

LAYOUT SETTINGS are on the bottom right of the PAGE tab.

- RIGHT AND LEFT: The page style is used for both right and left pages.

- ONLY RIGHT or ONLY LEFT: The page style is used only for right pages or only for left pages.

STOP

Caution

The PAGE LAYOUT field may be over-ridden by the NEXT STYLE field on the ORGANIZER tab. Ordinarily, this override would mean that you could ignore the PAGE LAYOUT field.

However, in some versions of LibreOffice, some combinations may cause blank pages or other formatting problems. For this reason, you should make sure that no conflicts exist, such as a NEXT STYLE field that forces a page style set to LEFT ONLY to appear on a right page. Otherwise, a page style created in one version of LibreOffice may not display as you intended in another version.

Setting margins

Margins are set on the PAGE tab of a page style. All margins have three purposes:

- To let readers hold hard copy without hiding some of the text with their fingers.

- To provide space for readers to add comments in the case of essays, proposals, and printed drafts.

- To frame the document unobtrusively so that readers can focus on its content.

The third is by far the most important. Unlike the other two, it applies to all documents, no matter what their medium.

STOP

Caution

None of these purposes should ever be ignored in favor of the time-honored student efforts to fit text into a certain number of pages.

These efforts are not only obvious, but usually distract from the text by being too broad or too narrow.

STOP

Caution

The default settings for all margins in Writer is 57 points (about 3/4 inches or 2 centimeters). For almost all cases, this is at best a minimum for a margin that fulfills any of its functions.

Choosing margin proportions

Theories about ideal margins often are based on everything from how reams of paper were folded to make books in the Middle Ages to analogies of musical scales, with accompanying diagrams that look capable of summoning demons.

One popular theory holds that the ideal margin settings are based on the Golden Section, a set of proportions first fully described by Euclid that are said to be naturally pleasing to the human eye.

Applying the Golden Section to page margins means that, starting from the outer margin moving to the top, then the inner and the bottom margins, the proportions of the margins should be 2:3:4:6. You could also start from the inner margin, but the result is often a narrow margin that may binding reduces even more

This ratio means that, using a basic unit of 20 points, the inner margin would be 40 points, the top 60 points, the outer 80 points, and the bottom 120 points.

These proportions do produce a pleasing page, but publishers sometimes regard them as wasteful, especially with the large bottom margin.

To be truthful, the only time that you are likely to see the Golden Section used to format pages is in poetry and in small print runs of prose, in which printers are willing to charge more in return for a well-designed page.

In the end, the Golden Section is a prestige ideal rather than a practical one – and one that not everyone believes is worth the effort of applying its elaborate theory. If you decide to use it, choose a thick, quality paper and a simple but elegant font for the body text of the document. Anything less seems out of place.

A view of non-printing characters showing margins set using the Golden Section.

A more flexible set of rules can be distilled from the majority of theories and layouts:

- Make the TOP margin greater than the INNER margin.

- Make the OUTER margin equal or greater to the inner margin. For printed documents, the OUTER margin should be wide enough so that the pages or book can be conveniently held.

- Make the BOTTOM margin taller than the TOP margin.

  All margins should be multiples of the line spacing.

  You can find other page margins that are successful, but these guidelines reflect the most common margins. Just as importantly, they are flexible enough that, unlike the Golden Section, you can use them without adding to the printing cost by increasing the number of pages.

Considering binding and trimming

If your document is going to be printed and bound, the INNER margin requires extra space for the binding. This space will make the two-page spread look lopsided on your monitor, but prevents words disappearing into the gutter (the center of a spread, where the edges of the pages are bound) in the finished product.

The exact space needed for binding varies with the type of binding, and the fittings chosen. For example, a spiral bound book can use spiral coils of different sizes.

You should consult your printer, but in most cases you will probably need at least 20–45 points extra on the inner margin for the binding, and possibly more.

Tip

If you are unsure what binding you will use, too wide an INNER margin is easier to adjust than too narrow a one.

Caution

Depending on the printer used, you may also need extra space on the other margins for trimming. Consult your publisher and printer as necessary.

Designing headers and footers

Headers and footers are spaces at the top and bottom of the page that contain document information. In Writer, their spacing is in addition to the margin; they do not fill part of the margin.

Unlike in Microsoft Word, in Writer, headers and footers are classified as part of a page style. Even when you manually format from INSERT > HEADER or FOOTER, your selection is based on the pre-defined page styles.

Headers and footers often appear together, but using just one is just as common. Decide what information you want to display on the page, and how it will be divided up, and you may find that just one will do. Typically, each header or footer has up to three pieces of information.

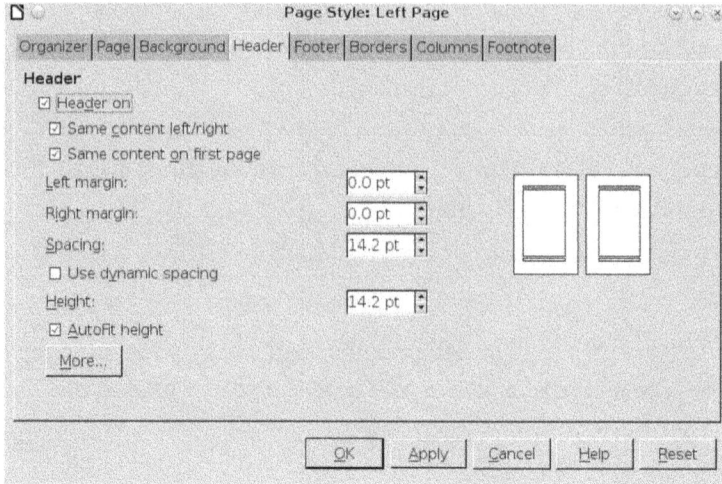

The HEADER and FOOTER tabs for a PAGE style have identical features.

If you do choose both, an obvious arrangement is to reserve one for just the page number, which is the most used information likely to be in a header or footer.

STOP
Caution

You can use a single footer, then unselect the check boxes SAME CONTENT LEFT/RIGHT and SAME CONTENT ON FIRST PAGE rather than designing each page style separately.

However, do not use both approaches together. The result can be unresolvable formatting conflicts.

Turning on headers and footers

To add a header or footer, go to the HEADER or FOOTER tab for a page style and select the ON box on the top left.

The immediate result is a single line for text in the top or bottom margin. The text area is immediately visible in Apache OpenOffice, but in LibreOffice you need to click anywhere in the margin for the minimal guides to be visible. Although you can add additional lines, more than one line gives a sloppy look that you should avoid in any published document.

Choosing tabs or tables

Many users simply use tab stops to add information, using a right tab for information that ends at the right margin. However, this arrangement can require constant readjustment as you revise, especially if you use fields or alter font sizes, making it more trouble that it's worth.

A more robust solution is to add a single-row table with invisible cell borders and as many columns as you need. This technique means fewer spontaneous changes than with tabs, and, therefore, less work. You will especially appreciate the convenience of tables if your document is likely to last several years and through several versions of LibreOffice.

Formatting headers and footers

Below the box for turning on a header or footer are the basic formatting options:

* LEFT MARGIN and RIGHT MARGIN: The margins for the header and footer are in addition to the page margins. Usually, these can be set to zero, since headers and footers are rarely indented more than the body text.

Tip

You cannot enter a negative number to make a header or footer extend into the left or right margin.

Should you ever want this arrangement, you would have to give your paragraph styles indents on the left and right, so that they use a shorter line than the header or footer.

- SPACING: The distance between the header and footer and the main text frame. This field should be a multiple of the line height. If the distance is wide enough, you may not need a line or any other sort of divider to separate the header or footer from the body text.

- HEIGHT: The line height of the footer. Often, this will be the line height of the body text. If you are using the footer or header to include a recurring image, then the HEIGHT will need to be at least the height of the image.

Adjusting the border and background

The BORDER/BACKGROUND tab for headers and footers is full of settings that need to be used cautiously.

To start with, unless you are looking for a retro-1990s look or deliberately practicing bad typography, ignore the settings for adding a shadow to the footer or header.

The same is often true for the BACKGROUND, except for the most delicate difference in shading between the page and the header and the footer, or if the only point of the header or footer is to add a graphic in the same place on every page. Consider using a transparency to make the background more subtle than a solid color.

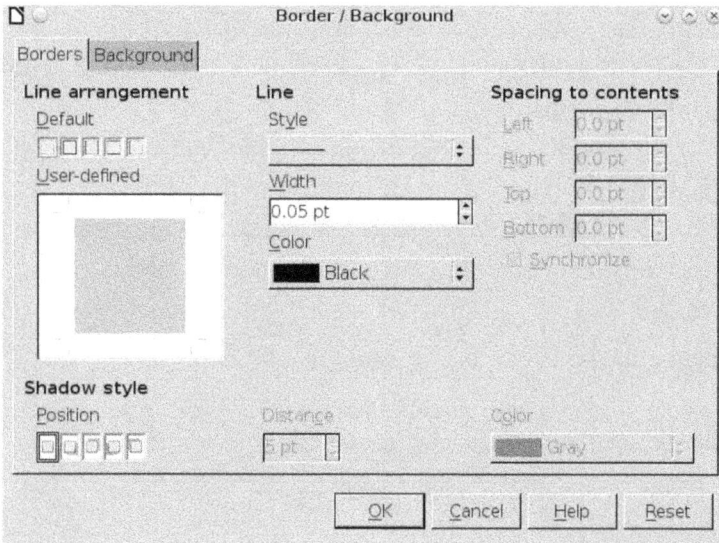

Border / Background

Borders | Background |

Line arrangement
Default

Line
Style

Spacing to contents
Left   0.0 pt

User-defined

        Right   0.0 pt

Width
0.05 pt

Top   0.0 pt

Color

Bottom 0.0 pt

Black

Synchronize

Shadow style
Position

Distance
5 pt

Color
Gray

OK   Cancel   Help   Reset

Click the MORE button on a HEADER or FOOTER tab to reach the BORDER/BACKGROUND tab.

Most of the time, you can also forget anything more than a single line between the header and the footer and the page's main text frame – and even that line should be set to the thinnest setting possible, although you might choose to color it.

In fact, you might manage without even a thin line if the space to the body text is large enough and the font used in the header or footer is different from the body text.

The most useful settings on the tab are for SPACING TO CONTENTS, and even they are only necessary if your use of borders makes the header or footer look cramped.

Adding header and footer paragraph styles

At this point, you may want to revisit your paragraph styles for headers and footers. You have HEADER LEFT, HEADER RIGHT, FOOTER LEFT, and FOOTER RIGHT by default. However, you might want to create HEADER CENTER LEFT and HEADER CENTER RIGHT as well. Or, if you are using tabs instead of tables, consider character styles of the same names.

No matter how you arrange headers and footers, their information should have a similar font size to the body text. The page number, perhaps, can be larger. Making the text smaller than the body text only reduces the usefulness of headers and footers.

Adding content to headers and footers

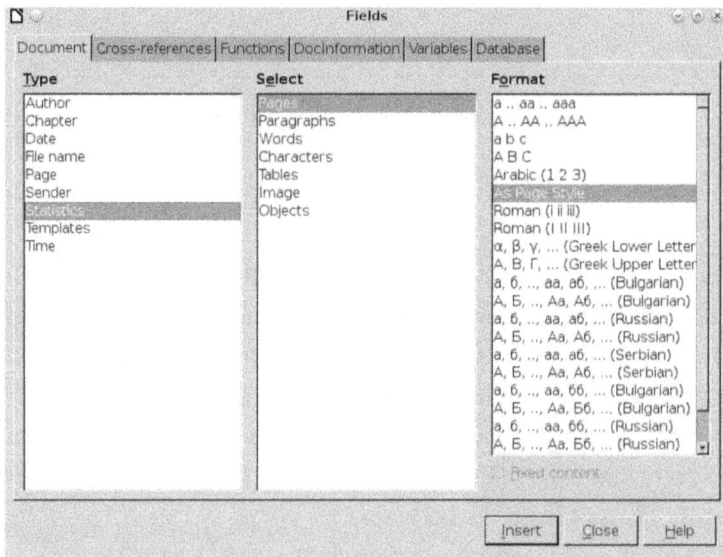

Fields are a common source of header and footer contents.

The contents for headers and footers generally include static information such as the document name, chapter name, and writer's name. Other possible contents includes the fields available in INSERT > FIELDS.

While you are writing, you might want to use temporary contents, especially fields from INSERT > FIELDS > DOCUMENT, such as the word count or template. As you finish the document, you can delete or replace these temporary fields.

Other content is available at INSERT > FIELDS > OTHER. Most of the fields you might consider using are on the DOCUMENT tab and the DOCINFORMATION tab.

The table below suggests likely fields.

General	Development	Internal
AUTHOR	FILE NAME	CREATED
TITLE	REVISION	MODIFIED
CHAPTER	TEMPLATE	SENDER
PAGE	STATISTIC > WORDS	LAST PRINTED
TITLE	PAGE COUNT	MODIFIED

Fields for headers and footers. Many fields have the advantage of updating automatically, or of taking information directly from your personal information or from FILE > PROPERTIES.

Tip

You may want to change header and footer content as a document is being prepared.

When you create the document, you might want to include word count and author in the headers or footers.

However, before you publish, you probably want to delete these fields, and replace them with ones for the chapter title.

Using running headers and footers

Running headers (or footers) constantly change according to the latest instance of a particular paragraph style. In this way, they provide a guide for readers scanning to locate a passage.

For example, you could have a header for left pages that repeats the text of the previous HEADING 1 paragraph style. If HEADING 1 was used only for the chapter title, then the header would always include the chapter title. You could then have a right page that repeats HEADING 2 texts to help readers see where they are in the chapter.

Running headers or footers can be set up using any paragraph style set as an outline level. By default, that means using heading styles. See "Adding header and footer paragraph styles," page 211.

STOP Caution

If more than one paragraph style is assigned to the same outline level, you may have unexpected results.

To set up a running header or footer:

1 Set up a paragraph style on the TEXT FLOW tab so that it starts a new page. The default is HEADING 1, but TITLE or a custom style called CHAPTER NUMBER is less confusing.

2 From TOOLS > OUTLINE NUMBERING > NUMBERING, assign the paragraph style you are using to an outline level if you have not already done so..

3 Place the mouse cursor in the position for the page number.

4 Select INSERT > FIELDS > DOCUMENT > MORE > CHAPTER > CHAPTER NUMBER. Then click the INSERT button.

5 Repeat steps 3 and 4 for every page style in the document that includes page numbering.

Making vertical headers and footers

Headers and footers are generally horizontal. However, you may find that on landscape pages (ones wider than they are tall) that the length of headings and footers makes for difficult reading.

You might also choose vertical headers and footers on portrait pages (ones taller than they are wide) to give a novel effect.

The disadvantage of vertical headers and footers is that page styles do not automatically repeat them on every instance of a page style, the way they do horizontal ones. Instead, you have to recreate them on each instance, or copy and paste them. These choices tends to restrict them to shorter documents.

To create vertical headers and footers:

1 Add the landscape page if it is not already in use.

2 Create the text for the header or footer, using the appropriate paragraph style and adding fields. Position it about halfway down the landscape page.

> ## Tip
> If you are working in a document that already has portrait pages, you can copy and paste a header or footer on another page.

3 Select the line that will become a header or footer and select CHARACTER > FORMAT > POSITION > ROTATION/SCALING > 90 DEGREES or 270 DEGREES. 90 DEGREES positions the text so that it begins at the bottom and moves up, while 270 DEGREES positions the text so that it begins at the top and moves down.

STOP Caution

Tabs, borders, shadows, and other formatting other than the paragraph style will be stripped when you click the OK button.

4   Select the now-vertical line and click INSERT > FRAME to place it in a frame.

5   Position the frame outside the inner or outer margin, where it will act as a header or footer. If you are working in an existing document, check another page style to see how far the header or footer is positioned from the main text body in other page styles. Turn on the grid to help you position the frame.

6   Size the frame so it occupies the full space between the top and bottom margins. To be exact, you can subtract the top and bottom margins from the page height to get the exact size that the frame should be. However, at a high enough zoom, the text boundaries may be enough to guide you.

7   Right-click on the frame and select FRAME from the right-click menu to add any borders or shadows, or to turn them off.

8   Repeat as needed.

Setting page numbers

INSERT > FIELDS includes PAGE NUMBER in its sub-menu. Selecting from the sub-menu, you can insert a page number based on the setting for the current page style set from the PAGE > LAYOUT SETTINGS > FORMAT FIELD. You can then align the page number by editing its paragraph style.

The sub-menu also includes a PAGE COUNT field, so by typing one or two characters, you can quickly have "2 of 3" or "2/3."

However, to gain full control of page numbering, you need to go to INSERT > FIELDS > MORE FIELDS > DOCUMENT > PAGE. There, you can override the page style's setting with another numbering format chosen from the pane on the right. For instance, you might want to start with an introduction numbered in Roman numerals, then continue with the body of the text numbered in Arabic numerals.

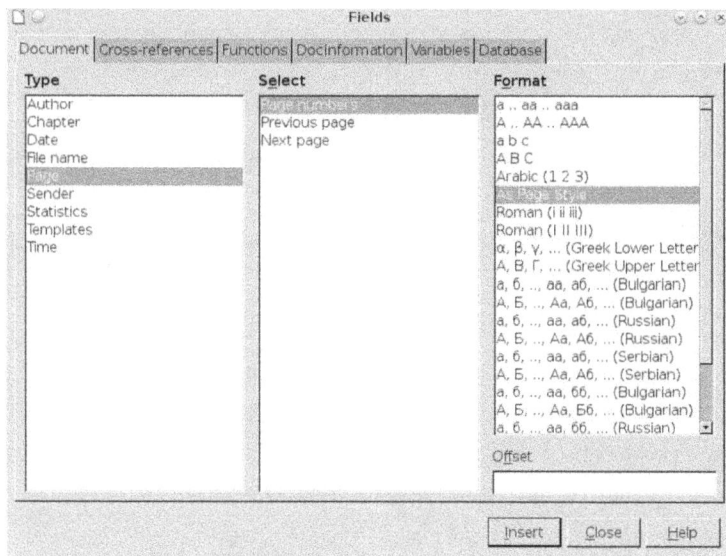

For a complete set of options, set page numbers from INSERT > FIELDS > MORE FIELDS > DOCUMENT > PAGE.

You also have the option of adding an offset – of subtracting or adding pages from the actual page count. An offset is most commonly used when a document has a number of pages that are either unnumbered or use a different numbering system, such as front matter or an introduction.

Adding chapter numbers to page numbers

Technical documentation or any other material that is frequently revised sometimes restarts the numbering with every chapter. Under this system, for example, the third page of chapter 5 would have the page number 5–3.

This style may be used so that, when revisions are published, users can replace only a chapter instead of the whole document – an arrangement especially useful with ring binders.

Setting page number formats

LAYOUT SETTINGS > FORMAT sets the page numbering format for the page style. However, just as the PAGE LAYOUT field may be over-ridden by the NEXT STYLE field on the ORGANIZER tab, so the FORMAT field is over-ridden by the settings you choose for INSERT > FIELD > PAGE NUMBER field.

Depending on the version of LibreOffice, this over-ride may cause formatting problems, so make everything consistent.

Adding chapters in page numbering

To include the chapter in the page numbering:

1   Set up a paragraph style on the TEXT FLOW tab so that it starts a new page. The default is HEADING 1, but TITLE or a custom style called CHAPTER NUMBER is less confusing.

2   If necessary, from TOOLS > OUTLINE NUMBERING > NUMBERING, assign the style you are using to LEVEL 1. In the AFTER field, add a separator, such as a hyphen.

3   Place the cursor in the position for the page number.

4   Select INSERT > FIELDS > DOCUMENT > MORE FIELDS > CHAPTER > CHAPTER NUMBER. Then click the INSERT button.

5   Select INSERT > FIELDS > MORE FIELDS > DOCUMENT > PAGE > PAGE NUMBERS (or simply INSERT > FIELDS > PAGE NUMBER) to add the page number.

6   Follow steps 3 and 5 for every page style in the document that includes chapter-page numbering.

Restarting page numbers

The most common scenario in which page numbering restarts is when a document begins with an introduction – usually numbered in lower case Roman numerals, then continues with the rest of the text – usually numbered in Arabic numerals.

To restart the page count:

1   Create INTRODUCTION START, INTRODUCTION LEFT and INTRODUCTION RIGHT page styles, modeled on the main default pages. On each of these custom styles, set PAGE > LAYOUT SETTINGS > FORMAT to lower case Roman numerals.

2   Immediately before the page on which the page count restarts and the main body of the text begins, select INSERT > MANUAL BREAK.

3   Select PAGE BREAK for the TYPE.

4   Select the page style to use after the break. Probably, you will want to use FIRST PAGE.

5   Select CHANGE PAGE NUMBER, and set the number to RESTART AT. Negative numbers are not allowed.

Setting up multiple page columns

Multiple columns are useful for newsletters, and for printing indexes or other tables whose entries rarely require an entire line.

Without multiple columns, many indexes and tables would occupy far more pages than necessary.

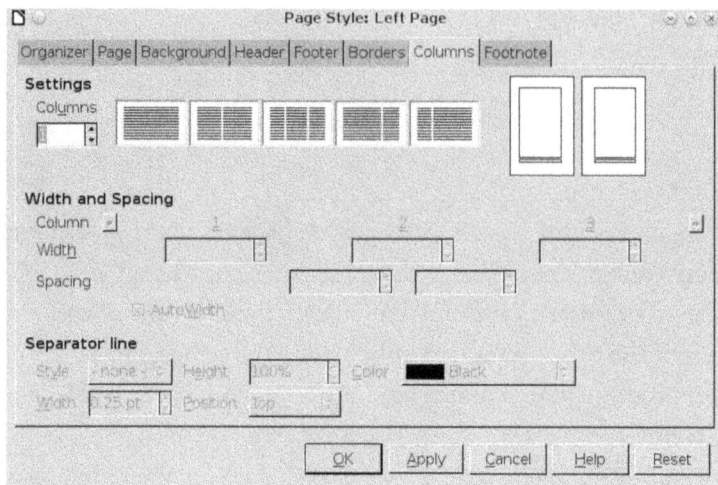

The COLUMNS tab contains several tools for setting up multiple-column layouts.

On the most commonly used formats – A4 or Letter sized paper with a portrait orientation – you probably have room for a maximum of 4–5 columns, unless some of them are extremely narrow.

STOP Caution

Too many columns may result in poor hyphenation and problems with alignment. See "Setting hyphenation," page 118.

Fortunately, this is exactly what the COLUMN tab assumes. You can add more columns, but the tools assume no more than 4–5.

You can set the number of columns by entering an exact number plus a layout under SETTINGS. In most cases, all columns are given the same width.

If you prefer, you can set each column width separately using WIDTH & SPACING. At all times, the total with of all columns must equal the total available. Among other possible confusions, this arrangement means that you must reduce the free space in one column before you add space to another column.

Below the WIDTH & SPACING is SPACING, which sets the spacing between columns. The greater the spacing, the easier the text will be to read.

Use a SEPARATOR line only if the SPACING is extremely tight and relying on white space alone would make reading difficult. In effect, adding a line between columns is an acknowledgment that your design does not work, but you have some overwhelming reason not to correct it.

Combining single- and multiple-column layouts

Writer is designed with uniform pages in mind. As a result, you cannot create a page style with more than one column format.

If you need such a layout, begin with a single-column design, then add a multiple-column section. Unfortunately, you will need to add the section on each instance of the page style.

Another option is to add manual frames and set up the text flow you want. See "Setting text flow between frames," page 262.

Setting up footnotes

Footnotes are positioned automatically by LibreOffice – usually with acceptable results, although occasionally the only solution is to convert them to endnotes instead. However, you can control much of the footnote layout by the settings on a page style's FOOTNOTE tab.

The most important setting is the height for the footnote area. You can set a specific MAXIMUM FOOTNOTE HEIGHT, or NOT LARGER THAN PAGE AREA — which means that no footnote can be larger than a page long. Usually, this is not a problem, since a footnote longer than a page is probably important enough to be moved to in the main text or an appendix.

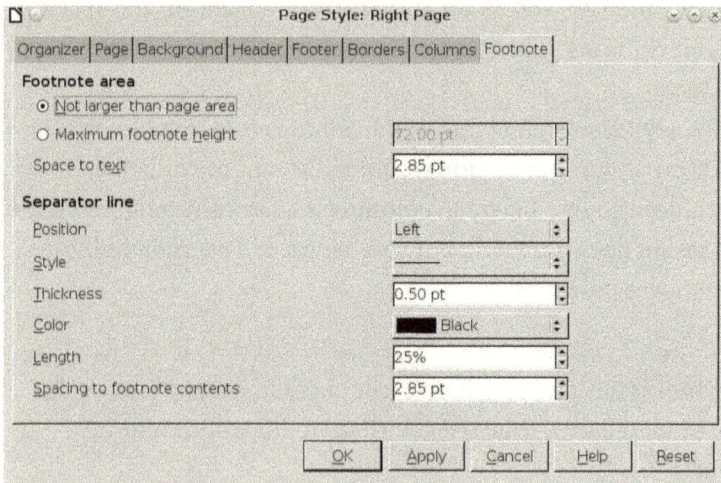

If your document has no footnotes, ignore the FOOTNOTE tab.

Typically, you will want at least two lines' spacing as SPACE TO TEXT, and at least one line between the SEPARATOR LINE and the SPACING TO FOOTNOTE CONTENTS.

A separator should be as thin and as short as possible. With proper spacing, it may not be needed at all. However, be careful that the separators for the footer and footnote do not result in two solid adjacent lines.

Setting the page background

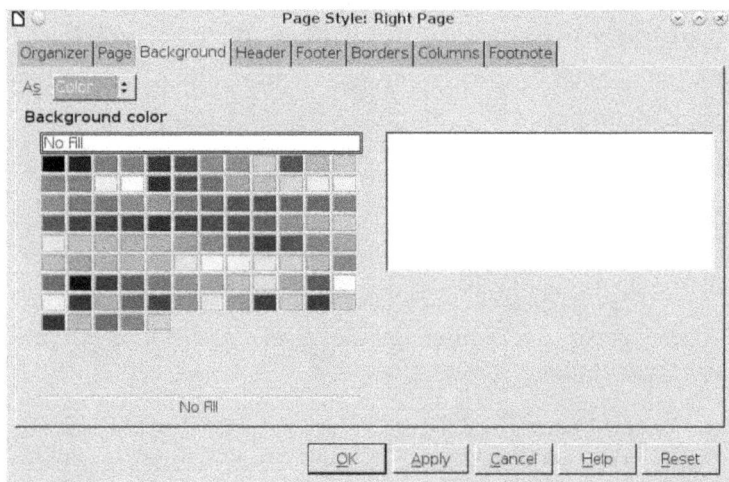

The BACKGROUND tab is available for page styles, but is often unnecessary.

Backgrounds are useful either to mark part of the document as different or for short works like brochures. If you can't give a reason for a special background, then you can be confident that it is not really needed.

The trouble is that page backgrounds are seriously limited in functionality. For one thing, they cover only the space inside the margins. You can set all the margins to zero, but you will need a printer capable of bleeds (the technical name for printing to the edge of the paper). On most home printers, you will still have about a centimeter or so around the edge of the page where you cannot print. This non-printing area severely limits the usefulness of adding a background.

For another, in a printed document, changing the background from the default white can mean slower printing and wasted ink.

A more efficient solution is to print on colored paper, although you might have trouble matching batches of the paper exactly.

If you go ahead despite these limitations, the basic principle remain the same as for paragraphs or any other unit of design that can use a background. See "Highlighting and setting backgrounds," page 134.

Tip

A color or graphic background usually does not need a border unless some point along its edge blends into the paper color.

When that happens, use the minimal border that serves its purpose – and never add a shadow, except for a retro look.

Using recurring images

The greatest weakness of LibreOffice page styles is that they have only limited ability to include a recurring image such as a logo each time a style is used. In fact, there are only four work-arounds, three of which are less than ideal:

- Place the recurring image in a header or footer. On a first page, you might even be able to position the image more or less the way you want it by extending the height of the header or footer. Often, however, the usefulness of this option is limited.

- Associate the graphic with a list style. You will still need to apply the list style at each position, and you are very limited in how you can position the graphic. See "Applying list styles," page 274.

- Add a graphic background. Make all of the background the same color as other pages, and position the graphic where you want it to appear. The graphic will have no text wrap, so you will have to design carefully so that no text comes near it.

- Anchor the image in the header or footer, but place the image outside the header or footer, setting the anchor to As PARAGRAPH or As CHARACTER. You can then position the image anywhere on the page, and it will be repeated each time the page style is used. This tactic is usually the most effective.

Moving in the new dimension

Immigrants from other word processors sometimes overlook page styles. However, page styles are the means of adding everyday features such as page numbers and headers and footers.

Just as importantly, they help you design in large blocks, such as the page or the two-page spread. This ability gives you a perspective that most word processors entirely lack. You might want to use sections for slightly smaller blocks, but once you are comfortable with page styles, you will probably find few uses for sections unless you want to password-protect part of your document.

Take the time to understand page styles, and you will find that Writer really comes into its own.

9

Getting in the frame

Frame styles are the least understood type of style in LibreOffice. Often, you don't need to understand them, because Writer adds frames automatically to contain objects such as images.

In many ways, frame styles are as much for Writer's automatic formatting as they are for users. Most of the time, they are so completely in the background that users have a hard time distinguishing frames from the images and other objects they enclose.

Another reason for uncertainties surrounding frames is that keeping images where you place them can be difficult. Generally, images stay anchored to the page, paragraph, or character to which you assign them, and some users never have problems.

At the same time, almost as many find that Writer in particular is notorious for spontaneously switching images so they are move on the page for no apparent reason. Changing anchors, moving objects, copying and pasting – sometimes any editing whatsoever seems to send objects shifting out of control.

For this reason, this chapter includes both how things are supposed to work (and should work for you, with any luck), and the precautions and work-arounds you may need. Although the work-arounds may give you fewer formatting options, they do keep images where you put them.

Tip

LibreOffice currently prefers the word "images," but you sometimes find the terms "graphics" and "picture" used instead. In the most recent versions of Writer, the INSERT menu uses MEDIA as well.

How frame styles work

When an object is added to Writer, it is automatically enclosed in a frame of a pre-determined type. The frame sets how the object is placed on the page, as well as how it interacts with other elements in the document.

You can edit the frame by modifying the frame style it uses, but you should avoid manual overrides whenever possible.

Unfortunately, however, elements not included in any frame style, such as an image's anchor, alignment, stacking, and wrap usually have to be edited separately for each frame, making this advice easier to give than to practice.

STOP Caution

If you are having trouble positioning something, the first thing you should do is check whether you are editing the image instead of the frame, or the frame instead of the image.

Understanding pre-defined frames

Because of the problems that sometimes occur with frame styles, creating custom styles is best avoided. Instead, stick with editing the pre-defined frame styles. Often, they will be all you need anyway.

The names of some pre-defined frame styles are self-explanatory, such as GRAPHICS, LABELS, and FORMULA.

Others require clarification:

- FRAME: Both a general frame and a text frame specifically. This is the default style.

- MARGINALIA: Frames that sit on the left side of the main text frame, creating the effect of notes in the margin. See "Creating marginalia and sideheads," page 258.

- OLE: The term is technically obsolete, but now refers to a document nested within a document, including charts. In this way, a document can be easily updated, and used in different situations.

- WATERMARK: Frames that position a graphic behind text. You will need to prepare the graphic for use before you add it. See "Creating watermarks," page 260).

Planning frame use

The addition of graphics and other objects is often an after-thought of writing, done with minimal thought about layout.

However, you can improve your layout by choosing a general strategy. Tactics to consider include:

- Placing images on separate pages from the text. In this case, you may want a separate page style whose use automatically creates a new page.

- Using no text wrap, so that there is text above and below the frame, but not to its left or right. If you lack time, this is always a low-maintenance tactic to use anyway, and is common in technical manuals. While not always ideal, it generally provides an adequate layout unless you are adding extremely small images, which tend to get lost in all the white space to their left and right.

- Deciding how much space to place around the frame. The space should be a multiple of the line-spacing.

- Using either a border or extra white space when images have the same background as the pages of your document.

Before you design, sketch out the alternatives for positioning multiple images on the same page.

Preparing images

You can adjust how an image displays with the tools on the IMAGE and CROP tabs, which are available when you select IMAGE PROPERTIES from its right-click menu.

These tools do not affect the image itself, only its display. The IMAGE tab has no undo function, but you can easily change the settings until you revert to the original.

On the IMAGE tab, you can flip an image vertically or horizontally. You can further refine the editing by setting which pages the image is flipped upon. Using these settings, you could add dingbats or perhaps decorative scroll work twice in a two-page spread so that they formed a mirrored image.

In the FILE NAME field, adding a path changes the image from an embedded image that is part of the document file to a linked, separate file. Changing the path replaces the image. See "Choosing linking or embedding," page 237.

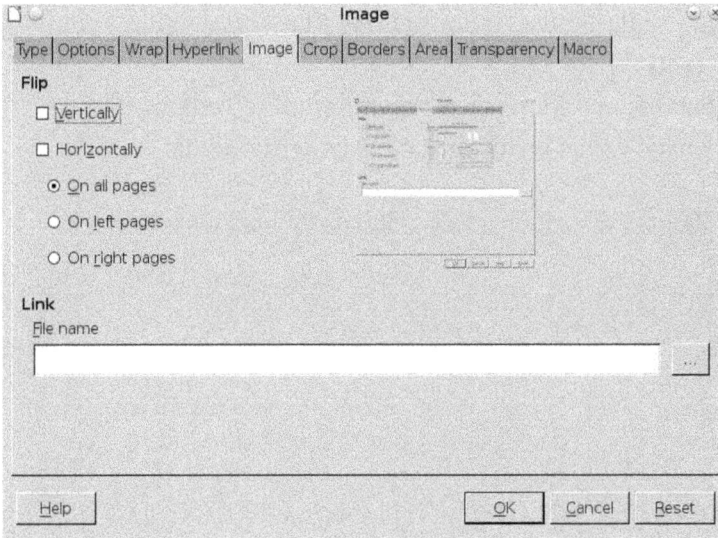

The IMAGE tab edits how an image displays in LibreOffice, not the image file itself.

Cropping is the displaying of only part of an image. Cropping helps readers to focus on the relevant part of an image, but at the risk of losing context. On style tabs and dialog windows, you can easily crop so tightly that readers have little idea where the items displayed actually are.

On the CROP tab, you can change the overall dimensions of an image, or display only part of the image. If you display only part of the image, you can select KEEP IMAGE SIZE or else scale the newly cropped image to a percentage of its original size. You can undo such changes by clicking the ORIGINAL IMAGE SIZE button.

All these tools can be handier than opening a graphics editor to make changes. However, given the potential instability of frames, the tools on the IMAGE and CROP tabs are just extra things that might go wrong. If you are having trouble with graphics staying in place, avoid these tabs. See "Using cropping or indicators ," page 234.

Another consideration is that LibreOffice's editing tools are less versatile than many third party graphics editors.

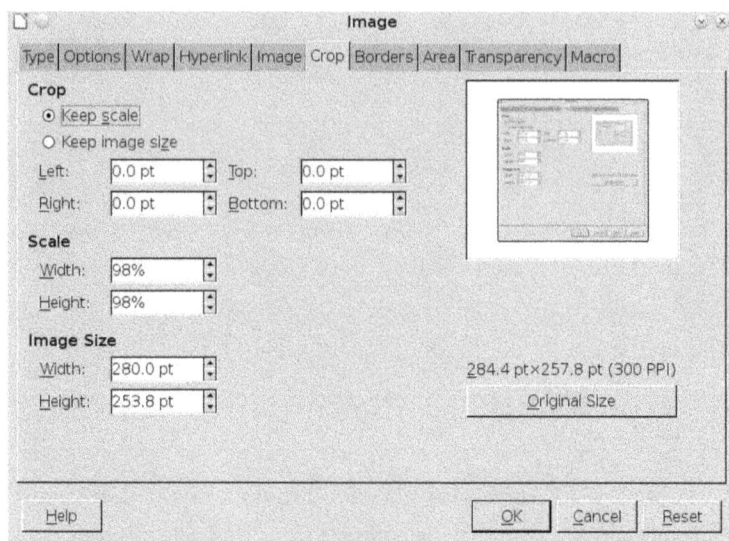

The CROP tab is a misnomer. It includes not only fields to crop the display, but also fields to adjust the display size.

Preparing images in graphics editors

Graphics editors can be a more versatile and reliable way of preparing images than the tools that LibreOffice itself provides. Editors such as GIMP and Krita are free to download for all the operating systems that LibreOffice runs on.

Before editing images, measure the distance between the left and right (or inner and outer) margins on all pages where images might display. You can determine this distance by subtracting the vertical margins from the page width given on the PAGE tab of each page style. You will need this measurement when sizing images. If some images are too large to display legibly at this size, consider adding a landscape page style for them.

You can open images in other applications by right-clicking and selecting EDIT WITH EXTERNAL TOOL, or directly from the graphics editor. If the image is already open, right-click to copy it, then paste it in a new file in the graphics editor.

Graphics editors allow you to change the size and colors of an image, and do many other operations besides. However, the four operations necessary for every image are:

- Setting the image's resolution and print size.

- Deciding to crop the image or to add indicators to point to features.

- Setting natural borders.

- Cleaning up the image.

Setting image resolutions

For an online document, a resolution of 96 DPI (dots per inch) is usually enough. For hard copy, use a minimum of 300 DPI, or 600 DPI or higher for quality printing.

Resolution is best set in a graphics editor. Many graphic editors will show an actual size and a printed size, displaying each in a number of different formats, including pixels, points, inches, and percentage. Getting the highest resolution is a tradeoff: the higher the resolution, the smaller the actual or printed size of the image. Most images can be enlarged by 50%, but few can be increased to 200% without becoming badly distorted unless they are very simple. Experiment to find the best compromise.

Most editors work at the screen display of 96 DPI. If you are making original graphics, one solution is to make everything three times the size you need, then reduce it so that it is the right size at 300 DPI.

Using cropping or indicators

Editing a graphic helps readers know what to focus on. You have two main choices: cropping or adding indicators.

Cropping is the reduction of the image to whatever is essential. Leave some context so readers can locate what you are discussing.

Some writers put jagged edges around a cropped image, as though it were torn from a page, which is a vivid effort, but a time-consuming one.

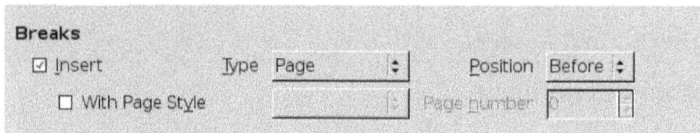

Breaks

☑ Insert   Type   Page   ⬍   Position   Before ⬍

☐ With Page Style   ⬍   Page number   0   ⬍

A cropped image of the TEXT FLOW tab for a paragraph style.

By contrast, indicators draw attention to parts of the image by their bright colors and the fact that they obviously do not belong.

Types of indicators include bars, arrows, and an oval. Bars and arrows are quickest to insert, while adding an oval usually involves making its fill area transparent so that the part of an image it encircles is visible.

Choose one type of indicator, and note its colors and dimensions so that you can use them consistently.

Tip

You can also add indicators such as arrows, lines, boxes, or callouts within the graphics editor, or by using VIEW > TOOLBARS > DRAWING.

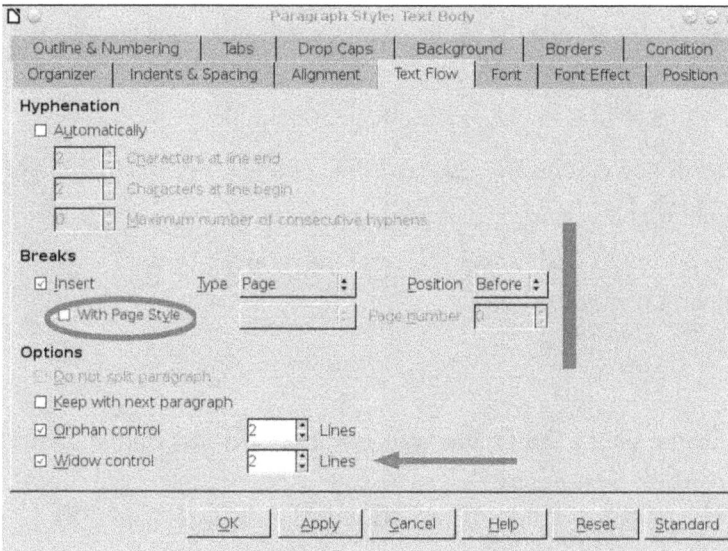

Indicators call attention to elements that you want readers to find easily as they follow your discussion.

Setting natural borders

You can add a border to an image in LibreOffice. However, a natural border can be just as effective. If possible, crop the image so that all its edges are a different color from the document's background.

For example, some operating system or desktop themes place a shadow around dialog windows. Include the shadow and you have a natural border that needs no further attention.

Cleaning up the image

As a final step in image editing, remove any unnecessary clutter. For example:

• If you take a screen shot of a menu, white out any irrelevant text and dialogs in the background.

- Check for details in the background that might accidentally violate someone's privacy.

- Crop any blank space in an image if possible.

- See if you can improve the contrast of an exceptionally dark or light image.

- Experiment with image size, making it no larger than necessary for legibility.

Inserting images

Throughout LibreOffice, frames are usually less trouble if you follow these best practices:

- Add objects when the formatting and writing is done. The objects are less likely to move around.

- If possible, format the frame style, not individual frames.

- Adjust objects immediately after you add them, not later. If necessary, experiment with the exact settings first, making notes of all the settings. Then delete the experiment and add the frame again, applying the settings as the frame is added.

- Never copy and paste frames or objects. Delete a frame and start from scratch if you want to move an object.

- Never drag an object to resize or reposition it. Use the right-click menu.

- Never use spaces or empty lines to position objects. Instead, always use styles.

- Avoid putting two or more images one after the other, unseparated by text. The workaround suggested in this chapter is more reliable for placing two or more images together. See "Using the table workaround," page 255.

These precautions seem to work more reliably in Writer than in Calc, Draw, or Impress.

Choosing linking or embedding

When you select an image from the file manager using INSERT > IMAGE, LibreOffice defaults to embedding the image as part of the document file.

However, in some versions of LibreOffice, you have the option to use the INSERT AS LINK box in the bottom left corner of the file manager. If you select this option, your document will use the image's original file each time it loads.

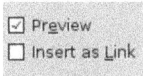

☑ Preview
☐ Insert as Link

Located at the bottom left of the Insert Image window, the INSERT AS LINK option is easy to overlook.

The fact that LibreOffice defaults to embedding images suggests that its original programmers saw embedding as the easiest solution. In fact, professional writers and designers argue all the time about these two approaches. Both embedding and linking have pluses and minuses. Which you prefer is not so much right or wrong as a matter of how you prefer to work and how others prefer to receive your work.

Pluses and minuses to consider include:

Embedding

- Document size is bigger, because images are included.

- Images cannot be lost, because they are part of the document at all times.

Linking

- Document size is smaller, without images.

- Images can be easily lost, so create orderly directories to reduce the possibility.

- When you share, you know the document is complete. There are no additional files to find.

- Images can be edited from within LibreOffice, which is more convenient.

- Images are updated by selecting CHANGE IMAGE from their right-click menu.

- When you share a document, you have to send image files as well.

- Images must be edited in a graphics editor, which gives more options.

- Images are updated by overwriting the existing separate image file with a new one. If you do not use TOOLS > UPDATE > UPDATE ALL, Writer updates the image the next time the document opens.

Tip

CHANGE IMAGE may not work if you have try to swap in an image with the same name as the original. Instead, delete the original image and then insert the replacement.

Formatting frames and images

The right-click menu includes items for both frame and image. Although you can modify many features from the right-click menu, some observers suggest that using the dialog windows seems to help keep objects where you placed them.

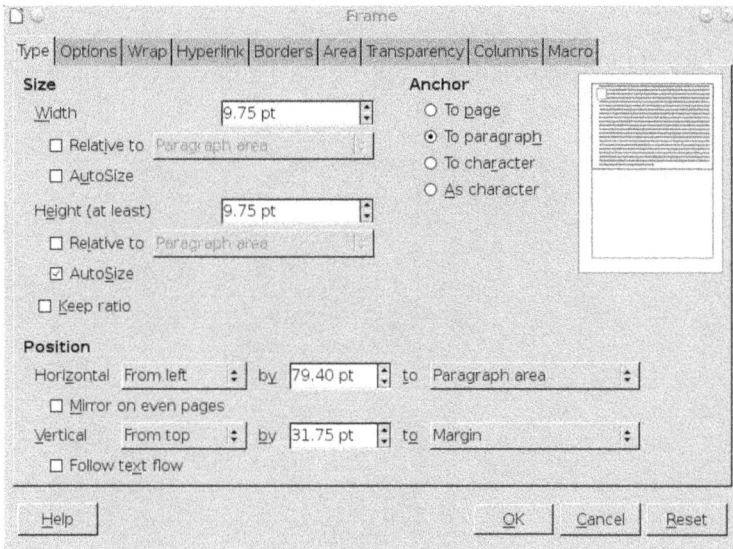

Frame

Type | Options | Wrap | Hyperlink | Borders | Area | Transparency | Columns | Macro

Size

Width `9.75 pt`

☐ Relative to `Paragraph area`

☐ AutoSize

Height (at least) `9.75 pt`

☐ Relative to `Paragraph area`

☑ AutoSize

☐ Keep ratio

Anchor

○ To page
◉ To paragraph
○ To character
○ As character

Position

Horizontal `From left` by `79.40 pt` to `Paragraph area`

☐ Mirror on even pages

Vertical `From top` by `31.75 pt` to `Margin`

☐ Follow text flow

Help | OK | Cancel | Reset

Frames and images share an almost identical dialog window. The main difference is that the window for frames includes a COLUMNS tab. Be sure that you select the one you intend to modify.

Resizing frames and images

Resize frames and images on the TYPE tab of the dialog window. You have several options for resizing:

- Set WIDTH and HEIGHT separately. This choice can easily distort the image, so you are better off with other alternatives.

- Select KEEP RATIO, then add either the WIDTH or HEIGHT. The other dimension will change automatically to remain proportional, saving you calculations.

- Use the RELATIVE fields to set a WIDTH and HEIGHT that is a percentage of the paragraph's or page's width and height.

- Select AUTOSIZE for WIDTH and HEIGHT when first adding a frame. This option may have no effect if you edit the frame dimensions later.

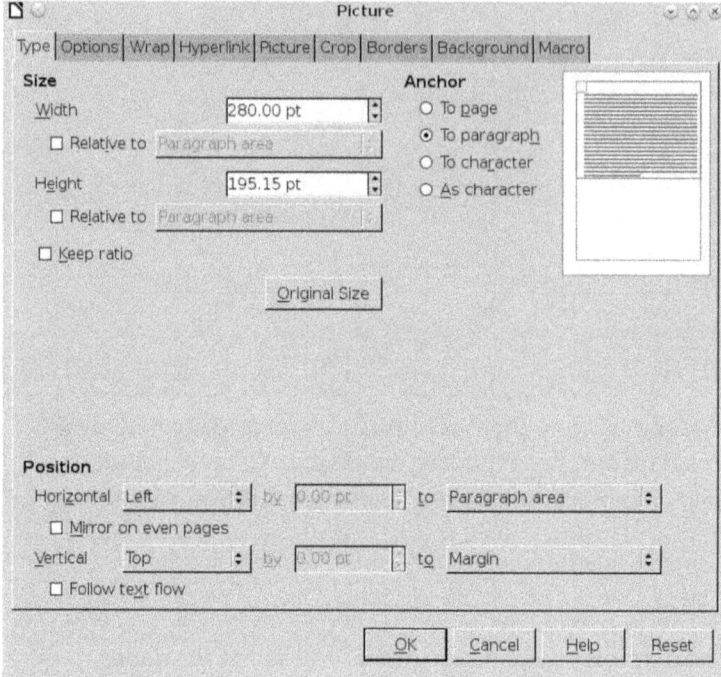

The TYPE tab includes various options for resizing, anchoring, and positioning images.

To help keep images in place, make any adjustments when first adding an image. If necessary, experiment first, making notes about the size you want, then delete your experiments and add the image again.

Positioning frames on the page

The POSITION options on the TYPE tab are the equivalent of the horizontal and vertical ALIGNMENT options on the right-click menu. You should adjust these as you are adding an image, reserving the right-click menu for experiments.

The horizontal options are LEFT, RIGHT, CENTER, and FROM LEFT (which works with an indent field called BY).

Each of these alignments can be relative to various reference points. Usually, the most useful reference point is LEFT PAGE BORDER.

By contrast, in many cases, you should use ENTIRE PAGE only if the document is intended for on-line use or your printer is capable of bleeds (that is, printing to the very edge of the page).

The vertical options are TOP, BOTTOM, CENTER, and FROM TOP (which also includes a space above field called BY). Usually, the most useful reference point will be MARGIN, the least useful ENTIRE PAGE.

STOP Caution

Do not use the FOLLOW TEXT FLOW option. It is included for compatibility with old OpenOffice.org documents, not for use today.

Setting anchors

An anchor is a reference point for positioning frames and images. You set the anchor on the TYPE tab for an image or frame.

The TYPE tab offers four options for the anchor: TO PAGE, TO PARAGRAPH, TO CHARACTER, and AS CHARACTER. The first three choices indicate what an object is positioned in relation to.

By contrast, AS CHARACTER indicates that the object is treated as a character. This choice means that the line that an object is placed upon has a height that is tall enough to display it fully.

Usually, any problems with AS CHARACTER can be solved by setting the line spacing for a paragraph style with AT LEAST.

Writer defaults images to TO PARAGRAPH when you insert an image. However, setting the anchor to AS CHARACTER seems the choice least likely to have objects shift spontaneously.

By contrast, if you keep TO PARAGRAPH, the image will be positioned relative to the anchor's paragraph, but can flip above the anchor sometimes.See "Using the Haugland workaround," page 253.

Choosing text wrap

Text wrap refers to how body text is positioned in relation to a frame. Text wrap features set how exterior text moves around the frame, and the spacing between exterior text and the frame. Usually, generous spacing improves the look of the page.

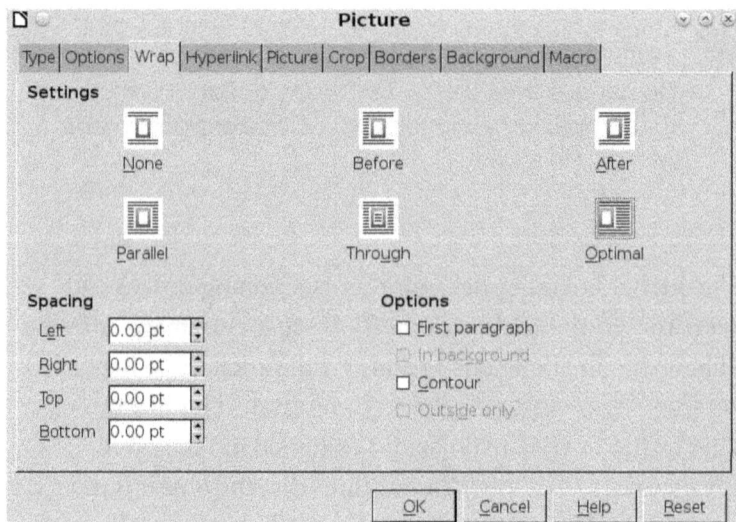

IMAGE > WRAP positions an object in relation to the text around it.

Writer has six settings on the WRAP tab for both frames and images:

- NONE: The frame interrupts the text, so there is no text to the left and right of the frame. This is a favorite strategy in technical manuals, because it requires minimal time positioning. However, it can make small images look even smaller because of the white space beside them. It is a good, average choice, but not always ideal.

- BEFORE: Text wraps above, below, and to the left, leaving white space on the right. This setting is especially useful for frames against the right margin.

- AFTER: Text wraps above, below, and to the right, leaving white space on the left. This setting is especially useful for frames against the left margin.

- PARALLEL: Text wraps equally on all sides of the frame, starting on the left, then jumping across the image to the right. Unless the text is very short, avoid this wrap, because most readers will have to concentrate to read the text.

- THROUGH: The frame is placed on top of the text, hiding it. If you use this option, you should also select WRAP > OPTIONS > IN BACKGROUND so that the text is visible. You might also make the image partly transparent so that the text is more readable.

- OPTIMAL: Automatically wraps text on all sides of the frame. If the frame is less than 2 centimeters from any margin, the text is not wrapped on that side.

Generally, OPTIMAL makes a reasonable default setting if one side of the frame is close to the left or the right margin. However, if the frame is centered, it requires readers' eyes to jump continually across the frame and should be avoided.

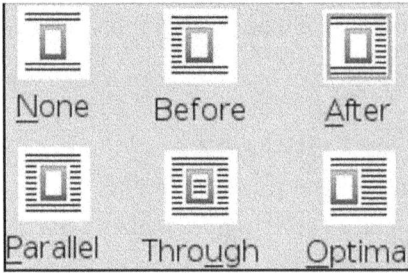

The six types of text wrap available in Writer.

Tip

Most of the text wrap settings leave a very even gap between the frame and body text. Select WRAP > OPTIONS > CONTOUR if you want the text wrap to conform more closely to the shape of the object in the frame.

Setting white space around a frame

The WRAP > SPACING fields set the white space on each side of the frame. These settings are often ignored, but they are as important as the text wrap setting. Too little spacing and the page looks cramped, while too much spacing weakens the association of the frame's contents with the body text around it.

As a general rule, the minimal white space around a frame should be half the line height in the body text. As much as three times the line height may also work, but anything more usually looks sparse.

Developing a white space policy

Consistency is essential to design. For this reason, you need to decide exactly how images and other objects fit into the text.

The basic space above and below is easy. However, what happens when the space above an image is added to the space below a heading? The result is too much white space. Even worse, the result can be that the heading, which you carefully set up so that it sat closer to what was below it than above, is now carefully poised midway between. To prevent such problems, you may decide that, in certain cases, an image should use less white space than usual.

Example: Developing a white space policy

Here is a sample policy that was used in one draft of this book (the final one is somewhat different):

- Images, tables and paragraphs all have a minimum of 8 points of white space above and below them.

- If another heading or other element gives enough additional white space above or below, then an element may not add any white space itself. The point is to be consistent and not to have any large gaps.

- The default width of all images is 280 points, the width between the margins.

- Images may be less than the complete page width when a dialog window is smaller than usual or is cropped.

- Images below a bullet or numbered item, or an indented paragraph, will align with the start of the text above them. This rule means making images 8 points narrower than normal, and setting the tables used to be indented 16 points FROM LEFT in the TABLE tab.

- Large images or tables will be on separate pages, introduced by a heading that forces a new page break.

Setting other wrap options

In addition to the basic text wrap choices, the WRAP tab includes several settings that modify how the settings work:

- FIRST PARAGRAPH: Starts a new paragraph below the frame if you press the ENTER key. Since this choice adds space according to the size of the object, you will have more control if you ignore this setting and adjust the white space exactly using the SPACING fields.

- IN BACKGROUND: Available with the THROUGH text wrap setting only. Treats the frame as an object in a stack of objects, sending its contents to the back so that the body text is at the front. This option is the equivalent of right-clicking on the contents and selecting ARRANGE > SEND TO BACK.

- CONTOUR: Wraps the text more closely to the shape of the object in the frame than choosing a text wrap setting alone can. This setting can give a more exact wrap, but it can also give the page a distractingly busy look, especially when the frame is small or has a complicated shape.

- ONLY OUTSIDE: Like CONTOUR, but ignores blank spaces in the object. It cannot be used with frames (that is, TEXT FRAMES), presumably because text is too regular for it to make any difference in the wrap.

Setting frame and image borders

Novice designers can be obsessive about frame borders, adding them everywhere. The result is usually cramped and awkward-looking.

Although the BORDERS tab contains numerous options, borders are mostly useful when at least one edge of an image is the same color as the page background, so that one blends into the other.

Even then, extra space around the image can be just as effective.

Setting frame backgrounds

While the dialog windows for frames and images include a BACKGROUND tab, often a background has no useful function.

A carefully selected background color might prevent an image blending into the page background, but a border or extra space is often an easier solution.

Setting general options

The ambiguously named OPTIONS tab in the Image dialog window contains miscellaneous options to do with editing and printing. Often, you can ignore these settings:

- NAME: For the frame or image. Writer adds an automatic name, such as FRAME15, but a more descriptive name is useful if you use the Navigator to jump around in a document. Using the file name for an image's name can help you stay organized.

- PROTECT: Prevents editing of CONTENT, POSITION, and SIZE. These options are useful when a document has multiple editors. PROTECT does not help an image stay in place.

- EDITABLE IN READ-ONLY DOCUMENT: Allows editing in a restricted document.

- PRINT: Includes frame or image when you print.

- TEXT DIRECTION: Applies only to non-Western European languages within a frame. Ignore this setting in English or other Western European languages.

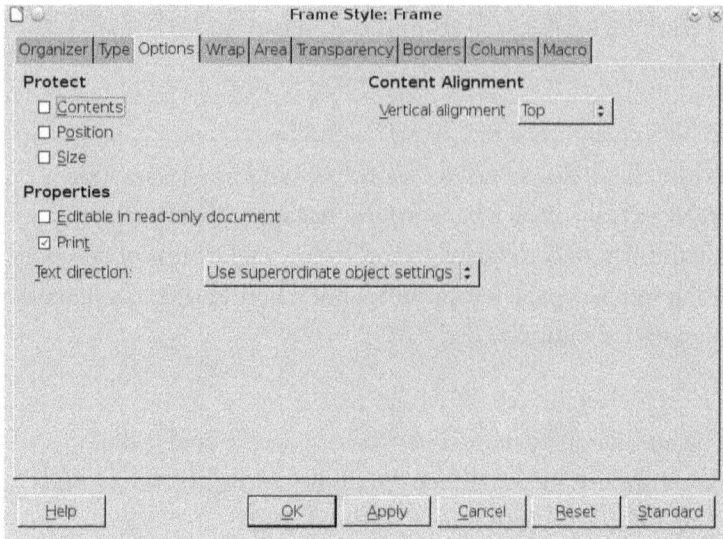

The OPTIONS tab for frame styles.

Adding columns

You can set multiple columns for a text frame on the COLUMNS tab in the dialog window.

You may prefer to insert a section from INSERT > SECTION... instead, since sections have more options than frames.

Adding hyperlinks and macros

In online documents, you can add hyperlinks (links) and macros that run when you click a frame or image.

You need the frame name from the OPTIONS tab to configure a hyperlink.

You can use some pre-defined macros, but to record a macro in LibreOffice, you first need to select TOOLS > OPTIONS > LIBREOFFICE > ADVANCED > OPTIONAL (UNSTABLE) OPTIONS > ENABLE MACRO RECORDING (LIMITED).

Caution

Remember that the tenth time users hear a sound or see a macro effect, many will wish for a way to turn it off.

Adding captions

The purpose of an image may be clear from the text around it, especially if the paragraph above introduces it with a colon.

However, at times, a caption adds clarity by repeating key words and concepts from the text. A caption may also explain the relevance of the image, or parts of the image whose relevance is not immediately obvious.

Used carefully, a caption may help to give detailed information in less space than it would take in body text. The only trouble may be that readers are not aware of the fact, and might miss key facts by skipping over the image.

Another consideration is that in online documents or when the caption is separated from the text that an image illustrates, the caption might be used as a cross-reference.

When you compose a caption, you may think that it is embarrassingly obvious. Sometimes, that may be true, and you may want to consider whether to use captions at all.

Most of the time, however, what is obvious to you after you have planned and written is much less obvious to readers. Generally, the worst that can happen is that readers skip over what seems irrelevant to them, without blaming the writer in any way. Under these circumstances, when in doubt, using a caption is always a reliable option.

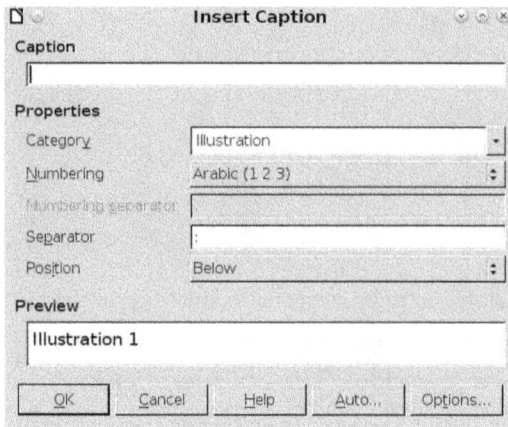

Insert Caption

Caption

Properties

Category	Illustration
Numbering	Arabic (1 2 3)
Numbering separator	
Separator	:
Position	Below

Preview

Illustration 1

OK	Cancel	Help	Auto...	Options...

Writer's caption options are especially useful when you plan on a table of contents for particular types of objects. Captions are automatically detected and used to create the content entries.

To add a caption:

1   Right-click anywhere in the image and select CAPTION from the context menu. The INSERT CAPTION dialog window opens.

2   Add the caption to the CAPTION field.

3   Consider whether you want to set the CATEGORY and NUMBERING fields and the separator between the number and the text. These are time-honored features for any objects added to a document, but many modern documents avoid them altogether.

Tip

You can add categories by typing them into the CATEGORY field. Once you add a new category, it is available to use again.

4 To prefix the image number with the chapter number, click the OPTIONS button and select the OUTLINE LEVEL that includes the chapter number.

You may also want to select a special character style for the chapter number, although usually there is no reason for more than a bold weight.

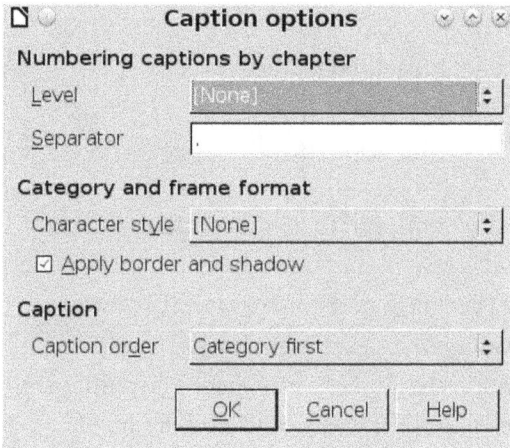

The CAPTION OPTIONS window opens off the main CAPTIONS dialog window.

5 Consider whether to select APPLY BORDER and SHADOW to the caption in the OPTIONS sub-window. Avoid using them if you cannot explain what purpose they serve. Often, you can do without either one.

6 Set the caption order, placing either the number (complete with chapter number preface) or the category first.

To add a chapter number, you must assign a numbering style to one paragraph style, and then assign the paragraph style to an outline level. HEADING 1 is often used for this purpose.

7 Set the caption POSITION to ABOVE or BELOW. A caption below an image is more common today, but a caption above may be useful if you need to explain something before readers look at the image.

You can edit the caption directly, or change its formatting by selecting CAPTION again from the right-click menu.

Formatting captions

Caption paragraphs are formatted using the CAPTION paragraph style. Contrary to common usage, the CAPTION paragraph style defaults to italic, but a regular weight is more common.

Similarly, the style does not need to be smaller than the body text. If anything, a smaller font for captions removes much of the convenience of adding the image in the first place. If you want to save space, use a narrow or condensed font style for captions.

In addition, the caption should have less space between it and the image than between it and the text below or above it. Proximity is one of the basic ways that design indicates that two parts of the document are related.

Adding automatic captions

Autocaptions immediately add a caption to all specified objects, using the CAPTION paragraph style.

To set up Autocaptions, select the types of objects for them, then follow the directions above for adding a caption.

Tip

You can select multiple Autocaptions to format at the same time.

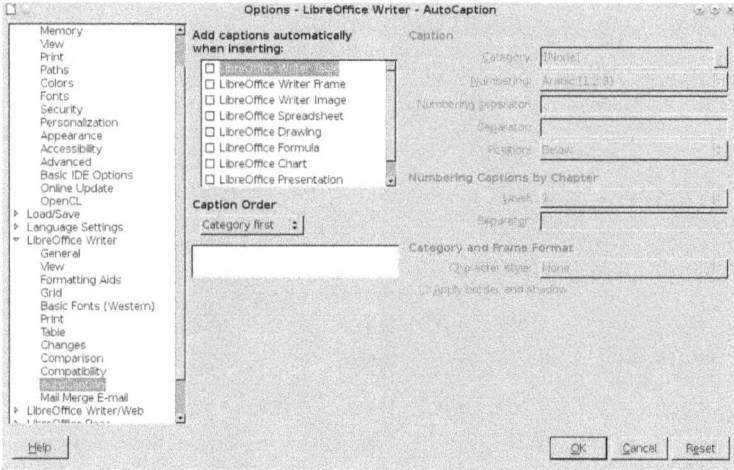

Set the objects to which you automatically want to add a caption from TOOLS > OPTIONS > LIBREOFFICE WRITER > AUTOCAPTION.

Making images stay in place

Many people have no trouble with graphics. Many others find that they shift constantly. Although no one has suggested a reason for these different experiences, they may be due to the different work habits of users, or to the operating system or LibreOffice version being used.

However, two work-arounds are known for Writer – but not, unfortunately, for other LibreOffice applications: the Haugland work-around and the table work-around. Since the table work-around limits some options, use it only after the Haugland workaround fails.

Using the Haugland workaround

In 2009, Solveig Haugland, one of the first people to write about OpenOffice.org, devised a solution for making images "reasonably manageable." Her solution is still the most reliable anyone has found.

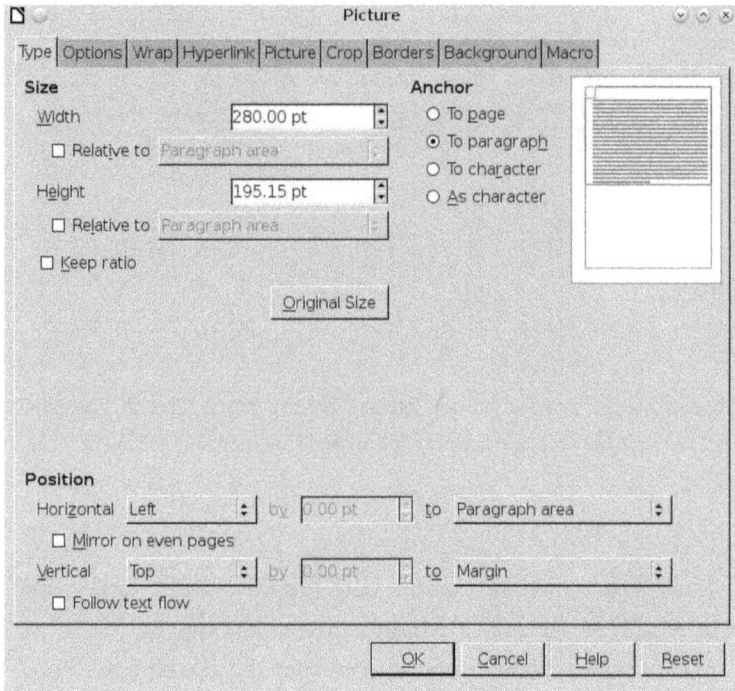

Haugland's workaround works mostly with the TYPE tab in the IMAGE dialog window.

Here is Haugland's solution, reworded and slightly reworked:

1   Create a new line, and click INSERT > IMAGE to add the image.

2   Click IMAGE from the right-click menu and go to the TYPE tab. If the frame is visible, you can select FRAME > TYPE instead.

3   Adjust the width and height of the image, using the SIZE fields on the TYPE tab. You will probably want to select the KEEP RATIO check box, to avoid distorting the image.

4 Using the right-click menu, set the anchor to As CHARACTER. This choice lets Writer treat the image the same way it would a letter or number.

5 Set the horizontal and vertical alignment if necessary. The vertical alignment rarely needs adjustment, while the horizontal alignment can generally remain on the left side.

6 Make any other formatting changes, and close the IMAGE dialog window.

7 If you find you need to make changes later, the safest approach is to delete the image and add it again with the changes.

Using the table workaround

If you continue to have problems with frames and objects staying where you placed them, try replacing them with tables. In effect, the table acts as a frame, except that for some reason images in a table are less likely to move around. This solution is similar to using tables for layout on a web page.

This workaround only gives you the option of wrapping text above and below the table. However, that limitation can free you to do things like putting the caption in a row to one side of the image to reduce the space occupied by the image.

To use the table workaround:

1 Create an IMAGE SPACER paragraph style with INDENTS & SPACING > LINE SPACING set to FIXED, and a line spacing of 0 points.

2 Check that tables are turned off in TOOLS > OPTIONS > LIBREOFFICE WRITER > AUTOCAPTION.

3   Place the cursor on a blank line. If necessary, change the paragraph style to DEFAULT STYLE to eliminate unnecessary numbers, bullets, or indentations.

4   Select TABLE > INSERT TABLE, and make a table with these characteristics: 1 column and 2 rows (or 1 column and 1 row if you are not using captions).

5   Before inserting, unselect HEADING and BORDER and select DON'T SPLIT TABLE OVER PAGES.

STOP Caution

The boundaries of the table are not the same as its borders. In some versions of LibreOffice, or with some settings, the boundaries may be visible in the editing window, but they will not print.

In others, the boundaries may show even in FILE > PRINT PREVIEW. To see how the table looks, right-click within it and unselect TABLE BOUNDARIES.

6   With the cursor in the table, right-click and select TABLE PROPERTIES to add the space above and below the table.

Like most measurements, these should usually be multiples of the line spacing. However, if the paragraphs above or below have spacing, adjust the table spacing to eliminate extra spacing.

7   If you want an indentation from the left, set the ALIGNMENT to FROM LEFT, and set the indentation in the SPACING > LEFT field.

This formatting aligns the image with indented text, which is a useful way of showing what text the image is connected to.

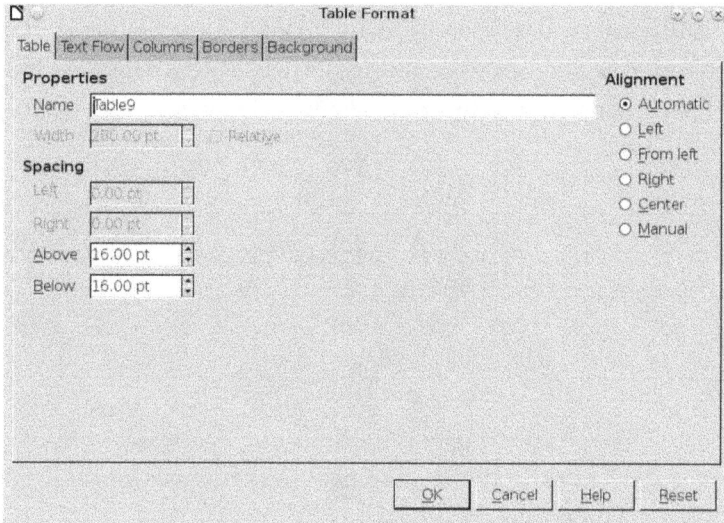

Use the ALIGNMENT and SPACING settings to place the table
that will contain the graphic.

8   Place the cursor in the top row of the table and click INSERT >
    IMAGE to add the image.

9   Right-click on the image, and click IMAGE > WRAP. Set the TOP
    and BOTTOM spacing to o to place the image in the upper left
    corner of the table. In this way, you only have to move the
    table, and can forget about the image.

10 Below the image in the top row, apply the IMAGE SPACER
    paragraph style. The bottom of the image is now aligned with
    the bottom side of the top row.

11 Using the CAPTION paragraph style, add the caption in the
    second row. Be sure that your formatting positions the caption
    closer to the image than to the text below the table. Do not use
    automatic captions (see "Adding automatic captions," page
    252).

Although full wrap options are unavailable with this work-around, you can use two columns, instead of two rows, and place the second column to the left or right of the image.

Tip

If you have multiple images to place together, put one image in each row or column.

Advanced uses of frames

The basic formatting of frames is straightforward. However, some of the advanced uses of some types of frames are less obvious. This section covers some of them.

STOP

Caution

These advanced uses may not work if frames are not staying in place.

Creating marginalia and sideheads

Once formatted, most frames are applied automatically. A major exception are marginalia – headings that are placed to the left of a body of text in a second column. Marginalia can give plenty of white space to a page, creating an inviting and original design, all of which outweigh the fact that marginalia usually take up more pages than a more conventional layout.

Marginalia were first named during the Middle Ages, when paper was so expensive that none of it was wasted. Instead of taking notes on a new piece of paper, clerks would add comments or even drawings in the margins. In Writer, marginalia are technically not placed in the margins – they just give the appearance of being so. That means that you can often get away with a narrower left margin than usual, since marginalia leave plenty of white space.

The main disadvantage of marginalia is that each one must be added manually. However, you may think the results are worth the final effort, since marginalia make headings easier to find.

Lorem ipsum dolor sit amet	Lorem ipsum dolor sit amet, consectetur adipiscing elit. Donec in libero consequat, hendrerit turpis quis, mollis velit. Maecenas maximus nunc faucibus sollicitudin convallis. Sed velit nisl, fermentum accumsan tempus ut, mollis sed justo. Aliquam eu tellus
	Vivamus tincidunt vel quam et aliquet. Mauris sed tortor dolor. Pellentesque accumsan est quis odio convallis suscipit. Fusce eu hendrerit ante, ut ornare turpis. Fusce eget tortor tellus. In justo e
	Aliquam posuere arcu quis mollis sollicitudin. Fusce ultrices congue quam, nec varius diam. Maecenas malesuada est eget nunc viverra, quis tempus orci rutrum. Praesent tortor augue, auctor sit amet augue et, faucibus elementum massa.
Vestibulum efficitur blandit felis nec ultricies	Nam nec nisi augue. Vestibulum ante ipsum primis in faucibus orci luctus et ultrices posuere cubilia Curae; Proin auctor elit augue, vitae bibendum nulla pulvinar nec. Pellentesque habitant morbi tristique senectus et netus et malesuada fames ac turpis egestas. Nullam tortor dui, semper vitae ante sit amet, tempus

Marginalia frames used to create sideheads to replacing normal headings.

To add sideheads:

1   Set INDENTS & SPACING > BEFORE TEXT in the TEXT BODY paragraph style so that the text will begin to the right of the marginalia frame. Be sure to leave a generous gap between the frame and the text.

2   Add the main text to the document.

3   Select INSERT > FRAME to add a text frame. Use the following format:

- Anchor it To PARAGRAPH.

- Make the frame borderless. The boundary of the frame will be visible when editing but it will not print, nor will it be visible in FILE > PRINT PREVIEW.

- Set the frame style to MARGINALIA.

4   Adding the frame adds the FRAME CONTENTS paragraph style. Edit the FRAME CONTENTS style to format the contents of the marginalia frames.

5   Give each marginalia frame the same width as the first one.

6   Add images and other objects so that they align with the start of the text.

Tip

Marginalia frames can also be used for commentary, or even as a high-maintenance alternative to footnotes. However, for each of these purposes, the setup is the same.

Tip

If a work-around is necessary, try using a table, adding a two-column row whenever you want a side-head, and using the FROM LEFT alignment in the second row to separate the text from the side-head.

Creating watermarks

Originally, a watermark was a logo that identified the manufacturer of paper.

Today, it refers to a faint image in the background of a page. Sometimes a modern watermark is a logo or a graphic relevant to the text, while at other times it is a short text that gives the status of the text – for instance, "Draft" or "Confidential – Your Eyes Only."

The text and objects in the document appear over top the watermark. The WATERMARK frame style positions a graphic frame for use as a watermark.

To create a watermark:

1   Create a frame and add an image or text to it.

Tip

You may want to create the image in a graphics editor first, and make it semi-transparent so that the text will be more visible.

2   Set the frame to use the WATERMARK frame style.

3   On the WRAP tab, select SETTINGS > THROUGH and OPTIONS > IN BACKGROUND.

Tip

Two other ways exist to add a watermark. The first is to add a basic frame with text or an image, and select from the right-click menu ARRANGE > SEND TO BACK.

The second is to add a bitmap as the Area for a paragraph, then lighten it using the TRANSPARENCY TAB. In this case, the watermark does not underlie the entire page.

If you need a work-around, create a transparent graphic with the dimensions of the space between the margins. Then add it to a page style as a background.

ullamcorper. Ut est diam, tempus vitae ipsum in, ultricies luctus metus. Sed vulputate sapien ut leo eleifend, ac feugiat urna accumsan. Phasellus porttitor velit nibh, sed convallis nunc mattis id. Mauris ultrices libero eget tortor iaculis suscipit.

Vivamus tincidunt vel quam et aliquet. Mauris sed tortor dolor. Pellentesque accumsan est quis odio convallis suscipit. Fusce eu hendrerit ante, ut ornare turpis. Fusce eget tortor tellus. In justo elit, vulputate vitae neque a, commodo imperdiet elit. Mauris ornare, lectus sed mattis maximus, risus odio tempor diam, in mollis mauris nisi non augue. Donec id nisl ac mi vehicula congue. Quisque convallis odio in erat sollicitudin luctus. Nulla posuere purus in est elementum, vel molestie erat vulputate. Cras aliquet ut orci ac varius. Sed non nunc in nibh maximus condimentum. Pellentesque habitant morbi tristique senectus et netus et malesuada fames ac turpis egestas.

Nam nec nisi augue. Vestibulum ante ipsum primis in faucibus orci luctus et ultrices posuere cubilia Curae; Proin auctor elit augue, vitae bibendum nulla pulvinar nec. Pellentesque habitant morbi tristique senectus et netus et malesuada fames ac turpis egestas. Nullam tortor dui, semper vitae ante sit amet, tempus volutpat libero. Etiam sit amet arcu ut purus euismod egestas. Curabitur vitae risus eget arcu sollicitudin sodales. Aliquam posuere arcu quis mollis sollicitudin. Fusce ultrices congue quam, nec varius diam. Maecenas malesuada est eget nunc viverra, quis tempus orci rutrum. Praesent tortor augue, auctor sit amet augue et, faucibus elementum massa.

Nunc iaculis quis lectus ut semper. Etiam nisi ipsum, dapibus in iaculis non, elementum vel neque. Sed rutrum metus vitae enim ullamcorper, vel sollicitudin nunc commodo. Aenean ornare massa sed felis porttitor, sit amet tincidunt lorem suscipit. Class aptent taciti sociosqu ad litora torquent per conubia

A watermark used to indicate that a document is a draft.

Tip

Whenever possible, do not insert a watermark that you will need to edit later. If you do need to edit a watermark, select it and click FORMAT > ARRANGE > BRING TO FRONT.

Use the Navigator if you have trouble selecting the watermark or its frame.

Setting text flow between frames

In advanced layouts, using multiple text frames can be easier than using sections or columns. For example, if you create a

Designing with LibreOffice

brochure on a single piece of paper, the inside pages (pages 2-3) are two connected frames.

To have text flow from one frame to another:

1 Create two or more frames using INSERT > FRAME, leaving both empty.

2 Select the first frame.

3 Click the LINK FRAMES icon on the FRAMES tool bar. The tool bar displays only when a frame is selected.

4 Select the target frame (the one that text will flow into from the first frame).

When the frames are connected, a blue line runs between them when one frame is selected.

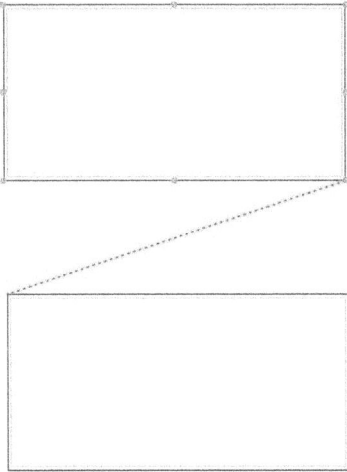

The diagonal blue line indicates that the two frames are connected. In other words, text from the first frame will flow automatically into the second frame.

5   Edit the frames as needed – for example, making them borderless, or coloring the borders or background.

Tip

If you anchor two text frames in the header of a page style, then position the frames on the page and link them, the same arrangement of frames appears on every instance of the page style.

Troubleshooting the connection of frames

If you are having trouble linking, the reason could be:

- The target frame has contents.
- The target frame is already linked from another frame. A frame can only receive text from one frame and flow into one other frame.
- The two frames are in different sections, or in different headers or footers.
- One frame is nested in the other.

Tip

If you need a work-around, try using tables.

Working around the problems

If you think working with frame styles or images is needlessly complex – you are right. Part of that complexity is because LibreOffice offers more options than your average word processor, but the largest part is the difficulty of keeping images where you place them.

10

Structured prose: lists and tables

Lists and tables are sometimes called structured prose. The name contrasts them to the relative formlessness of body text.

Structured text is easy to read, but takes up more space than body text. This extra space is no problem online, but can add to the pages and therefore the expense of hard copy.

In most word processors, list options are included in paragraph styles, while table styles are not provided at all. By contrast, Writer treats bulleted and numbered lists as a separate type of style, and tables as a sort of pseudo-style, or at least a gallery of saved formats.

Writer's separate list styles have several advantages:

- Lists have more formatting choices, which would be harder to offer if all the choices were squeezed into a single tab for paragraph styles.

- The same list style can be used with multiple paragraph styles, avoiding duplication of design work.

- A paragraph's list style can be changed with a single selection.

Table styles are due to be added to Writer in the future, but for now tables are formatted in a mixture of manual and style-like editing.

Understanding the types of list

With list styles, you can create:

- Bullet lists: Unordered lists whose items start with a bullet, special character, dingbat, or graphic.

- Numbered lists: Ordered lists whose items start with a number, upper or lower case letters, or upper and lower case Roman numerals.

- Outline lists: Hierarchical summaries of an argument or piece of writing, in which each level has its own numbering system.

All these types of list are in common use today, especially online.

However, what most people do not appreciate is that each has its own set of conventions about how they are structured and used – conventions that are rarely taught in schools, and that most people never observe or learn.

Understanding bulleted lists

Bullets are probably descended from midpoints, the all-purpose separator used in medieval European manuscripts. However, midpoints were used to cram as much as possible on each line because parchment and other writing materials were expensive.

By contrast, bullets take up more space. They take full advantage of the cheapness of wood or rag pulp paper compared to vellum for printing.

More recently, of course, the rise of online reading means that space is no longer an issue, so bullet points can be used at will without increasing the expense of publication.

Nobody has documented exactly what happened, but the name suggests that bulleted lists started being used after the invention of guns loaded with balls.

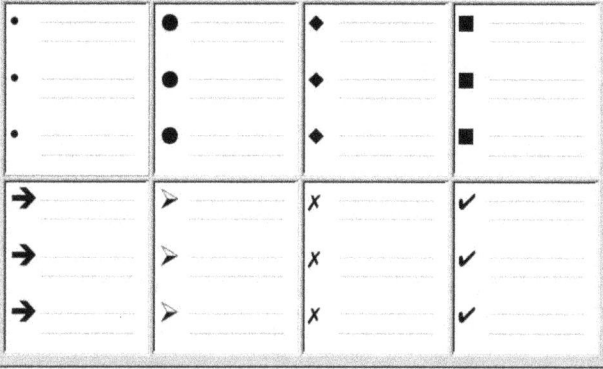

Writer's pre-defined bullet types.

However, we do know that, by the mid-twentieth century, bulleted lists became popular in technical documents. More recently, slide shows have further spread the use of bullets.

Learning the conventions for bullets

The use of bullet lists follows well-defined rules. Bullet lists:

- Are used only when the order of the points is irrelevant. You might want to arrange points for rhetorical effect, starting with one fairly important point and ending with your strongest point, but readers do not actually need to know one point before another. The HTML tag for bullet lists, <UL> (unordered list), emphasizes this convention.

- Have three points or more. If you have two points, they both stay in the body of the text.

- Are introduced in the last sentence in the body text above them either without any punctuation, or with a colon.

- Consist of points that are all grammatical completions of the last sentence in the paragraph before them. That means that each point has a similar grammatical structure to the others. In this bullet list, for instance, each point starts with a present tense verb.

- May be sentence fragments, but should be consistent with each other. For example, they could be all nouns or participles.

- Start with a bullet on the left margin, then indent for the text. If they are lists within lists, then the bullet has the same indent as the text in the top level list. The extra indentations of raw HTML and Microsoft Word are the exceptions, not the convention.

- Can start with either an upper or lower case letter, so long as the convention is consistent throughout the list and the document.

- End each point with the same punctuation. No punctuation, commas, semi-colons, and periods are all valid choices. What matters is the consistency of list items and of all lists within the document.

- Are generally no more than 6–8 items long. Much longer, and the ease of reading is lost.

- Do not use an "and," "or," or any other word to introduce the last point in the list, even though that would be grammatically correct.

- Are sometimes considered too informal to use. When in doubt, avoid them.

Understanding numbered lists

While people number lists all the time, the convention is that numbered lists should only be used when the order of the information matters.

For instance, in a procedure in a technical manual, one step might be impossible – or even dangerous – without doing another one first.

1)	1.	(1)	I.
2)	2.	(2)	II.
3)	3.	(3)	III.
A)	a)	(a)	i.
B)	b)	(b)	ii.
C)	c)	(c)	iii.

Writer's pre-defined numbered lists.

Learning the conventions of numbered lists

Numbered lists have fewer conventions than bullet lists, but they do have a few:

- They are used when the order of items is important. If the order is irrelevant, use bullet lists instead.

- Like bullet lists, they are used only for three items or more. Two-step procedures stay in the body of the text.

- They are generally introduced in the body text by a summary of the overall task they describe that ends in a colon. For example, "To install the software update, follow these steps:" or, simply "To install:"

- Each step can have multiple paragraphs, most of them unnumbered, describing what happens when it is performed or the alternatives.

- The steps in a procedure should be less than a dozen (some suggest 6–8, based on the maximum number of items the average human can easily remember). Any more are intimidating and harder to remember.

Tip

If each step has multiple paragraphs or you have more than about a dozen steps, you may need to break down the list into smaller lists or else present the points as ordinary body text.

Understanding outline lists

Outline lists summarize the structure of a much longer, typically unwritten document. In finished technical and legal documents, they are used in headings to make the structure obvious, although this use is becoming less common than it was a couple of decades ago.

Writer gives several options for outline lists. List styles create an outline method that uses a single paragraph style. When such a paragraph style is in use, you change the level and the numbering by pressing the TAB key to descend a level, and SHIFT+TAB to ascend a level. This single style outlining is by far the quickest to apply and learn.

1.	1.	1.	1.
1.	a)	(a)	1.
1.1.a)	1.a.•	1.a.i.	1.1.1.
•	•	A.	1.
1.1.a.••	1.a.•••	1.a.i.A.•.	1.1.1.1.1.
I.	A.	1	➤
A.	I.	1	→
I.A.i.	A.I.a.	1.1.1	➤→♦)
a)	i.	1	•
I.A.i.a.•	A.I.a.i.•	1.1.1.1.1	➤→♦••

Writer's pre-defined outline list styles. Remember that bullets imply that the order is unimportant.

The conventions for outline lists are:

- Usually, a different numbering system is used for each level to help distinguish them.

- Levels can be ordered using Arabic numerals, upper and lower case Roman numerals, and upper and lower case letters.

- Upper case Roman numerals are usually reserved for the top level, and upper case letters are used before lower case ones. Another alternative is Arabic numbers followed by lower case letters. However, these rules are not fixed.

- In technical manuals, you used to see multiple levels in a heading (for instance, I.A.2 or 1.1.1). These headings have largely fallen out of practice except in a few specialized cases such as legal documents, for the obvious reason that they are hard to remember. Also, if each heading is indented, as was common in the days of typewriters when formatting choices were limited, after two or three levels, almost no space is left for text.

Naming list styles

LibreOffice uses LIST 1-5 for default bullet lists, and
NUMBERING 1-5 for numbered lists. However, these names are too
limited to remember easily. Instead, add your own styles and give
them descriptive names like ARABIC NUMERAL BLUE or LOWER CASE
INDENTED.

Along with each basic paragraph style, LibreOffice also
includes list styles ending in CONT. (Continue), END, and START.
You can use these styles to customize lists.

For example, the START list style might have extra space above
it to separate the list from the body text, and the END list style
extra space below it.

The CONT. style is sometimes used for unnumbered
paragraphs in a list that have a different format. However, the

name suggests using it with a list style with the NUMBERING field set to NONE on the OPTIONS tab, and (CONTINUED) or the equivalent in the BEFORE field.

The text in the BEFORE field will be added automatically whenever you apply the style.

Tip

If the paragraph has no other content than the BEFORE field, you need to type a space before you press the ENTER key. Otherwise, the paragraph disappears.

If you decide not to use these styles, you can right-click on each of them in the STYLES AND FORMATTING window and hide them. You can go to the HIDDEN view and unhide them later if you decide you need them after all.

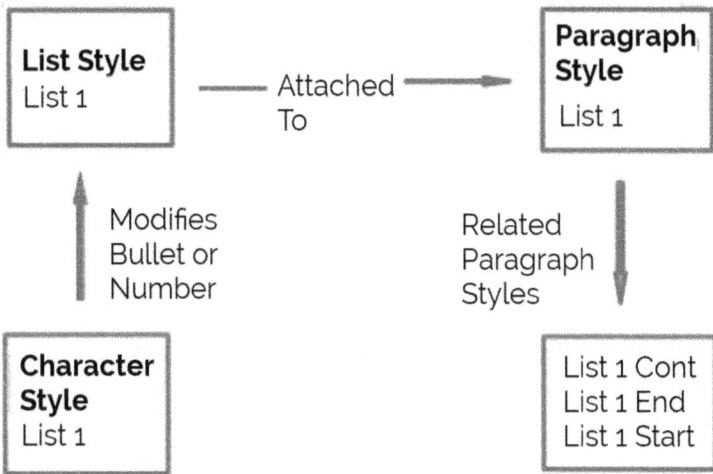

```
┌──────────────┐                      ┌──────────────┐
│ List Style   │ ──── Attached ────▶  │ Paragraph    │
│ List 1       │        To            │ Style        │
│              │                      │ List 1       │
└──────────────┘                      └──────────────┘
       ▲                                     │
    Modifies                             Related        │
    Bullet or                            Paragraph      ▼
    Number                               Styles
┌──────────────┐                      ┌──────────────┐
│ Character    │                      │ List 1 Cont  │
│ Style        │                      │ List 1 End   │
│ List 1       │                      │ List 1 Start │
└──────────────┘                      └──────────────┘
```

Give related styles similar names and you can locate the ones you need more quickly.

Applying list styles

You can apply a list style just as you would any other style, placing the cursor in a paragraph, and then selecting the list style from the STYLES AND FORMATTING window.

However, the most effective approach is to create a paragraph style that is attached to the list style. Go to the NUMBERING STYLE field on the OUTLINE & NUMBERING tab for the paragraph style, and select the list style from the drop-down list. This method also has the advantage of requiring fewer mouse clicks to apply the style.

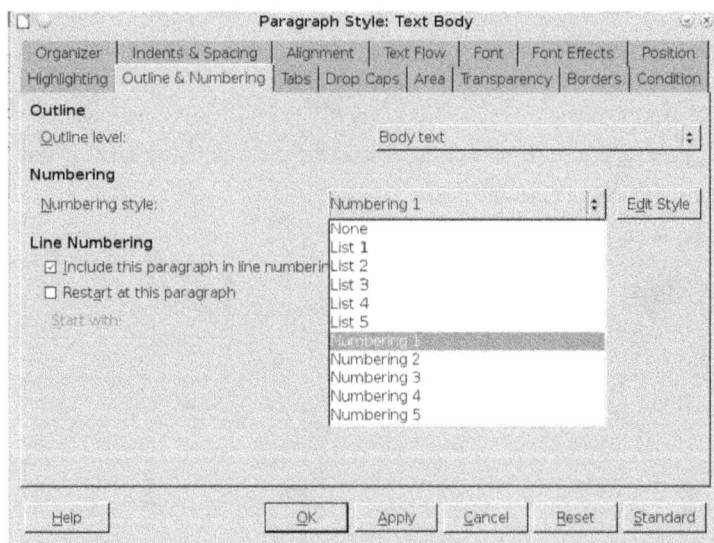

Select OUTLINE & NUMBERING > NUMBERING STYLE to select from the drop-down list the list style to associate with a paragraph style.

Formatting list styles

You have two ways of formatting bullets and numbers in list styles.

The quick way is to select a style from the BULLETS, NUMBERING STYLE, OUTLINE, or IMAGE tabs for a list style. Each of these tabs give a variety of options, although not an exhaustive list.

However, I suggest you avoid using any choices on the IMAGE tab unless you want a retro mid-1990s look.

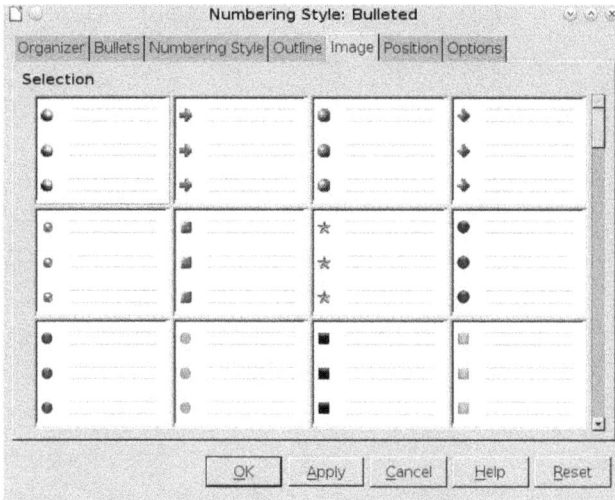

The bullets on the IMAGE tab are too old-fashioned to use.

The second and more practical way is to customize bullets or numbered lists for yourself, using the OPTIONS and POSITION tabs.

Both the POSITION and OPTIONS tabs have ten levels. This setting is mostly useful for creating a single outline numbering style, in which the numbering changes each time you press the TAB key (see "Understanding outline lists," page 270).

For most bulleted and numbered lists, either set the LEVEL to 1, or leave the LEVEL at the default 1-10.

If your design gets muddled, restart by clicking the DEFAULT button on the POSITION tab or RESET button on the OPTIONS tab.

Positioning bullets, numbers, and list items

The POSITION tab sets up the spacing before bullets or numbers, and between the bullet or number and the text.

When a list style is linked to a paragraph style, editing the fields on the POSITION tab in the list number dialog results in changes to the INDENT > BEFORE TEXT and INDENT > FIRST LINE settings on the INDENTS & SPACING tab for the paragraph style.

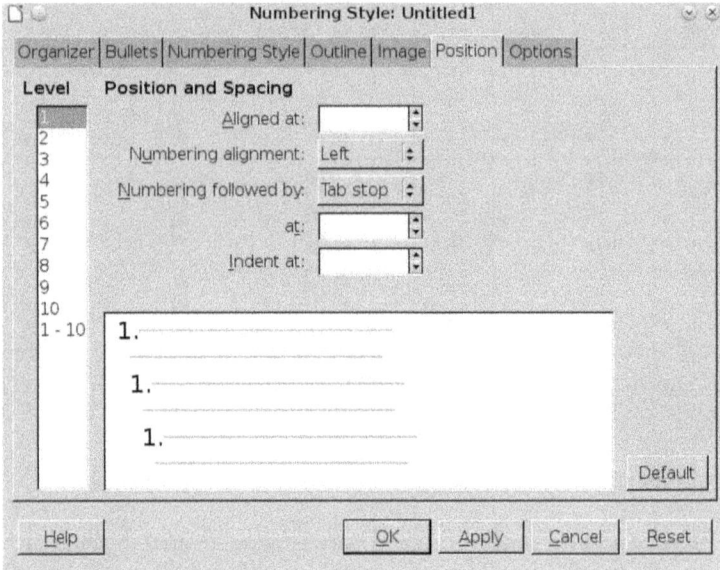

The POSITION tab is one of two tabs in the list style dialog window for customizing lists.

The reverse is also true. However, to avoid complications, make all the changes on the POSITION tab for the list style. Not only is that the logical place to look for changes on the list style, but adjusting the paragraph settings usually involves negative entries for the FIRST LINE field, which can complicate editing immensely.

Understanding position fields

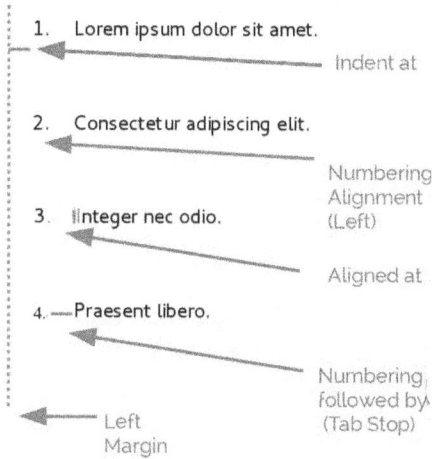

1. Lorem ipsum dolor sit amet.
   — Indent at

2. Consectetur adipiscing elit.

   Numbering
   Alignment
3. Iinteger nec odio.   (Left)

   Aligned at

4. Praesent libero.

   Numbering
   followed by
   Left   (Tab Stop)
   Margin

Fields on the POSITION tab for list styles and what they refer to. In this case, the list is indented from the left margin, which often is not the case.

When you are defining a new list style, the important fields on the POSITION tab are:

- ALIGNED AT: The vertical position for numbers, measured from the left margin. In most cases, you can leave this field at 0 (at the left margin). However, if you use any NUMBERING ALIGNMENT except LEFT, numbers set this field to another value.

- NUMBERING ALIGNMENT: How the bullet or number is aligned. Most of the time, you can leave this field at the default of LEFT, but if you are having trouble positioning text, changing the alignment to CENTER or RIGHT can sometimes solve the problem, especially for lists or levels that require two-digit numbers.

Left	Center	Right
1. Lorem ipsum dolor sit amet.	1. Lorem ipsum dolor sit amet.	1. Lorem ipsum dolor sit amet.
2. Consectetur adipiscing elit.	2. Consectetur adipiscing elit.	2. Consectetur adipiscing elit.
3. Integer nec odio.	3. Integer nec odio.	3. Integer nec odio.

The dotted line is the margin in this example. If the value of the NUMBERING ALIGNMENT is 0, then choosing CENTER or RIGHT can force the numbers into the left margin.

- NUMBERING FOLLOWED BY: Sets the space between the number or bullet and the text. Although the choices include SPACE or NOTHING, the choice that offers the most control is TAB STOP. Set the exact tab in the AT field directly below the drop-down list.

- ALIGNED AT: Sets where the numbers or bullets are on the line. In many cases, this setting is 0 points – that is, against the left margin.

- INDENT AT: Sets the start of the text. This setting should be equal or greater to the tab stop set for NUMBERING FOLLOWED BY.

STOP

Caution

This setting should not be more than about two line-heights, or else the connection between the bullet or number and the text might be lost.

Formatting ordered (numbered) lists

To create a numbered list, select a numbering style from the NUMBER field on the OPTIONS tab. The selections in the drop-down list begin with typical choices for Western European languages: Arabic, upper and lower case letters, and upper and lower case Roman numerals. Scroll down, and options for Bulgarian, Russian, Serbian, and Greek are available.

Numbering Style: Arabic Numerals

Organizer | Bullets | Numbering Style | Outline | Image | Position | Options

Level   Numbering

Level		
1	Number	1, 2, 3, ...
2		I, II, ...
3	Character Style	A, B, C, ...
4		a, b, c, ...
5	Show sublevels	I, II, III, ...
6		i, ii, iii, ...
7	Separator	A, .., AA, .., AAA, ...
8		a, .., aa, .., aaa, ...
9	Before	Bullet
10		Graphics
1 - 10	After	Linked graphics
		None
	Start at	A, Б, .., Aa, Аб, ... (Bulgarian)
		a, б, .., aa, аб, ... (Bulgarian)
		A, Б, .., Aa, Бб, ... (Bulgarian)
	All Levels	a, б, .., aa, бб, ... (Bulgarian)
		A, Б, .., Aa, Аб, ... (Russian)
	☐ Consecutive r	a, б, .., aa, аб, ... (Russian)
		A, Б, .., Aa, Бб, ... (Russian)
		a, б, .., aa, бб, ... (Russian)
		A, Б, .., Aa, Аб, ... (Serbian)
		a, б, .., aa, аб, ... (Serbian)
		A, Б, .., Aa, Бб, ... (Serbian)
		a, б, .., aa, бб, ... (Serbian)
		A, B, Г, ... (Greek Upper Letter)
		α, β, γ, ... (Greek Lower Letter)

Help   Reset

Select a numbering style from the OPTIONS tab.

Adding characters before and after numbers

You can set up to 40 characters before or after the actual number using the BEFORE and AFTER fields. These characters are added automatically whenever the list style they are attached to is applied.

Common characters after a number might be a period, a parenthesis, or both. Alternatively, you might put a parenthesis both before or after the number, or text such as STEP # in the BEFORE field. In a LIST CONT. style, you might add (CONTINUED) before.

More elaborately, you might set a paragraph style to start at the top of the page, then attach to it a list style with text so that the paragraph style will automatically add text.

In a numbered list, you can choose the number of outline levels in the list by adjusting the SHOW SUBLEVELS field. For example, if you decided to show three sublevels, the first use of the third sublevel would be numbered 1.1.1.

STOP

Caution

Using the BEFORE, AFTER, and/or SHOW SUBLEVELS fields means that the settings on the POSITION tab need to be adjusted so there is enough space between the number and the text.

Step #1:

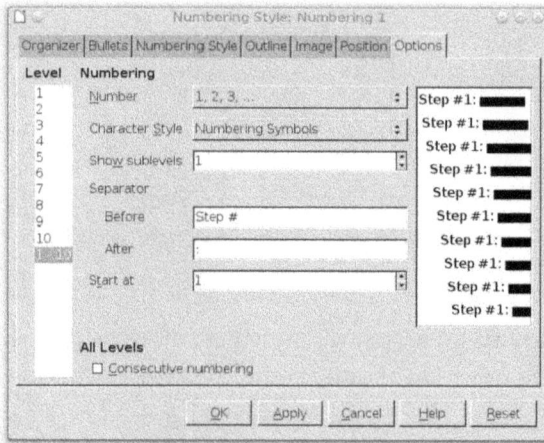

Characters before and after numbers in a list, created using the BEFORE and AFTER fields, increase the versatility of list styles.

Setting the character style

By default, the CHARACTER STYLE field for numbered lists is set to the NUMBERING SYMBOL character style, and for bulleted lists to the BULLETS character style.

For most purposes, you probably have no reason to change these defaults. Unless modified, these character styles use the same font and font size as the DEFAULT STYLE character style, and apply to both the number and any text in the BEFORE or AFTER fields.

Common modifications include making the numbers or bullets larger, giving them a corporate color, making them bold, or using a condensed version of a font.

STOP Caution

You may need to change the text indent if you use a larger font, especially for two or three digit numbers. The line height may also need to be increased.

Working with two-digit list numbers

Numbered lists with two digits can displace list items, upsetting your carefully calculated designs by offsetting the text too much.

9. Lorem ipsum dolor sit amet, consectetur adipiscing elit.

10. Fusce molestie, nisl eu suscipit imperdiet, nibh orci sodales erat, in scelerisque justo lacus vitæ leo

Unless extra spacing is provided, the list items are displaced when the numbering enters two digits.

You have several options to correct this problem:

• Never have a list with more than nine items. Rewrite lists that have more, combining steps or dividing one list into two or more shorter ones. This arrangement may make your instructions the easiest to remember.

- Add extra space between the number and the list item using the INDENT AT field. Do not add so much space that the association between numbers and list items is lost.
- Adjust the size of the numbers using OPTIONS > CHARACTER STYLE.
- Set the NUMBERING ALIGNMENT to RIGHT. Watch that this change does not extend numbers into the left margin.

Restarting a numbered list

The OPTIONS tab for a numbering style includes a START AT field. However, notice that this field refers to the first time that the list style is used in a document. It is not a tool for re-starting the numbering.

To restart the numbering in a list, right-click on a paragraph with a list and select RESTART NUMBERING from the menu.

Reversing number order

People occasionally ask for numbered lists that count down from the starting number, instead of up – presumably for Top 10 lists and other countdowns. Unfortunately, LibreOffice provides no way short of a custom macro for reverse order in lists.

A reverse order list must be entered manually. Since LibreOffice does not recognized reverse order lists, it will not automatically generate numbers.

Designing unordered (bulleted) lists

The default character style for bullets is BULLETS. It gives you a standard bullet for the Default style. However, you might want to change the symbol using the CHARACTER field. Selecting the

CHARACTER field opens a dialog window from which you can choose any symbol supported by the current font.

To choose a truly unusual bullet, set the character style to use a dingbat font. However, be careful: too detailed or unusual a dingbat distracts from the contents.

STOP

Caution

When you use an unusual character style for bullets, be sure to include the font used when you share a file.

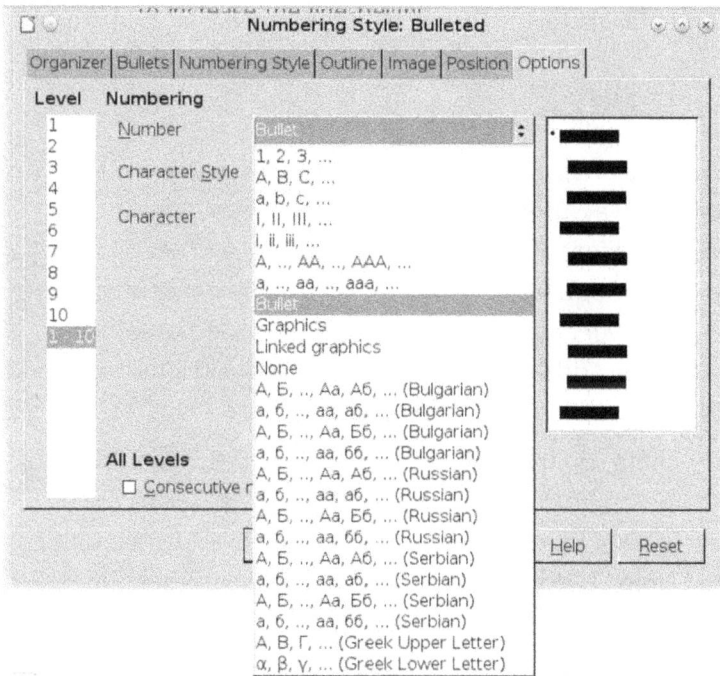

The field name is deceptive: To set up a bullet list, select OPTIONS > NUMBER > BULLET in a list style.

If your design includes nested bullets – that is, bullet lists within bullet lists – you might want to create an additional list style with a name like BULLETS2.

However, if you do use more than one bullet list style, make sure their designs are compatible. In fact, indenting the nested bullets and nothing more is enough to distinguish them from the top level bullets.

Example: Making a checklist

Depending on the characters you choose, bulleted list styles can serve as more than unordered lists. For example, a bullet list can be made into a checklist by selecting the font or character used for the bullet.

If you want a checklist to be used with a pen, set up the list style in the usual way, using a character style that uses the OpenSymbol font that ships with LibreOffice, and assign the character U+E00B (a shaded open box) as the bullet (that is two zeros, not lower case "o"s). Print the list, and it is immediately ready for use. Add some corporate branding and letterhead, and the To Do list can be used in business.

If you want to use the list on the computer, create two list styles, one that uses the character U+2752, and one that uses the character U+E531 (a box with a check mark). Create the list using the first style, then tick off an item by applying the second style to it.

Depending on the purpose of the list, you can also create a third list style that uses the character U+E532 (an X mark) to indicate items that were not completed.

❑ Lorem ipsum dolor sit

☑ Etiam dictum mattis

☒ Nulla facilisi

With three list styles, you can create both manual and computer-based checklists. Change the PARAGRAPH style and its associated LIST style as each task is completed or marked as undone.

Using images as bullets

Using an image instead of a standard bullet is a convenient way to add some originality to your document. However, you are limited by the small size at which most bullets display. Mostly, you need simple images with strong contrast as a substitute bullet. Often, a black and white image will be more effective.

Images used for bullets are also a way to position an image on a page. In particular, they can be used to create tip and warning signs in a technical manual or an informal text.

In either case, select a graphic to use from POSITION > NUMBER in the dialog window for the LIST style.

Choosing GRAPHICS embeds the picture within the document file. By contrast, LINKED GRAPHICS only adds a link to the graphic. See "Choosing linking or embedding," page 237.

STOP

Caution

If the image is cut off, you need either to adjust the image size, or else change the line spacing to AT LEAST so the top half of the characters in a line is not chopped off..

After you choose GRAPHICS or LINKED GRAPHICS, the window lists a set of fields for editing the bullet:

- The SELECT button opens a file manager to select the picture.

- The WIDTH and HEIGHT fields set the size at which the picture displays. They do not affect the original picture file.

  Remember that too large a height requires changing the paragraph LINE SPACING setting to AT LEAST so that the letters are not cut off at the top.

- KEEP RATIO, when selected, ensures that changing either the WIDTH or HEIGHT field changes the other proportionally.

- ALIGNMENT can usually be ignored, but can help with the spacing between the bullet and the text.

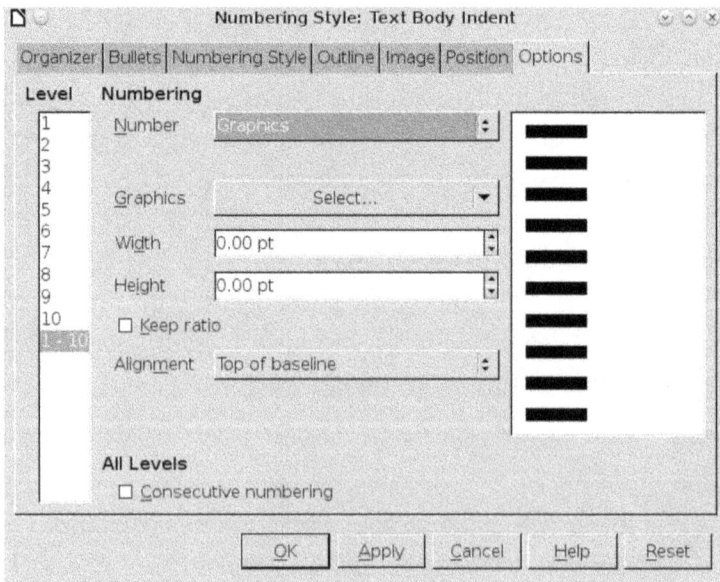

The fields for using a picture as a bullet appear after you have selected OPTIONS > NUMBER > GRAPHICS or LINKED GRAPHICS.

Example: Repeating graphics using lists

Graphic bullets are especially useful for reoccurring graphics. For example, in a technical document, you could use a graphic to mark a note, caution, or warning, as this book does.

To use bullets for repeated graphics:

1   Create the style, setting it up to use the graphic (see "Positioning bullets, numbers, and list items," page 276).

2   Create a paragraph style to link the list style to. If you want a logo at the top of every page, create an automatic page break on the paragraph style's TEXT FLOW tab.

3   Apply the paragraph style as needed.

4   Type the text to accompany the graphic. You must enter at least one character or a space, or else the graphic disappears when you press the ENTER key, leaving the indent but no bullet.

Setting up and designing tables

Tables began to be used in the eighteenth or nineteenth century, when scientists first appreciated their ease of reading and how they could suggest new relations between data.

Charles Babbage, who designed (but never built) the first computer, was especially fascinated with tables, especially for mathematical purposes, publishing his own tables of logarithms early in his career. Part of the intended purpose of his never-built Analytical Engine was to use and generate tables more efficiently.

LibreOffice does not have currently have styles for tables. For now, the next best thing is to to use TABLE > AUTOFORMAT.

Tip

You do not need to have the same number of rows and columns as in the table from which you made the AutoFormat. AUTOFORMAT does its best to apply the format despite differences.

Planning tables

As you design a template, decide what table formats the document will have.

The most common are:

- Plain: Uses borders, with the thinnest possible lines.

- No borders or background: This style is ideal for comparisons in point forms. It needs a reasonable amount of white space to replace the borders.

- Shaded: Uses a background for alternate rows in place of borders. The different colors help readers follow information horizontally within the table.

Tip

Keep the spacing around tables consistent. Most times, you will want to use the entire space between the horizontal margins. Watch, too, for extra space added by paragraphs above and below the table.

- Place sample tables of the appropriate widths in TABLE > AUTOFORMAT (see "Using AutoFormats," page 298).

Lorem ipsum	Dolor sit amet	Consectetur	Duis sit amet
Viverra quam eu.	Duis eget purus felis.	Tempor lorem tempus efficitur bibendum eget.	Pellentesque habitant morbi tristique senectus.
Fames ac turpis egestas.	Cras ornare justo non commodo tristique.	A feugiat tortor consequat eu.	Bibendum massa nec, tempor libero.

Lorem ipsum	Dolor sit amet	Consectetur	Duis sit amet
Viverra quam eu.	Duis eget purus felis.	Tempor lorem tempus efficitur bibendum eget nequ	Pellentesque habitant morbi tristique senectus et netus et malesuada .
Fames ac turpis egestas.	Cras ornare justo non commodo tristique.	A feugiat tortor consequat eu.	Bibendum massa nec, tempor libero.

Lorem ipsum	Dolor sit amet	Consectetur	Duis sit amet
Viverra quam eu.	Duis eget purus felis.	Tempor lorem tempus efficitur bibendum eget neque.	Pellentesque habitant morbi tristique senectus et netus et malesuada .
Fames ac turpis egestas.	Cras ornare justo non commodo tristique.	A feugiat tortor consequat eu.	Bibendum massa nec, tempor libero.

Basic table designs. When designing a template, choose a few designs and stay with them, rather than designing each table as the need arises.

The three shown here are classical designs that should serve as basic patterns for most purposes, and are compatible if two or more are used together. As you can see, modern typography favors simple designs. They may go out of fashion, but they will always remain functional.

For convenience, the boundaries of the borderless table in the middle are shown within Writer, but do not print.

To see how a borderless table looks when printed, view it from FILE > PRINT PREVIEW.

Tip

LibreOffice usually offers a choice of tables with different backgrounds for row headings and ordinary rows.

However, modern convention favors minimizing the use of backgrounds.

Designing tables

The goal of tables is to present information efficiently. Cluttered or over-designed tables work against that goal. If you are working in a Western European language like English, these rules should ensure that your tables serve their function properly:

- Headings should be horizontal or at the most slightly angled, but never vertical. Vertical headings may save space, but they reduce readability, which is the main point of having a table.

- Fonts should be the same size as body text, although they may be in a different font or weight. Making them smaller saves space at the cost of readability and convenience.

- Cell borders, shading for alternate rows, and other elaborate design elements should be minimized.

- Remember to use white space to help with the design, especially when setting the distance from a cell's borders and its contents. A cramped table defeats the purpose of using a table in the first place.

Tip

In particular, leave space at the bottom of table cells. Select all the cells in the table, and select TABLE > SPACING > BELOW. Two line heights will often be ideal.

Adding a table

To create a new table:

1 Select TABLE > INSERT TABLE or press CTRL+ F12. The INSERT TABLE dialog window opens.

2   Either name the table so you can find it in the Navigator, or else accept the default name. The default name is TABLE, followed by a number. The number indicates the order in which the table was added, not the table's order from the start of the file.

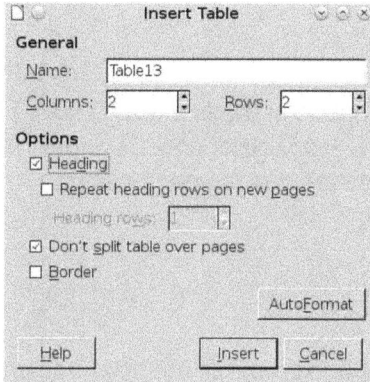

The INSERT TABLE dialog window includes the most commonly used table options, so you do not have to format after the table is inserted.

3   Select from the common options listed:

•   HEADING: Defines one or more rows as a TABLE HEADING row at the top of the table. Once HEADING is selected, you also have the option of REPEAT HEADING ROWS ON NEW PAGES, and of selecting the number of heading rows in the fields below.

•   DON'T SPLIT TABLE OVER PAGES: Prevents tables from printing on two or more pages unless the table is so long that is impossible. This setting keeps information together, but can also create problems with page breaks unless tables are always given their own page.

- BORDER: Adds a default border around all cells and table edges consisting of a solid line, black in color and .05 points thick. You can adjust this setting on a table's BORDER tab.

- Optionally, click the AUTOFORMAT button to choose an already-defined format.

Tip

Note the options you choose in the first table and, so far as possible, use them in every other one. Consider saving the table as an AUTOFORMAT. See "Creating AutoFormats," page 299.

Tip

If you want the same options most of the time, you can set some of them in TOOLS > OPTIONS > LIBREOFFICE WRITER > TABLE.

Editing table parts

When you right-click in a table and select TABLE PROPERTIES from the right-click menu, you can edit all parts of the table that are currently selected. If the cursor is simply in the table, you edit the entire table.

A more exact way to edit is to use the CELL, ROW, and COLUMN sub-menus on the right-click menu. From these sub-menus, you can select, insert, or delete parts of a table, as well as adjusting their width or height.

In the CELL sub-menu, you can split a single selected cell, or merge two or more selected cells, altering the general table design for your specific purposes. For example, you might want a table heading to straddle more than one column.

To delete an entire table, place the mouse cursor anywhere in the table and either click TABLE > DELETE > TABLE from the main menu or select the table as well as the space before and after the table and press the DELETE key. Using the menu is generally easier.

Adjusting table spacing

By default, tables occupy the entire width of a line. If you ever need to know the exact space between margins, you can right-click on TABLE PROPERTIES and read the WIDTH field on the TABLE tab to get the information.

To adjust a table's overall width, select from the right-click menu TABLE > TABLE > WIDTH. Alternatively, if you prefer, you can adjust the ALIGNMENT and SPACING options.

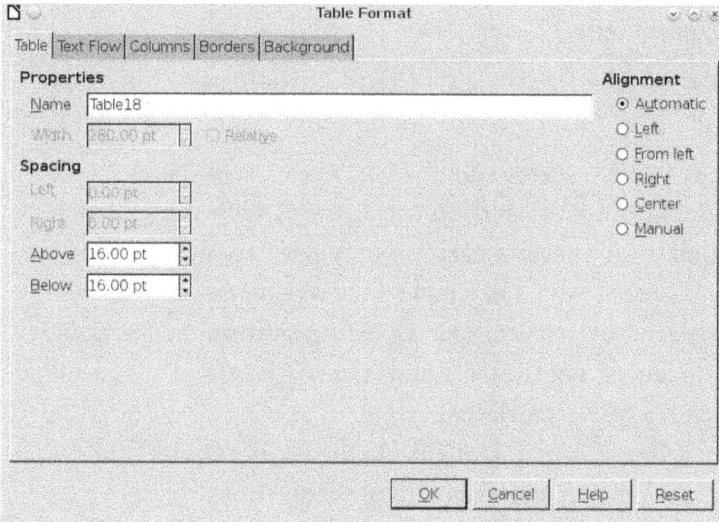

The TABLE tab of the TABLE FORMAT dialog window has fields for positioning a table horizontally and vertically.

The available options depend on your choice of alignments:

- AUTOMATIC: The table fills the entire line width.

- LEFT: The left side of the table aligns with the page's left margin. You can use SPACING > RIGHT to indent the right side of the table.

- FROM LEFT: The table shifts by the amount in the SPACING > LEFT field. This option may shift the table into the right margin, where part of it may be unprintable.

- RIGHT: The right side of the table aligns with the page's right margin. You can use SPACING > LEFT to indent the left side of the table.

- CENTER: The table aligns with the center of the line. If the table's width equals the full length of the line, this setting has no visible effect.

- MANUAL: Use the SPACING fields to adjust the table on its left and right.

If the table is surrounded by text, place a table closer to the paragraph above it than the one below it to show their relation.

Similarly, if the next paragraph style is a caption, position the caption closer to the table than the next paragraph.

To adjust the vertical spacing before and after tables, right-click on any part of the table and select TABLE PROPERTIES > TABLE > SPACING > ABOVE and BELOW.

By default, content is aligned to the top of cells on the TEXT FLOW tab. You can also align it to the center or the bottom, although in practice there is rarely a reason for doing so.

Adjusting column spacing

You can redistribute horizontal space among the existing columns by using the cursor to drag at cell borders. This method may seem inexact, but with both vertical and horizontal rulers in the editing window, it can actually be as exact as any choice.

Alternatively, select TABLE PROPERTIES > COLUMNS from the right-click menu and balancing the COLUMN WIDTH fields.

Adjusting row spacing

You can redistribute vertical space between the existing rows by using the cursor to drag at cell borders or selecting ROW > HEIGHT from the right-click menu.

Setting text flow options

Positioning a table in hard copy can be difficult, because you frequently get uneven page breaks. Sometimes, rearranging rows can improve the break, but often you need to manually intervene with one of the available tools, most of which are listed in the TEXT FLOW tab of the TABLE FORMAT dialog window.

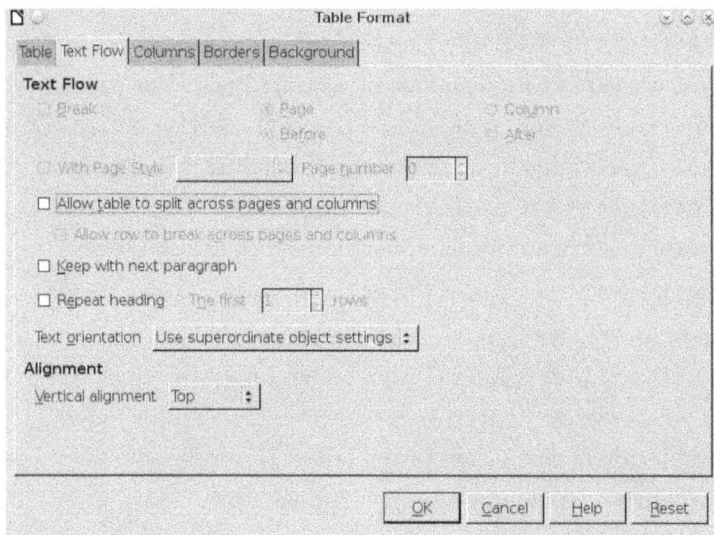

The TEXT FLOW tab of the TABLE FORMAT dialog window contains options for how a table displays on the page.

- REPEAT HEADING: Repeats the top row(s) of a table on each page if the table continues on another page. Usually, you need only the first row when it serves as a table heading. Repeating multiple rows will usually only be needed when you have complicated headings that take up more than a single row.

- ALLOW TABLE TO SPLIT ACROSS PAGES AND COLUMNS: A multi-page table tends to defeat the purpose of making information easily read. However, a table that does not split often makes for uneven page breaks.

- ALLOW ROW TO SPLIT ACROSS PAGES AND COLUMNS: This option has the same trade-off as allowing the entire table to split, but to a lesser extent.

- KEEP WITH NEXT PARAGRAPH: Since a table usually requires an introduction, this setting should only be needed occasionally. However, it is available if it will be useful for captions if you prefer not to place captions in a frame.

- REPEAT HEADING: Repeats the top row(s) of a table on each page if the table continues on another page. Usually, you need only the first row when it serves as a table heading. Repeating multiple rows will usually only be needed when you have complicated headings that take up more than a single row.

- CONVERT: TABLE > CONVERT in the main menu converts text to a table, or a table to text. Converting text to a table requires markers to mark columns and rows, and is rarely worth the effort. However, converting a table to text saves time when you decide to change the presentation of information or are working with data that uses tabs to create columns.

Adding spreadsheet behaviors

Writer's tables have limited capacity to act as a spreadsheet:

- NUMBER FORMAT: Available from the right-click menu, NUMBER FORMAT opens a dialog window where you can set how numbers are interpreted and presented. For example, if you set the format to DATE, you could choose from such formats as YYYY-MM-DD or DD-MM-YY.

- NUMBER RECOGNITION: Selected from the TABLE menu. Identifies input specifically as numbers and right aligns it.

- ADDING FORMULAS: Selected from TABLE > FORMULA in the main menu, this option opens a tool bar for inserting a couple of dozen common spreadsheet formulas.

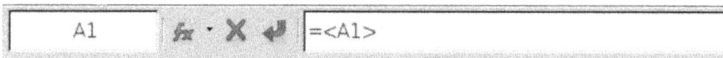

| A1 | f_x · X ↵ | =<A1> |

The FORMULA BAR allows basic spreadsheet functions to be used in Writer tables.

- ALIGNMENT: Available from TOOLS > OPTIONS > LIBREOFFICE WRITER > TABLE > INPUT IN TABLES, ALIGNMENT places numbers in the lower right corner of a cell, as in a spreadsheet.

> ### Tip
> If you need a more complex spreadsheet, create one as a separate file, then embed it using INSERT > OBJECT > OLE OBJECT.

Adding captions

If the sentence which introduces a table is clear enough, a caption may be redundant.

However, if a table needs a caption, or you want to refer to the table by a number, right-click and select CAPTION from the right-click menu. If you always want a caption, set up AUTOCAPTION for tables in TOOLS > OPTIONS > LIBREOFFICE WRITER > TABLE > AUTOCAPTION.

✎ **Tip**

Adding a caption to the table adds a frame around the table and the caption.

If you are having trouble with frames staying in place, add a row with no borders to the bottom of the table and place the caption there.

Using AutoFormats

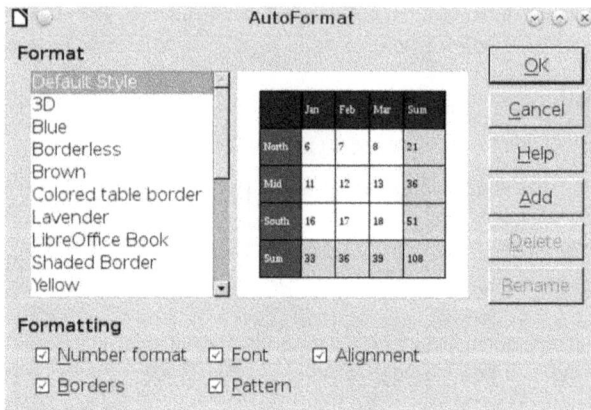

Table AutoFormats are a partial substitute for styles, but the pre-defined formats include many obsolete designs.

AutoFormats are the closest that Writer gets to table styles. As with styles, AutoFormats can be either pre-defined or customized. Unlike styles, AutoFormats cannot be edited, except for being renamed. If you want to use the same name as an existing AutoFormat, you must delete the existing AutoFormat first.

Like many galleries in Writer, table AutoFormats include many styles that were popular in the mid-1990s, but have fallen out of fashion since. Think twice before using multi-colored AutoFormats, or the gray 3D AutoFormat.

Follow the same restrictions when creating customized AutoFormats. You might want to use corporate or project colors for borders or a colored header, but usually nothing more.

Lorem ipsum	Lorem ipsum
dolor	45,000
sit amet	32,000

Lorem ipsum	Lorem ipsum	
dolor		112000
sit amet		54000

Lorem ipsum	Lorem ipsum	
dolor		10000
sit amet		17000

Obsolete table formats are found throughout LibreOffice. By modern standards, they are ugly and over-elaborate.

Creating AutoFormats

Creating an AutoFormat is similar to creating a new paragraph style from a selection:

Manually format a table as you choose, then, with the cursor anywhere in the table:

1   Click the formatting options you want to store in the AutoFormat from the list at the bottom of the AUTOFORMAT dialog window.

2   Click the ADD button. Note that in some versions of LibreOffice, once you click the button, you can no longer select formats.

3   Name the new AutoFormat. Until you close the dialog window, the new AutoFormat displays at the top of the window's list.

Tip

In addition to the formatting listed in the window, you also save font selection and spacing options.

Tip

As an alternative to AutoFormats, in some versions of LibreOffice you can save a table in EDIT > AUTOTEXT.

STOP Caution

You can delete any AutoFormats one at a time, including pre-defined AutoFormats. Deleted AutoFormats are deleted not just from the current document, but from Writer and all documents.

Using tables as workarounds

In many ways, Writer's tables are simpler versions of frames. The major differences are that you cannot wrap text around tables, and text cannot flow from cell to cell like it can from frame to frame.

However, as detailed in Chapter 8, Writer's frames are often unstable, shifting objects without warning. When frames fail you, a table may be the solution you need. For example, tables can successfully anchor text in headers and frames, as well as keeping pictures and other objects in their positions.

In such cases, a table gives you more limited options than a frame or another formatting feature such as tab stops. However, if your main goal is to keep text or objects where you place them, tables do appear to be more reliable than frames.

New aspects of literacy

The use of lists and tables is no more than a few hundred years old. For much of this time, they were used by only a minority of scientists and engineers.

Now, however, both lists and tables have become commonplace in online documents. Neither is taught at any level of education, but how and when to use lists and tables is rapidly becoming part of the knowledge that defines basic literacy. Learn the conventional ways of using them, and you can be sure of presenting your thoughts in the best possible light, both inside LibreOffice and at the podium.

11

Styled features and long documents

While you are designing, styles constantly prove their worth. However, styles don't stop giving you advantages when the template is finished. In Writer, paragraph styles also make advanced features more efficient, especially in academic and formal documents.

Tasks such as outlining, navigating documents, adding cross-references, or creating tables of contents are possible without the use of paragraph styles. However, without styles, such features are so much more laborious that doing them manually is a waste of time, except in a few cases where they are unavoidable.

This chapter begins with Writer's advanced features, focusing on both how paragraph styles enhance them, and how you can use them to customize your documents and give them a professional touch. You might say that the chapter is mostly about the unexpected dividends that taking the time to use styles can pay you.

The rest is about the tools for designing long and academic documents. Some of these tools do not rely heavily on styles (if at all), but you may need to be aware of their quirks as you design.

Using outline levels

If you have noticed TOOLS > OUTLINE NUMBERING, you may have assumed that it is a manual method of creating outlines.

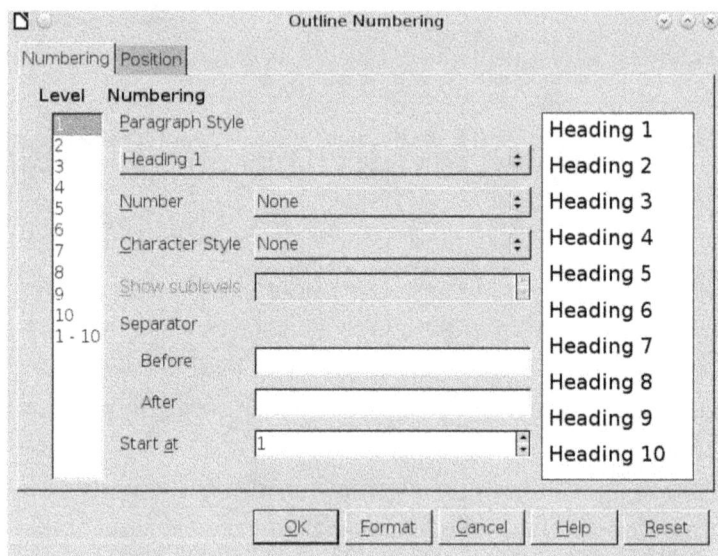

The OUTLINE NUMBERING dialog window is used for more than just formatting outlines.

However, outlines are only the most basic use of outline numbering. More importantly, outline numbering also defines the paragraph styles used for each level. These styles are picked up by other Writer tools to simplify your work.

By default, each outline level is assigned a heading paragraph style, with HEADING 1 assigned to outline LEVEL 1, and so on with each heading style corresponding to the same outline level.

However, what most users never notice is that you can assign any other paragraph style to any outline level, by using the OUTLINE LEVEL field on the OUTLINE & NUMBERING tab for a paragraph style. You can also change the default style for an outline level by editing the PARAGRAPH STYLE field in TOOLS > OUTLINE NUMBERING.

Once a paragraph style is assigned to an outline level, it can be used for:

- Writing an outline.

- Outlining in the Navigator.

- Setting up cross-references in the most efficient manner.

- Creating tables of contents and formatting indexes and bibliographies.

Writing an outline

You can outline using heading paragraph styles with a list style attached to them, or a single paragraph style with an outline list style attached.

However, the most obvious method is to use TOOLS > OUTLINE NUMBERING. The settings for this tool resemble the choices on the OPTIONS tab of a list style. The formatting can be customized separately for each outline level, or for all levels at once.

See "Understanding outline lists," page 270.

Outlining in the Navigator

The Navigator is one of the most under-used features of LibreOffice. However, the longer the document, the more useful it becomes as you edit and revise

To open the Navigator, select VIEW > NAVIGATOR, or press the F5 key, or select the Navigator in the sidebar.

On the simplest level, the Navigator lists all of a document's objects, including outline levels – headings by default, other paragraph styles as well if you edit outline levels. Clicking a list item in the Navigator jumps to it in the editing window.

However, what may be less apparent is that the headings listed in the Navigator can help to restructure a document.

Tip

Tables, frames, and other objects are most useful for navigation if you give them descriptive names rather than accepting defaults like TABLE6 or IMAGE12. One choice is to give all pictures the same name as their original files. That way, finding the files becomes easier.

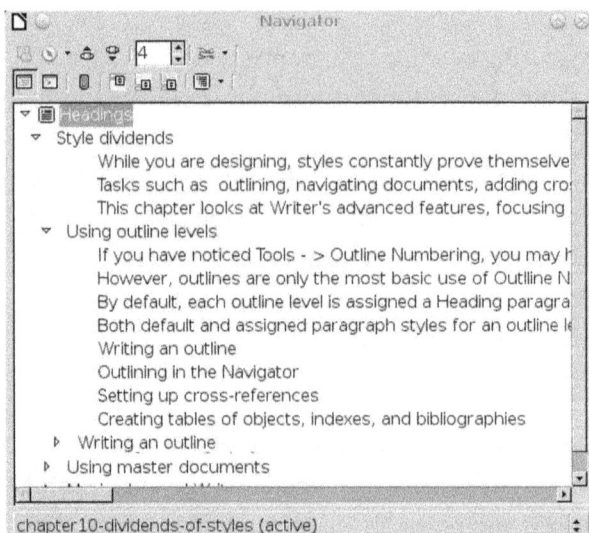

The Navigator becomes a more powerful outlining tool if you set an Outline Level to show the TEXT BODY paragraph style.

Changing outline levels using the Navigator

Headings should be hierarchical, so that the topic in a HEADING 3 paragraph style is contained by the HEADING 2 paragraph style directly above it. For example, the heading "The Human Body" might have sub-headings below it of "The Heart" and "The Lungs." This structuring strengthens the internal logic of a document, and helps readers find sections when they scan.

Such relationships are essential to the structure of a document. If you see a heading that should be raised or lowered in the hierarchy, highlight it and then click either PROMOTE LEVEL or DEMOTE LEVEL, the buttons on the bottom right of the tool bar.

Each time you click, the currently selected heading will be raised or lowered one level in the hierarchy. So will any outline levels subordinate to it, so that promoting a HEADING 2 outline level to HEADING 1 also promotes all HEADING 3 outline levels between it and the next HEADING 2.

Moving material using the Navigator

Similarly, as you work, you may find that part of the contents belongs somewhere else in the document.

Instead of cutting and pasting, you can click either PROMOTE CHAPTER or DEMOTE CHAPTER, the buttons on the top right of the tool bar, to move a heading and the text beneath it to a new place in the document.

Tip

In the Navigator, "chapter" refers to the part of the document between one heading and the next. "Promoting" moves the chapter closer to the start of the document, "demoting" moves it closer to the end.

All subordinate headings and any other paragraph styles underneath the selected heading will also move, keeping the same position in relation to each other, but changing their group position in the document.

In effect, the Navigator replaces ordinary copying and pasting. However, it is more effective than copying and pasting, because it provides a visual image of your actions.

Just as importantly, if you are interrupted, with the Navigator there is no danger of losing content because you have forgotten about it.

Using cross-references

Cross-references are updatable fields that refer to another part of a document. In online documents, they are links for easy navigation to the reference.

Manual cross-references would be difficult to maintain – especially their page references—so LibreOffice keeps them automatically updated as you add and delete material and close and open documents. You can also manually update by clicking TOOLS > UPDATE > FIELDS.

To add a cross-reference, you need two elements: the SELECTION or source, and the REFERENCE or target. The SELECTIONS are chosen either from the contents of outline levels or from bookmarks or markers added manually.

Usually, you should add cross-references as your document is being finished. That way, you avoid breaking links and having to re-create them as you move passages around or rename files. Also, you can keep the cross-reference dialog window open and do all cross-references in one effort.

Tip

If you plan to use cross-references for tables, images, and other elements, give each element a caption, then assign the CAPTION paragraph style to an outline level.

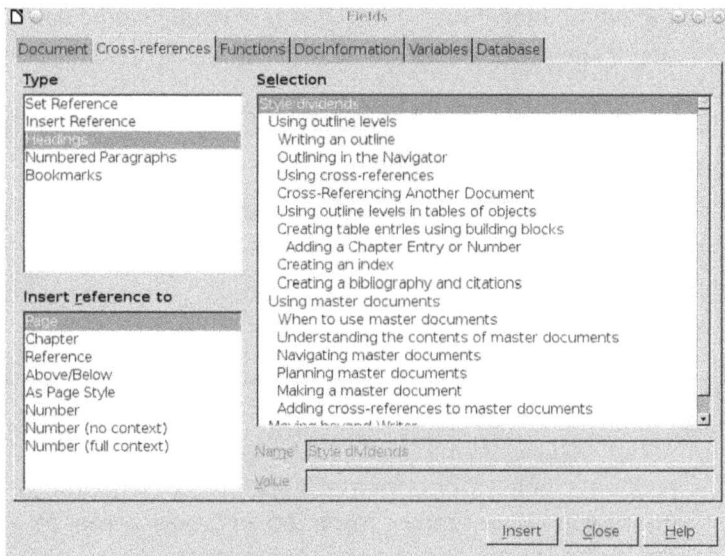

Outline levels simplify adding cross-references. The alternative is to set references, either manually or as bookmarks.

Cross-referencing within one document

Outline levels provide automatic markers to use with cross-references. Add headings as you write, then follow these steps when you add cross-references:

1 Place the cursor in the position for the first cross-reference.

2 Select INSERT > CROSS REFERENCE. The FIELDS dialog window opens on the CROSS-REFERENCES tab.

3   From the TYPE pane, select the sort of source to use. Use HEADINGS whenever possible, since you are adding them anyway and they tend to be relatively short. Otherwise, consider NUMBERED PARAGRAPHS or BOOKMARKS.

When all else fails, you can use SET REFERENCE to manually create a source. However, this method is so cumbersome and slow that it should be avoided if at all possible.

4   Choose the source from the SELECTION pane.

5   Choose the format for the reference from the INSERT REFERENCE TO pane. Click the INSERT button to insert the cross-reference into your document. The FIELDS dialog window remains open.

Tip

ABOVE/BELOW are informal, and should be avoided in academic or legal documents. Avoid using them unless the document is nearly completed, in case you move passages around and change their relationship.

6   In the document, add the words to introduce the cross-reference. For instance, if the structure you are using includes the chapter and page number, the cross-reference dialog inserts only the actual chapter and page number.

The complete reference may require something like, "See Chapter 6, page 79." Alternatively, you might want to mention the heading.

Tip

You can add the wording around the text as AutoText. For instance, you could have one AutoText entry or Custom field for "See Chapter " and another for ", page " (notice the spaces at the end of both).

Repeat for all the other cross-references. Close the dialog window when done.

Tip

Cross-references work differently in master documents. See "Adding cross-references between sub-documents," page 339.

Cross-referencing to another file

Adding a cross-reference to another document is a different process from adding a cross-reference within a single document, even if both the source and the target document are in the same master document.

The two basic methods involve using SET REFERENCE or hyperlinking using styles. Both methods are done manually.

Using styles saves time when you are cross-referencing another file. In fact, using SET REFERENCE to create a manual reference is sufficiently confusing that I recommend avoiding it altogether.

To add a hyperlink using styles, follow this procedure:

1   Open the target document for the cross-reference. The target document is the one which contains the cross-reference.

2 Open the Navigator by selecting VIEW > NAVIGATOR, or pressing the F5 key, or selecting it in the sidebar.

3 Select the source document (the document which you are referencing) from the drop-down list at the bottom of the Navigator.

4 Set the DRAG MODE tool to INSERT AS HYPERLINK.

5 Drag the heading you are referencing into the target document.

A hyperlink to the heading is placed in the target document. The hyperlink is active and can be used online to jump to the source document.

Tip

If you want the hyperlink to resemble regular text, edit the INTERNET LINK and VISITED INTERNET LINK character styles to remove the colors and underlining. This change will affect all hyperlinks, not just cross-references.

6 If necessary, add:

* The introductory text. You can define fields or AutoText to avoid having to type it.

* The page number. It must be added and updated manually.

* The document name. Add it manually, or by dragging and dropping the title of the source document.

Tip

The text displayed for a hyperlink is not automatically updated in the target document when the source document changes. Use TOOLS > UPDATE to update manually.

Using outline levels in tables and indexes

"Indexes and Tables" is the term LibreOffice uses to describe fields that are generated from the contents of a document.

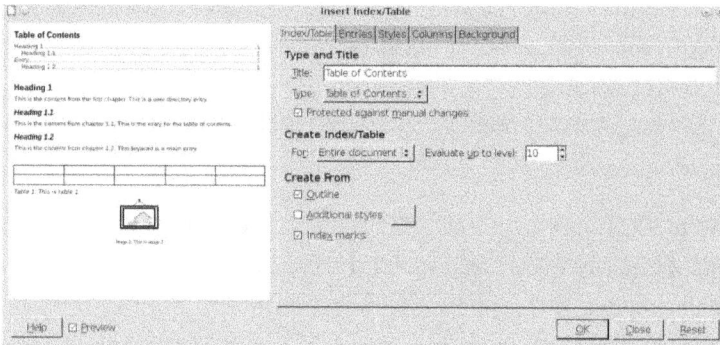

INSERT INDEX/TABLE includes tools for extensive customization of tables of contents and similar tables.

The most common are a table of contents (TOC), which is created from outline levels. and tables of illustrations and tables, which are created from captions.

However, you can create all sorts of indexes and tables, such as:

* Alphabetical Index: A list of keywords and their appearances in the text – in other words, a regular index.

- Table of Illustrations: A list of images, generated from caption categories.

- Table of Tables: A list of tables, generated from caption categories.

- Table of Objects: A list of other elements, such as charts.

- Bibliography: A list of reference materials used in the document.

You can also add user-defined index marks to create other tables.

Creating a table of contents

Each kind of table has its own list of customized features. However, the procedure for building most of them is similar to the one for creating a table of contents:

1 If necessary, customize a page style for the table, and add it to the document.

2 Go to INSERT > INDEXES AND TABLES > INDEXES AND TABLES > INDEX/TABLES > TYPE and select the type of table. Your selection determines both the default title and some of the advanced options. However, many of the advanced options may be unnecessary.

3 Select INDEX/TABLES > ADDITIONAL STYLES to add additional paragraph styles to the table of contents. Any selection you make does not add styles to the outline levels.

Tip

Styles already assigned to outline levels cannot be given different outline levels.

4   If your table entries are single words or phrases of a few words, you might be able to save space by setting 2–4 columns on the COLUMNS tab.

5   On the ENTRIES tab, customize the table entries using the building blocks in the STRUCTURE field.

Tip

Keep the LS (Link Start) at the beginning of the ENTRY field, and the LE (Link End) at the end of the field.

These two links make the entire entry a hyperlink to the text, that you can use in an online document or when editing.

Other fields appear in the tab as you make selections. The preview pane on the left shows what your design will look like on the page.

6   Click the OK button to add the table. You can right-click the table to edit or update it later.

7   Edit the paragraph styles for each table entry. These styles consist of a heading paragraph style (for instance, CONTENTS HEADING for a table of contents), and styles for each outline level of table entry (such as CONTENTS 1-10 for Index/Tables).

Usually, you can model the CONTENTS HEADING paragraph style on the document's HEADING 1 or 2 style, and the entry styles on TEXT BODY, using the INHERIT FROM field on the ORGANIZER tab. There is no need to use different font sizes or colors to distinguish the style for each entry level – the left indent is enough.

An alphabetical index will have an index separator style for the alphabetical delimiters at the start of each section.

Structuring table entries with building blocks

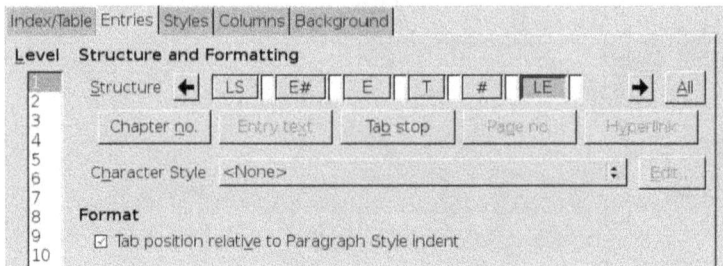

Use building blocks to customize tables of contents.

Unlike most word processors, LibreOffice provides the tools for customizing each entry for a TOC or similar table. These tools are located at INSERT > INDEXES AND TABLES > INDEXES AND TABLES > ENTRIES. You can also modify indexes and tables by customizng their paragraph styles.

The tools consist of a STRUCTURE field in which you can arrange building blocks such as PAGE NUMBER and CHAPTER NUMBER, characters, and spaces to create a standard entry.

Below the field are the unused building blocks. When you add a block to the field, it may become grayed out and unselectable.

Similarly, when you delete a block from the field, it reappears in the unused list below the STRUCTURE field.

When a building block is selected, it looks sunken in the STRUCTURE field. In addition, formatting choices for the building block appear in the window.

Each outline level can be customized separately, or together by pressing the ALL button on the right side of the window. If the levels have common elements, format them together, then edit each level separately for unique features.

As you design, remember:

- Use the LS (Link Start) at the beginning of the ENTRY field and the LE (Link End) at the end of the field to make the entire entry a hyperlink.

- The spacing of all tabs is added to the BEFORE TEXT indentation on the INDENTS AND SPACING tab for each entry's paragraph style (CONTENTS 1-10). To avoid difficulties, leave the BEFORE TEXT field set to o.

- You can reliably use only one tab in the ENTRY field. Otherwise, spacing can become erratic.

- You can add manual spaces and text as well as building blocks to an entry. Manual spaces are inelegant, but can sometimes be a workaround to the one-tab limit.

Avoiding the default TOC design

Table of Contents

Style dividends..1
   Using outline levels...3
      Writing an outline..4

The standard word-processor design for a Table of Contents. Its need for crutch-like leader dots between the text entry and the page number is enough to prove it a crippled design.

TOCs in LibreOffice default to a format that has become standard in many word processors. In this style, each entry consists of text and a page number placed by a tab on the right margin. In between are fill characters, usually a period.

If you have regularly generated TOCs using word processors, you might not see anything wrong with the default TOC design in Writer. Probably, you have seen the design too many times to be bothered by it.

However, to anyone with design knowledge, the result is a failed design. Starting the TOC entry at the left margin and placing the page number against the right margin disassociates them, and the leader dots are needed to try to reconnect them.

The result is ugly. It is also clumsy. Since periods are used to indicate a stop, not a continuation, the periods do not lead the eye across the page. A design that does not disassociate the text entries and the page number in the first place is far more efficient, and simpler as well.

Fortunately, while LibreOffice defaults to this design, you can work with the building blocks and paragraph styles to create a more functional design in any number of ways. For instance:

* Reduce the space between the entry text and the page number using the paragraph style.

Table of Contents

Larger fonts and no leader dots improves the design. But watch for entries that spill over on to another line, spoiling the symmetry of the design for no reason.

* Select the # (Page no.) block and give its character style a larger font size and/or a color to make it stand out more. The

larger page number helps to keep the association between the text entries and page numbers.

Table of Contents

Increasing the size of the page number helps some, but the basic problem remains: The distance from some page entries still makes the table of contents harder to read than necessary.

- Click on the T (Tab) block. Fields for the fill character and tab stop position appear below the list of unused building blocks. Replace the fill character with an underscore, and at least your eye is guided continuously across the page, which is an improvement on leader dots. However, having a fill character at all still seems like a needless addition.

Table of Contents

An underscore leads the eye across the page, but still tends to separate the text entries from the page numbers.

- Go to INSERT > INDEXES AND TABLES > INDEXES AND TABLES > COLUMNS and set the table to use two columns. This solution shortens the distance between the text entry and the page number, but may be impractical if any entry text is more than a few words long and spills over onto another line.

Table of Contents

A two-column table of contents lessens the space between text entries and page numbers. However, to work without the problem of long entries taking up two lines, it requires short text entries, or perhaps a landscape oriented page with columns.

- Delete the TAB block and manually add spaces between the E (Entry text) and # (Page no.) blocks. Manual spaces are generally not a good way of laying out design elements, but in this one case, they do not create any problem beyond the need to keep count. They are inelegant, but work.

Table of Contents

A ragged right table of contents keeps text entries and page numbers together so that they can be easily read. However, two ragged margins looks cluttered.

One way to avoid ragged right looking cluttered is to format the Contents paragraph styles so that all entries have the same margin on the left. However, this solution hides the hierarchal structure of the headings.

- Reverse the order of the text entries and the page numbers, with a tab or a couple of manual spaces between them.

Table of Contents

1 Style dividends
   2 Using outline levels
      4 Writing an outline
      5 Outlining in the Navigator

Placing the page numbers before the text entries keep their relation clear and gives the most space for long text entries.

Tip

You can also add a special character or dingbat between the text and page number.

Adding a chapter number

In Writer, you can add chapter numbers to page numbers in the body of a document (see "Adding chapter numbers to page numbers," page 218). However, although the building blocks on the ENTRY tab include a chapter number, your ability to add chapter numbers in a table of contents is limited.

The chapter number building block can only be used in the top level entry in the table of contents. The building block draws its information from the top outline level (usually, the HEADING 1 paragraph style) if the outline level or the paragraph style includes numbering. In the same circumstances in a master document, each top outline level continues the numbering from the previous heading at the same outline level.

Other outline levels cannot display the chapter number, even if you add the building block to its structure on the ENTRIES tab.

Table of Contents

10-1 Style dividends & others
  2 Using outline levels
    4 Writing an outline
    5 Outlining in the Navigator

A table of contents that adds the chapter number as a prefix.

As an alternative, ignore the building blocks and attach a list style to the CONTENTS 1 paragraph style. The list style could also be used to add the word "Chapter" before the number.

Creating an index

An index is created in much the same way as a table of objects. The main difference is that it is built from tags of individual words or phrases, rather than from paragraph styles, which would not provide the type of information that an index requires. These tags display in the document as fields.

Adding index entries

The simplest way to add an entry is by selecting words or phrases and marking them with INSERT > INDEXES AND TABLES > INDEX ENTRY. However, it is laborious and time-consuming.

Instead, you can automate the creation of index entries by selecting APPLY TO ALL SIMILAR TEXTS to add other occurrences of an entry in the document. Use MATCH CASE and WHOLE WORDS ONLY to modify the selection of similar texts.

No matter how you prepare them, indexes can have a main entry, and up to two sub-entry levels. Any more sub-entries would generally be overly-complicated for writers to maintain and readers to follow.

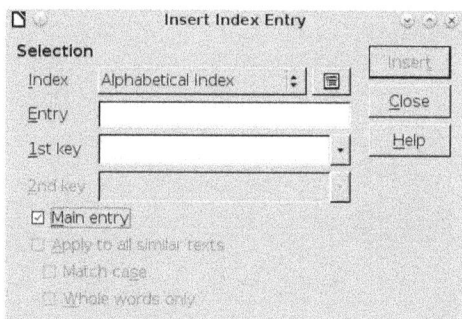

The INSERT INDEX ENTRY dialog window stays open after you insert an entry, letting you move on immediately to the next entry.

Generating an index

After all the entries are created, open the INSERT INDEX/TABLE dialog window to generate the index.

Tip

A standard index is called an ALPHABETICAL INDEX on the TYPE field in the INSERT INDEX/TABLE dialog window. Since this is a non-standard usage, you might modify the title to "Index."

If your entries are short, you can save pages by clicking INSERT > INDEXES AND TABLES > INDEXES AND TABLES > INDEX/TABLES > COLUMNS, and setting the index to use two columns.

If you want to add headings with letters of the alphabet, select INSERT > INDEXES AND TABLES > INDEXES AND TABLES > INDEX/TABLES > ENTRIES > ALPHABETICAL DELIMITER. Alphabetical delimiters are sub-headings, with one for each letter of the alphabet.

Alphabetical Index

A selection from an alphabetical index.

Creating a concordance

A more systematic way to create an index is to use a concordance file. A concordance is a file that lists words to add to the index. It is a plain text file with one word or phrase defined on each line.

Each line has a strict structure, consisting of seven fields, separated by a semi-colon:

SEARCH TERM; ALTERNATIVE ENTRY;1ST KEY;2ND KEY;MATCH CASE; WORD ONLY

No space is entered between the semi-colon and a field's contents. A key is a higher level heading that a search term is placed beneath. For instance, if your search term is "styles," you might want to use the keys "LibreOffice" and "office applications."

If you choose not to have an alternative entry, a first key or a second key, leave the field blank, so that one semi-colon immediately follows another.

The last two fields are structured somewhat differently. If you want only entries that have the same upper or lower case letters as your entries, enter 1 in the second to last field. Similarly, entering 1 in the last field sets the index to only include instances where the entry is a whole word, and not part of a larger one. You can also just leave the last two fields blank, as you can with any of the others.

For example, entering:

MACAW;ARA;PARROTS;;0;0

Would produce an entry for "macaw" with

- A listing under "macaw."

- An alternate listing under "ara" (the scientific name).

- A listing of "Parrots, Macaw."

- No second key (notice the two semi-colons).

- Inclusion of instances that start with a lower or upper case letter (both "macaw" and "Macaw").

- Inclusion of instances in which the term is a whole word or part of a longer word.

Whether creating a concordance is faster than adding entries manually is debatable since the tasks are so different. However, a concordance is certainly more systematic and possibly less tedious.

The disadvantage of a concordance is that it can produce an index that includes instances of common words that are irrelevant for your purposes. In many cases, a useful index may require a combination of manual entries and a concordance.

Creating citations and bibliographies

Like tables of contents and indexes, bibliographies are generated with the INDEX/TABLE dialog window. However, the contents are based upon citations that refer to entries in the TOOLS > BIBLIOGRAPHY DATABASE.

The bibliography database has to cover many different media and circumstances, which is why it contains so many fields. It also includes fields such as ISBN that no citation style uses, but might be useful to you as you do your research.

In practice, however, any single entry in the bibliography needs only about half a dozen fields filled in, no matter what citation format you use. What differs is the fields needed for each type of source material and the order of the fields in each citation style.

However, all citations use the IDENTIFIER field (first on the left) to set the format for a citation in the document. In this column, you can add the citation in the correct form for the citation style.

For example, in the APA style, a citation to this book would use "Byfield" in the text and follow the information cited with (2015).

All necessary information, including the IDENTIFIER field should be entered before any citation is created. In theory, you can add a citation manually by highlighting text, but doing so makes consistency much more difficult.

Tip

Writer has a single bibliography database for all documents. Since formatting entries can be tedious, consider creating a template with citations for each type of source material.

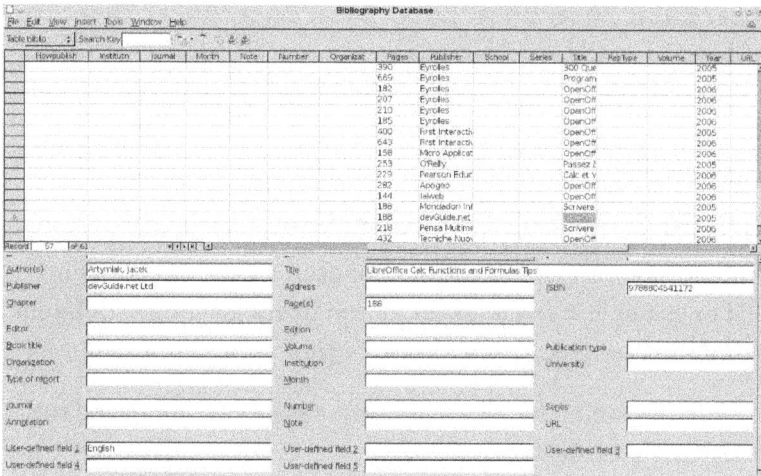

The bibliography database is the source for citations in the text, no matter what citation style you use.

STOP Caution

Confusingly, the IDENTIFER column and the SHORT NAME field below the table are the same field, and should have the same content.

To complicate matters even more, the sample entries for both the IDENTIFER column and the SHORT NAME field are meaningless, although they have been in OpenOffice.org and LibreOffice for over a decade. Replace them with the proper format for the citation style you are using.

Building citations and bibliographies

This procedure is an overview of the steps in creating citations and bibliographies. More detailed information follows:

Bibliography

LibreOffice Documentation Team, *LibreOffice 4.2 Impress Guide*. Friends of Open Document, 2013

LibreOffice Documentation Team, *LibreOffice 4.3 Writer Guide*. Friends of Open Document, 2015

Weber, Jean Hollis, *Self Publishing Using LibreOffice Writer*. Friends of Open Document, 2013

A short bibliography generated by Writer. The book titles use a character style so they appear in italics.

1   Enter the correct information for each source you are using. For example, a reference to a journal article requires different information from a reference to a book.

2   Add the format for citations in the IDENTIFER column and the SHORT NAME fields.

3   Position the cursor in the text and click INSERT > INDEXES AND TABLES > BIBLIOGRAPHY ENTRY. Use the drop-down list in the SHORT NAME FIELD to chose the citation from the ones you have prepared in the bibliography database, then click the INSERT button. The INSERT BIBLIOGRAPHY ENTRY dialog window remains open, so you can insert citations without having to re-open the dialog for each one.

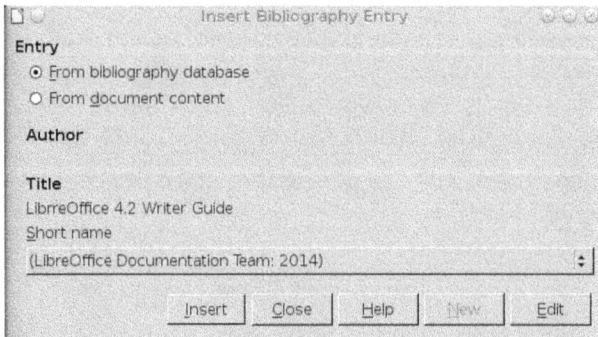

By collecting references in the bibliography database, you can add consistent citations to your document.

4 Place the cursor where you want the bibliography to appear in the text, and select INSERT > INDEXES AND TABLES > INDEXES AND TABLES. Usually, a bibliography appears at the end of a document.

5 Format the bibliography. At a minimum, you will need to:

- Set the TYPE field to BIBLIOGRAPHY on the INDEX/TABLE tab. The TYPE refers to the kind of source, such as a periodical or a web page.

- Use the POSITION field on the ENTRIES tab to structure each type of source used in the document.

- On the ENTRIES tab, set SORT BY. In most modern citation styles, you will want CONTENT (alphabetical descending order), but you can add other sorting criteria, or use ascending alphabetical order.

For example, the default is to arrange a bibliography in the order in which citations appear in the document, rather than alphabetical.

Similarly, the STRUCTURE field begins by default with the SHORT NAME for each item, which is not needed.

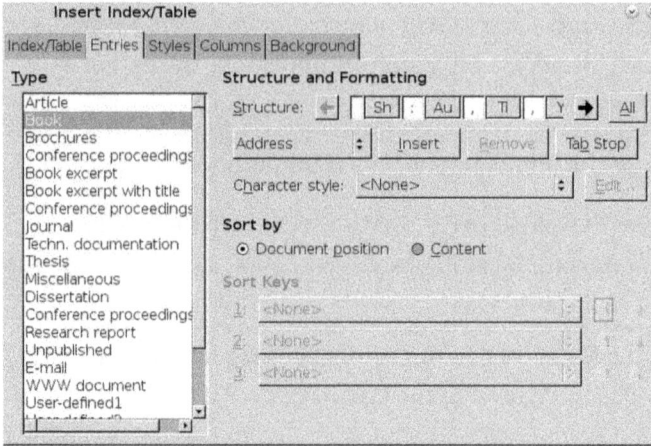

Create a structure for each type of source material used in the document.

6   Adjust the BIBLIOGRAPHY paragraph styles. Usually, they will be similar to the TEXT BODY styles.

Preparing bibliographic formats

Before adding citations, you need the correct information for the citation style you are using. Similarly, you need to have the correct information for each bibliography entry.

Most citations styles developed in different fields of academic study. They are a matter of convention, since they all give similar information.

There are five main styles. If you are taking a class or writing for a journal, ask your teacher or editor which format they prefer.

Otherwise, use the format for your field of study:

- APA (American Psychological Association): Psychology, education, and other social sciences.
- MLA (Modern Languages Association): Literature, art, and humanities.
- Chicago: History and specific publications.
- Turabian: A variation of the Chicago style for general use by university students.
- AMA (American Medical Association): Medicine, health, and biology.

Citations within the text require entries in different fields in the bibliography database, and different presentations in the text.

Today, all except the AMA style favor parenthetical citation, in which minimal information is presented in parentheses in the text. Parentheses are less distracting when you read and keep citations from being an exact duplication of the bibliography.

The AMA style uses footnotes or endnotes instead.

The following table shows what fields to use for three common sources: books, articles, and web pages. Fields are arranged from top to bottom in the order that they appear.

STOP Caution

LibreOffice's bibliography database has not been updated for years. Meanwhile, citation styles have changed dramatically, many becoming simpler. For this reason, in case of conflict, use the information and order given here or online in preference to the defaults on the ENTRIES tab.

Format	Book	Journal	Web page
APA	AUTHOR(S)	AUTHOR(S)	AUTHOR(S)
	YEAR	YEAR	YEAR OR [DATE]
	TITLE	TITLE	TITLE
	[CITY]	JOURNAL	Retrieved from:
	PUBLISHER	NUMBER/SERIES	[WEBPAGE]
		PAGE(S)	URL
MLA	AUTHOR(S)	AUTHOR(S)	AUTHOR(S)
	TITLE	TITLE	TITLE
	[CITY]	JOURNAL	PUBLISHER
	PUBLISHER	NUMBER/SERIES	YEAR or [DATE]
	YEAR	YEAR	
		PAGE(S)	
Chicago	AUTHOR(S)	AUTHOR(S)	AUTHOR(S)
	YEAR	YEAR	YEAR
	TITLE	TITLE	TITLE
	[CITY]	JOURNAL	PUBLISHER
	PUBLISHER	NUMBER/SERIES	Accessed: YEAR
		PAGE(S)	or [DATE]
			URL
Turabian	AUTHOR(S)	AUTHOR(S)	AUTHOR(S)
	YEAR	YEAR	YEAR
	TITLE	TITLE	TITLE
	[CITY]	JOURNAL	PUBLISHER
	PUBLISHER	NUMBER/SERIES	Accessed: YEAR
		PAGE(S)	or [DATE]
			URL
AMA	AUTHOR(S)	AUTHOR(S)	AUTHOR(S)
	TITLE	TITLE	TITLE

[CITY]	JOURNAL	PUBLISHER
PUBLISHER	YEAR	YEAR
YEAR	NUMBER/VOLUME	Available at: URL
	PAGE[S]	Accessed: YEAR
		or [DATE]

Preparing citations

Citations in the text need to be prepared beforehand. Edit the IDENTIFIER and SHORT NAME (which are different names for the same field) using the format indicated in the table below. Fields are listed from the top in the order in which they should appear:

Format	Datab.	Citations	Other
APA	YEAR	(YEAR)	Mention the author at the start of the sentence that includes the citation.
MLA	AUTHOR	(AUTHOR pages)	Add title if different sources are used by the same author.
Chicago	AUTHOR YEAR	(AUTHOR, YEAR, pages)	Older version uses footnotes or endnotes.
Turabian	AUTHOR YEAR	(AUTHOR, YEAR, pages)	
AMA	–	Footnote or endnote	Footnote or endnote.

The bibliography database fields need for in-text citations, and the citation formats.

Creating footnotes and endnotes

Parenthetical citations have the advantage of letting you view them without losing your place in the text. However, footnotes and endnotes are still used for citations in the AMA format as well for personal preferences.

To use the bibliography database for footnotes and endnotes, set up the citation in the IDENTIFIER column of the bibliography database. The citation may be much longer than most parenthetical citations, but you can still use the column.

To position a footnote or endnote, click INSERT > FOOTNOTE/ENDNOTE. After the number, complete the footnote or endnote by selecting the citation from the drop-down list for INSERT > INDEXES AND TABLES > BIBLIOGRAPHY ENTRY > SHORT NAME.

Using master documents

Master documents are meta-documents: documents made from a collection of Writer documents. Like many advanced aspects of Writer, they work best with a consistent use of templates and styles.

You view the structure of a master document through a specialized version of the Navigator that you can toggle on and off on the tool bar's left.

A master document contains links to its sub-documents. When sub-documents are opened, they are reformatted according to the master document's template. You can print from a master document, and edit text created in one, but all sub-documents must be opened separately to edit them.

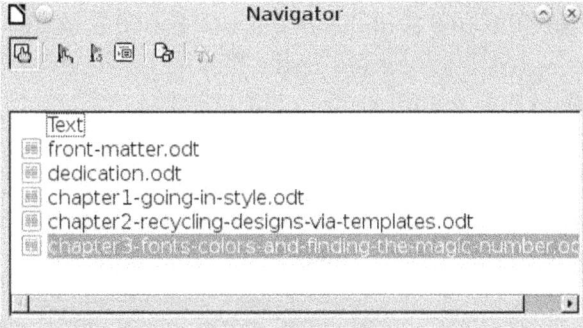

```
┌─────────────────────────────────────────────┐
│ ▯ ◌           Navigator            ◌ ⊗ │
│ ┌──┐ ┌─┐ ┌─┐ ┌─┐ ┌─┐ ┌─┐               │
│ │  │ │ │ │ │ │ │ │ │ │ │               │
│ └──┘ └─┘ └─┘ └─┘ └─┘ └─┘               │
│ ┌─────────────────────────────────────────┐ │
│ │  Text                                   │ │
│ │ ⊞ front-matter.odt                      │ │
│ │ ⊞ dedication.odt                        │ │
│ │ ⊞ chapter1-going-in-style.odt           │ │
│ │ ⊞ chapter2-recycling-designs-via-templates.odt │ │
│ │ ⊞ chapter3-fonts-colors-and-finding-the-magic-number.od │ │
│ │                                         │ │
│ └─────────────────────────────────────────┘ │
└─────────────────────────────────────────────┘
```

The Navigator includes a special view for the contents of master documents.

Tip

The reformatting applies only within the master document. If the sub-documents use their own template, they format differently when opened separately.

When to use master documents

Consider using master documents when:

- Your computer's memory is limited, so you are working with small documents.

- Material is used in different places. A sub-document can be included in more than one master document.

- A document (such as a book) has multiple authors. Authors can work on sub-documents (such as chapters) by themselves, then you use the master document for assembling the complete document.

- You want to produce two or more documents that are similar except in some parts. You can add all the files for all the sub-documents, then hide or unhide individual sections.

Understanding master documents' contents

Master documents are built from three sources:

- Sub-documents: Smaller, individual files. You can edit one by selecting it in the Navigator, and selecting EDIT from the right-click menu. Sub-documents help multiple authors to work on the same master document at the same time.

- Indexes and tables of objects inserted into text areas of the master document. Like any text, they can be replaced by sub-documents.

- Text: Areas between sub-documents that are part of the master document. In Navigator's master document view, each text area is only labeled as TEXT, so their use should be minimized to avoid confusion. You might find the parts of the master document easier to keep track of if you avoid text and use sub-documents instead.

Navigating master documents

Master documents have a special view in the Navigator. To toggle the view, click the TOGGLE button in the upper left of the tool bar. A new set of icons appears in the toolbar.

The Navigator icons for the master document view.

Tip

The Navigator only inserts items above the current one, You can rearrange items after adding them.

Planning master documents

To use master documents efficiently:

- If possible, use the same template to create the master document and all its sub-documents. A sub-document with a different template may have formatting problems when you switch between using it by itself and using it as a sub-document. If you are using a sub-document in more than one master document, ignore this advice and hope for the best.

- Place a master document and all of its sub-documents in the same directory.

- Ordinarily, you probably want each part of a master document to start on a separate page. You can set this format up automatically using the BREAKS section on the TEXT FLOW tab of paragraph styles to start a new page after the paragraph style that begins all the sub-documents, such as HEADING 1..

- The convention is to start each new part of a long document on a right, odd-numbered page. The reason is that most readers' eyes fall on the right page first. If you want a page to be a right page, add a blank text in the master document. Do not uses spaces to add another page, or you may run into difficulties.

- Aside from tables and indexes and page breaks, minimize the content that is added to the master document directly, rather than to sub-documents. The more content that is added directly to the master document, the more likely it is likely to crash.

- Use page styles and/or manual page breaks to use different numbering for different parts of the master document. For example, one common format is use lower case roman numerals for front matter such as copyright pages and tables of contents, and Arabic numbers for the main text. Often, too, numbering is restarted with the main text.

STOP Caution

Currently, master documents can have problems with page breaks. If you have difficulties, assemble long files by copying and pasting.

Creating master documents

Master documents can be fragile to work with. Creating one in this order should minimize problems:

1 Create the sub-documents as you can, even if they are blank. The sub-documents should all use the same template. You can create master documents from sub-documents with different templates, but you might have formatting problems.

2 Use the same template to create the master document. Click FILE > SEND > CREATE MASTER DOCUMENT and save. You can use a blank document, or a sub-document. If you use a sub-document, then it will be first in the master document, and will not be deletable.

Tip

Master documents all have an .odm extension. However, you can start the name with "master-document" for quicker identification, at least while you are working.

Caution

Unless your default template is the one that the master document uses, do not create a master document from FILE > NEW > MASTER DOCUMENT. You want to ensure that you are dealing only with the template you want.

Unless the master document and sub-documents share the same template, the sub-documents reformat each time you use the master document, increasing the chances of corruption.

3 The Navigator is open when you finish saving the master document. Use its features to add and position all the sub-documents (as described above).

4 Add any tables of contents, indexes, and bibliographies directly to the master document when all the sub-documents are complete.

Adding cross-references between sub-documents

Adding cross-references between two sub-documents in a master documents is similar to adding a cross-reference in another document. However, because headings do not display, you must set references manually, in an awkward work-around:

1 Open the sub-document you plan to reference (the source document). You can open it by itself, or from the master document.

2 Highlight the text for the reference, and click INSERT > CROSS-REFERENCE > SET REFERENCE.

The FIELDS dialog window opens to the CROSS-REFERENCES tab. The selected text is entered in the VALUE field.

3 Enter a name for the reference. Then click the INSERT button. In the text, the selected text now has the gray shading that marks a field.

Choose a name that is unique not only in the current sub-document, but all other sub-documents. The easiest way to ensure uniqueness is to make the name and the value identical. You can also keep a separate note of each name in a spreadsheet.

Tip

To view the reference, change to the Navigator's view of the master document and look under REFERENCES.

4 Save the source sub-document with the reference.

5 Open the target document and select INSERT > CROSS REFERENCES > INSERT REFERENCE.

6 The FIELDS dialog window opens to the CROSS-REFERENCES tab.

STOP Caution

> Because the reference is in another document, it is not listed in the SELECTION pane.

7 Type the reference's NAME in the target document.

8 Make a selection from the INSERT REFERENCE TO pane. CHAPTER is the chapter number, REFERENCE the text of the reference.

9 In the target document, enter the lead text, then select the format followed by the INSERT button.

Because the target sub-document cannot find the reference in the source sub-document, the message ERROR: REFERENCE SOURCE NOT FOUND displays.

STOP Caution

> This error message may cause problems with pagination when the sub-document is open by itself. You can ignore the problems if the sub-document is only going to be used in the master document.

10 Save the target sub-document with the cross-reference. When you re-open the master document, it will be able to locate the reference, and the cross-reference will now display instead of the error message. Pagination problems due to the error message are also corrected.

If you open the sub-document with the cross-reference from outside the master document, the cross-reference fields show the error message again.

STOP

Caution

Cross-references are based on the names of sub-documents. If you change a sub-document's name – for instance, to indicate a draft – you have to re-insert any cross-references to it.

Moving beyond Writer

After ten chapters, the importance of styles in Writer should be proved beyond any doubt. When you do not use styles, you waste time and limit your possible actions. It's that simple.

12

Designing and delivering slide shows

The emphasis in designing shifts with Impress, LibreOffice's slide show application. As in Writer, templates remain important, but styles become relatively minor. Instead, the attention turns from formatting to structuring content – often, to the challenge of avoiding designing a slide show that is all summary, so that you are constantly twisting your head away from the audience to read directly from the slides.

Why are slide shows boring?

Used well, Impress can help a talk succeed. The trouble is, just as many people never learn how to use a word processor properly, many fail to understand the uses and limitations of a slide show.

Information designer Edward Tufte points out that presentations are designed for a lecture format. In fact, with comic exaggeration, he likens them to a Soviet May Day rally.

Unless well-planned, a slide show discourages questions from the audience, as well as conversations between members of the audience.

Spreadsheets: MS Excel vs. LO Calc

- Both in arms race to extend columns and rows
- Calc careful to match functions, because Excel is so widely used:
- Sometimes, 2 functions, with LO version having more features
- Roughly equivalent feature set: Main difference is in names of some features.
- Some claim Excel better for expert users.

A slide from a summary presentation. Slides like this one are only effective when a presentation is running unattended.

This one-way flow of information tempts many speakers to believe that a presentation should be a complete summary of their ideas. Their talks follow from bullet to bullet in the most unimaginative way possible. In many cases, presenters could have sent their slides and stayed at home for all that their physical presence adds.

Sometimes, a summary slide show makes sense – for example, if the presentation is meant to run unattended as a continuous loop at a trade show. But many exchanges of information, such as a planning session or learning a language, fit poorly into a lecture format.

Even more importantly, many – maybe most – ideas cannot fit into a structure of separate bullet points and slides without risking over-simplification.

These problems explain why announcing that you will not be using slides in your talk is an almost guaranteed way to win your audience's applause.

Because of these problems, some critics discard the idea of presentations altogether. Amazon, for example, has gone so far as to ban presentations in its business.

But such reactions are too harsh. Forewarned of the problems, you can still make your slides an enhancement of your talk, and not a substitution that overwhelms it.

Deciding when to use a slide show

A slide show is a medium with serious limitations. With no more than 75 words per screen, a slide by itself cannot easily communicate complex information. Even more seriously, slides can discourage any exchange of ideas between the speaker and the audience.

With work, you can reduce these tendencies, although you will always be straining against them. However, before you choose to use a slide show (assuming that you have a choice), you should ask yourself whether one is necessary.

Use a presentation if:	Don't use a presentation if:
• Your purpose is to deliver information without interruptions, and/or without a speaker.	• One of your goals is audience participation.

- Audience participation is limited.

- Members of the audience require individual attention or discussion is important.

- Your topic is simple or well-unified.

- Your topic is complex or abstract, and the connection between ideas is essential for understanding the whole.

- Your topic is technical.

- Your topic involves an understanding or appreciation of language.

- Your talk includes diagrams or illustrations.

- Your audience does not need diagrams or illustrations, or you are presenting them in handouts or some other way.

- Your talk has a series of questions and answers, as in a vocabulary drill.

- Your talk is about high-level, abstract concepts.

- The presentation is going to run looped and unsupervised.

- You are delivering the talk live.

- You want to emphasize key words and show how they are spelled.

These guidelines limit slides to information that is hard to present any other way, in effect using the presentation in the same way that lecturers once used an overhead projector with transparencies. If followed, these guidelines should free you from the obsession of summarizing by encouraging you to add a slide only when it helps the audience's understanding.

Designing a presentation

In early releases, OpenOffice.org used to start Impress with a wizard that made clear the design is both format and structure. Recent releases of LibreOffice no longer follow that practice, but you might still consider starting your building of a presentation by running FILE > WIZARDS > PRESENTATION. You can make Impress default to using the wizard by clicking TOOLS > OPTIONS > GENERAL, NEW DOCUMENT > START WITH WIZARD check box.

Regardless of whether you use the wizard, remember that designing an effective slide show consists of six steps:

1   Plan the presentation structure.

2   Use the MASTER view to set up features such as backgrounds, footers, Presentation styles, and transitions.

3   Set the slide design as needed for individual slides.

4   Use the Draw-like features in Impress to create any charts and diagrams or tables. Alternatively, you may want to insert charts and diagrams made in another program and imported in a standard graphics format.

5   Add any notes for your talk.

6   Choose slide show settings from SLIDE SHOW > SLIDE SHOW SETTINGS.

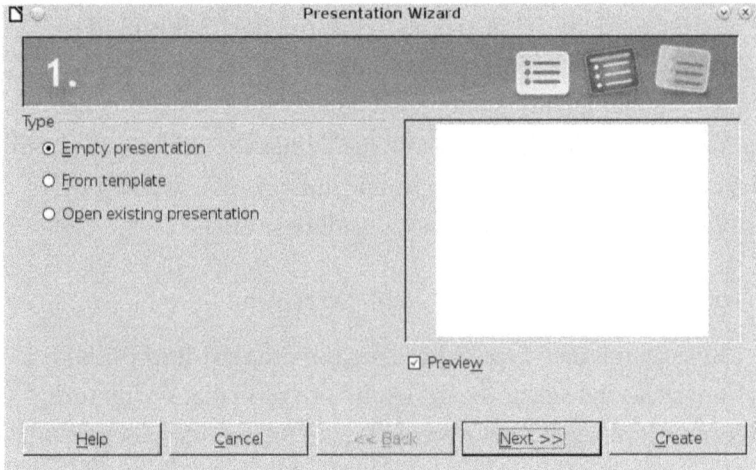

Impress' Presentation Wizard helps you to structure your presentation.

In all these stages, keep everything simple and make design choices to enhance legibility. Just as the average text-based document rarely needs more than two fonts (plus, of course, their font styles or weights), so a slide show rarely needs more than one type of slide transition, or more than a few slide designs.

Each slide show is, in fact, an exercise in design under restricted conditions. Compared to the possibilities of a Writer document, a presentation is extremely simple, with limited choices to make.

For instance, instead of setting up a complex format feature by feature, you are more likely to choose a slide design. In effect, you are designing a series of posters that are readable at a distance.

To an extent, you can add some flexibility by adding graphic text, which is treated as an object instead of as regular text. However, as you design, take constant reality checks. If you start feeling that you are struggling against the structure of Impress –

for instance, by trying to wrap text around a graphic, or to set up text to flow from frame to frame – you should probably give up and accept the limitations of a slide show.

Tip

If you really want a complex format, design slides as Writer pages, and then export them to PDF. You will need to be careful that you don't use font sizes that are too small, but many alternative presentation apps use PDF slides, and the audience probably never notices.

Outlining slide shows

People plan in different ways. A tree of main points, mind mapping, scribbling main points – all can be effective ways for different types of people to plan. Too many, though, plunge into developing a slide show with only a limited idea of the structure.

This approach is inefficient, because it means that you are trying to get ideas down at the same time that you are structuring, giving only half your mind to each of two tasks, each of which deserves your full attention. Instead of thinking and structuring well, you most likely end up doing both poorly.

Even worse, this practice encourages slide shows that are complete summaries of your talk.

The best place to begin a presentation in Impress is in the Outline view. Each top outline heading is a new slide, the others a bullet point on the slide. You can descend a level in the outline by pressing TAB, and ascend a level by pressing SHIFT+TAB.

Tip

The OUTLINE view is simple yet powerful enough that you might consider using it for all your outlining, even for text documents.

Normal | Outline | Notes | Handout | Slide Sorter

- MSO more mature
- No cost = low quality
- If you can't find a feature, it doesn't exist
- LO is just a clone

⁴ **Reality:**

MSO & LO are comparable office apps

⁵ Talking points

1. Interface and organization

2. Core applications

3. Other features

⁶

1. Interface and Organization

⁷ Classical vs. Ribbon

Use Impress' OUTLINE tab as the starting point for a slide show.

Alternatively, outline in Writer, then transfer the outline to Impress by selecting FILE > SEND > OUTLINE TO PRESENTATION.

However, whichever way you work, do not stop with the outline. When you have the complete outline, go back and mark the items that should be enhanced by illustrations or emphasized by giving them a slide. Aside from structural slides such as the title page, only these points will have a slide.

Designing with LibreOffice

No firm rule exists, but if more than about one-third of your points are listed as having a slide, you are probably still too close to a summary presentation. Rework the outline until points marked to become slides are as few as possible.

You should now have an outline consisting consists of only useful slides, and that you cannot simply read when presenting.

Making a structural template

If you find yourself continually doing similar types of presentations, you can save structural templates. At the very least, you might want to save a structural template with the first few slides. These include:

- The title page: Use the TITLE SLIDE layout, with the presentation's title at the top and your name below it. In a long slide show, you might want title pages for each section.

- Biography: Placed near the start, this slide is not a general life history, but proof that you are an expert on your subject, and that your ideas are worth listening to. If you have a reputation among audience members for your expertise, you might omit the biography.

- Talk outline: A summary of the major sections of your talk after the title page and biography. You can make it more informal by wording the sections as questions. Listeners can follow your presentation better if they have a sense of the structure of your talk.

- A sub-title page: Sub-title pages can be shown briefly to let listeners know what stage your talk is at. Usually, if you use sub-titles, you should also use a talk outline.

- Conclusion: A summary, a call to action, or an example that emphasizes your main point. Whatever tactic you choose, the conclusion is your last chance to leave an impression with listeners.

- Bibliography: In a formal or academic presentation, you may want to show your sources and comment on them briefly. In other circumstances, you might omit the bibliography, but, if you do, be ready to provide your sources for those who ask for them.

- Question: The last slide in the presentation, the Question slide indicates that you are opening the topic to general discussion. Generally, you want to time your presentation so that the audience has at least fifteen minutes to discuss it.

Tip
Adding tables can be laborious in Impress, so add a slide with a table in the colors you want.

Add content as necessary between these slides. Use the template as the source for other, more specialized templates.

Designing with master slides

Master slides are Impress' equivalent of Writer's page styles. They set the look of your slides in one place rather than for each slide. However, unlike page styles, each master slide also has its own set of styles for text.

Most presentations need only a single master slide. However, you may want design elements such as reversing the background and foreground colors on title and biography pages to emphasize their differences from the body of the presentation.

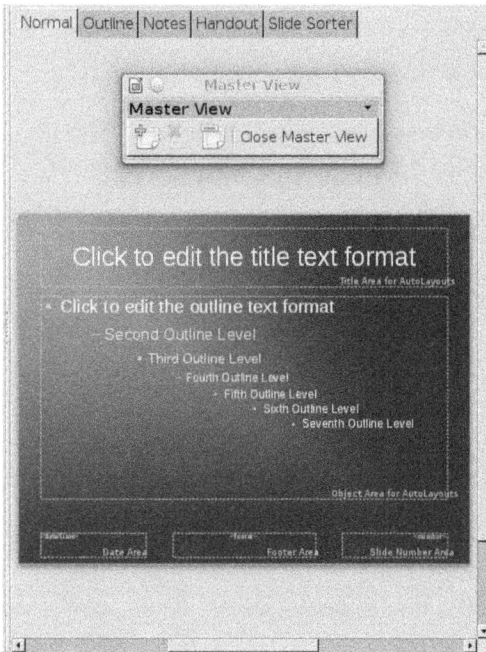

Edit master slides from VIEW > MASTER > SLIDE MASTER.

Creating master slides

To create each master slide:

1 Find a background template. You might find one in the
PRESENTATIONS BACKGROUNDS folder of the Template Manager,
or else create one using Draw or a third-party application like
GIMP.

2 Select a presentation structure from FILE > NEW > TEMPLATES.
LibreOffice has a separate folder in the Template Manager for
structures, marked simply PRESENTATIONS.

3 Select VIEW > MASTER > SLIDE MASTER. The Slide Master view
opens.

4 Optionally, click the RENAME MASTER icon in the floating window in the top middle of the editing window.

5 Right-click anywhere on the master slide and select PAGE SETUP to set the slide dimensions.

6 Right-click anywhere on the master slide and select SET BACKGROUND IMAGE FOR SLIDE or the AVAILABLE FOR USE pane in the sidebar. Use the file manager to select the file for the background.

7 Optionally, enter information in the footer.

8 Adjust the presentation styles as needed.

9 If you want to create another master slide, click the NEW MASTER icon in the floating window. When finished, click CLOSE MASTER VIEW in the floating window.

Choosing slide backgrounds

When you select backgrounds, you face the usual design challenges of any background (see "Highlighting and setting backgrounds," page 134).

On the one hand, a single-color background risks looking amateurish. On the other hand, a background full of gradients or different colors risks leaving large portions of the screen with too little or too much contrast for adding text. The ideal background is somewhere between these extremes, with the more complicated parts of the design either extremely simple, or else confined to the corners or the top and bottom of the slide, leaving the center free for displaying text.

Test possible backgrounds against a variety of different colored texts. Setting the background to be partly transparent can often make a major difference. Just make sure that the two contrast, so that the text is as readable as possible.

If you plan to distribute your slides in grayscale, also check how your slides look in black and white.

Just as importantly, you might want a background that uses personal or corporate colors.

Finding backgrounds

LibreOffice comes with a selection of backgrounds, in the Presentation Backgrounds folder of the Template Manager. You can also find many more choices with a quick web search, although the quality of the selections varies. Just because a background is available online does not mean that it is suitable for use.

The most common problem with downloaded backgrounds is that they are too busy for text to be readable against them.

Tip

Remember that you can also use PowerPoint backgrounds. You should have no trouble importing most PowerPoint backgrounds – although when you save you are asked if you want to convert to Open Document Format.

Designing backgrounds

If you are unable to find a suitable background, you can design your own, or modify an existing one in a graphics editor. Impress rescales slides as needed, but rescaling distorts not only screenshots, but also text on logos. For this reason, do not rely on rescaling without thoroughly checking the results.

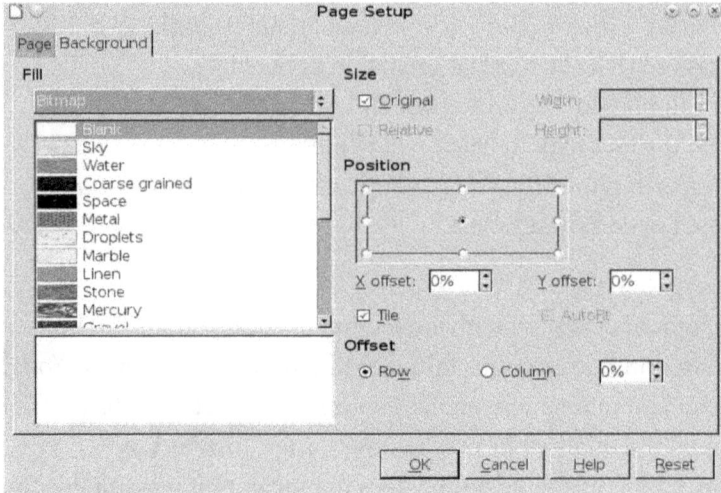

Use FORMAT > PAGE > BACKGROUND to design and choose a patterned background.

Tip

If you need to add a logo to the slide background, consider placing it where the footer would otherwise go.

Writer does its best to adjust images, but to guarantee avoiding distortion, use one of the standard monitor ratios: 16:9 for wide screens, or 4:3 for older screens.

You can also use the tools on the BACKGROUND tab to reduce an image's size, position it, or offset it.

To design your own patterned backgrounds, go to VIEW > MASTER > SLIDE MASTER, and from the menu select FORMAT > PAGE > BACKGROUND to choose a color, gradient, cross-hatching, or bitmap tile for the background for all slides with the same master slide. Click the GALLERY button on the sidebar for more patterns and images. If other options fail, create a patterned background.

A tiled background using a brick pattern. The design is intricate, but small enough that foreground text is readable.

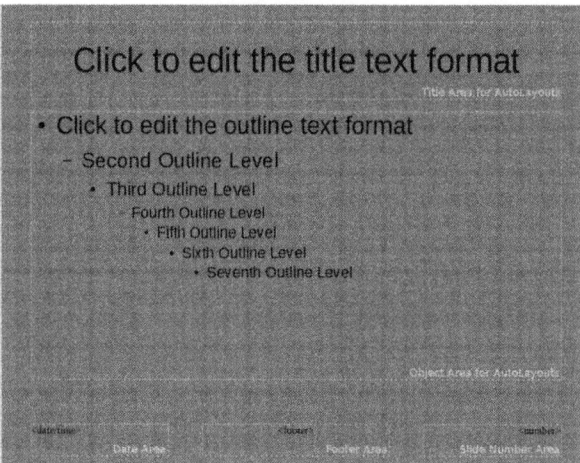

A hatched background. Be careful that a hatched background has enough contrast with the foreground text and is readable. Take particular care when printing in black and white.

A gradient background. This gradient leaves most of the slide's center with a strong contrast, leaving the lesser contrast to the sides where there is less text.

When you are finished designing, save the result by selecting FILE > TEMPLATES > SAVE AS TEMPLATE > PRESENTATION BACKGROUNDS. The background is then available for use in other presentations.

Adding footer information

All slides include three frames for footers: from left to right, date and time, optional fields, and slide number.

In practice, only the slide number is used regularly these days, and, sometimes, not even it. Instead, the footer area often holds a company logo and ignores the frame altogether.

The footer section of Impress' MASTER VIEW provides a simple arrangement for basic information.

Setting Presentation styles

Impress has two types of styles for fonts. Drawing Object styles (called Graphics styles in OpenOffice and earlier versions of LibreOffice) treat text as one feature of objects, and are covered in Chapter 13 when Draw is discussed.

The more common font styles are Presentation styles – the styles for each level of bullet point on the slides. Most options for Presentation styles are explained in Chapters 5 and 6 in the discussion of paragraph styles.

Most people change little except FONTS and FONT EFFECTS. Unlike styles elsewhere in LibreOffice, you cannot create new Presentation styles. However, each master slide can format its Presentation styles differently. If you want a design that Presentation styles cannot handle, use a Drawing Object style.

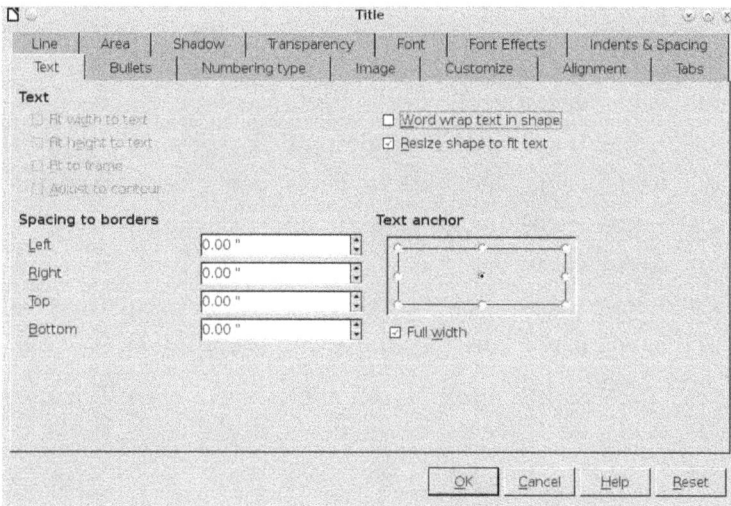

The PRESENTATION STYLES dialog window formats the bullets in a slide show.

Selecting fonts for slides

Since slides are presented at a low resolution, sans serif or slab serif fonts are generally preferable to serif ones for content. Titles and sub-titles are generally large enough that they can use any fonts.

Because backgrounds vary more in slide shows than in text documents, experiment with the colors on the FONT EFFECTS tab to get the one that stands out most from the background.

The default font sizes for slides are 44 points for a title and 18 points for an OUTLINE 1 style. If you can possibly make the OUTLINE 1 style larger, do so.

By contrast, the temptation to make a font size smaller than the defaults is a sure sign that you are cramming too many details on the slide and need to rethink.

Adjusting lists

The Outline styles in Impress default to bullet lists. You can customize them using the BULLETS, NUMBERING TYPE, IMAGE, and CUSTOMIZE tabs, but, as with list styles in Writer, avoid the retro-styled IMAGE tab. The CUSTOMIZE tab allows adjustment of spacing or the selection of custom bullets and numbers or larger-sized ones for special circumstances.

However, in many cases, the default spacing is adequate. That means that you may be mostly using the BULLETS and NUMBERING TYPE tabs to set up lists.

Tip

If you do not want lists, set the NUMBER field on the CUSTOMIZE tab to NONE. This one customization alone adds greatly to the flexibility of your design.

Tip

As with headings in text documents, restrict your OUTLINE styles to 3 or 4 levels. You can use some of the rest to create numbered lists or lines with neither bullets or numbers.

An especially useful style to create is an Impress equivalent of the paragraph style TEXT INDENT – that is, one with no bullets or numbers, indented to start where the text in the list starts.

You will not be able to rename the styles, but their limited number should make them easy to find.

Setting alignment

Presentation styles include an ALIGNMENT tab, so those who want justified text in slides can have them. However, at the large font sizes that slides use, justified lines frequently have too many hyphens and irregular spacing between words.

Instead of giving yourself one more worry, accept the default Left alignment for content. Your audience will never notice.

Tip

Titles are centered on slide designs that include both titles and contents. However, giving them a left alignment simplifies the design while emphasizing that they belong to the content that follows.

Setting indents and spacing

Line spacing, indentations, and spacing above and below lines are all set on the INDENTS & SPACING tab.

These settings are useful for large font sizes, but needing them in other circumstances is often a sign that you are adding too many words per slide and risking readability. Nothing requires that the words fill the entire slide.

Setting wrap

The TEXT tab for Presentation styles sets how content fits into Impress' pre-existing frames. Most users are likely to be content with the defaults – especially since many of these settings can have unexpected results when you change slide designs.

Deciding on tabs or tables

Mostly, you can let slide designs determine how content is arranged on slides. If you find the default slide designs too limiting, you are likely trying to make slides do something that they were never intended to.

However, if you decide that you do have a reason for more complex layouts, you can use the TABS tab for a Presentation style, or else a table.

Of the two choices, a table positions information more securely. You can add a table by positioning the cursor and selecting INSERT > TABLE.

Tip

After you have added a table, a table design pane opens in the sidebar.

When you add a table, the PROPERTIES pane adds a TABLE DESIGN tab. Many of the check boxes under TABLE DESIGN can be useful for formatting, but, unfortunately, the default colors are unlikely to match your slide show. In particular, the default black text will probably need to be changed.

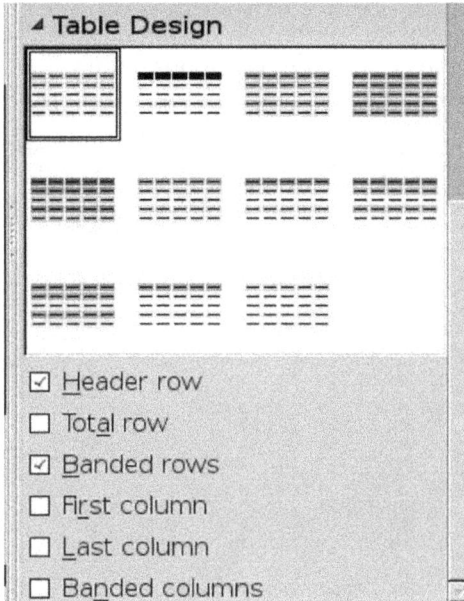

⊿ Table Design

☑ H̲eader row
☐ Tot̲al row
☑ B̲anded rows
☐ Fi̲rst column
☐ L̲ast column
☐ Ba̲nded columns

When using Impress' TABLE DESIGN tab, a plain gray table is the least garish choice.

Selecting a slide transition

LibreOffice offers nearly sixty different transitions available from SLIDE SHOW > SLIDE TRANSITION or the SLIDE TRANSITION tab in the sidebar. You can set the speed of each transition, and a sound to accompany it, and apply it to the entire presentation, or just to the movement between two particular slides.

This variety has a certain fascination, and every now and then you might find a match between your topic and an available transition.

For example, CHECKERBOARD DOWN might be suitable for a slide show that discusses chess or uses a chess metaphor. Or a small sound clip might emphasize the start of a major topic.

However, obsessing over slide transitions is not the best use of your time. Few ever notice the visual slide transitions – the audience will judge your talk on its content and its delivery. Whenever possible, choose a transition and click the APPLY TO ALL SLIDES button, and move on as quickly as possible.

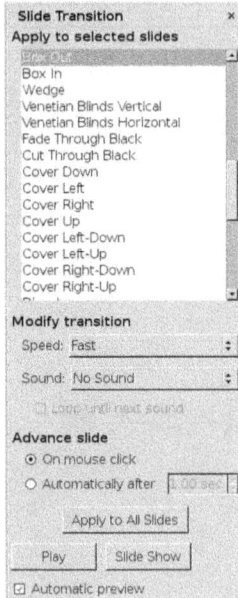

Slide Transition	×
Apply to selected slides	

Box Out
Box In
Wedge
Venetian Blinds Vertical
Venetian Blinds Horizontal
Fade Through Black
Cut Through Black
Cover Down
Cover Left
Cover Right
Cover Up
Cover Left-Down
Cover Left-Up
Cover Right-Down
Cover Right-Up

Modify transition

Speed: Fast

Sound: No Sound

☐ Loop until next sound

Advance slide
⊙ On mouse click
○ Automatically after 1.00 sec

Apply to All Slides

Play   Slide Show

☑ Automatic preview

Elaborate transitions are rarely worth the effort to pick them.

Setting slide layouts

Slide layouts are applied to individual slides. On the sidebar, you can select from twelve different layouts, each with frames for different combinations of text and objects.

The layouts allow you to place text and objects with a degree of symmetry without requiring much time. In practice, however, the last six have far too many frames to be useful except for handouts. At best, they make your slides hard to read.

Tip
The frames on slide layouts can be adjusted by dragging on their edges with the mouse. You can also delete (but not add) frames.

You can use Drawing Object styles to add your own unique designs, but selecting from the pre-defined layouts is almost always a better use of your time.

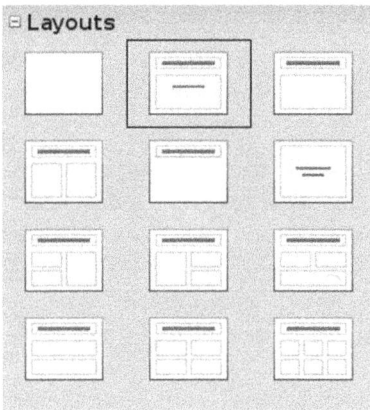

While you can design your own slide layouts, there are few reasons not to stay with the default ones..

Adding other elements

Impress slide shows are primarily words and images. However, you can also add:

- Additional images (INSERT > IMAGE).

- Objects (INSERT > OBJECT): A separate LibreOffice file that can be updated as needed.

- Animated GIFs (INSERT > ANIMATED IMAGE): Animations can be constructed using SLIDE SHOW > CUSTOM ANIMATION, setting up the separate images one at a time. They are especially useful for before and after pictures when giving instructions.

- Movies and sound (INSERT > MEDIA > AUDIO OR VIDEO): Both are set to play only on a certain slide. That means that, if you want a continuous narration, you must break it down slide by slide, and set each slide to change only after the narration is complete. Do this by right-clicking on the slide and filling in the field SLIDE TRANSITION > ADVANCE SLIDE > AUTOMATICALLY AFTER. In this circumstance, each slide needs its own transition setting.

Tip
Use SLIDE SHOW > REHEARSE TIMINGS to help sync movies and sounds with your narration.

If adding these elements sounds too complex, don't worry – few presentations use them, and you can deliver an effective slide show without them.

Example: Displaying one line at a time

Many animations are not worth the time they take to develop, although sometimes they can take the place of before and after pictures.

I remember, for example, an animation that showed how the links in chain mail slide into place so that each ring is connected to six other rings.

These uses aside, one of the most common animations is displaying bullet points or lines one at a time. This animation helps the audience to focus on the current point being discussed, instead of encouraging their thoughts to drift to the other points.

Showing bullet points one at a time is especially handy for oral quizzes or in-class vocabulary reviews, or any sort of question/answer structure.

You could get a similar effect with two slides, but putting the question and answer on the same slide helps to keep the answer in context. Just as importantly, having only two items on one slide lets you use a larger font size.

To advance the slide show one line at a time:

1   Enter the question or vocabulary item on the first line. Since only two items are on the slide, you can make the font size much larger than usual.

2   Select CUSTOM ANIMATION from the SLIDE SHOW menu or sidebar. The CUSTOM ANIMATION pane opens.

3   Place the cursor at the start of the first line. In the CUSTOM ANIMATION pane, click the PLUS button and select ENTRANCE > APPEAR from the dialog box.

4   Check that EFFECT APPEAR > START on the CUSTOM ANIMATION pane is set to ON CLICK.

Tip

You can adjust animations from the DIRECTION and SPEED fields, but in this case you probably don't need to.

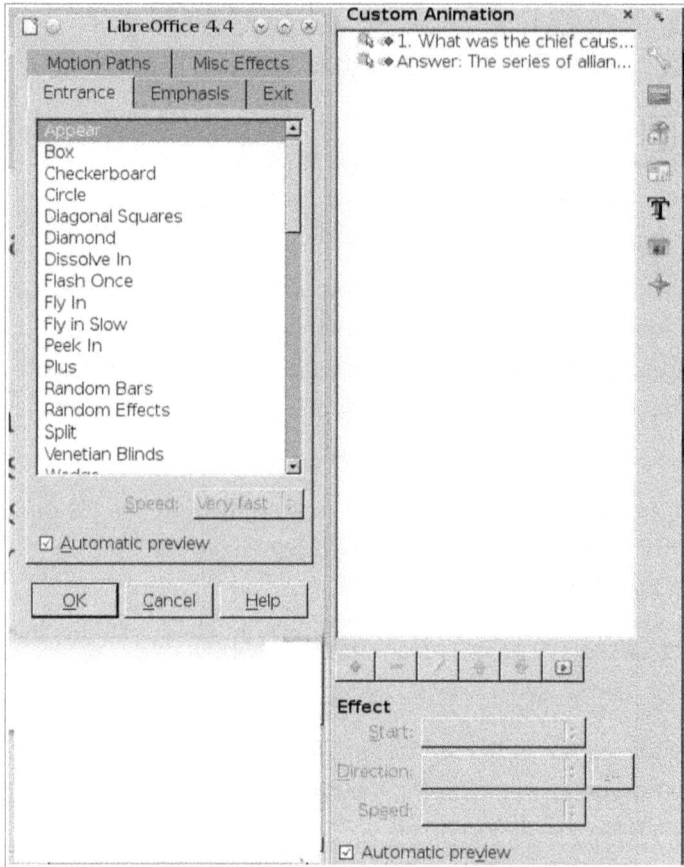

The CUSTOM ANIMATION pane and its dialog window. Make sure that any animations you add are not just bells and whistles, but illustrate something that cannot be easily shown any other way. Usually, animations are particularly useful when you need to show motion.

5   Repeat steps 1–4 for the paragraph for the answer.

    When you present, move the mouse cursor to the start of a line and click the mouse once to reveal the line.

1. What was the chief cause of
World War I?

Answer: The series of alliances that
  created two rival camps in Europe:
  England, France & Russia in one,
  and Germany and Austria-Hungary
  in the other.

A slide that uses animation to reveal a question in one line, then
the answer in the second line. During the presentation, each line
will be hidden until you click on it.

Preparing notes and handouts

Many versions of LibreOffice have a console built in that let
you read the NOTES tab as the slide show runs. If yours does not,
consider installing the Presenter Console extension.

Handouts are generally copies of the slide show printed out to
give to the audience. Once part of any well-organized slide
presentation, they have been largely replaced in recent years by
putting the entire presentation online. In theory, presenters can
prepare any sort of handout, but, typically, unless you do a
detailed summary presentation, handouts usually give only the
vaguest sense of your talk and are only minimally useful.

Tip

If you do decide to use handouts and cannot print them in color, check their appearance in black and white for contrast.

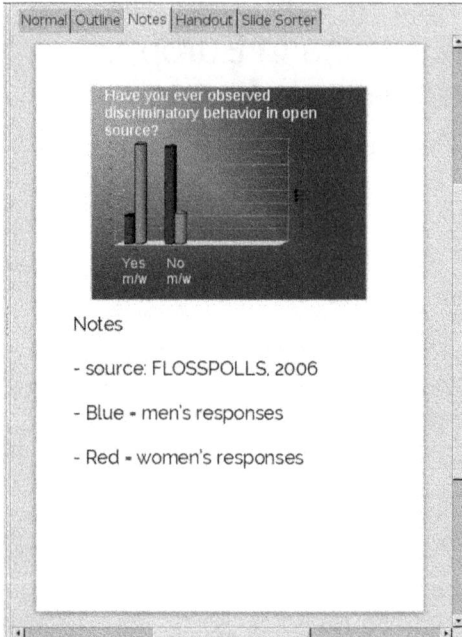

Impress' Notes tab is for information you want to remember while presenting. Put the information in bullet or number lists to keep yourself from reading the notes.

Unless you are an accomplished speaker, you will sound much worse reading your notes word for word.

Setting presentation options

Most of the options in the SLIDE SHOW dialog window are obvious from their description. However, the implications of some are not always clear:

- Like the HIDE FONT EFFECT, the RANGE pane is useful for single-sourcing similar presentations in the same file. Within the same presentation, you can store several different shows, each for a different audience or circumstance.

- Create custom slides shows from SLIDE SHOW > CUSTOM SLIDE SHOW.

STOP

Caution

Until you create a custom slide show, the USE CUSTOM SLIDE SHOW option is not active.

- TYPE > AUTO sets the time between repetitions of the presentation when it runs unattended.

- The NAVIGATOR VISIBLE check box gives you another way to move back and forth between slides. However, other formats for switching slides make it unnecessary.

- PRESENTATION ALWAYS ON TOP floats Impress above any other open windows, preventing you from fumbling in front of your audience. This option can keep you from fumbling in the middle of a presentation when a mouse slips.

- MULTIPLE DISPLAYS sets the display on which the presentation runs. Usually, you will need to adjust this option so that the presentation runs on the projector.

Other options are a matter of taste or necessity.

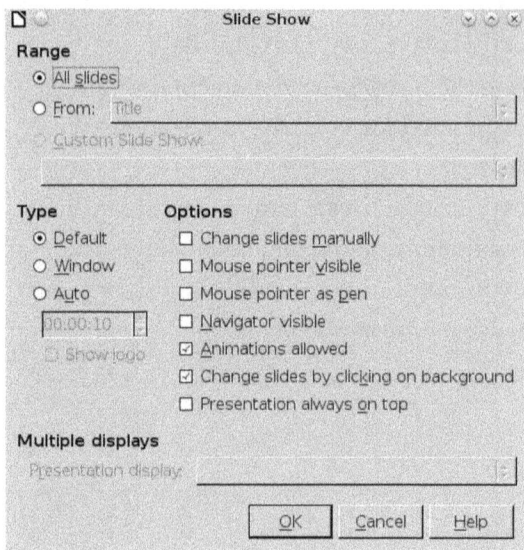

SLIDE SHOW > SLIDE SHOW options provide the finishing touches to a presentation.

Saving templates

Designing a slide show is not as complicated as designing a document that may be printed. The distance at which slides are seen is very forgiving and obscures details.

All the same, nobody wants to do the same job twice unless they have to. Save your background and structural templates and copies of complete presentations using FILE > TEMPLATES > SAVE AS TEMPLATE. Even if your next presentation is on an entirely different subject, you can probably cannibalize large pieces of your previous presentations and save yourself time.

Delivering a slide show

Slide design can only do so much to make your presentation effective. Practicing your talk – even how you will move on stage to keep listeners' attention – is equally important. Having designed an effective slide show, you must also design an effective means of delivery. After having made the effort to create a genuinely useful slide show, you should make sure that your delivery does not ruin your previous work.

In particular, you want to discourage yourself from reading from the screen, and your audience from reading the screen instead of paying attention to you.

If you create your slide show as suggested in this chapter, such problems should be minimized. However, you can reduce potential problems even further if you:

- Always carry a backup of your presentation.

- Create at least a rough outline of how you will deliver your presentation if a slide projector is unavailable.

- Reduce your nervousness by arriving and setting up before the talk starts. The less nervous you are, the less likely you are to let the limits of the medium control the presentation.

- Know your material well enough that you only occasionally need to refer to your notes or slides.

- Continually position yourself (from the audience's perspective) to the left of the screen you are using for the slide show. If you are speaking in a language that reads left to right, listeners' eyes are more likely to move toward you.

  If you are using a lectern, position it to the left of the screen, if possible. You do not need to stay in that position, but when you start to refer to a slide, move to that position, and keep coming back to it as you continue to discuss the slide. With any luck, you will draw at least some listeners' attention toward you and what you are saying, and away from the slide.

- Move around as you deliver your presentation in order to distract the audience from looking at the screen. In fact, you can signal changes of topic by changing your position.

- Get somebody else to change slides, or be well-enough rehearsed that you can set the slide show to advance automatically. The less you interact with the slide show, the less likely you are to start reading slides.

With these hints, you should be able to control your slide shows, rather than being controlled by them.

Understanding design constraints

Slide shows are a design challenge with well-defined conditions. Structurally, the conditions mean that building a presentation is a contest in which either you succumb to the internal logic of the form, or learn how to make the conditions serve your own purposes. Aesthetically, the conditions mean that the choices are heavily constrained, which can help you learn more about design.

13

Designing drawing content

Draw and Impress share a set of graphic editing tools. These tools are partly reproduced in the Drawing tool bar of other applications. Like stand-alone graphic editors as Inkscape, these tools work with vector graphics, which are formats stored mathematically and which therefore can be expanded to any size.

However, you can also import bitmap formats such as .JPEG and .PNG, which store information as pixels, from editors like GIMP.

Despite their names, Draw and Impress are not meant to be a complete set of tools for editing graphics. Designers have done professional works in Draw, but mainly it is intended for diagrams and simple pictures. Flow charts, architectural layouts, construction plans, organizational charts, circuit diagrams, icons – these are the sorts of documents that Draw, Impress, and the Drawing tool bar are meant to handle.

You can also import graphics prepared in another application, and do simple layout. However, if you want to draw or edit an image, programs like Inkscape or Krita have more tools.

Learning design principles

Diagrams and layout have fewer limits to their design than a page of text or even a spreadsheet. For this reason, you can work with them better if you know some basics of design.

Whole books are written about design, and perfecting your expertise can be a life-long study. However, the best starting points I have ever seen are the four principles that Robin Williams uses in her books. See Appendix B, "Learning more about typography," page 485.

Each principle helps to guide readers through the document, but their use remains contextual. In some situations, using more than one principle at once can strengthen the design, but in others they can work against each other. Sometimes, too, one principle may be strong enough that you can ignore other ones.

Williams' four principles are:

- Alignment: Shows whether elements are or are not connected by their alignment. For example, list items have a common alignment, while the return address is the only part of the letter to have a right alignment because it is unconnected to the rest of the letter.

- Contrast: Emphasizes differences between elements on a page by design differences. For example, use a different, larger font for headings than for body text, or a background color for a side bar in a financial report that is different from the background for the body text.

- Proximity: Groups items that are related to each other together. For example, a document's title and author might appear in the same header or footer. By comparison, word count and the author's name do not belong in the same header or footer unless you have no other place to put them.

- Repetition: Unifies the document by repeating design elements. For example, if you use a particular shade of blue for the headings, use the same blue as a background for table headers and for a line that separates the header from the text.

These principles can be thought of as the tactics of design. To them, I would add several strategic guidelines. These guidelines are partly a matter of typographic standard practices, and partly a reflection of current design trends that show no signs of disappearing any time soon.

These strategic principles are:

- A simple design is preferable to a complicated one.

- If you don't have a reason for a design element, delete it. Replace it with the simplest possible alternative. Sometimes, you may not need to replace it at all.

- Layout that calls attention to itself is bad layout. Design enhances documents. It is not an end in itself.

- Modern design favors the asymmetrical rather the balanced design. This strategy directly contradicts most beginners' instinct, which is to always create a symmetrical design.

There is much more to design than these brief comments. But learn to apply these ideas, and you will be thinking like a designer.

Example: applying design

To help make Williams' four principles more concrete, here are four illustrations based on the designing of business cards, showing a card before and after a principle was applied.

The After cards, while not necessarily the best of all possible designs, are at least noticeable improvements over the Before cards.

(Photo credit: Nathan Wilson, "Tagwa")

Alignment

Before

Sarah Drummond, Project Manager
Devilfish Software

#131 - W. 32nd Avenue
South Vancouver, B C VOX OXO
Canada

sdrummond@ganglion.com
O: (123) 456-7890
C: (123) 987-6543

After

Sarah Drummond
Project Manager
Devilfish Software
#131 - W. 32nd Avenue
South Vancouver, B C VOX OXO
Canada
sdrummond@devilfish.com
O: (123) 456-7890
C: (123) 987-6543

Separating the name and company from the rest of the contact information serves no useful purpose. The design is simpler – and therefore stronger – with all contact information in a single column, and the name and company are still prominent because they are at the top of the column.

Contrast

Before

Sarah Drummond, Project Manager

Devilfish Software

#131 - W. 32nd Avenue
South Vancouver, BC VOX OXO
Canada
sdrummond@devilfish.com
O: (123) 456-7890
C: (123) 987-6543

After

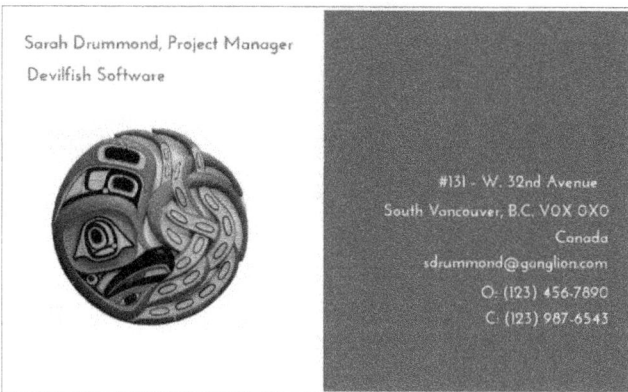

Sarah Drummond, Project Manager

Devilfish Software

#131 - W. 32nd Avenue
South Vancouver, B.C. VOX OXO
Canada
sdrummond@ganglion.com
O: (123) 456-7890
C: (123) 987-6543

Since the design already splits into two columns with two different types of information, why not make the design more interesting by giving one column a different background color? Using the red color makes sense because it is the dominant color in the octopus panel.

In this case, placing the name and company in one column helps because it provides a top and bottom contrast to accompany the left and right contrast.

Proximity

Before

After

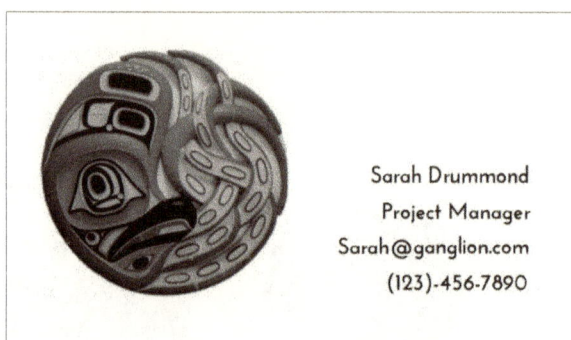

The Before card looks as though the designer thought: "Four pieces of information? Four corners? Cool!" and plunged ahead. But there is no connection between the pieces of information and their positioning, which means that the reader's eyes have no hint about where to start. Instead, eyes tend to fall on the octopus panel in the middle, which is the most visually interesting element, but also the one that contains the least information.

The After card introduces some proximity, placing all the information together, and giving it a common alignment.

Probably, I would use another principle to improve the design, but at least the After card is less cluttered and more easily read.

Repetition

Before

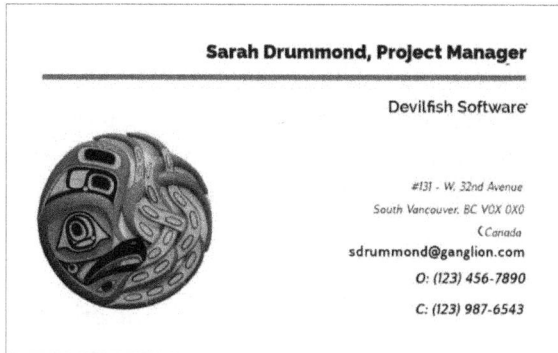

After

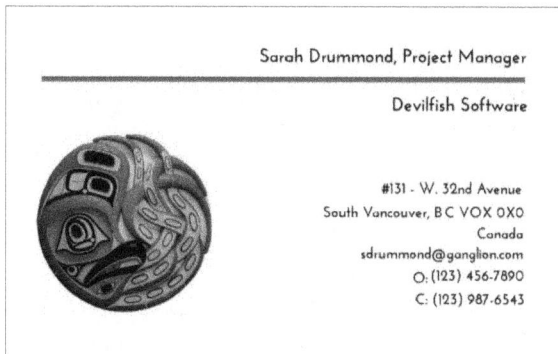

Remember the suggestion to limit the number of fonts? Here, the Before card's design uses two different fonts and several weights and font sizes. Probably, the idea was to differentiate different types of information, but the encoding is not immediately obvious. Even more importantly, the result is chaotic, even though a right alignment is used consistently throughout.

By contrast, the After card uses the same font and weight throughout, with only two different font sizes. The result is far less confusing to the eye.

Finding content

The Drawing tool bar includes a generous supply of primitives or basic drawing shapes among its icons. They include basic geometric shapes, callouts to annotate diagrams, arrows, and even a library of basic flow chart shapes. By grouping or stacking shapes, you can make more complex shapes as well (see "Stacking shapes into other shapes," page 394).

Often, though, you need more than the primitives. For instance, while the flow chart library contains most of the basic shapes for creating flow charts, some of the shapes you need may be available from other buttons on the tool bars. Many people, too, will need to do a web search to find a guide to when each shape should be used.

In addition, while Draw and Impress are ideal for creating diagrams, they sometimes lack the necessary libraries for some types of diagrams. Some, such as those for architectural or electrical diagrams, are missing from both the tool bar and the Clip Art Gallery. Instead of developing the libraries for yourself, you can save time by looking for libraries that already exist. Try:

- LibreOffice and Apache OpenOffice extensions (see Appendix A, "Downloading LibreOffice," page 483).

- The libraries of other free-licensed diagram applications, such as Dia or Calligra Suite's Flow.

- The OpenClipart site (http://openclipart.org/).

VIEW > CLIP ART GALLERY (also found in the sidebar as GALLERY) is a convenient place to store these libraries.

Producing content

The odds are that if you use Draw much, you will need to produce your own content using the Drawing tool bar. The Drawing tool bar contains mostly basic shapes like rectangles or ovals, or primitives, as designers call them.

Tip

The Drawing tool bar is complete in Draw and Impress only. Writer and Calc versions of the tool bar are missing a few tools such as connectors.

To draw a primitive, select an item from the Drawing tool bar, and then move the cursor to the editing window, clicking and dragging to size the object.

In many cases, an additional tool bar for the shape opens at the top of the editing window for manually editing the shape. However, applying a style instead simplifies revisions.

Tip

If you want a square instead of a rectangle, or a circle instead of an oval, press the SHIFT key as you drag the primitive.

After you insert an object, you can move and resize it by clicking then dragging it. When you do, a frame with eight handles appears around the object. As you drag an object, it appears in snap lines so that you can position it more exactly in relation to other objects.

Click any other part of the object than the handles, and you can move an object without changing its size and proportions. If you want to resize the object or change its shape, drag it by the handles that appear when you click it.

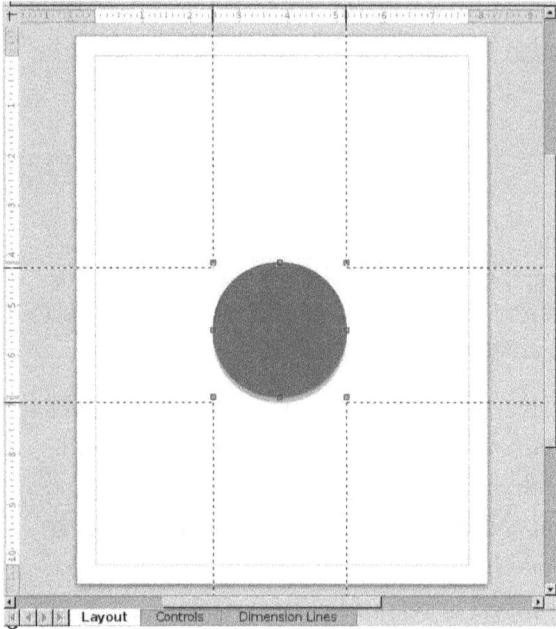

A basic shape being moved. The snap lines are useful for exact positioning, even with the grid turned off, because you can see the exact position on the horizontal and vertical rulers.

After you add a primitive, you may need to click the SELECT button, the first on the left of the tool bar, to restore the drawing tools to their default state. Otherwise, you might not be able to add another shape.

For most primitives, these instructions are all you need to know. However, some primitives require additional notes.

Understanding dimension lines

Dimension lines show the space between two end points on a diagram. The end points are emphasized by two guides or vertical lines, and a measurement is generally used as well.

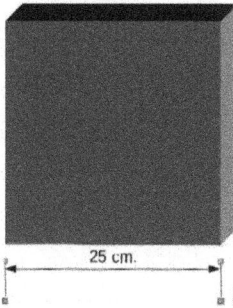

A dimension line for a three-dimensional shape.

Understanding text inside a shape

Before release 4.4, to add text inside a shape required that you draw the shape and the graphic text separately, then position and group them so that the text was overlaying the shape (see below).

However, in 4.4 and above, you can simply select an object and start to type.

Text outside a shape is still added by creating a text box first.

Understanding connectors

Connectors are lines attached to two objects by means of glue points. When you move an object that has a connector, the connectors are modified to keep them attached to the objects at the other end.

Other objects at the other end of the connector remain in place unless you select both objects, which drags the objects and the connectors between them as though all elements were grouped.

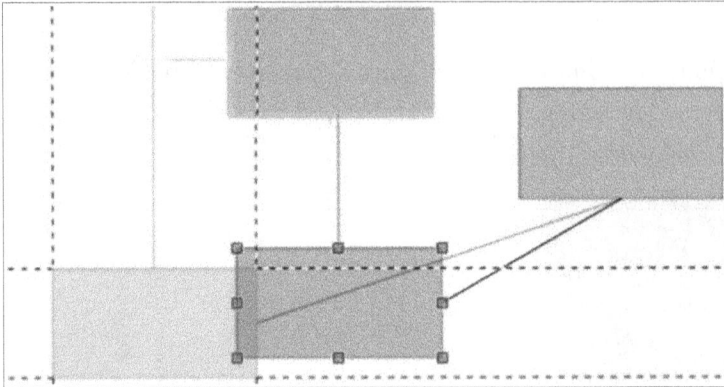

A rectangle attached to two others with connectors. Lines at the center of one side are connectors, while broken lines are the snap lines for positioning the object being moved. The paler rectangle indicates the object's original position.

Understanding curves

The CURVES button is for drawing freeform shapes, usually (but not always) with curved sides. Depending on your selection, a curve can be open, or filled with a color.

When you draw a curve, click once to change directions, and twice to stop drawing. When you are done, selecting the curve reveals the points that you can drag on to adjust the shape.

Understanding freeform lines

A freeform line is one that follows the direction of the cursor as you move it in the editing window. The Writer and Calc Drawing tool bars have a separate button for freeform lines, but in Draw and Impress, they are the last option when you select the CURVES button.

With patience and practice, you can use freeform lines to produce more advanced content. However, while you are learning Draw, you might want to avoid the effort.

Understanding callouts

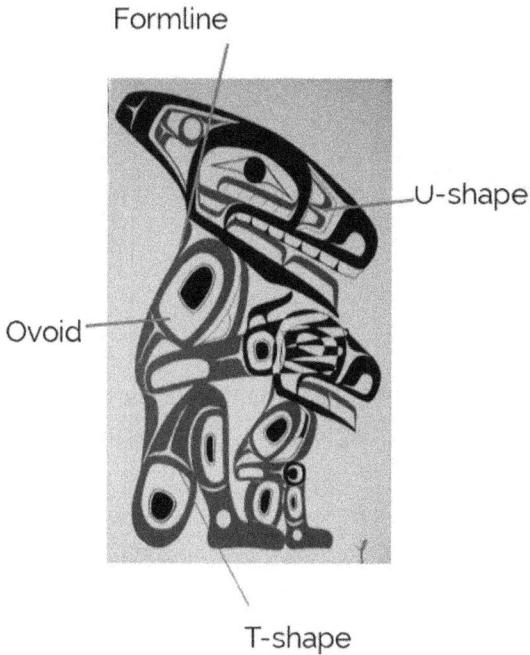

Callouts describing some of the basic shapes in Northwest Coast formline design. In this example, the text blocks have been made borderless. Photo credit: Todd Stephens, "Jorja and I."

Callouts are used to indicate and explain parts of a diagram. They consist of a line pointing to part of the diagram and a text box, both of which are edited together. The lines act like connectors, changing shape if you drag the text box around.

By default, callouts have borders. However, borders are usually unnecessary. To remove them, right-click the object and select LINE > STYLE > NONE.

Understanding points

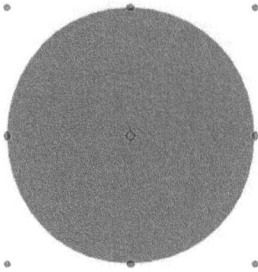

Drag on points to edit a shape.

Points are controls for manipulating a shape. They are synonymous with the frame handles, but they rotate rather than move the shape.

To edit points, select the shape in the editing window, then select the POINTS button and click the shape so that the handles turn red. Dragging on a handle changes the shape of the primitive.

Understanding the Fontwork Gallery

The Fontwork Gallery is available from the Drawing tool bar. It is midway between manual formatting and graphic styles. The Fontwork Gallery offers a quick way of formatting graphic text that is not on a flat baseline, but follows a curve or other shape. It is useful mostly for short, highly formatted documents such as a brochure or newsletter.

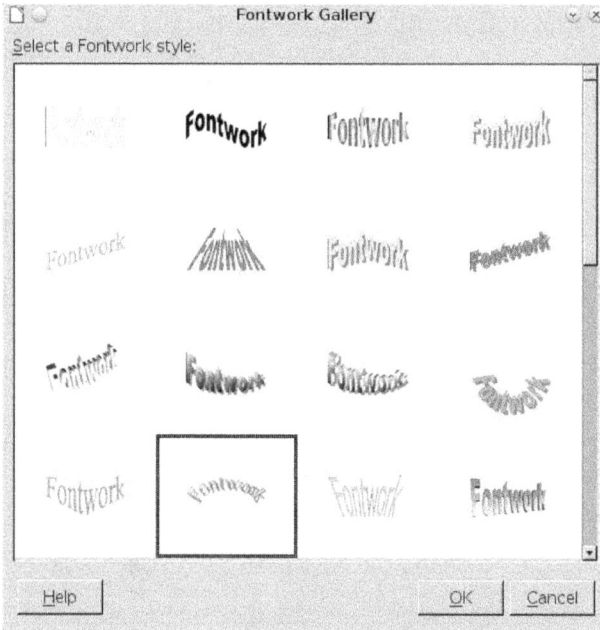

Help   OK   Cancel

Fontwork is a library of formats for editing graphic text.

The Fontwork Gallery includes forty pre-defined samples. Often, you will not find exactly the sample you need, but if you pick the one closest to it, you can modify it. Sometimes, all you need to modify it will be the standard object tool bar. However, you can also use the Fontwork tool bar that opens to the right of the standard Drawing tool bar that appears on the bottom of the page when you select the sample in your document.

Begin by replacing the default text with your own. You will probably want to replace the color of the FILL and the AREA as well.

The text can be formatted by clicking it, but often you will find making changes easier by using the icons on the Fontwork tool bar:

- FONTWORK SHAPE: Choose the shape of the baseline. The baseline for text is the imaginary line on which the bottom of an "m" or "n" rests upon.

Tip

If you need an effect not available from the tool bar and are having trouble editing, set the shape to flat to make your changes, then return to the original shape.

- FONTWORK SAME LETTER HEIGHTS: Toggles letters to same height or restores original letter heights. Setting letters to the same height is not the same as converting all the letters to upper case, but produces its own distortions.
- FONTWORK ALIGNMENT: Align the entire sample, or each word.
- FONTWORK CHARACTER SPACING: Sets the spacing between letters, choosing one of several broad categories ranging from VERY LOOSE to VERY TIGHT, or choose a custom percentage.
- TILT UP, DOWN, LEFT, RIGHT: Angles the sample. This tool is not available in some versions of LibreOffice.

Caution

Text pasted into a Fontwork sample is displayed unformatted until you finish creating the sample.

A Fontwork sample ready for the text to be edited,

You can get quick and interesting effects by using a dingbat set with Fontwork.

The Knavery dingbat set used with Fontwork.

Understanding 3D objects

Any primitive can be made into a rotatable 3D object by selecting it and then clicking MODIFY > CONVERT > TO 3D.

You can do some basic editing on 3D objects by clicking on them until the handles turn red, then dragging by a handle.

A set of editing tools for 3D objects is available by selecting 3D EFFECTS from the right-click menu, or by toggling on EXTRUSIONS on the Drawing tool bar. You can rotate objects, adjust depth and perspective, and adjust surfaces.

A rotatable 3D rectangle.

STOP Caution

Like shadows on text frames, 3D objects are easy to overdo. Avoid using 3D shapes unless they result in a diagram that is genuinely easier to read than a 2D one.

Understanding tables

Tables are not on the Drawing tool bar. Instead, use INSERT > TABLE. The tool is similar to the one in Impress, but defaults to gray column headings and row. To get more options, either take a screen shot of a Writer table, or add the Writer table to the Draw or Impress document using INSERT > OBJECT > OLE OBJECT.

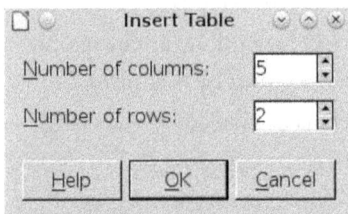

Compared to the table options in Writer, those for Draw and Impress are basic.

Grouping shapes

As you build a diagram or drawing, you often want to keep certain shapes together. In an organization chart, for example, you might want to keep all the positions on the same level together. By keeping them together, you can move them without having to reposition each one individually. In effect, you make a single shape out of originally separate ones.

In other cases, you might build a complex object from several simple ones. You would group them together because it is the complex shape, not its components, with which you work.

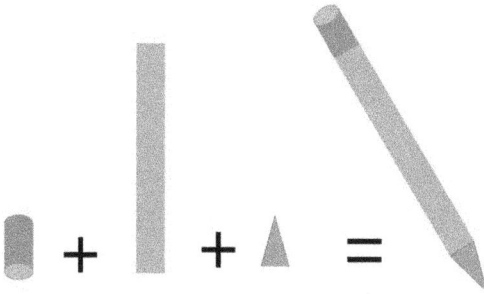

Arranging and grouping a cylinder, rectangle, and triangle produces a stylized pencil, suitable for use as an icon in a document, perhaps for tips.

To group shapes, select them one at a time while pressing the SHIFT key. With each selection, the frame and handles expand to include the new shape. Then select GROUP from the MODIFY menu or the right-click menu from one of the shapes. The option changes to UNGROUP so you can undo the group.

Tip

If the diagram is too crowded to select shapes to group, try selecting smaller groups first, then grouping groups. The only drawback to this technique is that ungrouping may become more difficult.

Tip

You can edit an individual shape in a group by selecting ENTER GROUP from the MODIFY menu or right-click menu.

Grouping shapes is an under-appreciated feature of LibreOffice. Very few people seem to use it, so it is rarely explained in any meaningful way in manuals or online help, which in turn means that fewer people consider using it. Yet, with ingenuity, it can produce results that cannot be created with any other feature.

Stacking shapes into other shapes

You can build complicated shapes by combining basic shapes in different ways. All require careful planning.

Often, the effect you want depends on which shape is on the top or bottom of the stack. Sometimes, two menu selections can give the same result.

Tip

Using the MODIFY menu to ROTATE, FLIP, or CONVERT shapes may help to make primitives more versatile. In particular, converting graphic text to a bitmap may give you more options.

Stacked shapes can be made into a single complex shape in several ways:

- Overlap stacked shapes, then choose ARRANGE from the main or right-click menu. The shape changes as shapes are sent back or forward in the pile.

  Shapes become more visible towards the front, and more hidden towards the bottom, while in between their visibility depends on the colors and transparencies in the stack.

  Once you have the shape you want, group the objects to preserve the more complicated shape.

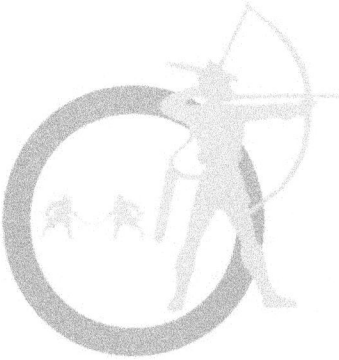

A custom drop capital "O" shows how shapes can be stacked into more complex ones.

This one consists of:

a) A circle with a thick line and transparent area..

b) An archer dingbat set. stacked on top of the circle.

c) Two sword fighter dingbats. The one on the left is converted into a polygon using the MODIFY > CONVERT sub-menu, then flipped horizontally to face the other.

- Create a shape from overlapping objects by selecting MODIFY > SHAPES > MERGE. The result is a shape with the outlines of the objects. Overlapping areas disappear, and the area color is the fill of the object at the bottom of the stack.

When shapes are merged, a single new shape results that is easier to keep track of.

- Create a shape from overlapping objects by selecting MODIFY > SHAPES > SUBTRACT.

When the circle and a dingbat set are stacked, SUBTRACT leaves a cutout showing the color of the paper.

The same effect could be made by changing the dingbat's color, but a white character on a white background would be easy to lose.

- Create a shape from overlapping objects by selecting MODIFY > SHAPES > INTERSECT. The top objects and the visible parts of objects lower in the stack disappear, leaving only the parts that overlap.

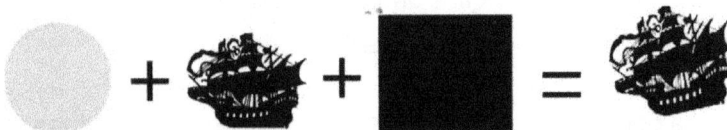

In this example, the circle and the ship are in the middle of the stack, and the rectangle at the bottom overlaps them on all sides. When INTERSECT is chosen, the visible portion of the rectangle disappears, leaving the objects in the middle merged to form a flaming ship.

Connecting lines and curves

The bottom of the MODIFY menu arranges items in combinations of general curves, lines, and shapes. Unfortunately, it can be confusing, because menu items are arranged in no particular order, and with few indications of which item is to be used with which shapes.

To connect two lines, select them, then click MODIFY > CONNECT. Be careful that they are actually touching, because

otherwise LibreOffice draws a connection that may be crooked.
To split lines, click MODIFY > BREAK.

Connect two curves with MODIFY > COMBINE, and split them
with MODIFY > SPLIT.

STOP

Caution

Do not try to use CONNECT or COMBINE with closed
shapes. If you do, the result is an abstract shape with
few practical purposes.

Adding images

Draw, Impress, and the Drawing tool bar treat images as
another form of primitive. All standard graphic formats are
supported, but Draw is especially useful because of its support of
vector graphics – images that are stored as a series of
mathematical relationships rather than pixels and are therefore
easier to resize.

On the right-click menu, images have several tools that
primitives lack:

- CROP IMAGE: Display only part of the image, or resize the image
  display. The original picture file is not affected in either case.

- CHANGE IMAGE: Replaces the current image with another one.

- SAVE IMAGE: Copies the image to its own file.

- COMPRESS IMAGE: Reduces the resolution, and therefore the
  size of the LibreOffice file.

- EDIT WITH EXTERNAL TOOL: Opens the image in the system's
  default graphics editor.

Designing fills

Object areas can be decorated with different types of fills: colors, gradients, hatchings, and bitmaps. These fills can be used to create an abstract design for custom Impress slides or for filling drawing shapes.

From a Drawing Objects style, you can only use the fills that are already defined for LibreOffice as a whole. However, you can customize styles from FORMAT > AREA within Draw. When saved, your custom designs become generally available in LibreOffice.

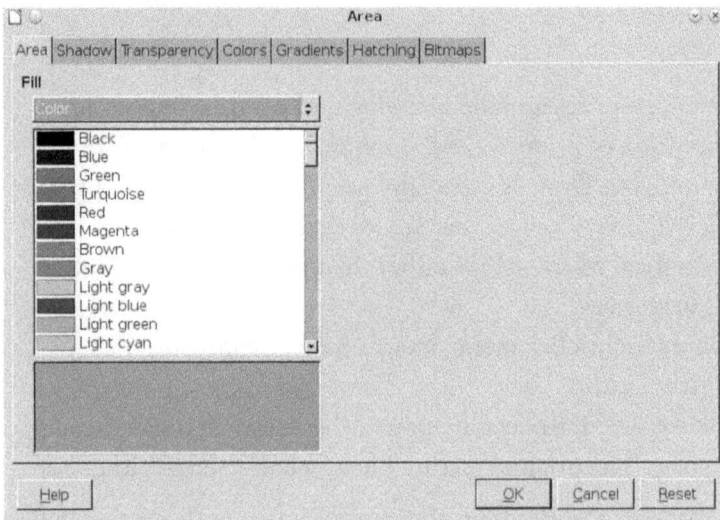

In FORMAT > AREA, fills are designed for use throughout LibreOffice.

Designing area colors

The COLOR tab of FORMAT > AREA is a duplicate of the tab at TOOLS > OPTIONS > LIBREOFFICE > COLORS. A color added in FORMAT > AREA becomes available for use throughout LibreOffice.

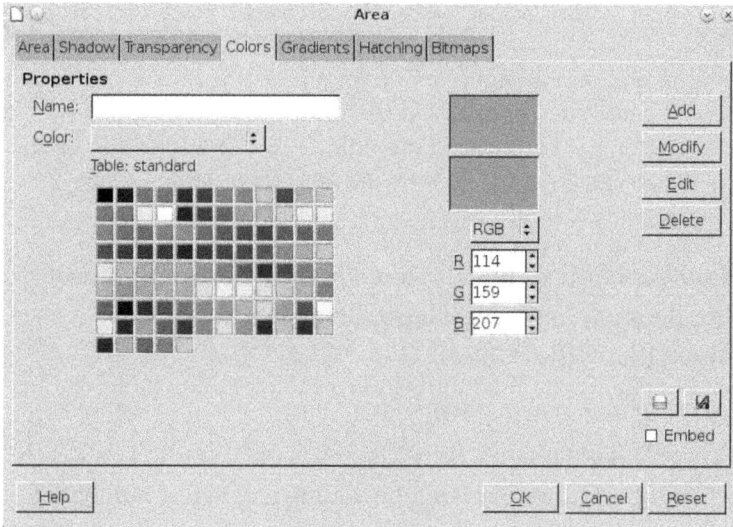

FORMAT > AREA > COLORS creates new colors with the RGB color model for use throughout LibreOffice.

If you need to add a specific color, sample it in a graphics program to get its RGB definition. For example, in the screen shot above, the blue color indicated has a definition of 114-159-207 on a scale of 256.

Tip

Color definitions are ways of blending a few colors to make the rest. RGB uses red, green, and blue, CMYK cyan, magenta, yellow, and black. The CMYK model is generally considered the most accurate.

The fact that RGB is used online and CMYK for hard copy explains why printing exactly the colors you see online can be challenging. There is no exact correspondence between the two color models, so results can be different between the screen and paper.

Your custom color fills are stored in the /user/config directory of your personal configuration path in a file with an .soc extension (StarOffice Colors).

Designing area gradients

A gradient is a gradual transition from one color to another. In between the starting color and the ending color are a number of intermediate colors, or increments.

Gradients are a popular choice for presentations and desktop wallpapers on computers. The reason is obvious: with a little experimenting, you can create an original, abstract design that is suitable for almost any subject matter.

Drawing Object styles use only gradients already defined in LibreOffice. You can create a custom gradient from FORMAT > AREA > GRADIENTS in the main menu.

LibreOffice gradients can have up to nine settings. At first glance, these settings may seem mathematically complex for such a simple goal. However, you can ignore all except the colors and still produce an original gradient.

Admittedly, you can create more complex designs with the other fields, but the most productive attitude is to regard the other fields as options you can play with and mix and match, rather than anything with which you have to deal.

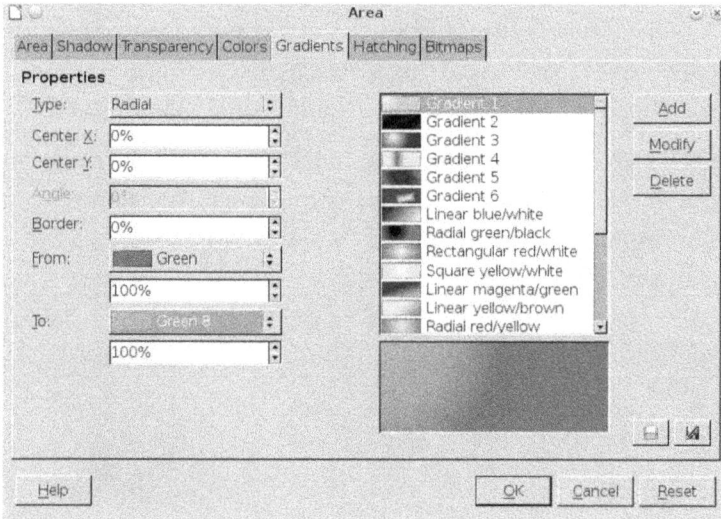

FORMAT > AREA > GRADIENTS creates backgrounds in which one color shades into another. The result is often abstract designs suitable for Impress slides, or even desktop wallpapers.

LibreOffice supports several different types of gradient:

- LINEAR: The gradient is horizontal, starting with the first color at the top and ending with the last color on the bottom.

- AXIAL: The gradient is horizontal, starting with the first color in the center and ending with the last color at the top and the bottom.

- RADIAL: The gradient is diagonal, starting with the first color in the lower right and ending with the second in the upper left.

- ELLIPSOID: The gradient is diagonal, starting with the first color in the lower right and moving through intermediate colors in curved bands to end with the second color in the upper left.

- SQUARE: The gradient is diagonal, starting with the first color in the lower right and moving through intermediate colors in square sections to end with the second color in the upper left.

- RECTANGLE: The gradient is diagonal, starting with the first color in the lower right and moving through intermediate colors in rectangular sections to end with the second color in the upper left.

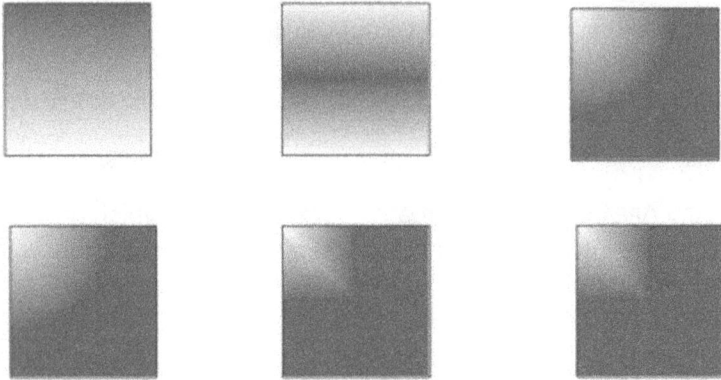

Gradients available in LibreOffice. From top left: LINEAR, AXIS, RADIAL, ELLIPSOID, SQUARE, RECTANGLE.

Tip

The illustrations above are based on gradients with an angle of 0, and no X or Y offset. If a gradient starts in a different position, it will look slightly different.

All gradients are defined by the colors they begin with (FROM) and end with (TO). Gradients can also have a border, at which the current color partially fades, as well as an angle.

Some, such as RADIAL gradient, also have an X (horizontal) and Y (vertical) offset from the upper right-hand corner. Use the preview to experiment until you get the positioning that you want.

Your custom gradient fills are stored in the /user/config directory of your personal configuration path in a file with an . sog extension (StarOffice Gradients).

Designing area hatchings

Hatchings are patterns of vertical, horizontal, and/or diagonal lines. Their usefulness is easy to under-estimate, but they can sometimes be effective fills, especially when printed in black and white.

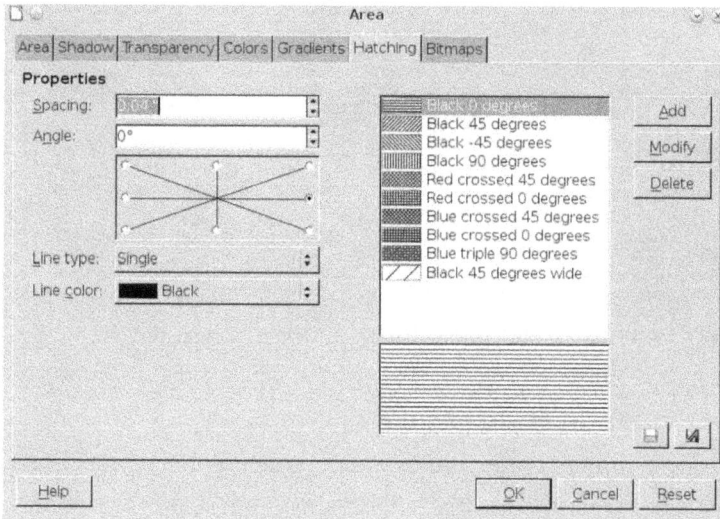

FORMAT > AREA > HATCHING creates linear hatchings for fills throughout LibreOffice.

Designing area bitmaps

Bitmaps refer in this context to tiles that are used to create a repeating pattern. You can build your own tile, pixel by pixel in the Pattern Editor, or load a fill from another source.

Your custom fills are stored in the /user/config directory of your personal configuration path in a file with an .sob extension (StarOffice Bitmap).

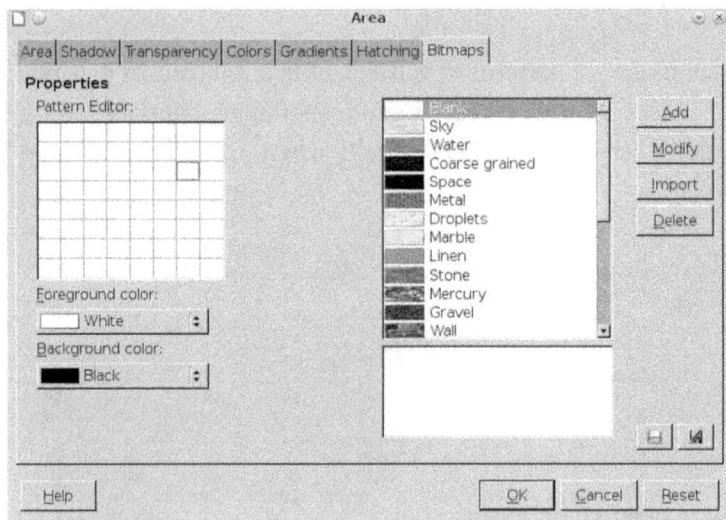

FORMAT > AREA > BITMAPS are tiles used for a quick area fill.

Gathering shapes

Draw is limited compared to stand-alone graphic editors like GIMP or Krita. However, as you find or develop shapes to use in a project, you may discover that Draw and the Drawing tool bar are more versatile than you first imagined. Draw's usefulness, like any graphic editor's, depends on how familiar you are with it and how much effort you are prepared to make.

14

Drawing Object styles and charts

Drawing Object styles (also known as Image styles and formerly as Graphic styles) define the characteristics of a drawing object in Draw or Impress. They are not available in any other LibreOffice application, even though you can use the Drawing tool bar to add manually many types of drawing objects in Writer and Calc. Typically, you apply them after inserting a shape.

STOP Caution

The Drawing tool bar has icons in Draw and Impress that it does not have in Writer and Calc. In particular, the Draw and Impress version has CONNECTORS and ARROWS.

Another point to be aware of: Drawing styles are for formatting only. They do not affect shape or size. That means, for example, that the pre-defined OBJECT WITH SHADOW style can format both a rectangle and shapes that are identical except for dimensions.

This chapter concludes with a discussion of how to design graphs and charts using LibreOffice's Chart sub-system. Available in most LibreOffice applications, Chart remains one of the few tools in the entire office suite that uses manual formatting only. All the same, charts remain important in business, academic or scientific documents, and are highly customizable.

Planning graphic styles

Like other LibreOffice applications, Draw includes pre-defined styles. Some of these are for graphic text, but others are for general categories of drawing objects, such as OBJECT WITH ARROW. Most are not for specific shapes, sizes, or purposes, except for DIMENSION LINE.

Often, however, creating your own styles is more convenient, even if you start by modifying a pre-defined style. The best way to begin is by breaking down the diagram into its basic elements. Then assign one graphic style per element.

For instance, if you are building an organizational chart, you might have a style called POSITION BOXES to indicate each job. If you want to apply this style somewhat differently – perhaps using different colored shapes to indicate different departments or the project lead – use the INHERIT FROM and NEXT fields on the ORGANIZER tab to create subordinate styles with names like POSITION BOX or PROJECT LEAD.

Applying graphic styles

Unlike styles in Writer, graphic styles can only be applied after a shape is added to a document. Insert one of each of the shapes your document uses, then choose the style to apply from the STYLES AND FORMATTING window.

Once you have added the style to one type of object, you can copy and paste to create others of the same type, or else use EDIT > DUPLICATE.

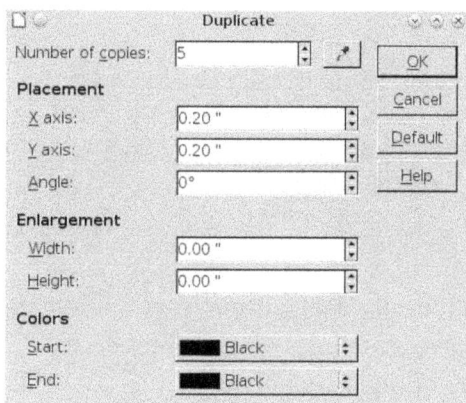

EDIT > DUPLICATE saves copying and pasting shapes.

Besides copying, the DUPLICATE window can enlarge and color copies, and offset them, so you can make a copy as you need it. When working in Draw or Impress, you might get into the habit of replacing CTRL+C with SHIFT+F3 for copying.

Formatting drawings

Shape choices determine each object's features. Many are similar to those found in other styles, but in a diagram they become more important.

For example, you may have few needs for a border or background in most Writer styles, but in Draw such characteristics (named LINE and AREA) become a primary concern.

As you work with shape characteristics, you will soon find that many of the available settings apply only to certain shapes. Others you may choose to ignore, either because the defaults are good enough for your purposes or because your drawing has nothing that could be affected by the setting. For example, if your drawing has no text, any text setting is irrelevant.

Tip

For detailed information about the ALIGNMENT, FONT, FONT EFFECTS, INDENTS & SPACING, and TABS tabs, see Chapters 3-5. Details about style features unique to graphic styles follow in this chapter.

Setting line formatting

Lines distinguish the outline of a shape from the area. They are approximately equivalent to Borders in other LibreOffice applications, although the features are not identical.

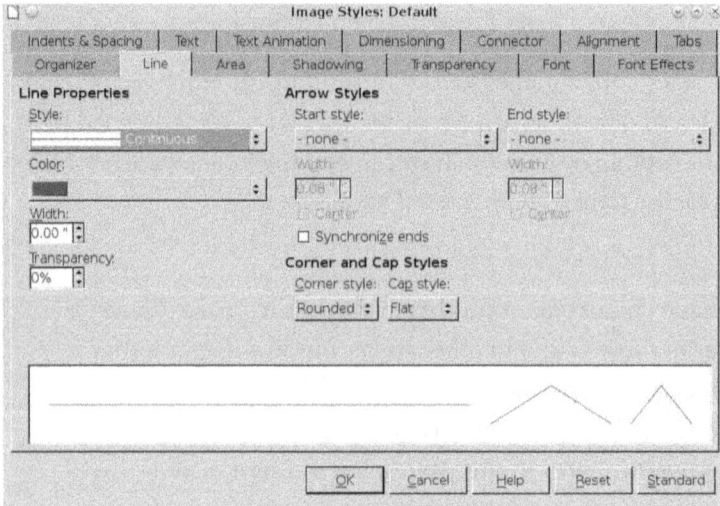

The LINE tab is analogous to the BORDERS tab in the styles for other applications.

If lines are irrelevant to your design, set the LINE STYLE to NONE, and you only need to be concerned about area formatting.

In addition to choosing the color and thickness of an object's outline, the LINE tab also includes options for arrows and line ends for both ends of a line. By default, arrows and line ends have the same proportions as the line itself, but you can make them thinner or thicker as you choose.

Tip

The Drawing tool bar also has block arrows that you can group with a line.

Customized lines are stored in the /user/config directory of your personal configuration path. The .sod file contains custom line formats, the .soe file custom arrows.

Setting dimension lines

You can modify dimensions lines from the DIMENSIONING tab of a graphic style. The LINE fields let you adjust the dimension line and the guides in relation to each other, although you will probably have little need to change the defaults.

You are more likely to want to change the legend, or measurement, positioning it in one of the ten default position shown in the right column of the DIMENSIONING tab.

Tip

The AUTOVERTICAL check box centers the legend vertically, the AUTOHORIZONTAL horizontally. Both must be turned off if you want to position the legend anywhere except the default central position.

Tip

If unit measurements are displayed, changing the unit may be a convenient way of changing the scale of a drawing. The alternative is to use TOOLS > OPTIONS > LIBREOFFICE DRAW > GENERAL > SCALE > DRAWING SCALE.

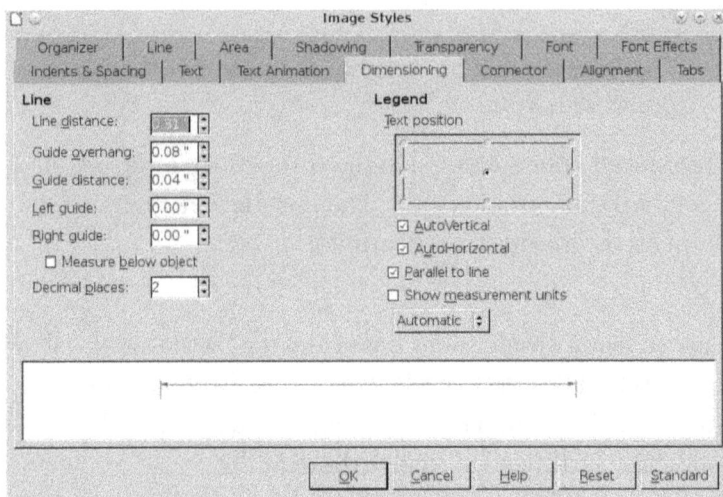

To draw a dimension line, click the LINES AND ARROWS button on the Drawing tool bar (the ninth from the left), and select DIMENSION LINE from the available tools.

Setting connectors

Connectors join shapes together. When you move an object that has connectors, the connectors are modified to keep them attached to the objects at the other end.

Objects at the other end of the connector remain in place unless you select both objects, which drags the objects and the connectors between them as though all elements were grouped.

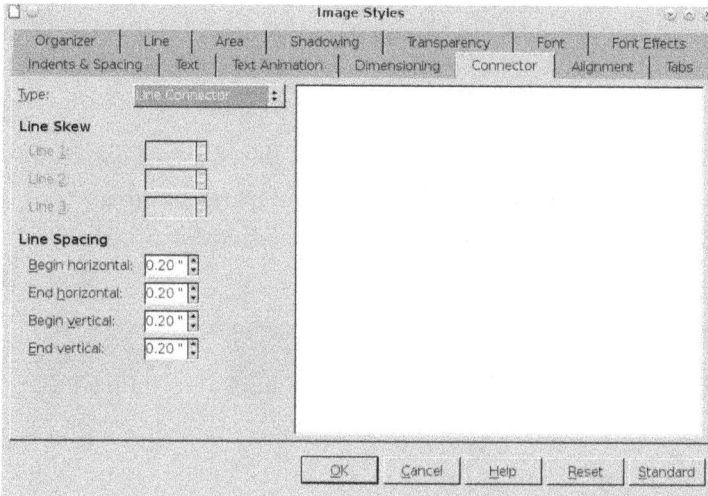

Connectors are lines attached to two objects by means of glue points. They keep objects attached to each other even when one is moved.

To add a connector, click the CONNECTOR button on the Drawing tool bar (the eighth from the left). You can choose between four kinds of connector:

- STANDARD: A connector with horizontal and vertical lines, possibly with one right angle in it. A Standard connector is useful in crowded hierarchical diagrams, in which several objects are subordinate to one above them, such as directors below executive officers in a company chart.

- LINE: A connector with a small segment at each end for adding a change of direction. Use Line connectors in diagrams that are even more crowded than the ones in which you use Standard connectors.

- STRAIGHT: A connector that consists of a single vertical or horizontal line. Straight connectors are by far the easiest ones to use, but you may not always have the space for them. Extend a connector to the center of one side of a shape, and it immediately converts to a Straight connector.

- CURVED: A connector with one curved line. Curved connectors are most suitable when you want an informal look to a diagram, perhaps to suggest that the relationships you are illustrating are approximate.

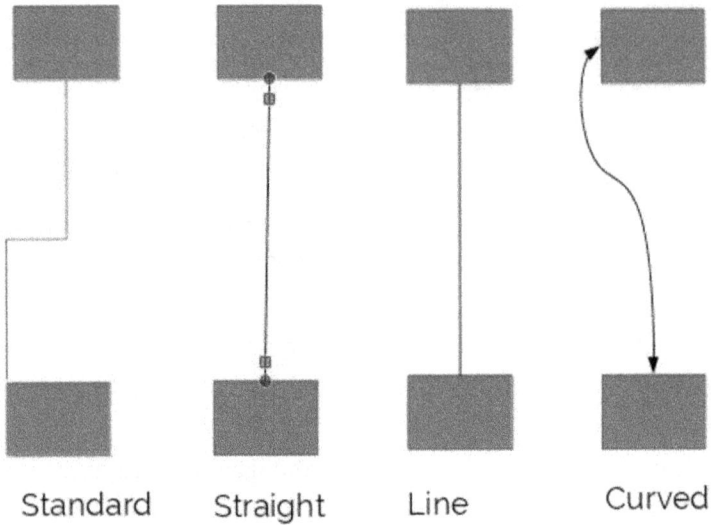

| Standard | Straight | Line | Curved |

The four types of connectors.

All connectors can end with an arrow or an open or filled circle. You can adjust the shape of a connector by selecting it and dragging on its handle, or by moving one of the objects to which it is attached. You can also select the GLUE POINT button on the Drawing tool bar.

To adjust a connector, go to the CONNECTOR tab of a graphic style. For a Line or Straight connector, you can also adjust the line skew – that is, the length of the line segments included – and the horizontal and vertical space for the line segments.

These settings are especially useful when repositioning has twisted connectors out of shape, or when you are adding the final touches to a diagram and trying to make everything consistent and uncluttered.

Even so, you may sometimes save time by deleting existing connectors and adding new ones.

Setting area options

The area of a drawing object can be formatted with COLORS, GRADIENTS, HATCHINGS, and BITMAPS. You are restricted to the fills already defined in LibreOffice. However, you can use Draw to define custom fills.

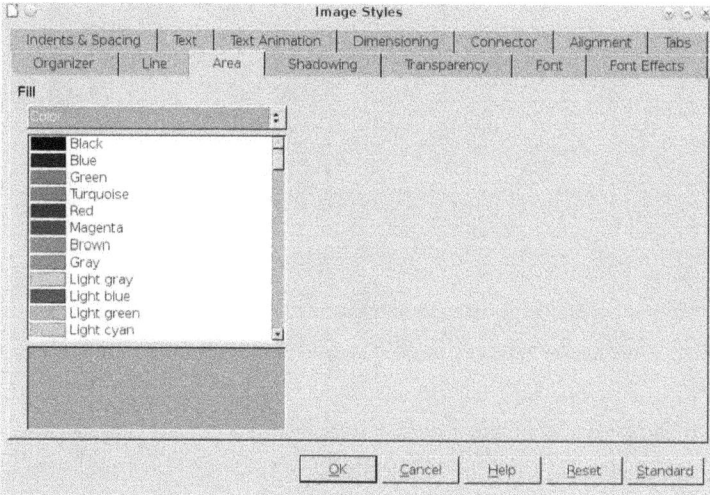

The AREA tab for graphic text is roughly equivalent to the BACKGROUND tab in some other types of styles. Formatting an object's area means choosing a fill for it.

To add a fill, go to FORMAT > AREA, and select the tab for the type of fill you want to add. See Chapter 13 for more details.

Setting shadows

Shadowing was popular in the early 1990s in graphic design. It is less common today, but can still be useful in creating a quick illusion of three dimensions.

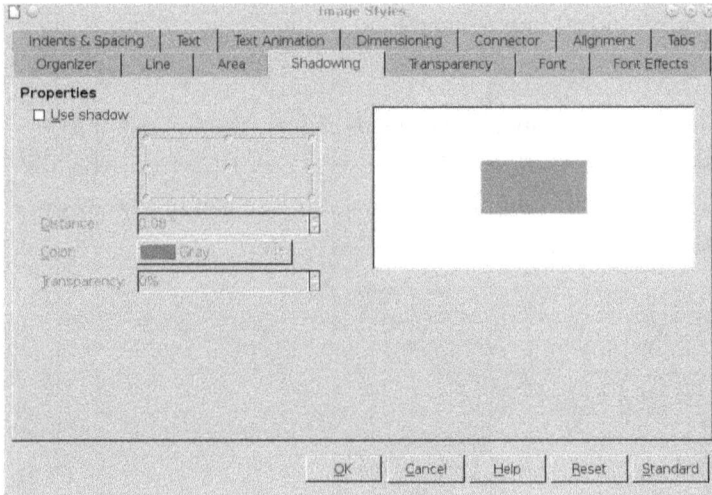

Shadows are easy to over-use, but can create a 3D look.

The SHADOWING tab lists settings to help customize a shadow. In many cases, all you need is to check the USE SHADOW box. However, you can also set the shadow's farthest distance from the object, the position of the shadow in relation to the object, and the color and transparency of the shadow for a subtler touch. Generally, a shadow's color should be black or a shade of gray.

Tip

The default position for the shadow is the lower right, assuming a light source in the upper left. If you change the shadow's position, use the same position for other shadows throughout the document.

Setting transparencies

Transparencies are useful for creating matching shades based on the same color, as well as for creating complex designs with overlapping layers.

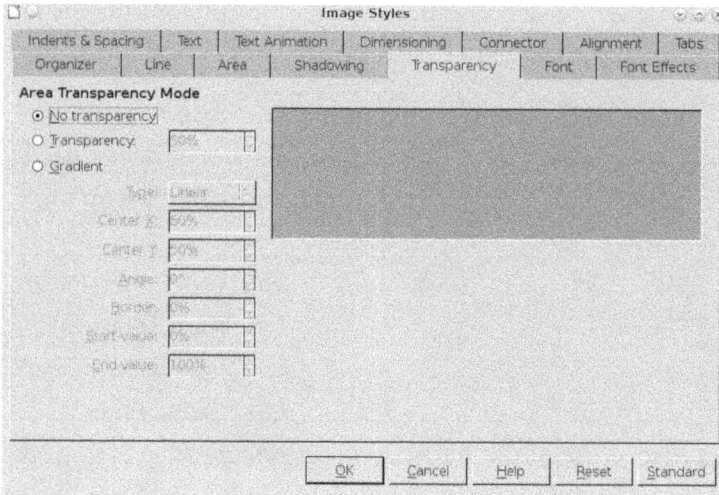

Transparencies expand your range of color.

The TRANSPARENCY tab expresses transparency as a percentage, with 0 being an unmodified or solid color, and 100% being completely transparent.

The TRANSPARENCY tab also includes options for creating a gradient, duplicating the options at FORMAT > AREA > GRADIENT (see above). In terms of graphic styles, the tab's gradient control allows you to customize gradients, while the AREA tab only lets you choose pre-defined gradients.

Setting text characteristics

The characteristics of graphic text are mostly the same as for text documents, with a few minor changes. Regardless of whether you are using regular or graphic text, the typographical conventions remain much the same.

For Tab	See	Notes
ALIGNMENT	"Selecting an alignment," page 114.	No options in Draw for last Justified line.
FONTS	"Choosing basic fonts," page 80.	Choose fonts at least the size of body text, if not slightly larger for diagrams. Sans serifs often make for clarity. If possible, use a font used elsewhere in the document.
FONT EFFECTS	"Font effects," page 79.	In most cases, ignore all except FONT COLOR.
INDENTS & SPACING	"Setting horizontal spacing," page 120.	Use indentations, especially for the first line, instead of tabs.

For Tab	See	Notes
TABS	"Setting tab stops," page 137.	Awkward with graphic text, and not really needed with the right spacing. Consider alternatives, such as tables, especially when the design is frequently changing.

Using text animation

From the TEXT ANIMATION tab in a graphic style, you can set LibreOffice's equivalent of the BLINK and MARQUEE HTML tags, either making text blink off and on, or scroll in one of several ways in the text frame. The tab includes settings for the direction of scrolling, the number of repetitions, and other settings.

However, LibreOffice users should learn from web designers' experience and avoid text animation in almost every circumstance. Blinking and scrolling are usually the antithesis of everything that a design element is supposed to do – instead of enhancing content, they distract readers' attention from it. In fact, they have little purpose except to call attention to themselves.

If you must use text animation, be merciful and set it to run only a few times before stopping. Having readers disagree with the opinions you express can be a natural consequence of writing, but annoying readers with your design is simply a poor tactic. Why undermine yourself?

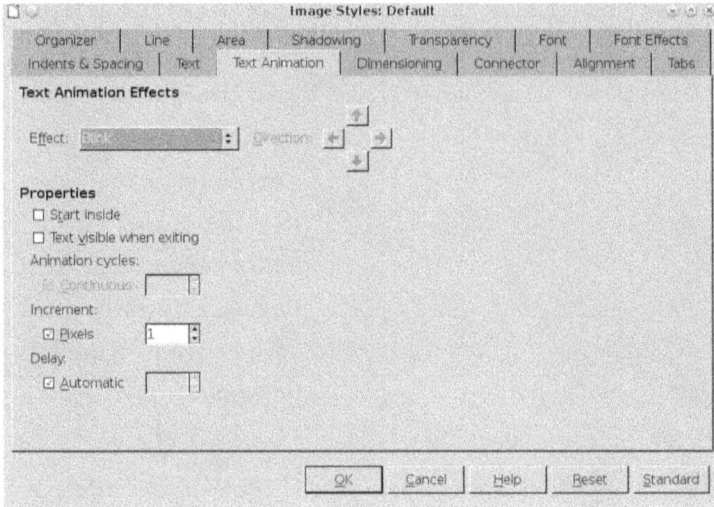

Avoid text animations as obsolete.

Creating a flow chart

Flow charts appear to have been invented several times between 1850–1930. They are meant to be informal documents, but you can vastly improve their look if you use basic design principles such as repetition and alignment to organize them.

As with any diagram, you can plan a flow chart by placing elements outside the margin of the document until you are ready to use them. However, sketching the design on a piece of paper might be just as easy.

Either way, when you are finished planning, turn on VIEW > GRID > SELECT GRID and SNAP TO GRID, and follow these steps:

1   Decide what basic shapes you need, and create a style for each. In this case, I needed a style for:

- Flow chart objects (Decision, Action, and Start/Finish). I only need one style, because drawing styles are not concerned with shape. I borrowed rounded rectangles from the tool bar's RECTANGLE button.

- Text.

- Lines starting with an arrow.

- Lines ending with an arrow.

- Lines starting and ending with an arrow.

    Styles should include settings for font effect, lines, area, and possibly transparency.

2   Create one each of the basic flow chart elements. Using the grid, size and position each shape and apply the style.

Tip

Expect to have to reposition objects, and possibly resize as well. In either case, you may come to appreciate the advantages of styles.

3   Copy and position each flow chart element as needed, making one column for DECISIONS (diamonds) and another for ACTIONS (large rounded squares). Use the grid to help keep elements horizontally and vertically aligned.

4   Add text to each object. In LibreOffice versions prior to 4.4, adding text requires creating text boxes and positioning them inside the flow chart elements, grouping them for convenience. In 4.4 or higher, simply start typing inside each element.

5 Add lines with arrows and their captions. Keep the line length and position as regular and as few as possible, unless you are trying for an informal look.

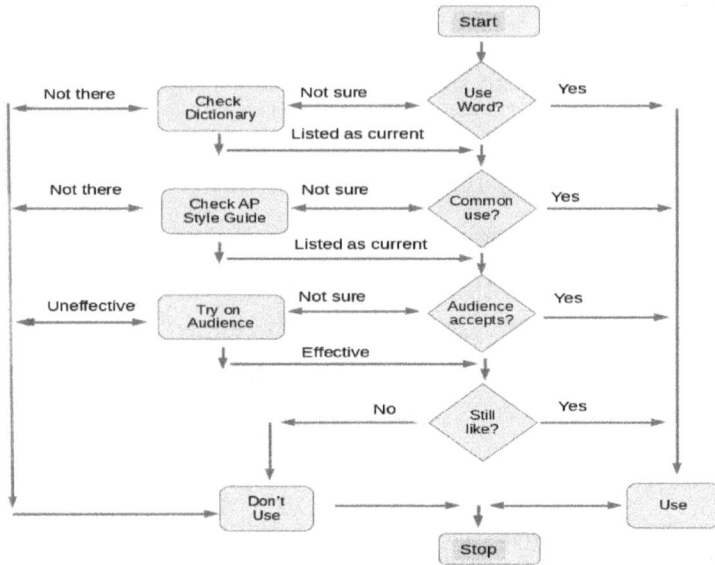

A flow chart for deciding whether to use an idiomatic word.

Adding charts and graphs

A chart or graph is a visual comparison of two or more pieces of data, such as the unemployment rate over time, or the distribution of results by population.

Charts and graphs are created in LibreOffice with the Chart sub-system. You can use charts in Writer by selecting INSERT > OBJECT > CHART from the main menu, or in other LibreOffice applications by selecting INSERT > CHART.

In Calc, adding a chart opens a wizard that guides you through formatting a chart. Unfortunately, in Writer, Draw, and

Impress, you must format manually without styles or much of anything else to help you.

Except in Calc, the Chart sub-system works much like the one for FONTWORK. When you select INSERT > CHART, LibreOffice adds a default chart to your document – specifically, a 2D bar graph.

The chart uses the default chart colors, which you can adjust in TOOLS > OPTIONS > CHARTS > DEFAULT COLORS or by right-clicking on the chart. By changing the colors used in a chart, you can make the chart fit with other decisions about color in the document, or reflect corporate or project branding.

All features in a chart are editable, but LibreOffice supplies no means to save formatting choices. If you want a chart to look similar to another one, you must copy and paste.

Formatting charts

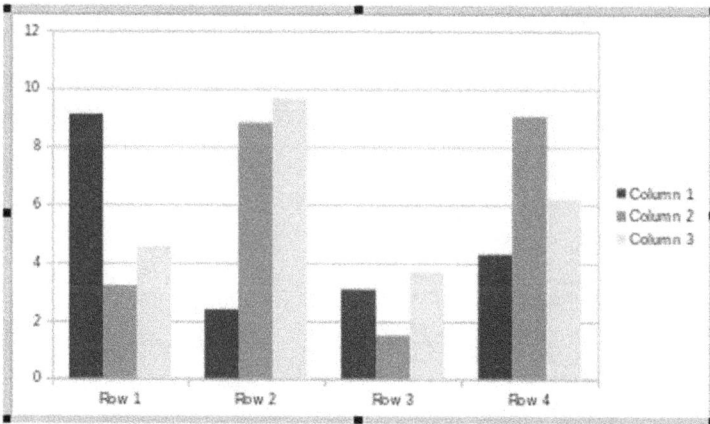

A chart is ready to edit when it has a gray border.

To edit the look and structure of a chart, click twice until the chart is outlined by a thick gray border.

Tip

When the gray border does not show, you can edit the separate elements of the chart, but not the general structure.

The default chart can be repositioned and resized by dragging on its handles. You can insert your own data by selecting CHART DATA TABLE from the right-click menu.

Tip

The default chart includes three Y axis values. However, many charts only require one.

Selecting chart types

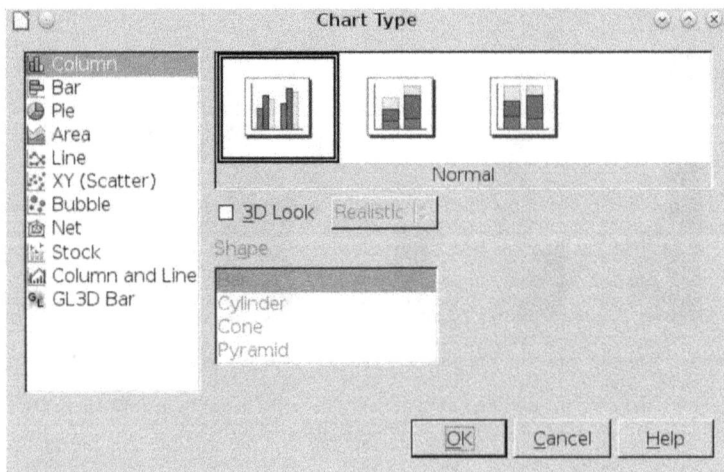

Charts are available in eleven types, many in both 2D and 3D.

You can change the default chart type by selecting CHART TYPE from the right-click menu, and choosing from the graphs shown.

The available charts are:

- COLUMN: The data displays in vertical columns.

- BAR: The data displays in horizontal columns.

- PIE: Chart data is depicted as wedges in a round shape. This chart type is popular for financial data and business reports.

- LINE: A graph of data points. If the data points are meant to show a progression (for instance, over time), then the points are usually connected.

- AREA: A line graph with several lines, and the space between lines shaded in with colors.

- XY (SCATTER): A type of chart for comparing the results of two or more trials of an experiment.

- BUBBLE: A graph that displays three dimensions: the X and Y axis and the size of the bubble that depicts the data point. Bubble graphs are a variation of an XY chart.

- NET: A chart in which every X axis has a separate Y axis. As a result, results are not a point or a line, but an enclosed shape. This type of chart can be difficult to read for an audience not accustomed to it.

- STOCK: As the name implies, a graph often used to show changes in stock values. It is described technically as a depiction of changes in the values of the X axis.

- COLUMN AND LINE: A chart that offers both a column and line representation of the same data.

- GL3D BAR: A bar graph that uses OpenGL for rendering three dimensional graphs. This choice only works when your video driver has hardware acceleration, which some Linux installations will not have.

Most of these types of charts have sub-types as well. Often, the differences in the sub-types are subtle, so you may have to look twice to see the difference. The same is also true for the three dimensional options for most types of graphs, which can have a SIMPLE or REALISTIC rendering.

Stick with the chart types you understand – if you don't know the uses of a graph, or are unable to see what is useful about a sub-type, you shouldn't be using it. The majority of users will probably use the COLUMN, BAR, PIE, or LINE formats for comparing data along two axes.

Choosing 2D or 3D

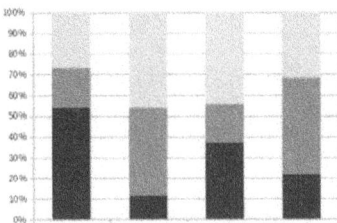

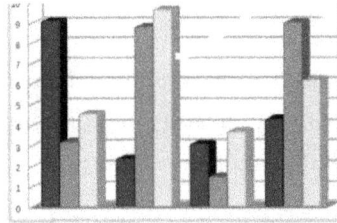

Two-dimensional and three-dimensional charts.

Three-dimensional charts were a new feature in early office suites. For a time, they completely replaced two-dimensional charts, just as justified alignment replaced left alignment, simply because they were new and seemed sophisticated.

However, in the last decade or so, a reaction has set in. Part of the reaction is a fad for two-dimensional icons and widgets on mobile devices, and part is that 3D graphics are no longer a novelty.

Whatever the reason, in many circles today, 3D graphs are seen as a sign of slickness that offers nothing that a 2D graph does not. An audience of developers may see a 3D chart as proof that style has triumphed over substance, while an audience of marketers might see a 2D chart as a lack of sophistication.

Editing graphs and charts

By clicking on a part of the graph or opening the right-click menu, you can manually edit all of its pieces.

The pieces differ with the type of graph, but may include:

- LEGEND: The key that describes what the colors refer to.

- WALL: The background.

- GRID: The lines against the wall that make values in the axes easier to read.

- AXES: The horizontal and vertical values.

- TITLE: The name of the whole graph.

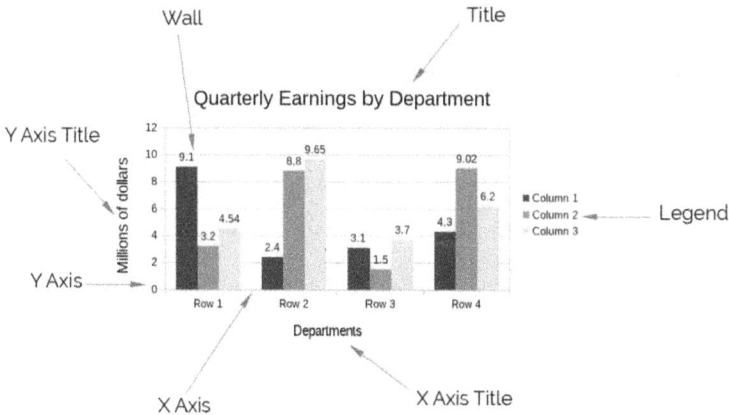

Editable parts of a chart.

Charts has no means of saving designs for later use, so copy and paste instead. If you use charts regularly, consider a template with samples of the charts you are most likely to use.

Creating a chart

In Calc, creating a chart is easy; adding a chart opens a wizard that lets you work through the stages of formatting.

However, in the rest of LibreOffice, creating a chart can be confusing at first, because the options change with how you click on the chart.

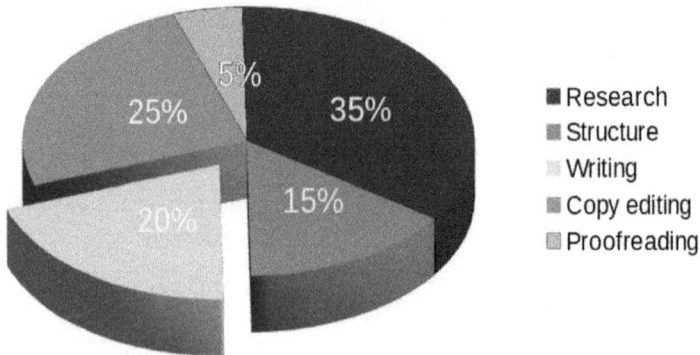

A 3D pie chart. The time spent writing is cut from the rest of the pie in order to emphasize it.

Following these steps should help minimize confusion:

1   Either accept the default colors, or change them at TOOLS > OPTIONS > CHARTS > DEFAULT COLORS. LibreOffice uses the colors in the order they are listed under DEFAULT COLORS.

STOP Caution

If you are printing in black and white, test colors for contrast.

2   Select INSERT > CHART in Calc, Draw, or Impress, or INSERT > OBJECT > CHART in Writer. LibreOffice adds a 2D bar chart.

3   Click twice on the chart so that it is surrounded by a gray border, then open the right-click menu to select CHART TYPE and choose the chart design to use.

4   Right-click on the chart when the gray border is visible and select CHART DATA TABLE to enter the data points for the chart.

5   With the gray border still visible, click an element to edit. When an element is selected, the right-click menu contains a menu item for formatting it, such as FORMAT LEGEND.

6   Click on the chosen elements or data series to edit their appearance.

7   With some chart types, you can select a data series, then right-click to select ARRANGEMENT. For example, if you are using a pie chart, you can select a data series and drag it out of the pie.

8   Click the chart so that the gray border disappears and the object handles appear. You can drag on the handles to move or resize the chart, or right-click to change features such as alignment, or edit the Line to create a border or Area to change the background.

Separating analysis and creativity

Using styles for diagrams means finding a new way to work. Instead of plunging directly into designing, it requires taking time first to think about what you need.

At first, this new work flow may make you impatient. However, by taking more time to plan before you begin, you will save time if – as seems likely – you modify your design while you work.

Even more importantly, planning styles first helps to separate the analytic aspects of work from the creative ones. If you try to structure as you create, you are trying to think in two different ways at once, which means that you are probably doing both inefficiently. By contrast, starting with styles helps you to separate these two ways of thinking – and, chances are, do each more efficiently.

If you have any doubts of the advantages of this work method, try it several times. Then try creating a complicated diagram manually, or even a chart. Once you are used to the new way of thinking, you are likely to have far fewer false starts than if you design manually – and, probably, wish that Chart was designed for styles, too.

15

Spreadsheet design

Spreadsheets are the electronic descendants of accounting ledgers. Yet although accounting ledgers are traditionally almost as regular in their formatting as text documents, the idea of styles has never caught on in spreadsheets as strongly as in word processors. There are several probable reasons for this difference:

- Spreadsheets' forty year history is hardly enough time for design conventions to develop and become accepted.

- Spreadsheets are valued more for their functional computing power than their formatting.

- Spreadsheets are not frequently revised.

- Spreadsheets often grow as needed, because they are mostly used online. It is no accident that one of the two types of styles in Calc is concerned with ways of squeezing the spreadsheet on to a printed page – a special use case that is of no relevance to many users.

- Calc styles are given only two sample defaults, making it harder for users to imagine how they might be used.

Don't mistake me – styles remain useful in Calc, especially for spreadsheets that are in constant use and maintained over long periods of time. Cell styles in particular are essential building blocks for a well-organized, self-automating spreadsheet.

Still, spreadsheets have less established forms than text documents. However, you may still want to apply the basic principles of design to your spreadsheet designs. See "Learning design principles," page 378.

Planning spreadsheets

Spreadsheets have a way of growing with no direction, but the more advanced planning you do, the more easily you will be able to find your data as you need it.

As with text documents, begin by designing a default spreadsheet template with corporate or personal branding colors and fonts. Then, using the default template as a basis, branch out and develop additional templates for the kinds of spreadsheets you use regularly.

A Calc spreadsheet includes one sheet by default. Begin with the first sheet, then add other sheets as necessary, right-clicking on the tabs to rename them to help navigation.

> Tip
> You can change the default number of sheets in TOOLS > OPTIONS > LIBREOFFICE CALC > DEFAULTS.

For example, if you are a computer programmer, you might start with a general list of potential employers, then eventually add another sheet specifically for high-tech employees.

Similarly, if you are regularly manipulating data, you will find that the pivot tables you create are added by default to a new

sheet. You can change the location of pivot tables from DATA >
PIVOT TABLE > CREATE > PIVOT TABLE LAYOUT > DESTINATION.

Building lists and data collections

Most spreadsheets, you will find, are either a text-based list or
a data collection. Spreadsheets are usually not categorized in this
way, but the distinction is useful when you are designing one.

A list spreadsheet could be as simple as a To Do list. It might
include when each task should be completed, or be a project
management plan that includes the stages of the project, who is
assigned to each task, and the dependencies that must be
completed before another task can start. This kind of spreadsheet
is often overlooked, but it is one of the more commonly used
types.

A data collection is what most people usually think a
spreadsheet is. It is a collection of information together with
calculations that help to analyze the data.

Such a collection could be as basic as a personal monthly
account that lists income and expenses, or as complex as a
collection of raw data whose average or future growth is
projected. Occasionally, you see a data collection arranged to
serve as a tutorial.

Tip

If a data collection has more than a few hundred entries,
you may decide to switch the information to a database.

Admittedly, current versions of Calc can contain over a
million rows, and 1024 columns. However, even with
modern computer memory, a database remains a more
efficient way of storing, retrieving, and manipulating

data. The tradeoff is that a database can require expert knowledge to make the most of it.

With both types of spreadsheet, you should generally organize by column. Not only is that the convention, but, if you plan on printing, columns are more trouble to position on the page than rows.

As you plan:

- Decide which sheets require what kind of design. For example, a sheet containing raw data needs a design that is straightforward and perhaps a single page, while a sheet containing analysis may require several sheets and not only headers, but also longer notes to guide users.

- Group related information on the same sheet.

- Leave space for labels – that is, cells that describe each data array. Labels assist users, and are often recognized automatically by Calc.

- Use borders, backgrounds, and empty cells to set apart one data array from another.

- Follow the basic principles of design described in Chapter 13 – formatting related types of information the same way and in the same order, and positioning them close together.

  For instance, if you are recording monthly sales figures, the text of cells that display the sales figures should have the same format. Cells for totals might be a different color, and should always be placed close to the sales figures they tally.

  Always, your main concern should be to make different categories of information easily distinguishable, structuring so that information is easy to absorb.

Do not worry about abstract aesthetics. Not everybody is equipped to admire the design of a text document, but very few have ever considered admiring the design of a spreadsheet. Unlike text documents, spreadsheets remain extremely practical.

Tip

Unless you can visualize the format clearly, start the design by sketching out its approximate layout on a piece of paper. The more complex a spreadsheet is, and the longer the spreadsheet is likely to be used, the more important planning becomes.

Designing spreadsheet lists

A list usually consists of cells formatted for text, not numbers. Basically, a spreadsheet list is a more powerful version of a table in a text document: its structure is meant to make information easier to scan, and to help users see relations between items that would be harder to see if the document consisted only of text.

For a list, assign individual colors to either the tasks or the people assigned them. To create sub-lists, set off cells from the rest of the sheet by blank cells, borders, or backgrounds. Make the colors as different as possible to make the sheet readable at a glance.

You might also want a sign-off column, either for initials or a signature, or perhaps a check mark borrowed from a dingbat font.

Lists are likely to make little use of functions. When they do, their functions are apt to be simple ones from the Mathematical and Statistical categories, such as SUM or AVERAGE.

Exercise: A trip-planning list

Don't under-estimate list spreadsheets. Even without functions, they can still be useful, and they are probably the most common type of spreadsheet used

Take, for example, this simple trip planner:

	A	B	C	D
1	Carribean Cruise, June 2015			
2				
3	Summary			
4	Depart: 2015-06-12,6AM SW Airlines from Seattle		June 12: Inflight	
5	Return: 2015-06-19,5:45PM, Air Canada, from Miami			
6			06:00:00 AM – Board plane	
7	Planning		06:30 AM	
8	Final payment for cruise		07:00 AM	
9	Arrange to board dog		07:30 AM	
10	Stop newspaper		08:00 AM	
11	Check carryon size limit		08:30 AM	
12	load novels on to tablet		09:00 AM	
13			09:30 AM	
14	Packing			
15	Tablet computer in carryon		10:00 AM	
16	phone in carryon		10:30 AM	
17	camera		11:00 AM	
18	8 changes of clothing		11:30 AM	
19	gifts for Gary & Lisa		12:00 PM	
20	tie		12:30 PM	
			01:00 PM	

A list spreadsheet for planning a trip. Sub-lists are separated by blank cells, borders, and title, and each day of the trip is broken down into half-hour sections. Large and colored headings help to organize information as well.

To create this trip planner:

1   Format the DEFAULT and HEADING 1 cell styles. Make the HEADING 1 style's FONT SIZE and FONT COLOR different from the DEFAULT style's.

Designing with LibreOffice

2   Merge the cells in row 1, and enter a total, using the HEADING 1 cell style.

3   Using empty rows and columns as separators, create ranges of rows for Summary, Planning, and Packing, increasing row and column dimensions as necessary. Use the HEADING 1 cell style for headers, and the cell's collective BORDER tab to put a box around each clump of information. Consider adding backgrounds, and new styles based on DEFAULT to go with them.

4   To the right of the first column, add a summary for each day of the trip, and a more detailed itinerary below. Copy and paste as needed.

The resulting spreadsheet can be filled out on the computer, or on separate pages for planning and each day.

You may have to customize the resulting template for each trip, but the result will still be quicker than starting from scratch. Much of the Planning and Packing sections can be reused, while recycling the calendar only requires a change of dates.

Designing data collections

Calc includes over 455 different functions for manipulating data, and more functions are available as extensions. Many functions are deliberately compatible with Microsoft Excel, so that Calc spreadsheets can be easily shared.

In addition to functions, plan for column headings, totals, and the results of the functions you will need. Format the cells for raw data and those for manipulations of the data differently.

Functions for data collections vary widely. Each has its own set of input variables, some entered manually and others that can be entered by dragging with the mouse on selected cells.

You can enter variables manually from the FORMULA BAR at the bottom of the tool bars, or with INSERT > FUNCTION LIST. However, the easiest way to add a function is to use the INSERT > FUNCTION dialog window, which opens a wizard for building functions and previews answers and errors.

The window is also useful for browsing functions to discover the ones you need. You can choose a category to browse, or press a key to jump to a category starting with that letter.

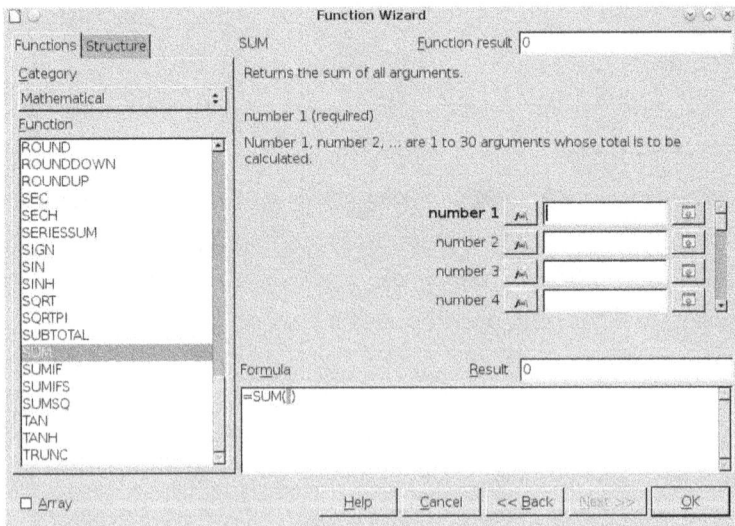

The Function Wizard (INSERT > FUNCTION) is the easiest way to construct a formula.

Exercise: Creating a mark book

A common misconception is that you need to be a mathematical wizard to take advantage of spreadsheet functions. In fact, functions can have simple everyday uses.

As an example of an everyday use for a spreadsheet, here are the steps to create a teacher's mark book, starting with the basic setup:

1   Format the DEFAULT cell style. In addition, create TOTAL, HEADING 1, HEADING 2, and VALUE styles. Use FONT SIZE and FONT COLOR to distinguish them from the DEFAULT style.

2   Merge columns A-G in row 1, and use HEADING 1 to enter the course name.

3   Set column A to a width of 12 centimeters, and column H to 1 centimeter. Column H will be used as a spacer.

4   Use HEADING 2 to name columns A-G. Starting from column A, the headings will be: STUDENT, ESSAY 1, MIDTERM, ESSAY 2, EXAM, TOTAL, and GRADE.

5   Use the VALUE style to format the row below the headings to enter the value of each assignment. Make the total out of 100 so that it is a percentage.

6   For convenience, enter the grading scale in column I. It is already set apart by the thin column H, but you can use the borders and/or background to further set it apart.

7   Format the TOTAL and GRADE columns with the VALUE cell style.

8 Leave enough rows for the number of students, then use the EXAM column below the list of students for the labels of any statistics you want to set. The TOTAL column will contain the actual statistics. A row separates the figures from the raw data in the sample, but you could use other formatting to set them apart. In the sample, I have used AVERAGE, MEDIAN, MAX, AND MIN.

	A	B	C	D	E	F	G	H	J
1	Introduction to Victorian Literature								
2									
3	Student	Essay 1	Midterm	Essay 2	Exam	Total	Grade		Scale
4	Assignment Value	(15)	(25)	(25)	(35)		-100		%
5	Allan, Robert	12	17	19	27	75 B			96-100: A+
6	Singh, Jack	11	21	23	29	84 A-			87-95:A
7	Wu, Monica	9	19	18	24	70 B-			82-85:A-
8									76-81: B+
9					Average	76.33333333 B+			71-75: B
10					Median	75 B			67-71: B-
11					Max	84 A-			62-66: C+
12					Min	70 B-			57-61: C
13									52-56: C-
14									47-51: D
15									46 or less: F

An excerpt from a data collection spreadsheet – specifically, a mark book for teachers.

Adding data and functions

When the basic layout is finished, enter the marks and functions:

1 Enter all the marks for each student.

2 In the TOTAL column for the student at the top of the list, add the function =SUM(INPUT RANGE). In the sample, the function is =SUM(B5:E5).

3 Drag on the lower right corner of the cell in the first student's TOTAL column until you reach the end of the list. This step

copies the function to each row and automatically updates each copy of the function so it works on its row.

4   Use the scale to assign the grade for each student (there is probably some way to convert the percentage automatically, but it is not immediately obvious).

5   Enter the function for each statistic. Use whatever functions you choose, but the sample uses:

* The average mark: =AVERAGE(INPUT RANGE).
* The mark midway between the high and the low: =MEDIAN(INPUT RANGE).
* The highest mark: =MAX(INPUT RANGE).
* The lowest mark: =MIN(INPUT RANGE).

    In each case, the input range is the contents of the TOTAL. column.

6   In the next column, add the grades beside each statistic.

Delete the marks and the student names, and you can save the spreadsheet as a template.

Adding spreadsheet tools

Discussion about spreadsheets usually centers on functions.

That emphasis is natural enough, but, as you plan, consider the available tools as well. Often, they can be as important to your purposes as the functions themselves.

Tools are scattered through the main menu, but most are located in the TOOLS and DATA menus. If, like many people, you are unfamiliar with them, taking a look at their purposes can help you plan your spreadsheets.

Some tools – DETECTIVE, GOAL SEEK, MULTIPLE OPERATORS, PIVOT TABLES, and SOLVER – are for use as you work with a spreadsheet. For that reason, they are not detailed here. By contrast, the ones here can be added to the spreadsheet as you design, either because they make using a sheet easier or because they need space allocated to them on a sheet.

Hiding and showing the display cells

Each row and column heading includes options to HIDE or SHOW. Changing these options can temporarily reduce complexity when you scan or study data, or select the data to print to hard copy.

	A	C
1		
2	Contract	American $
3	Tatlock Enterprises	$3,740.89
4	Anita Dibley	
5	Express Services	$7,128.50

A hidden column – in this case, Column B, which is for contracts paid in Canadian dollars. You can still tell that the Anita Dibley contract is in Canadian dollars, because its listing under American dollar is blank.

Grouping and outlining cells

As an alternative to hiding individual cells, you can select DATA > GROUP AND OUTLINE > GROUP to hide multiple cells. This feature clumps rows and columns together. Creating a group adds a tree structure to show the group by expanding the tree, or hide it by collapsing the tree.

Tip

Groups can be nested within groups.

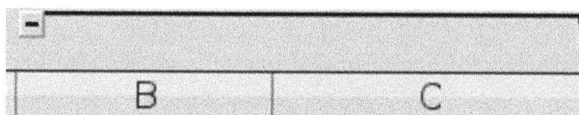

Here, Columns B and C are grouped, allowing them to be hidden or revealed together. The control for expanding and hiding are in the top margin on the left.

Filtering data

DATA > FILTER changes the data displayed in a selection of cells. Filtering does not delete the data in the selected cell – only which cells are displayed.

By filtering, you can focus on data more carefully by hiding information not immediately needed, or prepared different versions of a spreadsheet for printing or presenting to different audiences.

Calc includes three types of filter. The standard and advanced filters can be useful, but the most convenient filter for everyday use – especially in lists – is often AutoFilter.

Adding an AutoFilter requires a cell at the top of a range of cells, where it adds a permanent drop-down list for filtering. This cell can contain a heading, or, if you prefer, remain blank so that the control in the lower right corner is more obvious.

AutoFilters have several advantages:

- They are always on the sheet, next to the data they filter.

- Alone among filters, they can show empty and non-empty cells.

- The menu includes buttons for hiding and unhiding cells.

- You can create a standard filter from them.

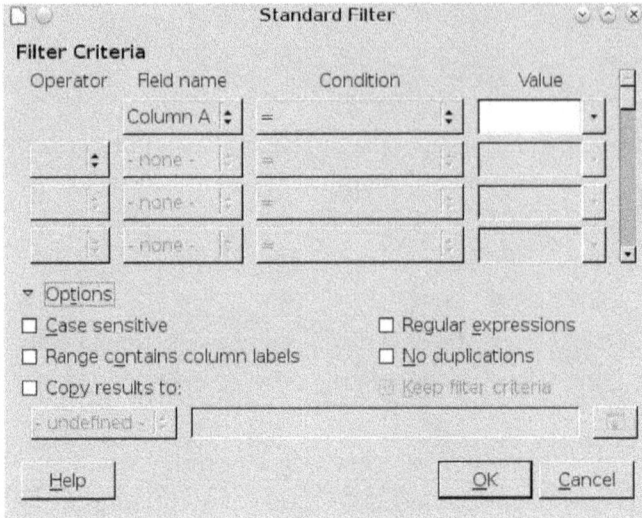

TOOL > FILTERS > STANDARD FILTER sets the Columns and conditions with which to filter information.

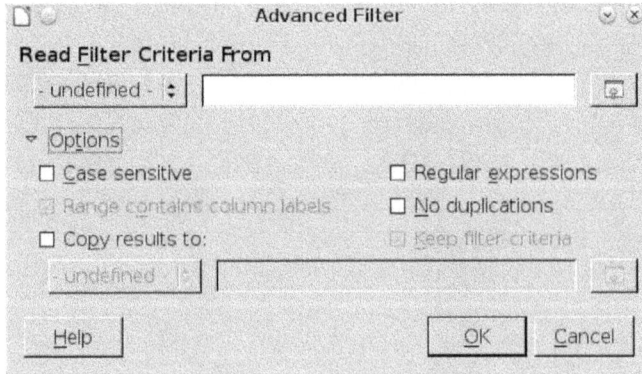

TOOL > FILTERS > ADVANCED FILTER reads filters from the spreadsheet. Otherwise, its options are similar to those of a standard filter.

A
Testers

1

2

3   Ch   Sort Ascending
     Sort Descending

4   Lu   Top 10
     Empty
     Not Empty

5   Au   Standard Filter...

6   ☑ Andrew
        ☑ Christine
        ☑ Lucas

7

8

9   ☑ All

10   OK   Cancel

DATA > FILTER > AUTOFILTER adds a convenient drop-down list for sorting a range of cells.

Creating subtotals

SUBTOTAL is actually a function listed under the Mathematical category of functions. However, because of its usefulness, the function has a graphical interface accessible from DATA > SUBTOTAL.

To work, SUBTOTAL requires a data array – that is, a selected range of cells with a label. When applied, it adds labels for subtotals and totals.

Using the SUBTOTALS window, you can select data arrays, then choose a statistical function to apply to them. You select where the labels for totals appear from the GROUP BY drop-down list.

Typically, the labels appear in the column to the left of the data array, with the totals below the data array. You may need to

add a column to your data to hold the totals unless you have
planned for them.

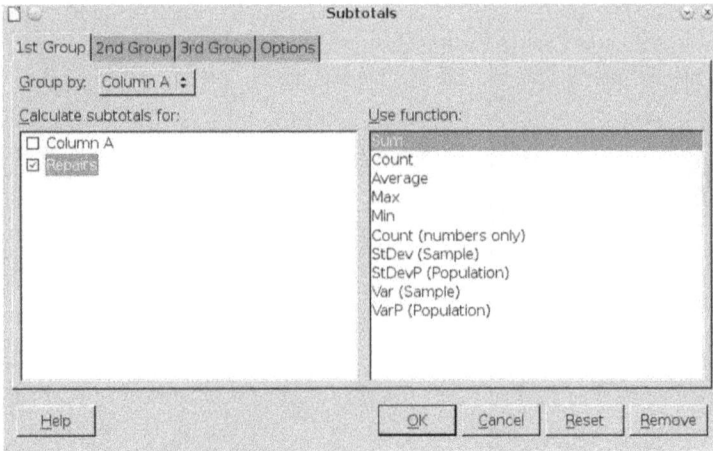

DATA > SUBTOTAL adds totals to a data array. However, it needs to
be set up in the correct position.

For efficiency, you can choose up to three groups of data
arrays to which to apply a function. When you click the OK
button in the window, Calc adds subtotals and grand totals to the
selected arrays.

Tip

Edit the labels for totals by modifying the RESULT and
RESULT2 cell styles so that they stand out and readers
can go directly to them.

You can also arrange the subtotals according to choices made
on the window's OPTIONS tab, including ascending and
descending order or using one of the pre-defined custom sorts
defined in TOOLS > OPTIONS FOR CALC.

	A	B
1		Repairs
2		$49.32
3		$731.12
4		$179.03
5	*(empty) Sum*	*959.47*
6	*Grand Total*	*959.47*

DATA > SUBTOTAL performs a function upon a data array, and adds labels for the totals.

Defining cell content and adding help

VALIDITY defines the type of contents that can be entered in a cell. Basically, it is a form of online help, either to aid your memory, or to assist others who are using the same spreadsheet.

You create your own messages. Imagine what you might need to know if you are using the spreadsheet six months from now, and provide as much detail as possible in the message. Point form or short phrases may be cryptic to your future self and other readers, so test your messages on somebody else.

Be as concise as possible, and revise your messages carefully. Remember, though, that too much detail is more useful than too little.

Contents for VALIDITY can include:

- The range and type of contents that can be entered (on the CRITERIA tab).

- The purpose of the cell contents.

- The proper formatting of contents.

- An explanation of the content rules you decide upon for the cell.

- A definition of invalid content, whether it will be accepted, and how to correct it (on the ERROR ALERT tab).

- A macro that starts when invalid content is entered.

Unless otherwise stated, most of this information can be entered on the INPUT HELP tab.

Tip

A validity rule is part of a cell's content. Selecting FORMAT or DELETE ALL from the DELETE CONTENTS window removes it.

To copy a validity rule along with the rest of the cell's content, use EDIT > PASTE SPECIAL > PASTE FORMATS or PASTE ALL.

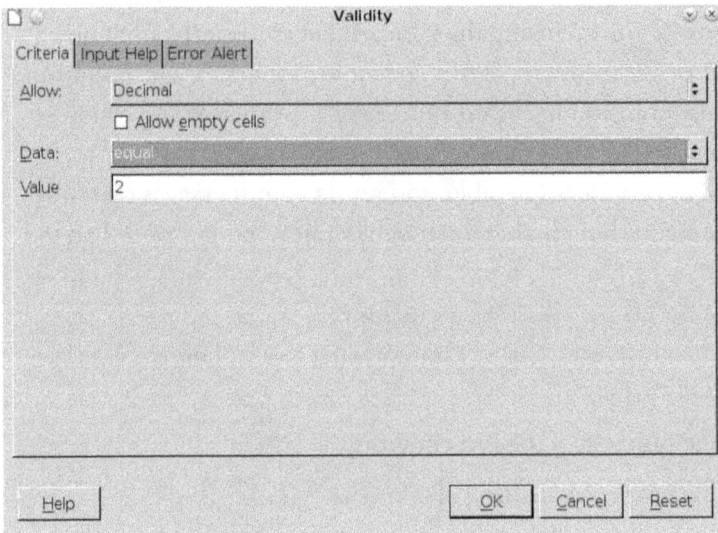

DATA > VALIDITY is a form of online help.

4.789

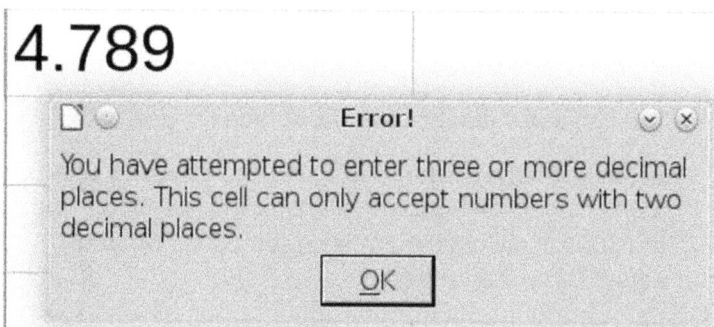

Error!

You have attempted to enter three or more decimal places. This cell can only accept numbers with two decimal places.

OK

You create your own Validity error messages. At the very least, explain in the first sentence what is wrong and in the second what needs to be corrected.

Creating pivot tables

A pivot table is a rearrangement of an existing range of data to give new insight.

At its most complicated, a pivot table can be used to analyze raw scientific data, showing the correlations between different fields. However, it can also be used in simpler cases, such as sales figures.

To create a pivot table:

1 Select the range of data on the spreadsheet, including the headings.

Spent	Country	Gender	Age
$750.41	Canada	M	25
$1,270.89	USA	F	46
$980.13	USA	M	32
$1,412.36	Canada	F	25
$673.19	Canada	O	54
$1,145.93	USA	O	35

A data range showing tourism expenditure, according to nationality, gender, and age, selected to create a pivot table.

Tip

You can use a database as the source for a pivot table.

Select from the main menu DATA > PIVOT TABLE > CREATE, then select DATA SOURCE REGISTERED IN LIBREOFFICE from the SOURCE dialog, then make a selection from the Select Data Source dialog.

2 Click DATA > PIVOT TABLE > CREATE. The PIVOT TABLE LAYOUT window opens. The headings in the original data are listed in the AVAILABLE FIELDS pane. They can be added to any of the other panes, but not all combinations will be relevant or make sense. Experiment to find the best arrangement.

The layout window for a pivot table.

3 Drag the available fields to the other panes to change their relationships. You do not need to use all the available fields. Choices are:

- PAGE FIELDS: Creates a drop-down list to filter what the Pivot table displays.

- COLUMN FIELDS: Creates columns from an available field.

- ROW FIELDS: Creates rows from an available field.

- DATA FIELDS: Information to manipulate in the pivot table.

    You need at least one column or row field, plus at least one data field. Page fields are optional.

STOP

Caution

Visualizing the results of a pivot table takes practice. You may need to experiment to get the results you want.

4   Click the OPTIONS arrow to select any other layout options. TOTAL COLUMNS and TOTAL ROWS are selected by default.

5   If necessary, click the SOURCE AND DESTINATION arrow to make any modifications. For example, by default, a new pivot table opens in a new sheet called something likE $'PIVOT TABLE_SHEET1_1'.$A$1, which would create a new sheet and place the first cell of the pivot table in the first cell of the new sheet. However, you might give the destination a more meaningful name, or place the pivot table on the same sheet as the source data.

6   Click the OK button to create the pivot table. The pivot table appears in the destination entered by default or edited by you.

Gender	Sum - Spent
F	$2683.25
M	$1730.54
O	$1819.12
Total Result	**$6232.91**

A pivot table that takes the source data and rearranges its information to show tourist spending by gender. Here, those tourists who identify as female are shown to spend the most money when traveling.

Tip

Pivot tables are uneditable, and do not refresh automatically. Click DATA > PIVOT TABLE > REFRESH to update pivot tables with the latest data or to correct a mistake.

Deciding on the styles

Calc offers only a couple of sample cell and page styles. However, you can create other styles. An analysis of your purposes can help you decide what styles to create. For instance, consider a separate cell style for:

- Column headings.
- Sub-totals and/or totals.
- A different cell color for each task or person in a list.
- Each cell of a different category on the NUMBERS tab for cell styles.
- Cells to be hidden when printing.

Page styles set how sheets are printed. They define page dimensions, format headers, footers, and margins, and how wide sheets are printed on multiple pages. Often, you may need only one style, selecting colors for branding or purposes and choosing the tactic for printing hard copy. At other times, pages may be color coded by purpose or customer, or include a sheet used as a title page.

Applying spreadsheet styles

To apply cell styles, you can select:

- Individual cells or a range of cells.

- One or more columns.

- One or more rows.

- An entire sheet (select the cell above row 1 and to the left of column A).

When the cells are selected, click the style in the STYLES AND FORMATTING window in the side bar.

To apply a page style, you technically need only to place the cursor anywhere on a sheet. However, to avoid printing blank pages, place the cursor in the last cell that has content, then click the style in the STYLES AND FORMATTING window. All cells above and to the left of the selected cell are formatted using the style.

Tip

Page styles are not visible in the editing window. You can view them from FILE > PAGE PREVIEW.

Setting up cell styles

Cell styles are the spreadsheet equivalents of paragraph styles in text documents. In other words, they are basic units for format and content.

The resemblance is so close that over half the tabs on cell styles are nearly identical to those on paragraph styles. You can read more about paragraph styles in Chapters 4–7.

Selecting fonts for spreadsheets

Choose fonts and font effects by the same criteria as you would for text documents. Most spreadsheets should follow the suggestions for online documents in "Other considerations for fonts," page 83.

A common fault in spreadsheets is to choose a small font size. However, a font size that prevents easy reading goes against the main purposes of putting information in a spreadsheet in the first place.

Generally, you should also avoid old style figures in favor of lining figures (the ones you are used to seeing). Old style figures, each with their own baselines, can be easier to read in text documents, but modern readers are likely to find them harder to read in rows of figures.

$12,361.00	$5,600.73	$12,361.00	$5,600.73
$34,256.17	$19,281.40	$34,256.17	$19,281.40
$780.93	$12,874.00	$780.93	$12,874.00
$5,400.00	$26,578.22	$5,400.00	$26,578.22
$79,852.56	$9,453.19	$79,852.56	$9,453.19
$34,385.73	$45,788.38	$34,385.73	$45,788.38

Left: Old style figures. Right: Lining figures. Old style figures look more polished in text, but are harder to read than lining figures in a spreadsheet or table.

Selecting borders

Borders in spreadsheets help to mark data arrays as separate from other figures on the sheet. However, blank cells or backgrounds can be used instead. Similarly, thicker than normal borders can set off totals or statistics from raw data.

You rarely see spreadsheets using any color except black for ordinary purposes, regardless of whether the sheet is used online or printed to hard copy. Other colors can be easily confused with the colored lines that Calc uses for display purposes but does not print.

Selecting backgrounds

Unlike text documents, spreadsheets use backgrounds freely for purposes such as classifying tasks or who does them in a list. Sometimes, they distinguish calculations and formula results in a data collection.

Go wild – if the background makes a useful distinction, no one will care if it is gaudy.

However, make sure that backgrounds contrast with foregrounds, so that cell contents can be easily read.

Setting how numbers are handled

By default, cells are set to contain any sort of information. Alphabetical characters are assumed to be text, aligned to the left, and numbers are assumed to be ordinary numbers, aligned to the right for convenience when reading.

Other formats, such as dates or currency, must be specifically set from the NUMBERS tab.

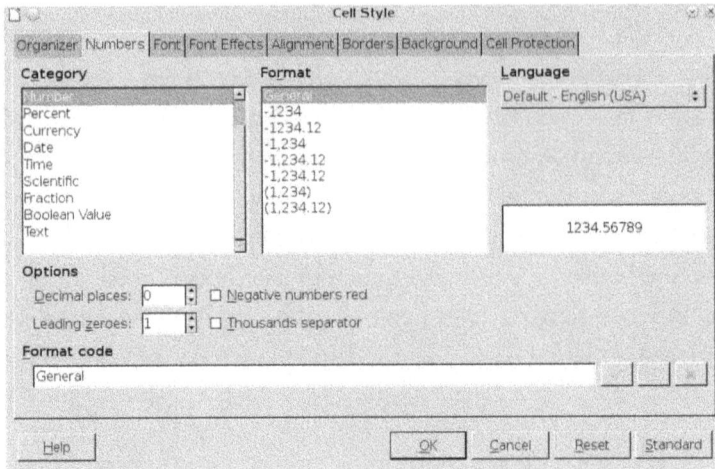

Cell Style

Organizer | Numbers | Font | Font Effects | Alignment | Borders | Background | Cell Protection

Category	Format	Language
Number	General	Default - English (USA)
Percent	-1234	
Currency	-1234.12	
Date	-1,234	
Time	-1,234.12	
Scientific	-1,234.12	
Fraction	(1,234)	
Boolean Value	(1,234.12)	
Text		1234.56789

Options

Decimal places: 0   ☐ Negative numbers red

Leading zeroes: 1   ☐ Thousands separator

Format code

General

| Help | | OK | Cancel | Reset | Standard |

The NUMBERS tab sets how cells treat numbers (and text, too). The available default formats depend on the locale to which LibreOffice is set.

When you select another format, the behavior of the cell becomes fixed. For instance, selecting TEXT means that numbers are treated as text characters, which might be handy in a list of numerical addresses that you did not want aligned to the right. Similarly, selecting DATE means that today's date is always presented in the format you select. Currency and other symbols are added automatically, depending on the format.

The available formats depends on the category. However, note that:

- Formats are often available with and without decimal places. If you choose a format without sufficient decimal places, your spreadsheet may read inaccurately when you use formulas.

- The default Date format for US English is MM/DD/YY. For instance, 01/31/15 is January 31, 2015. However, this format means that whether the month or the date comes first is unclear for days 1-12 of any month.

To avoid ambiguity, use the format YYYY-MM-DD, which is becoming increasingly common as an international standard.

- Most time formats assume a 24 hour clock, unless they end with PM.

You should also keep in mind the general options that may or may not apply to a particular number format option:

- Make sure you set the number of decimal places that you need. Otherwise, Calc rounds up or down, which may display imprecise results for formulas.

- Leading zeros set the digital places to the left of the decimal point. The default is 1, which means that you need to change it to 2 if you want to display 01 rather than 1.

- Negative numbers are red. This is a traditional setting for accounting, but make sure that your cell backgrounds and font color do not conflict with it.

- Thousands separator: Whether a character will be used to separate numbers larger than a thousand for easier reading.

The separator used depends on the locale. In English locales, the separator is usually a comma (for instance, 1,000), but in German it is a period (1.000) and in France a space (1 000).

Setting alignment

The ALIGNMENT tab has the options you might expect: LEFT, CENTER, RIGHT, and JUSTIFIED, all of them referring to how a line is positioned in a cell. However, the alignment options also include FILLED, which repeats contents so that the entire cell is filled, and DISTRIBUTED, a close relative of JUSTIFIED that distributes contents evenly across the cell. It also contains the equivalents for vertical alignment.

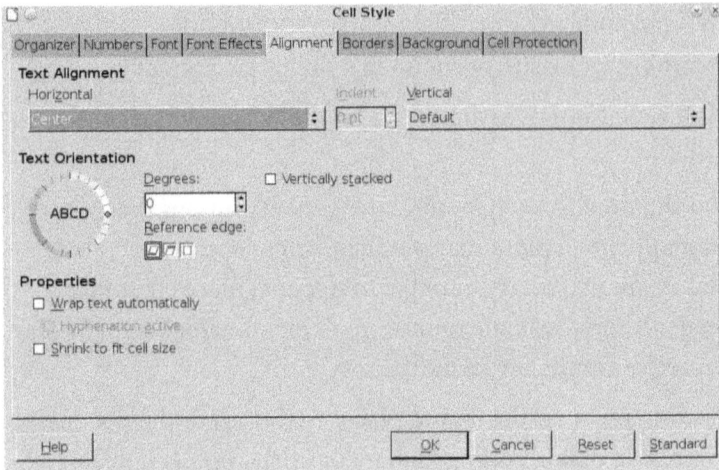

The ALIGNMENT tab also sets hyphenation and page wrap inside cells.

These options are useful if you care about the look of your spreadsheet. However, in practice, most people are focused on the information rather than the design, and tend to leave the defaults unchanged. In practice, most users are interested in the other options on the tab.

Rotating text

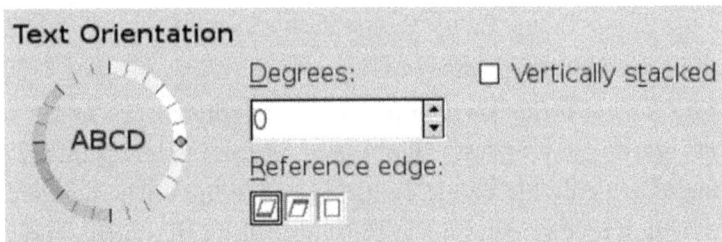

The ALIGNMENT tab includes settings for displaying text inside cells.

Confusingly, settings for how text displays are on the ALIGNMENT tab for cell styles.

TEXT ORIENTATION is useful largely for headings. By angling headings, you can often squeeze the entire text into a column that would otherwise be too small for it.

You can adjust text with the dial counter, or more precisely by entering an angle in the DEGREES field.

Rotate text as little as possible, turning the TEXT ORIENTATION dial counter-clockwise, so the text starts at its lowest point. More than a 45-degree angle should generally be avoided, and even more so VERTICALLY STACKED, which displays text vertically, character by character. Rotating text may allow more to be squeezed in, but often at the cost of reduced readability.

You can adjust rotated text by selecting its REFERENCE EDGE – that is, where the text starts. TEXT EXTENSION FROM LOWER CELL BORDER gives you the most space, and is usually a reasonable default. At times, TEXT EXTENSION INSIDE CELL may be reasonable, since it confines text to within the cell border, although it can quickly become too small to read easily.

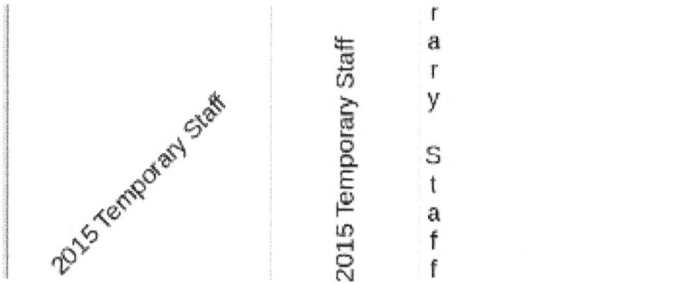

Rotating text. From left to right: a 45-degree angle, a 90-degree angle, and vertically stacked.

Adding hyphenation and text wrap

Properties

☐ <u>W</u>rap text automatically

☐ Hyphenation <u>a</u>ctive

☐ <u>S</u>hrink to fit cell size

Like text orientation, hyphenation and text wrap settings are found on the ALIGNMENT tab.

When spreadsheets first became popular, most users were satisfied with text appearing in a single line, extending into the next cell.

This presentation is known in LibreOffice as text extension. It is still the default way to display cell contents, and die-hards insist that it is the only way.

Tip

Text extension is used regardless of whether text is rotated or not.

	A	B
1	Project: GUI addition	
2	Brian Arthur Morley	
3	Fushan Betram Lei	
4	Moira Anne Hickley	

Text extension overlaps text into other cells as necessary.

However, the ALIGNMENT tab provides alternatives that many people today prefer.

The first is SHRINK TO FIT CELL SIZE. This option is useful largely for contents that almost but not quite fits into a cell. However, be careful: even with a zoom, it can result in text that is too small for easy reading.

A more readable solution is WRAP TEXT AUTOMATICALLY. This option makes text in a cell act like text in a Writer document, making it easier to read at the cost of changing the dimensions of the cell, which may not be practical if the cell needs to align with other cells.

Wrapped text can also cause unusual breaks in words. Generally, if a cell is set to use text, you should check HYPHENATION ACTIVE as well to make the text more readable.

Together, these two choices make cell content visible at a glance. They work best online, where cell width is not an issue, and you can use as much space as you want.

Staff
Brian Arthur Morley
Fushan Bertram Lai
Moira Anne Hickley

TEXT WRAP presents spreadsheet text in a more conventional format than text extension, displaying contents without spilling over into another cell.

Setting cell protection

Cell protection either protects cells from editing or causes Calc to skip over flagged cells when printing or performing other operations.

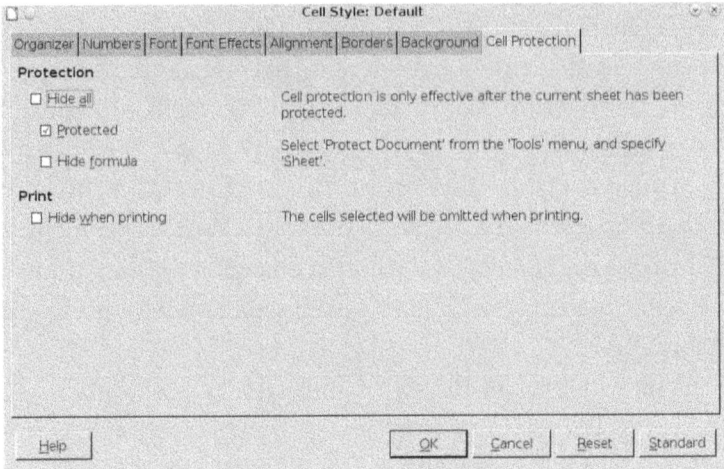

The CELL PROTECTION tab helps to control editing.

The CELL PROTECTION tab offers four options:

- HIDE ALL: Formatted cells are protected from editing, any formula in them is hidden, and the cells are not printed.

- PROTECTED: Formatted cells cannot be edited.

- HIDE FORMULA: Any function in a formatted cell is invisible.

- HIDE WHEN PRINTING: The contents of formatted cells are not printed. You should only make this choice when you know that you will always be printing the spreadsheet in the same way.

STOP

Caution

Cell protection is not activated unless you elect either SHEET or DOCUMENT from TOOLS > PROTECT DOCUMENT. Selecting either item a second time turns off all protection features.

Caution

Cell protection is useful mostly against accidental changes. For example, the spreadsheet might be used by clerks who need to enter data into specific cells, but who should not change anything else.

If you are seriously concerned about preventing other users from editing your spreadsheet, password protect the document, and/or limit the permissions on the file.

Setting conditional formatting for cells

Conditional formatting in Calc automatically changes the appearance of selected cells. The automatic format can be the application of a cell style, or of an indicator that visually presents data in much the same way as a graph or a chart.

Conditonal formatting is an extension of sparklines, which are small, undetailed graphs popularized by the information designer Edward Tufte. You can create a sparkline by shrinking a chart and removing the legends. However, conditonal formatting gives other graphical representations of data as well.

To use Calc's conditional formatting, select the cells to work with, then click FORMAT > CONDITIONAL FORMATTING > CONDITION, and select an item from the sub-menu. All types of conditional formatting can be configured from CONDITION. COLOR SCALE and DATA BAR are shortcuts to options available under CONDITION. If necessary, you can edit the range of cells affected at the bottom of the CONDITIONS window.

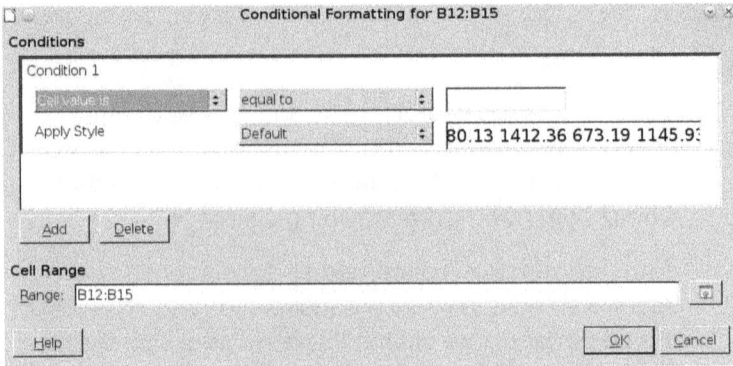

FORMAT > CONDITIONAL FORMATTING > CONDITION > CONDITION.

The CONDITIONS area has three fields. From left to right, they are:

- The general condition.
- The filter to refine the condition.
- The numerical value that must be present to activate the conditional formatting.

By changing the general condition, you can set the following types of conditional formatting:

- CELL VALUE IS: Applies the selected cell style when the numerical value is met. This type is useful for emphasizing target values in a range of cells. It cannot be used for cells formatted for text.

- FORMULA IS: Applies the selected cell style to cells in which the designated formula is used. The formula is typically one that viewers of the sheet wish to find easily.

- DATE IS: Applies the selected cell style to cells in which the designated filter is used, from Today to Last Week. This type is especially useful for locating recent information.

- ALL CELLS > COLOR SCALE (2 ENTRIES). Creates a gradient of two colors. The fields refer not to formulas, but to target values. The color scale is especially useful for showing high and low values in a range of cells at a quick glance.

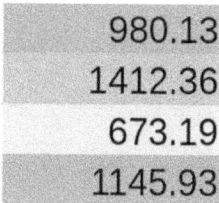

980.13
1412.36
673.19
1145.93

A color scale, with yellow indicating the lowest value and cyan the highest. Mid-ranged values are different shades of green.

- ALL CELLS > COLOR SCALE (3 ENTRIES): Like a color scale for two entries, except that a third target value is added, often a midpoint using the value PERCENT.

- ALL CELLS > DATA BAR: A gradient that creates a graph-like representation, typically showing how far above or below a cell value is of a designated norm.

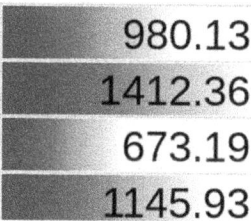

980.13
1412.36
673.19
1145.93

A data bar in which high values are indicated by more blue,

- ALL CELLS > ICON SET: Adds a set of icons to summarize the contents of cells. For example, traffic icons or emoticons might designate if results were above, below, or equal to projections.

☺	980.13
☺	1412.36
☺	673.19
☺	1145.93

An icon set annotates results. Here, emoticons indicate that two results were neutral, and two results better than neutral.

Once you have set conditional formatting, you can select MANAGE from the sub-menu to see a summary and edit the selections.

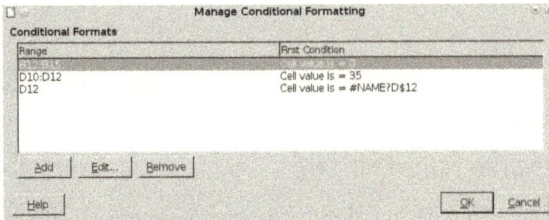

Click MANAGE in the CONDITIONAL sub-menu to add, edit, or remove conditional formatting.

Tip

If conditional formatting does not work, check that TOOLS > CELL CONTENTS > AUTOCALCULATE is selected. It should be on by default.

Using page styles

Page styles tend to be used less in spreadsheets than in text documents because spreadsheets are mostly online documents. Often, spreadsheets are made with no thought of them conforming to any printed page size.

Moreover, if you plan to print to hard copy, you may want to pay more attention to typographical standards than you would if a sheet is used entirely online. Users tend to apply the standards of text documents to any printed page, and what is acceptable online may not be on paper.

In addition, you may need to worry about how the sheet will look when printed. Often, colors that contrast well look too similar when reduced to black and white.

Conversely, if you are printing in color, a contrast that works well online may look distractingly garish on paper, because the color models for printers and monitors are different.

To help cope with such considerations, Calc page styles have many of the same options as Writer documents, giving you the versatility you need for printing well-formatted sheets. Borders, backgrounds, headers, and footers can all be designed with the same considerations as pages in a text document, although if the printed spreadsheet is meant for informal use, you might omit headers and footers. For more detailed information, see "Planning page styles," page 199.

Printing sheets

Online, the dimensions of a spreadsheet have few restrictions. However, translating a spreadsheet from online to hard copy is frequently an onerous task, full of false starts as you try different solutions.

One way to make printing easier is to keep careful track of column widths to make sure that they fit comfortably on a page. For instance, allowing for margins of 2.5 centimeters on portrait-oriented, letter-sized paper, columns should have a combined width of no more than about 17 centimeters.

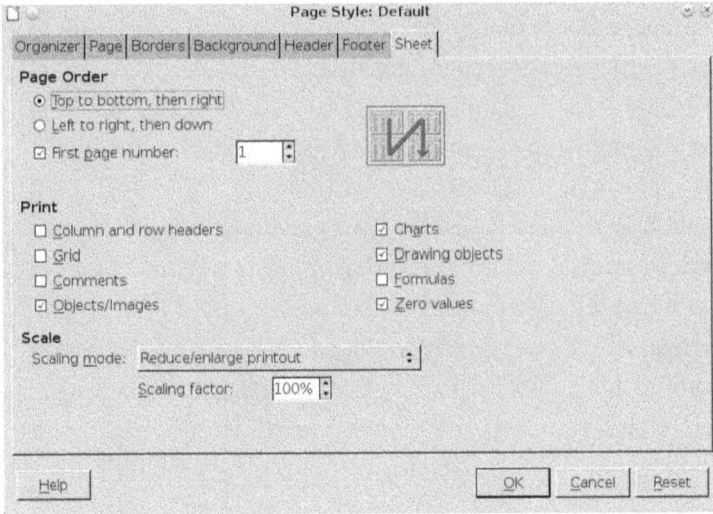

The SHEET tab has options for printing to hard copy.

Unfortunately, this practice would limit you to no more than
half a dozen columns, which is often impractical. Sometimes, you
can hide some columns or print only selected columns, but not
always. In many cases, page styles are the only alternatives.

Most of the options for spreadsheet pages are similar to the
page styles for text documents (see Chapter 8). However, the
SHEET tab has options that deserve a closer look.

Scaling spreadsheets

The scaling options on the SHEET tab should be your starting
point with page styles. It may even be your only point.

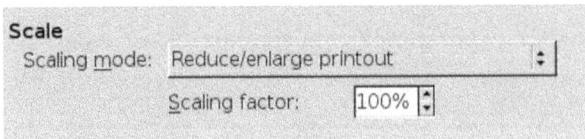

The SHEET tab includes options for fitting a spreadsheet on a
printed page.

Begin by experimenting with the REDUCE/ENLARGE PRINTOUT, entering either a percentage of the original size, or FIT PRINT RANGE(S) TO WIDTH/HEIGHT or FIT PRINT RANGE(S) ON NUMBER OF PAGES.

However, for all of these solutions, you are limited to no more than about one-third reduction in size if you are interested in readability. Anything more, and the contents will be less than 8 points high, and hard to read. At 300dpi or less, the result may not be printable, either.

For many spreadsheets, the most practical solution is to select from PAGE ORDER, choosing TOP TO BOTTOM, THEN RIGHT or LEFT TO RIGHT, THEN DOWN. These selections can be confusing, but the diagrams beside the selection may keep things clear.

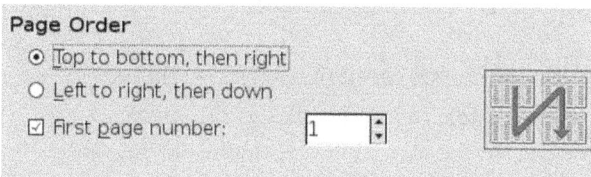

The page order options on the SHEET tab help to squeeze a spreadsheet onto a page.

If you continue to have problems, you might be able turn off the printing of elements such as comments or charts to save space.

STOP

Caution

Whatever combination of solutions you decide to use, plan and test in advance. Don't rely on printing a spreadsheet five minutes before you need it unless you have done so before and know how to get the results you want. You are likely to need several tries to print satisfactorily.

In the end, you may even want to tape pages together to reproduce the spreadsheet more accurately in hard copy.

Other options

The SHEET tab's PRINT pane includes selection boxes for what is printed. Most of these options are of limited use, except perhaps for comments on unfinished drafts or trial attempts at printing – after all, if the spreadsheet doesn't need objects, why add them?

The two possible exceptions are COLUMN AND ROW HEADERS (the alphabetical identifiers for columns and numerical ones for rows) and GRID (the cell borders). Printing them is only a matter of turning options on, but people have strong feelings about the choice.

Many users – especially inexperienced ones – feel that a spreadsheet requires borders for each cell and the row and column headers, and that a spreadsheet simply isn't a spreadsheet without one.

Others argue that such things distract from the contents. Sometimes, too – for instance, when you import into Writer – you may want the cells to look like a table rather than a sheet.

How you format printed spreadsheets may be a matter of personal preference or corporate style sheet. Or perhaps you have a practical reason for certain choices. For example, if you are writing a how-to about using a spreadsheet, you may want to use snippets of spreadsheets that look like an online spreadsheet. No firm conventions exist, except for one: once you have chosen the formatting, use it consistently.

Contract	Q1	Q2
2015-02-2-01	$12,361.00	$5,600.73
2015-03-07-01	$34,256.17	$19,281.40
2015-03-07-02	$780.93	$12,874.00

Contract	Q1	Q2
2015-02-2-01	$12,361.00	$5,600.73
2015-03-07-01	$34,256.17	$19,281.40
2015-03-07-02	$780.93	$12,874.00

Printing with (above) and without (below) cell borders and row and column headings.

You may especially want spreadsheets to look like tables when you use Calc to create a tutorial because, when you already have a collection of pictures and charts on the sheet, the grid may do nothing except add to the clutter. Like printing in general, whether you print the grid or the header may be an exercise in trial and error.

Formatting spreadsheets automatically

When you want to format only part of a sheet, you can use FORMAT > AUTOFORMAT. However, many of these pre-defined styles look dated, such as the 3D ones.

Instead use the ADD button to apply your own formatting. You may find AutoFormat more useful than using page styles for creating a general look.

> Tip
>
> You can apply an AutoFormat to an entire sheet by clicking the cell above the row 1 header and to the left of the column A header.

AutoFormat

Format

3D
Black 1
Black 2
Blue
Borderless
Brown
Colored table bord
Currency
Currency 3D

OK
Cancel
Help
Add
Delete
Rename

	Jan	Feb	Mar	Total
North	6	7	8	21
Mid	11	12	13	36
South	16	17	18	51
Total	33	36	39	108

Formatting

☑ Number format ☑ Font ☑ Alignment
☑ Borders ☑ Pattern ☑ AutoFit width and height

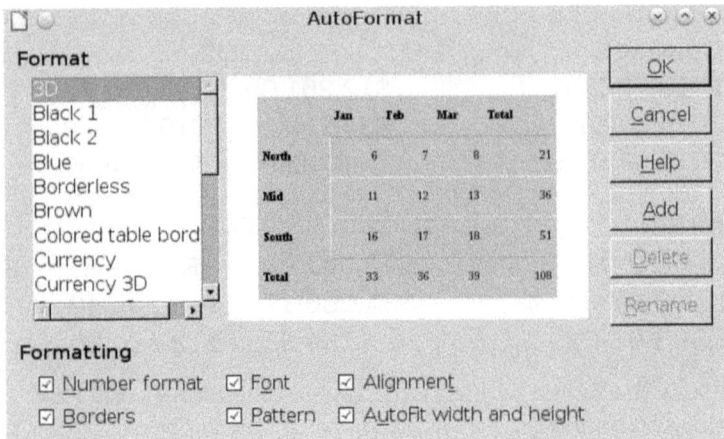

AutoFormats are an alternative to page styles for formatting some aspects of a spreadsheet.

Adding other elements

Spreadsheets are primarily lists or ledgers. However, you can also add other elements, such as pictures, charts, and formulas, especially when you are turning a spreadsheet into a tutorial.

Unfortunately, just as with frames in text documents, additional elements in Calc do not always stay where you place them. Even worse, nobody has found a workaround for the problem in Calc.

The best advice is to follow the precautions suggested in Chapter 10 for Writer frames. If you still have problems, consider not adding any other elements. They are almost always enhancements rather than necessities on a spreadsheet.

Working with conventions

Spreadsheet conventions differ greatly from those of text documents. Some of these conventions are expectations, worth noting because they are how others will judge your work.

Other conventions, however, are what have been found to work – usually, when reading a spreadsheet online.

However, despite the differences from text documents, spreadsheets still benefit from the use of styles. You may not use the page styles regularly, but, like all styles in LibreOffice, the cell styles will make revising your spreadsheets and using them over long periods of time much easier than manual formatting.

16

Putting everything together

Using styles, templates, and the tools associated with them makes formatting and writing a document easier. However, the last edit before you finish a document is also an important part of the design and composition processes.

By the time you finish designing and writing even a short document, you have probably lost perspective on it. You may be so familiar with the document that you are unable to notice if you have expressed everything you meant to say. In extreme cases, you may loathe the sight of the document – a stage which many professionals take as a sign that it is almost ready.

Yet regardless of how you feel, you need to regain perspective so you can do the final edit.

One way to regain perspective is to get a second opinion from someone who is interested in your topic and willing to take the time to read thoughtfully and respond honestly.

However, in practice, such people are rare. You might have to settle instead for reading your document aloud, reading it from a printout, or leaving it alone for several days. All these possibilities can help to distance you from your work enough to criticize it.

Start your final edit systematically, focusing first on content, then moving on to structure and design. The headings in this chapter will give you a checklist of steps to follow.

Checking copy

Ask yourself: Is your discussion complete? Are there opposing views you could include? Counter-arguments that you could answer? Terms, assumptions, procedures, or background that you have left out?

Are paragraphs the right length? If you are publishing online, then paragraphs should be no more than four or five sentences long for easy comprehension. In hard copy, paragraphs can be longer, but only if you need the extra length for a detailed argument. A paragraph that takes up more than half a page should usually be divided up regardless of the publishing format, because extremely large paragraphs can make readers skip them.

Check, too, for clarity. The ultimate test is to read a passage out loud at a regular, medium-quick pace. If you have trouble reading the passage, or a listener has trouble understanding it, you may want to reword or shorten sentences.

As you get down to the word level, consider whether every piece of jargon is necessary. Does a word convey precisely what you mean, or could you use a better one? Are you using the type of language and jargon that your readers would use?

Your favorite things

All writers have their favorite words and expressions. As you work, develop a list of yours, and watch for each of them as you edit copy. Consider alternatives so that they do not become too noticeable.

You may also find that you have become proud of some expressions or a single passage. Some writers believe that "a writer's best friend is the waste basket" and delete anything they are too proud of because they cannot be objective about it. That is probably extreme in some cases, but you should certainly consider the possibility.

Checking structure

How does your document develop? If you suspect that readers may not read the whole thing, you will want your most important points first, so they at least are read. By contrast, if you can count on readers to finish the document, you can put your most important point last, building up to it with less important points first.

> **Tip**
>
> If the document uses headings, select VIEW > NAVIGATOR or press the F5 key.
>
> Using the Navigator's controls, you can move headings and the sections of body text below them anywhere in the document much more quickly than you can copy and paste.
>
> If you change the position of points, their opening and closing sentences and transitions may need rewording.

More formal documents will probably have an opening paragraph or passage that sets up the topic and gives a little background. They will also have a conclusion that emphasizes the main points or what readers should get from your discussion.

This exercise can show you the value of choosing accurate headings. The more accurately that a document's headings reflect its contents, the more easily you should see the order in which passages should go. When the order looks clear to you, the chances are that it will be logical to readers, too.

One more point: LibreOffice automatically names headings, images, and other elements with unimaginative names like HEADING 1 or TABLE11. A counsel of perfection would be to give each element a distinctive name to help clarify the structure of the document.

However, giving names to every element is hard work. You may decide to give distinctive names to only key elements. Often, those key elements should be headings, because they are useful in many other ways. However, if a document does not include headings, choose another prominent element instead.

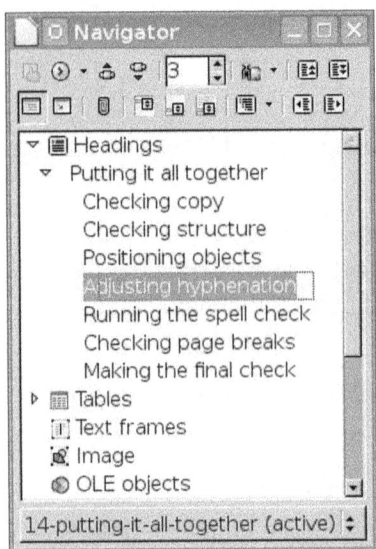

The Navigator is an ideal tool for restructuring material if your document has headings or descriptively named objects.

Checking design

Either print out a copy or use FILE > PRINT PREVIEW. Better still, do both. No matter how carefully you have developed and modified your template, it is still easy to miss problems in the design unless you look at pages as a whole – or, better, in a two-page spread.

Among the things you should check are that:

- Page styles follow in the order that you intend.

- Page numbering and different page numbering styles begin where you intended.

- New chapters start on a right page. Try not to be confused by the fact that Page Preview does not display two-page spreads accurately.

- Footers and headers arrange information in the intended order. For example, page numbers will be more noticeable if placed by the outer margin of each page.

- Paragraph styles for tables of contents or indexes, which you may have only created as a final step, are compatible with the rest of the design.

- When documents have been added to a master document or pasted together, the numbering of the first numbered list in each document may need to be restarted manually.

Positioning objects

Graphics, tables, charts, and other objects should be positioned as closely as possible to the text to which they refer.

Check, too, that formatting such as the structure of captions and the space above and below objects is consistent throughout.

The most common trouble spots are cases where a paragraph with space below is followed by a paragraph with space above, which results in more spacing than you may have intended.

Use the Navigator so that you go through the objects systematically, and you can recognize departures from the formatting conventions you have set.

Adjusting hyphenation

If you decide to hyphenate the body text, LibreOffice does the best it can while you work. But by the time you are finished editing and making changes, this on-the-fly hyphenation can be far from the best job that LibreOffice can do.

As you make your final check of the document, click TOOLS > LANGUAGE > HYPHENATION. This tool lets you choose where each line will break and what syllable each hyphen will follow.

STOP

Caution

Some versions of LibreOffice include spelling dictionaries, but not hyphenation dictionaries, so you may have to download and install a hyphenation dictionary before you run a check.

You will need a separate hyphenation dictionary for each language or locale in a document.

STOP

Caution

Running the hyphenation tool will add hyphens, even if none of your styles are set to use hyphens. Skip this step if you want to avoid all hyphenation and keep a ragged right margin.

Lorem ipsum dolor sit amet, consectetur adipiscing elit. Sed aliquet nulla eu sodales faucibus. Nulla lacinia sodales arcu, sed elementum dolor venenatis et. Curabitur eu faucibus lorem. Vestibulum dui mauris, element ... Class aptent taciti sociosqu ad litora torquent per co ... honcus quis sapien eget blandit. Vivamus posuer ... n congue vitae, faucibus non magna. Nullam sed con ... e lobortis dolor laoreet ut. Morbi hendrerit vehicu ... ec nec eleifend metus, eget placerat tellus. Vivamus ... ices, nunc vel aliquam facilisis, dolor urna volutpat a...

Hyphenation (English (USA))

Word

Vi=va mus

Hyphenate
Skip
Remove

Help   Hyphenate All   Close

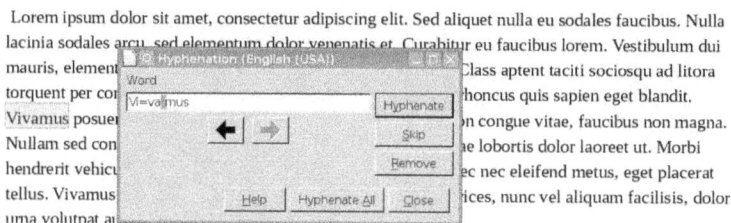

Running the Hyphenation Tool fine-tunes the hyphenation created in a work in progress.

Checking the spelling

Run the spell check in the TOOLS menu for each language used in the document. You can check the languages by looking at the FONTS tab of all your paragraph styles. LibreOffice also checks some grammar and layout, such as enforcing one space after a period instead of two.

However, always remember that a spell check is not a substitute for your own judgment. Not everything Writer flags is mis-spelled, and the grammar check is far from complete.

What the spell check can do is reduce the drudgery of catching typos and routine errors. Never think, though, that you have caught all the problems when you have run it. Spell checking should always be followed by at least one manual check.

As you spell check, make a note of your regular typos, and use EDIT > FIND & REPLACE to help you correct every instance of it. Finding and replacing common mistakes is much faster than spell checking, and allows you to see more of the context in which the mistake occurs.

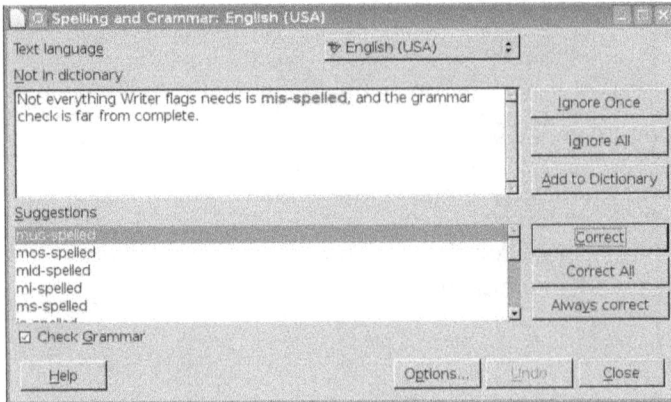

Spelling and Grammar: English (USA)

Text language　　　　　　　　English (USA)

Not in dictionary

Not everything Writer flags needs is **mis-spelled**, and the grammar check is far from complete.

Ignore Once
Ignore All
Add to Dictionary

Suggestions

mus-spelled
mos-spelled
mid-spelled
mi-spelled
ms-spelled

Correct
Correct All
Always correct

☑ Check Grammar

Help　　　　　　　　　　Options...　　Undo　　Close

Check the spelling once for each language used in the document.

Tip

If you have any last-minute additions, highlight the new material, and the spell check will review only it.

Checking page breaks

Reduce the zoom to 75% or less, and see where pages end. No matter how you format, thanks to graphics, tables, and other objects, you are likely to have pages that end more than a few lines before the bottom of the page.

Often, you can improve the page breaks by rearranging elements such as images and tables, or by dividing paragraphs so that another line or two are used. Perhaps you may decide that a comment you omitted is worth adding after all, or that a paragraph can be cut, although changing the content only to improve the design is a case of misplaced priorities.

In extreme cases, you might even add manual page breaks. However, like any manual formatting, the more you add, the harder the document is to maintain.

You will be extremely lucky (or painstaking) if every page breaks exactly at its final line. Instead, be satisfied with being 4 or fewer lines from the bottom of every page. The more manual changes you make, the more you are likely to require in the next editions of the document.

Problems with master documents

In the most recent versions of LibreOffice, master documents present some problems:

- Master documents can paginate differently from a stand-alone sub-document. You can sometimes see this problem by printing a range of pages to PDF first from the sub-document and then from the master document, and comparing the page breaks.

- If you have cross-references between two sub-documents, the target sub-document shows the message "Error: Reference not found" when you open the sub-document. The cross-reference only displays correctly from the master document.

- When you have a cross-reference between two sub-documents, the error message in the target sub-document can be much longer than the cross-reference in the master document. This discrepancy can cause the page break to change between the sub-document and the master document.

To overcome these problems, avoid tight pagination, leaving a line or two empty. Alternatively, use a master document when it is convenient in long documents or in group projects, and copy and paste a single long document at the very end of your final editing.

Updating

Select TOOLS > UPDATE > UPDATE ALL to ensure that all fields are up to date. This check is especially important for cross-references, which may have been repositioned as you edited.

Making the final check

Before you publish, set your zoom to 75% or select FILE > PRINT PREVIEW and take one last high-level look at the document.

At this point, you should see very few problems. If you do see problems, consider repeating the final editing process. However, if you have already done so several times, ask yourself at some point if you are tinkering in the hope of an impossible perfection.

STOP Caution

In some releases of LibreOffice, PRINT PREVIEW shows the borders around a table even if you have turned them off entirely. These borders do not print, but to view the tables properly, uncheck TABLE BOUNDARIES on the right-click menu.

When you see nothing to change, you know that your document is ready to print or post online. Be prepared to make some tweaks since working with a template reveals its shortcomings, and you may find situations that you never anticipated.

However, at this point, your work is ended and so is this book (or very nearly).

A

Downloading LibreOffice

LibreOffice has versions for Linux, OS X, and Windows.
Most Linux distributions include a copy in their package
repositories, sometimes with extensions and distinct icon sets.

The official page for downloading the latest release is:

http://www.libreoffice.org/download/libreoffice-fresh/

The site detects your operating system and language and
offers to download the appropriate version. Use the links at the
top right of the page to download versions for other operating
systems and languages.

The official page for downloading Apache OpenOffice is

http://www.openoffice.org/download/index.html

Extensions and templates

Hundreds of extensions and templates are available for
LibreOffice. Extensions can add much-needed features and
resources, while templates can save you designing time. However,
be aware that some extensions may not be kept updated and may

not always work with the latest release. Similarly, just because a template is posted does not mean that it is well-designed.

To get extensions and templates for LibreOffice, go to these links:

http://extensions.libreoffice.org/
http://templates.libreoffice.org/

For Apache OpenOffice's collection of extensions and templates, go to:

http://extensions.openoffice.org/
http://templates.services.openoffice.org/

Many extensions and all templates work on both LibreOffice and Apache OpenOffice. However, the two are different enough that compatibility is slowly lessening as each version is released.

B

Learning more about typography

You can find dozens of books on typography, including ones from modern masters such as Frederick Goudy and Adrian Frutiger. Many are concerned with hand-lettering, or typography in branding.

The books listed here are focused on typography as a practical art. They are on the conservative side, but together they show the foundations of modern typography and teach its basic principles. They vary from introductory books to advanced essays.

The most useful books I have found are:

- Robert Bringhurst. *The Elements of Typographic Style.* 2nd ed. (Hartley and Marks: Vancouver, 1996): Widely regarded as the Bible of typography, because most of Bringhurst's opinions are reasonable ones.

- Eric Gill. *An Essay on Typography* (David R. Godine: Boston, 1998): Thoughts by one of the shapers of modern design. Also available on Google Books.

- Jan Tschichold. *The Form of the Book: Essays on the Morality of Good Design*. Trans. by Hajo Haedler (Hartley and Marks: Vancouver, 1991): Thoughts about page design from the master typographer who designed Penguin's post-war cover format (and the only person known to be persecuted politically for his typographical standards).

- Jan Tschichold. *The New Typography*. Trans. by Ruari McLean (University of California Press: Berkeley, 1995): The classic statement of the principles of asymmetrical design that shape modern typography.

- Robin Williams. *The Non-Designer's Design Book* (Peachpit Press: Berkeley, 1994): By far the quickest, clearest, and most insightful introduction to typography that I know.

- Robin Williams. *The Non-Designer's Type Book* (Peachpit Press: Berkeley, 1998): A sequel to *The Non-Designer's Design Book*, focusing on the details of typefaces and how to use them.

C

Where to get free-licensed fonts

Like free or open source software, free-licensed fonts are ones that you can use, share, and edit as you please. Most are also available at no cost.

Free-licensed fonts barely existed before 2000. By contrast, hundreds are available today, although their numbers are still small compared to the thousands of proprietary fonts available from font foundries such as Adobe.

Many are clones or near-variations of classic fonts, but some are original fonts that are outstanding by any definition. Both clones and originals help you work without using proprietary fonts.

Free-licensed fonts are available under the SIL Open Font License (OFL) or the GNU General Public License (GPL) with font exception. Some are also in the public domain. Other licenses exist, but not all have been evaluated by the Free Software Foundation or the Open Source Initiative, and should be used cautiously.

If you use Linux, some of these fonts can be installed as packages from your distribution's repositories. Many of the others can be downloaded online, regardless of operating system.

Arkandis Digital Foundry
(http://arkandis.tuxfamily.org/adffonts.html)

The Arkandis fonts are meant to provide free-licensed versions of fonts for Linux. The selection includes Baskervald (Baskerville), Gillius (Gill Sans), and Universalis (Univers), as well as original fonts such as Mint Spirit, which was originally designed as the unofficial font for the Linux Mint distribution.

Barry Schwartz
(http://crudfactory.com/font/index)

Barry Schwartz is one of the outstanding designers of free-licensed body text fonts. His work includes three fonts based on the designs of Frederick Goudy, as well as Fanwood, an understated font which closely resembles Eric Gill's Joanna. You can get also get some of his fonts from The League of Movable Type (see below).

Cantarell
(https://git.gnome.org/browse/cantarell-fonts/)

The official font for GNOME 3. Originally criticized for some of its letter forms, Cantarell has evolved into a modern humanist font that can be used for body text and headings alike.

Dover Books
(http://www.doverbooks.co.uk/Fonts,_Lettering.html)

Dover Books publishes about 30 books with CDs of fonts and dingbats from Victorian times and earlier. They are marked as "permission free," which presumably means public domain.

Google Fonts
(https://www.google.com/fonts/)

Featuring over 630 font families, Google Fonts is intended

mainly for online use. However, you can also download fonts for print use. Updates are regular, so check regularly for new releases of updates of existing fonts.

The League of Moveable Type
(https://www.theleagueofmoveabletype.com/)

Describing itself as "the first ever open-source type foundry," The League of Moveable Type offers a small but select library of original font designs. If you find yourself getting lost in the sheer number of free fonts, anything from The League can be counted on to be of high quality, and usually includes small capitals and old style figures.

Liberation Fonts
(https://fedorahosted.org/liberation-fonts/)

Liberation fonts are designed to be the metrical equivalent of standard proprietary fonts. In other words, they occupy the same vertical and horizontal space, although they may otherwise be designed differently. Liberation Sans is meant to substitute for Arial and Helvetica, Liberation Serif for Times New Roman, and Liberation Mono for Courier.

Open Font Library
(http://openfontlibrary.org/)

With over 400 font families, the Open Font Library is second only to Google Fonts in its selection. Its front page includes a list of the most recently uploaded fonts.

Oxygen
(http://www.fontspace.com/new-typography/oxygen)

Created for the KDE desktop environment on Linux, Oxygen is a modern geometric font, made of simple shapes, but highly readable and pleasing to the eye.

Raph Levien
(http://levien.com/type/myfonts/)

A Google employee, Levien also develops fonts in his spare time.
Although not all the fonts displayed on this page are complete,
their consistently high quality makes them worth considering.
Most must be exported via the free-licensed font editor Fontforge
to a usable format .

SIL International
(http://www01.sil.org/computing/catalog/show_software_
catalog.asp?by=cat&name=Font)

SIL International is a missionary organization that specializes in
fonts for minority languages. It also developed the Graphite
system for the automatic use of ligatures, small caps, old style
figures, and other advanced typographical features. The SIL Font
License is the most widely used license for free fonts, and
responsible for much of the spread of free fonts.

Ubuntu
(http://font.ubuntu.com/)

Designed for the Ubuntu Linux distribution, this is a modern
humanist font. It is versatile, although its use in branding may
mean that a document that uses it will be automatically be
identified with Ubuntu.

D

Free-licensed equivalents for standard fonts

Like Linux desktops, free-licensed fonts started as imitations of proprietary equivalents. Today, original free fonts are becoming increasingly common, but the demand for free equivalents of proprietary fonts remains. This demand is unlikely to disapear because, although most professional designers think in terms of proprietary fonts, clients are often unwilling to pay for them. Moreover, free software advocates prefer free fonts to go along with their free applications.

Exact equivalents are rare because of fear of copyright restrictions. A match as high as 75% is rare. Some equivalents, such as the Liberation fonts, are only metrical – that is, they take up the same space as their proprietary equivalents, but the letters themselves are different. In other cases, the free fonts are inspired by their proprietary counterparts, but the designer never intended exact copies, and the most you can expect is a general resemblance. A few proprietary fonts, such as Optima, have no free equivalent at all, so far as I can see. For this reason, the listings in the table below are mostly the closest equivalents, and rarely exact replicas.

All of these fonts can be found from the sources listed in Appendix C.

Proprietary	Free Licensed
Alternate Gothic #1	League Gothic
Arial	Liberation Sans,* Pt Sans, Open Sans Condensed, Lato
Arial Narrow	Liberation Sans Narrow*
Avenir	Mint Spirit No2, Nunito
Baskerville	Baskervald ADF Standard, Libre Baskerville
Bembo	EB Garamond
Bodoni	Accanthis-Std, Oranienbaum, GFS Bodoni, Libre Bodoni
Cambria	Caladea*
Calibri	Carlito*
Caslon	Libre Caslon
Centaur	Coelacanth
Century Gothic	Muli
Comic Sans	Comic Relief
Courier	Liberation Mono*
Courier 10 Pitch	Courier Code
Courier New	Cousine
Didot	GFS Didot
Eurostile	Jura
Frutiger	Istok Normal 400
Futura	Mint Spirit No2, Nunito
Futura Light	Futura Renner Light

Garamond**	Crimson Text, EB Garamond
Georgia	Nimbus Roman No. 9
Gill Sans	Cabin, Gillius ADF, Hammersmith One, Railway Regular, Raleway
Goudy Old Style**	Goudy Bookletter 1911, Linden Hill, Sort Mills
Helvetica	Liberation Sans,* Pt Sans, Open Sans Condensed, Lato
Helvetica Narrow	Liberation Sans Narrow*
Joanna	Fanwood
Letter Gothic	Josefin Sans, Josefin Slab
Myriad	Junction, Pt. Sans
News Gothic	News Cycle
Stone Sans	Nunito
Stone Serif	Lustria
Tahoma	Lucida Sans, Nimbus Sans
Times New Roman	Liberation Serif, Linux Libertine
Trajan	Cinzel
Univers	Universalist-std
Verdana	DejaVu Sans

* Metrical equivalents.

** "Garamond" and "Goudy" are generic names for fonts inspired by particular designers, so the actual typefaces with these names can be very different from one another.

www.ingramcontent.com/pod-product-compliance
Lightning Source LLC
Chambersburg PA
CBHW021544210326
41599CB00010B/301